CW00470091

— Pick Your Own — STRAWBERRIES

John Martin Somers

Cover by Neil Aldir

This edition published in Great Britain in 2010 by Lulu, Inc.

Copyright © 2010 John Martin Somers and his licensors.
All rights reserved.

The right of John Martin Somers to be identified as the author of this
work has been asserted by him in accordance with the Copyright, Designs
and Patents Act 1988.

No part of this publication may be reproduced, stored in a retrieval system,
or transmitted in any form or by any means, without the prior permission
in writing of the publisher, nor be otherwise circulated in any form of
binding or cover other than that in which it is published and without
a similar condition including this condition being imposed upon the
subsequent purchaser.

All characters in this publication are fictitious and any resemblance to real
persons, living or dead, is purely coincidental.

A CIP catalogue record for this book is available from the British Library.

ISBN: 978-1-4457-6090-2

To my sadly missed compadres Mike and Gazza.
Station Inn stalwarts both.

Chapter 1

September 1993

I T STARTED RAINING again as they lowered the casket into the ground. A funereal day – the most appropriate weather of all for a funeral one would think, but a wet coffin is not a good start. The mourners were raining as well. They were there to bury dear old granddad who had died suddenly without even the good manners of a significant preceding illness and some of the family couldn't take it.

The four coffin bearers, immaculately dressed in sombre suits and top hats, stood heads bowed by the graveside having discreetly dropped the lowering webs on top of the casket. They remained in situ until the minister had completed the committal, then walked off in four different directions thereby giving way to the mourners who, having shuffled to the very edge of the hole in the ground, then instigated the filling in of it by morosely sprinkling soil on top of granddad's dead box. The bearers met up again, their job complete for the moment. One or two of them felt able to dispense with the fixed pallid and grizzly expression which was obligatory in their line of work and allow something more akin to a human likeness to replace it. Had Mr Woodcastle or Mr Snape witnessed this most serious breach of protocol the offenders would have been disciplined without question. Sobriety was everything according to the edict of this old established firm of undertakers. Any straying from this, even in the shadows, was unacceptable and amongst all members of staff, the coffin bearers were required to remain grim at all times. They, after all, cut the most poignant figures of all; their function to blend in with the mourners – indeed to represent them.

Should these mystical figures who delivered the departed into their grave, and in some peoples' eyes into the arms of the Lord, subsequently fall so carelessly out of character by allowing themselves to be spotted smoking and seemingly chatting together like gossiping shop girls as the mourners continued to grieve, this might reasonably be interpreted as disrespect, or at any rate unprofessional. Woodcastle & Snape, the Old Firm, were an entirely respectful and professional firm of undertakers.

They had been established in Pendlesham for forty-five years and had buried two of the town's Members of Parliament, three peers, countless numbers of town councillors and an even greater tally of wealthy elderly people (Pendlesham predominated in 'retired gentlefolk'). The most news-worthy of all burials was a young local rock musician who was known during his boringly inevitable short life as 'Tony Tasteless'. Tony had gone out in style following a long line of predecessors to a spectacular doom by leaping off the cliffs of Rocky Point, the 532 foot-high beauty spot which attracted so many people to the south coast determined to put an end to it all without the threat of a recount. A far greater number of visitors were the far less ostentatious breeds who made a trip to the same place in order to take in the stupendous views over the town or out to sea and whose descent was a tad more conventional (and significantly less terminal) than that chosen by young Mr Tasteless. The area of the town at the foot of Rocky Point, 'Maidens', was undoubtedly the most opulent part of affluent Pendlesham. It was awash with "old money". It was where men in blazers and old ladies who made jam lived and where everyone still thought Britain had an empire. It was a quaint noddy village, where nobody spoke about money because everyone had so much of it.

Rocky Point claimed one customer a fortnight on average. Some people didn't only jump, they drove their vehicle off as well. One severe case saw a woman securing her three young children on board before doing just this; a most distressing and selfish act which did nothing at all except maintain the steady rate of fatalities and rubber-stamp Rocky Point's clear position as England's premier suicide venue. This in turn attracted still more people to the cliff tops in the hope of witnessing a leap and it wasn't long before a philanthropic voluntary group called "The Lifejoys" felt obliged to get in on the act. This organisation, in its early days, had simply provided a voice on the telephone to anyone who was on the verge (or said that they were) of closing the book on themselves and the great book of life. This good but righteous voice grew louder and eventually became a face – several faces – and now The Lifejoys had become a nationwide charity, staffed still mostly by volunteers but also by full time workers. They even had an accommodation on top of Rocky Point itself, designed, of course, to enable them to offer a final glimmer of hope to those who were clearly not far away from the final curtain, or even to identify likely candidates en route to the edge and intercept them. Their tiresome presence extended to the placing of a number of small but solid square plaques near the edge of the cliff top. Quotations from the scriptures and other stomach-churning sources were printed on them, all bestowing the apparent virtues of the beauty of living and how throwing it away was so wrong, to say nothing of sinful. Nearly everyone ignored them. Others tripped over them and somebody on the immediate threshold of suicide is rarely dissuaded by being brought crashing to earth by a six-inch high monument hammered into the ground, pleading with them in effect not to fall over. It wouldn't take much of a cynic to suggest that this would have represented the last straw for most people. Perhaps something saying 'It's not your time to go yet, you fool!' would have brought forth a more desired result under those circumstances.

There was little doubt that the fun and games up on Rocky Point provided the Old Firm with a bountiful injection of business, being the senior undertakers on the scene, so to speak. Pendlesham District General Hospital, whose ambulances were on standby to inherit any mess cleared up by the Coastguard, were apt to contacting the Old Firm. This enabled them to grab the business themselves (in the case of a local person, this would usually go through on the nod) or more often than not the Old Firm could act as an intermediary between other respectable companies up country, a service for which the Old Firm naturally took a wedge of pie. This was not only acceptable to the out of town firms but there was actually quite a lively competition between the larger of them, all of whom had branches in the big cities, to get onto Woodcastle & Snape's 'approved list'. Needless to say, the Old Firm would only ever turn to this master list if they had failed to capture the business themselves; an act which, despite being mercenary, was always done subtly, like a wicketkeeper appealing for an improbable stumping. The wishes of the bereaved were paramount and it was this worthy value that was encrusted in everything the Old Firm did. It was what it stood for. A business, definitely, but most of all, a service.

The antiquated founders of the Old Firm were living still and so were their antiquated techniques. It was September 1993, but not for them the switch to an electronic system of administration and accounting. Loose-leaf ledgers and fountain pens (not much farther down the evolutionary scale from quills) were still used and computers were particularly and enthusiastically resisted as pre-war typewriters remained in use for the production of official letters. Not to write everything down on paper was an anathema to both the ancient partners, and although pocket calculators were grudgingly acknowledged as being useful, any information gleaned from them went straight onto a carbon paper sandwich.

Even the updating of the fleet of vehicles (although to call one hearse, three limousines and a removal vehicle a fleet was perhaps wishful thinking) had been a painfully slow and reluctant process and had been entirely due to the fact that the cars had become increasingly less roadworthy, rather than anything to do with style or even cost. The watchword for the Old Firm remained 'dignity'. Machines that bleeped at you and hearses that went faster were not dignified.

The premises at Woodcastle & Snape oozed dignity also. Modernisation would have been vulgar, totally unthinkable and had never been entertained. The entrance and reception areas were tastefully decorated and void of any memorials or floral displays. One's initial impression might well have been that of entering a dentists or opticians. But there was a compensation for this deception – an air of comfort and warmth. The private office was a cosy, warm, comfortable, carpeted room with only the imposition of a desk giving the gentlest of indications that this was where the bill was paid.

Along the corridor was the most evocative and sensitive room on the site. The Chapel of Rest or 'viewing room' was the beautiful little place where one's loved one was put on display in their coffin after they had been 'prepared' in a neighbouring room by the embalmer. Subdued lighting was ably assisted by a parade of candles, adopting a custodial position around the coffin and vases of fresh flowers, also strategically placed, completed the attempt to present a bright picture of an otherwise bleak landscape.

There was a service chapel too, although it had long since become more normal for the service as well as the committal to be held at the cemetery or crematorium rather than at the undertakers itself, although sometimes for reasons of cost, or in the case of very private affairs, the in-house chapel was still brought into play to tend to the spiritual needs of the departed (and of the mourners), after which the client was taken down the road for the more terrestrial side of the business.

There were other rooms, smaller and less important, but each was in the same vain and totally appropriate to its honourable function. Tradition went hand in black glove with dignity, whereas change – any change – was warded off, lest the feared malignant virus of vulgarity got a stranglehold.

The Old Firm had thus instilled in its staff the importance, indeed obligation, of staying put and to go about their business as if clients were still taken to their rest in a hearse drawn by equine horsepower rather than that of the combustion engine. The Old Firm was effectively stuck in a time warp of its own making, and as a consequence many of its staff were particularly tragic figures, not least the proprietors themselves, Herbert Woodcastle and Arthur Snape; an ancient pair indeed, the sort of one hundred-year-old guys who smelt of mothballs and wore mittens.

Equally as pitiful was one of the four coffin bearers, a man in his early fifties called Maurice Noddoes, who had become known, quite by his own instigation, simply by his last name and answered to this only. This eccentric and irritatingly loquacious man had originally trained as an actor hoping for a career on the stage and adopted solely his family name because he believed all great Thespians were monikered thus. Alas, he failed, giving up after two years in repertory had failed to get him noticed in Theatreland, or indeed anywhere else – even a bit part in *Casualty* had eluded him. He found work only as a ventriloquist and developed a talent for throwing his voice, an amusing party piece but hardly useful. He also picked up a knack for impersonation of both voice and mannerism of ordinary people, not celebrities necessarily. This of course only succeeded in antagonising his subjects, and even the insufferably vain Noddoes perceived the wisdom of keeping this talent under his hat on most occasions. His dream shattered (although his typically bloated actor's ego meant that he considered the dream merely suspended), he commenced a period of 'non-artistic' employment, even though his current job as a coffin bearer and particularly the associated duty as an extra 'mourner' was an acting part and nothing else. The same ego, however, ensured that this irony was completely lost on him.

A figure on a par for sadness with the wretched Noddoes was Frank Eddowes, a middle-aged man still rooted to his mother's nest, whose job it was to 'book-in' new clients, as well as ordering supplies of pencils, black ink, paper clips and coffins. He had occupied the same position for eighteen years. Frank's immediate superior was Arthur Snape himself. The only one of the partners who had ever taken a proletarian part in the running of the business, it was old Snape who provided the bereaved public with the initial contact to the comfort of the Old Firm. His was the reassuring voice and demeanour, which together produced a package which was wonderfully compassionate, even though nobody ever wanted it in the first place. Once Arthur had worked his spiel, the customer was turned over to Frank, who by that time was confronted with a person or people no less traumatized but degrees more relaxed and perhaps even encouraged.

The Old Firm retained two embalmers, who were also available to the District General Hospital as mortuary technicians. The senior man was Peter Foster, an unremarkable man who was the latest of a succession of Old Firm embalmers, all as unremarkable as each other, apart from the fact that they were embalmers and therefore slightly odd. Foster's deputy, who proffered to style herself instead as a 'beautician', was called Tessa Sharma, and Tessa was peculiar but very lovely. Her father had been a senior civil servant in his native India. There he met Tessa's English mother, who had a position as a legal advisor to a multi-national oil company and the articulate couple married and moved to Britain after they had both secured postings in England, Sharma ironically in the Indian High Commission in London. Not long after, they had a son and subsequently a daughter. The son, Peter, became a doctor, whilst Tessa, the daughter, set her sights on the same goal but very quickly became conscious of the fact that curing the sick was certainly not her cup of char. Instead she became immersed in the ways of the occult and death, eventually departing from her medical studies a trifle unconventionally by dressing up as a 'feline witch' and bursting in on a lecture to announce that she was not Tessa, in fact, but 'Sheba, the daughter of Selina and Sebastian, the imperial black cats of doom and wickedness' and that she had been 'commanded to denounce and relinquish the foul medicines and sorcery of the preposterous, who call themselves good'. Her collegiate brethren were, she advised them, 'the supreme opponents of Mother Selina and therefore destined to become inflamed forever'. The mecurial Miss Sharma concluded by informing the now subdued class that she now intended to 'vanish to associate with corpses' before sweeping out of the lecture hall, no doubt to snort some more gear. 'My home is with the dead, you foolish enemies!' she screamed after them.

The next morning, Tessa, as bright as a button, attended her lecture as normal, as if nothing had happened and was inexplicably expelled on the spot from medical school. Her parents, who were not after all called Selina and Sebastian but Caroline and Dinesh, were not very enamoured with her at all!

Tessa's male friends at the time were weirdos. There were the drugged-up, heavy metal biker types who wore their leathers to bed and never washed; then came the slightly smarter but much spottier vegetarian, summer solstice saddoes who, unlike the bikers (who were into heavy nightcaps before suicide) seemed to prefer living, Tessa's association with whom thereby contradicting her 'home is with the dead' bit, and finally there were the graveyard boys. These were lads who didn't look so bad – on the contrary, well dressed and from perfectly normal backgrounds – but who were far more likely to genuflect to Mother Sheba than either the bikers or the nut cutlet brigade. Tessa became a graveyard girl and started hanging around cemeteries with somebody called Rauss, who worked in a mortuary as an attendant. Rauss introduced Tessa to some contacts in the undertaking business and Tessa said 'yes, that will do for me, thank you very much' and joined the profession herself, seeking training as an embalmer in Wimbledon, taking to it like a duckling to water.

Paradoxically, this was when Tessa started calming down. For although she was now indeed 'associating with corpses', she soon came to realise that although her specialism was different, it certainly had nothing to do with evil, wickedness or black cats! The 'feline witch' thus disappeared and so did Rauss and his cretinous associates. Tessa's next boyfriend was called James, who ran a bookshop. He started taking the gorgeous Tessa to theatres and restaurants and all manner of 'normal' and nice places, followed by magnificent Vienna where they rode the Ferris wheel in the Prater together just like Harry Lime and Holly Martins. This time the door of the car remained closed.

Alas, Tessa soon made her mind up to move on. On the grapevine she had heard of a vacancy at Woodcastle & Snape down in Pendlesham for an assistant to Peter Foster. Tessa had met him at a function and liked him. It was not a promotion but it was certainly a fresh start. She applied and got it. Poor nice James was dropped.

The appointment of a young mixed-race female to the Old Firm, even to the background staff, was nothing short of groundbreaking. It might have been a different story had the young woman applied for a position as a member of the 'visable' staff, the probable prohibition of her appointment being put down to the 'preservation of tradition', when prejudice on both sexual and racial grounds would have come closer to telling the real story. Mind you, Tessa was certainly fortunate that the Old Firm had no idea about her antecedents, as any mention of medical school, claimed lineage to black cats or stories of moonlight sexual ravagings on gravestones would have seen her already controversial application thrown back in her face and any special interest group heading for the hills. Instead, Peter Foster came forward with a letter of recommendation to Mr Woodcastle, stating that in his professional opinion Tessa was an excellent choice. Woodcastle passed this on to Snape, who then interviewed Tessa and agreed that she was ideal, as well as being 'delightfully charming'…

Within a week of her joining the Old Firm, Frank Eddowes, the store's clerk, was infatuated with Tessa Sharma, the lady embalmer. In his mind, not always ground in reality, he resolved to mount a pursuit.

Chapter 2

Tom

THE STATION INN. A pub inside a railway station is rarely a hostelry of character. It is typically a mundane little affair, patronised almost exclusively by commuters, those either returning from work and stopping off only to fortify themselves before having to face another evening of domestic purgatory. Then there were those travellers waiting for a train back up, who nurse a single tiny drink in their hands for far too long whilst waiting for their service to be called; everyone united by being buried in a newspaper or magazine and not talking to anyone else; a cold, soulless place.

The Station Inn at Pendlesham was not like this. Indeed anyone who did not know it well was put right as soon as they walked through the door from the concourse and inhaled. This unapologetic den of iniquity nestled extraneously amongst a French-style sandwich bar, a newsagents, the station buffet, a barbers and a florists, most of which have remained staples of an English railway terminus for generations. This particular pub had a through door to a taxi rank and an upstairs bar, which was available for functions but which remained largely unused.

The 'Inn' was the incorrigible problem child of the concourse, frequented not by commuters at all but by a correlation of misfits, punks, tramps, woefully under-aged drinkers, dodgy young women and petty junkies. Loud, aggressive rock music thundered out of ill-placed speakers, as alongside the bar the regulars sat on tall, hard wooden stools watching newcomers try to score with Kate, the tall, brunette, all-smiling, moon-faced barmaid with only a mild habit. Particularly pithy was the small notice nailed up behind the bar, which ran: *"It is forbidden for vagrants, beggars, itinerant musicians and females of doubtful reputation to enter these premises – by order."* Had this ancient directive been strictly adhered to, this place would needless to say have been empty.

The establishment was run (perhaps 'kept going' would have been a better way of putting it) by a Peter Pan figure called Tom Beck who was knocking at the door of half a century but nobody had told him. Tom clung passionately and desperately to any shred that remained of his younger days, even to the ludicrous extent of running around in Bermuda shorts in the summer months and getting himself into silly little bits of trouble like getting caught by police carrying silly little amounts of silly little drugs. Yet Tom knew the business inside out and was no fool. He possessed a craggy charm which appealed to his teenaged customers; this a testament to his many years experience as a beatnik (Tom preferred 'bohemian') and this coupled with his appearance and tales of his mild recidivism, Tom hit the spot with the kids when many of his contemporaries, senior in age to the fathers of much of his clientele, were regarded with hostility in most instances. He genuinely continued to adore rock music supplemented by the occasional snort, and even more rarely took advantage of some of the better looking nubiles who hung around his bar looking for an inaugural step onto the drugs ladder, or maybe just a good rooting from a guy who knew what he was doing. There were times, however, when even the cutest of Tom's lines rebounded on him. A very lovely but extremely vacuous 'rock chick', who had steadily been drowning her favourite mixture all afternoon, came up to the bar again for another shot:

Tom: Pernod and lemonade?

Girl: Yeah.

Tom: Sex on the beach? And I don't mean the cocktail.

Girl: Piss off!

Tom did.

There were other instances:

Tom: I need your help, sweetheart.

Girl: Oh, yeah?

Tom: Yeah. You see, I'm playing with the orchestra down at the bandstand. I'm playing the triangle.

Girl: You're being silly.

Tom: Perhaps I can practice on yours?

Girl: Piss off!

Tom did.

Tom Beck had no intention of settling down or even of growing up. They would have to carry him out on his shield. The youngsters thought he was great.

Another one of the major players in the saga of this seedy pubescent drinking house was a guy who, like Tom, was also old by Station Inn standards. He was approaching thirty. He nevertheless fitted into the scene just as comfortably as Tom did due to him being a character who couldn't possibly have been disliked even had one worked at it. Enter one Eric Seebal.

Eric was far from a local boy, far by about six thousand miles, in fact; this measuring the distance to Pendlesham from Vancouver, British Columbia, where he had been born and brought up. Instead of heading south to the United States after graduating from college (a fact that he was never ready to admit to people), young Seebal stunned his émigré parents by odd jobbing it for two years before fleeing to the very country that they themselves had rejected in order to establish a fresh start in Canada.

'Why did you and Mom quit England, Dad?'

'We wanted a better life. We did it for you Eric, son!'

'You fucked up big style, Dad. Canada is a shithole. Damn it, man, I could have come from the same country as the Stones and the Pistols. I could have been a contender. Damn you, you bum you…'

Eric departed for London and hung around bars, getting hooked up in the minor music scene and smoking and snorting naughty things. He found work in some of these places too. As a further insult to his native land, he passed himself as an American, although claiming that he was from Seattle was certainly not far from the truth. It was after all a city he knew just as well as Vancouver.

Eric's main vice quickly and perhaps strangely became English ale, although the copious goblets he quaffed of the various kinds of this heavenly liquid had no effect on his lean, spawny body. He had become bored with hash and acid, then tried coke and didn't realise what all the fuss was about. A girlfriend then died from injecting smack and Eric turned his back on, not only Class A drugs, but London. He headed south for Brighton, got onto the wrong part of the train and ended up in Pendlesham. The first thing he did was to stroll into the Station Inn and order a pint of a local county ale which he had not come across before in the capital. He was served by Tom himself.

'Say, this is a great drop!' Eric said, after two thirsty gulps had done for about half of the pint.

'Yank, are you?' demanded the sixteen-year-old crack head standing next to him. 'I fucking hate Yanks!'

'Canadian', admitted Eric for the first time, recognising the danger signs immediately.

'Toronto?' asked Tom, as a rotund, balding bespectacled regular sat down on a stool on the other side of Eric from the Americanophobe who, after successfully putting together his one intelligible sentence for the day, had now decided to engage in a staring contest with the ashtray in front of him.

'No, no. Vancouver. I'm from the west coast,' Eric told him, pointing at the beer pump and knocking his now empty glass towards it with the other hand.

'You're a bit old to be a student,' probed Tom, tending to it.

'What makes you say that?'

'Does that mean you're not?'

'I'm a runaway,' confirmed Eric...

Tom's mention of students wasn't at all frivolous. Each summer, Pendlesham was invaded by foreign students, principally from Europe, and although hardly any of these young *"auslanders"* ventured into the Inn (they had been specifically warned against it by their group leaders after they themselves had been advised by the police that involvement in the premises would not further their students' understanding of English life for the better), foreign accents on the concourse were by no means a rarity, and having the owner of one occasionally stray into the Inn was not that unusual. Even the Danes and the Swedes have their recalcitrants. Admittedly, to hear a transatlantic brogue was a novelty. The only non-European students staying in Pendlesham tended to be the ultra-conformist Japanese, who didn't need telling what stepping out of line would mean. They avoided the Inn like the plague.

The fellow who had sat down next to Eric was called Tom, just like the proprietor. A loaner, this other Tom had been part of the Station Inn from the bar's inception in 1984 nine years previously and, on the wrong side of forty, was again a lot older than the rest of the folk who regularly went in there. Because of the name clash (something which had posed no problem to either Tom, but which had begun to confuse the less enlightened scrote), an 'occasional regular' called Stephen Mauve had taken some unsolicited action. Because Tom the customer's second name was 'Hoad', Stephen decided to mangle the names together to produce 'Toad'. This immediately distressed poor Tom who, with his tragic appearance already against him, had no desire to be named after a frog. Stephen therefore persuaded Tom that whilst he might claim that 'Toad' was probably unflattering, he certainly could not reasonably argue against being called 'Thoad' which, after all, was simply his initial attached to his last name. This was a nasty little ploy by Stephen, as he was hoping, of course, that the kids would struggle with the unusually sounding 'Thoad', resort to 'Foad' and eventually return to 'Toad'. But Stephen had outsmarted himself. 'Thoad' stuck just because it was such a strange name and it soon became clear that Stephen had inadvertently done Tom Hoad a massive favour. People would come into the Inn and pat him on the back instead of just ignoring him. All of a sudden he found himself with a celebrity, which totally astounded him and with this meant undisputed membership of the Inn's inner-sanctum, a boundary which ironically still remained impenetrable to Stephen Mauve.

Thoad was an otherwise sad man. Looking rather like Porky the Pig, he cut an odd figure perched up on his stool with his newspaper strewn over the bar. He always sat by himself, rarely spoke to anyone, and his only penchant outside the Station Inn (for the Inn did alas represent his entire outside world) was a passion for classic reggae – Desmond Dekker, Dave and Ansel Collins, The Upsetters, Dandy Livingstone, Prince Buster… He had a job for which he wore a jacket and tie but nobody seemed to know what it was. Everybody agreed that he was a 'nice bloke' (this, a summary rejection if a woman says it to you) but there were still plenty of unforgivable things written about him on the bog wall. Thoad was in all honesty less popular than pitied and deep down Thoad himself knew it. Despite all the pisstakes though, there didn't seem to be anywhere else he wanted to go.

Stephen Mauve was, as far as the Inn regulars were concerned, an even more paradoxical figure and someone for whom there was some open hostility. A crew cut, non-smoking capitalist, Mauve, 24, was an accountant with a degree in mathematics from the University of Warwick. He was good looking, fresh-faced, claimed a lovely girlfriend, who had never been seen in the Inn but had been spotted by some of the others elsewhere, had his own house, drove a BMW, was articulate, easy-going, amusing and loaded. His only saving grace was that he was one of the biggest pissheads Tom had ever come across. Even this was still not enough to save him on some occasions. His insistence in walking into the Inn in an Armani suit irritated nearly everyone. Tom had had to step in more than once when an atmosphere had resulted in Stephen being threatened with a twatting for simply being there, and although a lot of the baby girlies were attracted to him, none of them would have countenanced an approach in the Inn. To those who didn't fancy him, he represented, at least outwardly, everything they didn't and was therefore an interloper and fair game for a kicking from their male associates.

Although Stephen planted himself on one of the wooden stools at the bar and was on friendly if still distant terms with Tom, Kate and Thoad, he was largely ignored by all the other regulars, apart from those who didn't approve of him and were therefore liable to cut him. The Thoad episode had been the one moment he had gone anywhere near distinguishing himself. However, like Thoad, Stephen Mauve had no desire to go anywhere else. The reason for this was most odd. The young man who appeared to have everything, did not! Admittance to the inner-sanctum of the Station Inn elite – the Inn Crowd – was what he wanted.

Frank Eddowes, the Old Firm's store's clerk, also frequented the Station Inn. He, like Thoad, was practically a resident, and because of his job ('undertaker'), everybody thought he was great, despite being nearly as old as Tom and giving at least five years away to Thoad. Frank also liked the young girls, although unlike with the trendy Tom Beck, this could never be reciprocated and Frank scored only with women to whom he was introduced by the kids after money had changed hands. No curb crawler, he! But hand jobs only, usually.

Frank's perennial claim was that he 'looked after' his aged mother, but sadly the converse had always been true. Nellie Eddowes was the overbearing sort and she still exercised enough control over Frank's life to ensure that Frank was never really his own man. Subtle curfews were imposed on him and Nellie made certain that her son realised that he was no more important to her than her two cats, Hansel and Gretel, her 'babies', even though in *cat years* they were just as old as Frank. The affection Nellie had for these creatures naturally had an adverse effect on her real life middle-aged baby, who tried to respond by making a special effort to curry favour with his mother (for whom he had nothing but love) in order to inspire in her a remedy for what he saw as an imbalance in her feelings for him with those of the two tabby cats. His liaisons with professional ladies were naturally never mentioned.

Nellie had been a widow for fifteen years. Her husband Percy, Frank's father, had succumbed to an ear infection, which had initially been diagnosed as being benign but had then preceded to trigger off alarming complications, resulting in an unexpectedly serious and ultimately fatal disease. Both Nellie and Frank were devastated. The Old Firm took care of the arrangements at a special staff discount.

Chapter 3

Mr Snape

MR WOODCASTLE THREW a spanner in the works by dying one day in November. He had long been the most likely of the partners to slip away first and he didn't disappoint his backers. He'd had his three score and ten years plus tax. A heart attack got him.

There was a good deal of irony attached to the precise manner of Herbert's demise. He used to regularly attend the afternoon brass band concerts at the bandstand on the promenade, much beloved by Pendlesham's senior citizens. There were two reasons for this. Firstly, he genuinely enjoyed the performance of the military band, and secondly he made it his practice to wait until after the concert until everyone had left their seat. There were always some who did not leave. This was because they had dozed off. There were still others who also did not leave. This was because they had died of old age. In the case of the latter, Herbert would promptly drop a calling card into the blazer pocket or handbag of this fresh corpse before scuttling off. But on this occasion, it had been Herbert himself who had failed to rise. Who says that God does not have a sense of humour?

The news of his passing (Herberts, not God's) was delivered to the Old Firm staff by Arthur Snape before the commencement of business. Herbert Woodcastle had been really nothing more than a sleeping partner for some years, rarely getting involved in any of the practicalities, leaving much to the slightly younger Mr Snape. Now Herbert was down for some serious shut-eye.

'Thus, we shall give him a send off befitting his station,' promised Mr Snape keeping his emotions magnificently under wraps for the sake of the morale of his troops and the dignity of an Englishman. 'I have been authorised by dear Herbert's family to make good the arrangements,' he continued. 'Our noble industry will respond by celebrating a life devoted to the cause as well as mourning the loss of that life. To this end, I shall presently be delegating to each of you a specific duty, which when collectively performed will result in a ceremony which will send this great funeral director on his way to the saint with all the dignity and the respect commanded by my late lamented friend and partner. This shall be a congealing of the cream of the funeral industry. Best beef shall be eaten. Tributes will be paid. But gentleman…' (Tessa Sharma was also present) '… let us not forget that we are at first servants to those who seek comfort at the passing of a loved one. Let us now, without further ado, open our doors to them and set aside the personal tragedy which has befallen each and every one of us. Gentlemen… let us carry on!'

The staff wisely waited for the inevitable cringe-inflicting line, "It's what dear Herbert would have wanted", dutifully delivered by Mr Snape, before breaking out into applause.

'We shall not let you down, nor Mr Woodcastle's memory!' stridently offered Noddoes.

'I myself am mortified,' said Frank, and then immediately looked to the floor, hoping that his unfortunate choice of word would not be picked up by Snape, or ignored if it had been.

Peter Foster the embalmer then spoke:

'I await your instructions to perform the saddest task of my career,' he said, 'I only wish it were a dream.'

'We shall make him look beautiful' promised Tessa.

'A fitting tribute!' immediately added Noddoes, coming in again with his quivering Thespian voice.

The obsequious staff applauded once more and then, remembering Mr Snape's last directive and the fact that dear Herbert would have wanted it that way, dispersed and soon after opened for business and started doing deals with relations of dead people for live money.

Chapter 4

Amanda

FRANK EDDOWES SAT himself down upon one of the wooden stools alongside the bar in the Station Inn and started bevvying. The most recent matronly prostitute the youngsters had paired him off with had managed to relieve him of the agreed fee without relieving him. She had let him squeeze her sagging breasts, but that was about it. He had had to do everything else himself.

'One of your old boys has croaked, I hear,' said Tom on serving him. 'What are you doing for him?'

'We're giving him a really good send off, actually,' replied Frank. 'People are coming in from all over the place. Funeral people. It's an open casket job.'

'Christ, that's gross!' flinched Eric, who was planted on an adjoining stool. 'So what, if you drop flowers on the guy? It ain't nothing but a corpse, you know what I'm saying?'

'That's not nice,' said Frank.

'So it ain't nice,' blundered on Eric. 'Shit! He's had his life. Now he's like a piece of wood or a doughnut. How the fuck can you respect that – huh?'

'You didn't know him,' said Frank, who had gone into the session specifically in order to seek big time alcohol and had made an impressive start, 'and, to be honest, nor did I.'

'Get wise, Frankie,' carried on Eric for Frank's apparent own good. 'What you see on that slab or whatever, it ain't him! You're paying tribute to a doughnut. Just burn the shell and get it out of there!'

Frank shook his head and started draining his glass. Eric jumped off his stool en route to the cigarette machine on the wall by the little boys' room.

'You've got it all wrong, Frankie,' he called back. 'You're paying tribute to a doughnut. A *doughnut*! The guy inside is gone, baby! It's like an egg-shell without the egg!'

'I don't think he's trying to wind you up, Frank,' Tom said, noticing that Frank had been got to, or at least looked as if he had.

'No, no,' agreed Frank. 'I think there's a lot in what he says. I've often given thought to such things myself, actually. I suppose I just wasn't ready for this conversation, that's all. Everybody's just very sorry.'

'When's the planting?'

'Tuesday.'

'Is the other bloke going to retire now that his partner's gone?'

'Dear me, no!' said Frank. 'Old Snape practically ran the business by himself anyway. I don't think anything's going to change at all.'

Thoad had entered the Inn now and had caught Tom's eye. The proprietor acknowledged and then tended to a beer tap. Eric returned with his cigarettes and hopped back onto his stool just before Stephen Mauve, who had also just entered, could get to it. Stephen had to content himself with the place on the other side of Frank. He was once again on the outside of things.

'Hey, Frankie. No offence, okay?' Eric said, lighting up.

'Of course not,' said Frank, looking and feeling better. 'It's only a bloody job.'

'Sure.'

Stephen Mauve ordered his usual bottle of strong German larger, which he always drank from the bottle in another attempt to get accepted by the youngsters who did the same. He caught Thoad's eye and put his hand up. Thoad nodded back.

'I haven't seen Kate for ages,' he then said to Tom, who had broken off his conversation with Thoad to retrieve a packet of crisps for someone else.

'Tomorrow day-shift, mate,' said Tom, walking away again.

Stephen looked disappointedly down at his bottle and then brightened up slightly as a pretty young punk girl took the stool to the right of him. He returned to his bottle when she gave him the 'what is someone like you doing in here?' look which he was so used to by now but still did nothing to try to remedy by becoming a scruff. His girlfriend, Lucinda, would have been aghast enough had she known of his drinking regime, and indeed where he drank; if she were also to catch him dressing down in order to ingratiate himself with riff-raff, she would almost certainly have finished with him. Besides, Stephen quite liked being different, even though it must have been as clear as day to him that to lose his Armani influence would have taken him close to losing his unpopularity, particularly amongst newcomers.

The punk girl stared straight ahead as Tom plonked a small bottle of a clear but very strong cider in front of her.

'Cheer up, Amanda. He'll be back,' he said to her.

The girl smiled unconvincingly.

Stephen Mauve was just considering what an ill-fittingly feminine name 'Amanda' was for a rebellious, wayward girl, when she suddenly picked up his bottle of beer, spat in it and put it back down on the counter. Stephen responded to this immediately by picking up the bottle and draining it.

'One more time, please, Tom!' he announced stridently.

Amanda stared at him. 'That's disgusting!' she said, most surprisingly.

Tom put the new bottle down and Stephen lost no time in picking it up and pouring at least half of its contents down his throat. He then offered the bottle to the girl.

'One more time, please, Amanda!' he said.

The punkette had been outfoxed. She could spit in the drink and things would go around again. Instead she claimed her own bottle and stepped away.

'Cheer up, Amanda. He'll be back,' concluded Stephen and then indicated to Thoad that he required Tom's services again already.

It was a rare triumph.

Meanwhile, next door, Frank was getting very drunk. It was silly of him to try to compete with Eric, but he was always inclined to try.

'I only ever spoke to Mr Woodcastle once or twice,' he told the Canadian.

'Your boss is the other guy, right?' asked Eric, already knowing that this was true but recognising that Frank was approaching the slurring stage, which often accompanies the point at which the drunk professes love for everybody and therefore offering him an easy enough question because of it.

'Mr Snape is a decent enough old stick,' Frank continued, frowning at his pint. 'Once the funeral is over with, I really can't see much changing.'

'What happens when this Snape guy becomes a doughnut also? Has he got any kids? *Kids? Shit!* They must be older than Tom!'

'Get out of it' snapped Tom from behind the bar.

'He has, and I rather fancy that they are,' said Frank. 'And I also think that when Mr Snape does finally depart, heaven forefend, his family will disband the business and sell up, although I could be mistaken.'

'What makes you say that?'

'The business is worth more than a pretty penny. Simply thousands!' explained Frank, now slurring rather badly. 'I rather fancy that the middle-aged benefactors will want to cash in their dividend straight away. They would have waited long enough for it. Mrs Snape died some time ago, so she's out of the picture.'

'What about the family of the guy who's already a doughnut?' asked Eric, addressing a fresh pint.

'Nobody. No wife. Just nephews and cousins and that sort of thing, which is why old Snape was able to hijack the funeral so easily. He was undoubtedly closer to Mr Woodcastle than anyone.'

Eric leaned across to Frank to speak to him confidentially.

'Are we talking *fruits* here?' he asked, smiling broadly.

'Certainly not!' stammered Frank. 'That's terrible!'

Eric was being naughty again but he had a reason for it. An attractive and very unsubtly dressed girl with peroxide hair had just wiggled past and Eric needed to end the conversation with Frank so that he could go over and chat her up like he did every time he saw her. The girl's name was Cheryl and she was, most surprisingly, a hairdresser. She had had a string of boyfriends and was currently seeing one of the other Inn regulars, a pot-smoking scrote called Baz, who did painting and decorating in between periods of community service. Despite this, Cheryl was definitely interested in Eric, and Eric in turn fancied her like crazy.

'All I know, Frankie,' he concluded, climbing off his stool and placing a friendly hand on Frank's shoulder, 'is that when your guy Snape falls off his perch, there's gonna be one hell of a scrimmage for that company, okay?'

Frank gave an involuntary belch.

'I'm convinced the benefactors will sell up, in which case I'll be out of a job.'

'That's too bad.'

'Funerals are the only thing I've ever done. *My firm's* the only thing I've ever done, realistically speaking.'

'Maybe the old guy will live forever, Frankie!' Eric roared, finally walking away. 'Catch you later!'

'I certainly hope that he does,' slurred Frank, coupling this with another belch.

Eric, by the way, was never a difficult guy for Frank to find. An arbitrary visit to the Inn was all it took him. It wasn't that Eric was usually in there. The right way of putting it was that Eric was never usually *not* in there! Frank used to roll up and Eric was usually in there. But of course Eric wasn't *always* in there. He was only ever usually in there when Frank was in there. When Frank himself *wasn't* in there, Eric clearly seized his opportunity to go home or wherever else in order to eat, shit, fuck and sleep. But when Frank was back in there, so usually was Eric, or rather so Eric was usually never not.

Eric himself loved nothing better than winding Tom up big style:

'Say, Tommy. What star sign are you?'

'Aries, mate.'

'Oh, okay. Aries. That's good. That's good.'

'And you?'

'What about me?'

'What's *your* star sign?'

'Oh, okay. I'm Otto.'

'*Otto?*'

'Otto the otter.'

'What are you talking about, "Otto"? There's no such sign, you daft bastard!'

'Hey, sure there is, Tommy! Otto the otter. Comes right after Leo the lion.'

'Get out of it.'

'Tommy, I'm serious.'

'Bollocks!'

'Oh, hey, wait! Maybe this is just a Canadian thing!'

'Get out of it, you piss-taking bastard!'

A fresh pint arrived in front of Frank. He was now so pissed, he couldn't even remember ordering it. He stared at it crossly, as if it had just offended him and then looked to his left. Beyond the vacant stool, Thoad was there, reading his newspaper, which was spread over the bar as usual. Frank then looked straight ahead and saw and heard Tom talking animatedly behind the bar to someone he thought might have been Baz, but he wasn't sure. His vision was beginning to pack up. He smiled and nodded just in case it was him (it wasn't). Next, he glanced to his right and saw Stephen Mauve dismounting from his stool. He was probably only going to the toilet, but again, Frank wasn't sure.

Frank got the distinct impression that everybody was deserting him, but then instantly realised how silly this was. In fact, everybody was won-derful and they were all his friends. He fancied some nuts and started waving wildly at Tom. This unbalanced him and he toppled off his stool, falling heavily.

'I'm alright! I'm alright!' he immediately shouted, frantically waving away the assistance which was certainly not forthcoming. He scrambled up, walked towards the door, fell over again, got up, walked towards the door and went out.

It was not an unfamiliar exit for Frank, but this time it was supple-mented by Eric's exalted cry of "I hope he lives forever, Frankie!" triumphing over the heavy-metal, but still not enough to penetrate Frank's brain, as this had been taken over by something else – something which had no concern at all for the well-being of the rest of Frank's body.

Chapter 5

Frank's Mother

THE MONDAY EVENING, the night before Herbert Woodcastle's funeral, Frank had pledged to spend quietly at home with his mother and Hansel and Gretel, her two cats. The very last thing he needed was to go down and get shitfaced at the Inn again. His body badly required sleep – a full night's quality sleep, not alcohol-induced oblivion. He had had plenty of this ever since his most recent fall from grace (that is to say from a Station Inn wooden stool) and he certainly realised the wisdom not to clock up any more. Tonight he was going to be a good boy, he promised himself.

As Mr Snape had advised them, each member of the Old Firm staff had been given a specific role in the funeral proceedings. On the practical side of the funeral itself, these did not differ from normal, but first there were the pre-service 'celebrations' to negotiate, at which Mr Woodcastle would be on display to the guests, having been tended to by Peter Foster and Tessa Sharma so that he looked and smelled not quite as dead. Here duties *were* allocated: Noddoes had been given the job of greeter of the guests. His task would be to receive their calling card, announce them and that was the size of it. Even so, Noddoes took the bestowing of this honour on him with his usual actor's pomposity and somehow imagined that he had been appointed 'master of ceremonies', something for which only he was qualified. Perhaps Mr Snape was grooming him for a promotion now that a vacuum had been created by 'dear Herbert's' passing. A partnership! This would mean only one thing – the succession itself after Mr Snape's great heart was finally stilled.

Frank Eddowes would dearly have loved to have been given the job of greeter himself and felt badly wounded that he had not been. In addition, he felt considerably annoyed that as Mr Snape's assistant and secondary greeter of regular customers, he was not expected to assume those duties again on this very high profile occasion. He had not even been told why he had not been and why Noddoes had.

What really rubbed the salt in the wound was that it was clear that Frank had been subject to a direct swap of duties with the old luvvie. This meant that whilst Noddoes was doing his Ralph Richardson bit at the door, Frank was going to be required to stand suitably attired and head bowed over one corner of the open casket, whilst each of the other three points were guarded appropriately enough by one of the Old Firm's bearers. Noddoes too was a bearer and should have been at the fourth. Instead, he was standing where Frank should have been. Frank considered himself slighted. He was not a happy bunny.

Tessa had been asked to act as official 'hostess' on behalf of the Old Firm. Her task involved much more. She would be required to make certain that everybody was 'aware of the presence of dear Herbert'. Initially, she would receive guests from Noddoes, who would already have announced them, and then bring them over to a waiting Mr Snape standing behind the sherry table. She couldn't help feeling that she was in actual fact an usher rather than a hostess since her next duty involved her directing the guest to a viewing of an artwork (that of her's and Peter Foster's) and that she would thus be better employed carrying a torch and a tray of choc-ices. She wisely didn't suggest this.

Peter Foster himself was to be 'overseer' of the casket. This meant that he would be stood behind Woodcastle's casket with a self-satisfied look on his face and would acknowledge the guests and receive their compliments as they admired his handiwork, ready and willing to answer any questions these doyens of the industry might have with regard to this, his most important of exhibits. Once the preliminaries had been completed and tributes paid, including an address by Mr Snape, the funeral itself would take place at a local crematorium and that would be that.

The staff were expected at the undertakers for the usual opening time of nine o'clock, even though the Old Firm was naturally closed for business that day, and the guests were expected at eleven. Peter and Tessa had long since done the job on old Woodcastle and the departed was already waiting in the viewing room in his quality casket. He would need a bit of touching up in the morning, which Tessa would do with her beautician's kit, before being wheeled through to the private office, already emptied of its furniture, where he would be plonked onto a makeshift catafalque a couple of feet in front of the French windows, the curtains of which would of course be drawn for the occasion Mr Snape had decided would be a 'bleak and beautiful day'.

Frank looked over at the door from his armchair just in time to see Gretel walking out, probably to powder her nose. The male half of the feline duo remained in the lounge in a traditional picture box pose, curled up in front of the fire, albeit one of an electric barred variety rather than one of crackling logs. Mrs Eddowes sat in her own chair with the sound barely up on the TV and the subtitles on, and at this point Frank decided to go out and have a beer. He would only have a couple, say hello to Tom and Thoad and be back in time for the News. After this it would be bed, for although he was still pissed off (actually, crestfallen) at having been replaced by the insufferable Noddoes as Mr Snape's 'number two' for the funeral, Frank still recognised his duty to the Old Firm and this most certainly extended to being at his best for the events of the following day. Quite incidental to this was a medical need to keep his own promise to himself of a good night's sleep.

Frank rose from his chair and walked to the door.

'I'll be back before nine, mum,' he assured her.

Nellie Eddowes had heard something like this before: 'Don't you dare be getting pickled, now, Frank!' she warned him. 'You know what it is tomorrow.'

'Which is why I'll be back before nine,' repeated Frank, a little irritated. He had indeed let the business with Noddoes upset him again. Two pints and a chat with Tom would help him unwind and ensure that his exasperation would not prevent him from having the good sleep he needed for all sorts of reasons.

Frank removed his coat from the hook in the hall. He'd be back before nine for the News. As he went out, Gretel came back in through the cat flap.

Chapter 6

Mr Woodcastle

PETER FOSTER AND Tessa Sharma both arrived at the Old Firm soon after eight o'clock to put the finishing touches to their masterpiece. Old Snape had been there since seven and let them in. The final touching up was swiftly actioned by Tessa and her brushes tipped with rouge. Any nasal hair still remaining was clipped and removed, the sparse patches of hair on Mr Woodcastle's head brushed and the predominantly bald dome polished before the casket was sprayed and then left to set. Soon after this, the corpse was wheeled through to the general office and then lifted carefully onto the catafalque with the aid of one of the bearers who had drawn the short straw to come in early principally to perform that task.

The guest of honour had arrived!

Not long after this, other staff began to trickle in. Mr Snape welcomed them all with a sombre handshake and then waved them towards a trolley on which sat a large pot of coffee, prepared as an additional obligation by the early arriving bearer. Noddoes took his cup and saucer over to the open casket and peered in:

'Oh I say. He looks wonderful!' he exclaimed, knowing only too well that Mr Snape was scrutinising him.

'Thank you,' said Peter Foster.

'Bleak and beautiful,' craftily added Noddoes, quoting Snape directly, and then walked away before pushing his luck further.

Other staff members gathered around, and each in turn complimented the embalmers on their efforts with poor old dead Herbert. Peter nodded his thanks and Tessa smiled prettily whenever the praise was extended to her. Frank Eddowes stared at her and was overwhelmed once again by the feeling which was not so much an adult admiration for the young woman than a juvenile, indeed childish, crush. For it was a sad fact that Frank had never had a proper girlfriend in his life. He had had sex a few times, but never without parting with money and never for more than a few minutes and it was because of this that he remained at more than an arm's length away from the opposite sex. He knew that he was nuts about Tessa but had absolutely no idea what to do next except stare at her and blush like a twat. Had Frank been aware of Tessa's feelings towards him, he would have been despairing indeed. This wasn't because she didn't reciprocate Frank's admiration for her; this was because she wasn't even aware of it and, what's more, wasn't really aware of him!

But there was another reason for Frank's staring fit on this occasion. He had arrived at his place of work for the Old Firm's 'bleak and beautiful day' a full quarter of an hour late following a session at the Inn, which had seen him drink himself into a stupor to beat all stupors, despite the promise he had made to his mother and to himself not to get bladdered again. Not only had he supped steadily until closing time on his stool, but he had somehow ended up at an informal drinking party held by Stephen Mauve (a straw-clutching exercise to finally get himself accepted) where Frank poured a further quite disgraceful amount of alcohol down his scrag. Nobody else from the Inn bothered to go (Stephen assumed and hoped it was because he had chosen a Monday evening and this was largely true – even the Inn Crowd have to dry out sometime), but Frank, who would have agreed to parachute off Rocky Point at this stage of the game, jumped instead at the opportunity of more booze and a chance to explain to someone for the hundredth time how badly he had been treated by the Old Firm and how he couldn't give a stuff anymore about his job. He put his arms around Stephen Mauve's shoulder and opened his heart out to him. This was considered a major result by Stephen. A Station Inn regular in his home confiding in him so passionately! A foothold to ingratiate himself with Thoad, Eric and the others, perhaps?

When it was all over, Frank had drunk himself sober and was able to stagger home unaccompanied. By the time the key was thrust into the lock, it was nearly four o'clock and his mother had long since given up on him and gone away to her bed. Her punishment was to not get up to make him breakfast, the ultimate sign of displeasure, and it was this departure from the usually rigid regime which had proved to be the reason for Frank's tardiness rather than the fact that he was shot to pieces. After all, he had trotted off to work in similar states many times before and had always arrived right on the button. This time, he had been left to sort his morning out himself and had got himself into a bit of a tizz.

As for his actual level of sobriety, this was really quite passable, considering what he had been up to. Frank may well have had several antecedents for getting drunk very quickly, spouting nonsense and then falling over, but once initially intoxicated, he rarely deteriorated and therefore could and did continue drinking without really getting any worse thereby. Added to this was the principal weapon in his armoury, something for which he was renowned and something which was the envy of any drunk, or indeed any recreational drinker who occasionally went over the top: Frank Eddowes was a brilliant recoverer. He had many times stumbled indoors at well after midnight after, for example, a Saturday night session, completely hammered, but had then leapt refreshed from his pit at just after seven o'clock to make his mother a cup of tea (thereby partly reciprocating for her efforts throughout the week) and then trotted off in pursuit of the Sunday papers. By the time midday had come around again, Frank was more often than not back in the Inn for the lunchtime session before the magnetic lure of a Sunday roast presented a beckoning that not even Frank was able to resist. It was after this that he caught up with his sleep and was back on his stool in the Inn by seven o'clock for evensong. Frank Eddowes was a brilliant recoverer because he was obliged to be. He was an incurable pisshead.

As eleven o'clock approached, Mr Snape addressed his staff for the final time before kick-off. Everyone was in position now and Old Snape smiled and nodded in satisfaction.

'Dear Herbert would have been proud at such a sight,' he told them, meaning it. 'What a commendable body of men! And you too, my dear. I can almost sense dear Herbert smiling down from on high, despite the overwhelming bleakness of the landscape.'

'Indubitably, sir, this great funeral director is beaming down from his paradisiacal quarters, liberated from his mortal remains, resplendent though they be,' offered the 'Master of Ceremonies', again making a mercenary use of one of Snape's own phrases.

'"Mortal remains" *Tommyrot!*' thought Frank to himself, disgusted, not only at Noddoes' stomach-churning sycophancy, but also suddenly becoming very agitated again at the role-reversal with Noddoes that had been imposed on him and the fact that his rival was so obviously taking full advantage of this golden opportunity. The downward slope of having been drunk was beginning to set in a bit. This time, his famed recuperative powers had not been absolute, it appeared. Taking into account how much Frank had drunk, this was not the surprise of the century.

He craned his neck just enough to peer into the open casket. 'Eric's quite right,' he pondered. 'This isn't a dead body. This isn't a dead anything. This is a doughnut. We're paying tribute to a doughnut. This is all poppycock.'

'Poppycock!' he said out loud.

Everybody stared at him.

'I *beg* your pardon?' demanded Mr Snape.

Frank bowed his head again. 'Doughnut,' he said softly.

'Eddowes, what the blazes is the matter with you, man!' roared Snape. 'Pull yourself together!'

The bell then rang. The first guests.

Noddoes walked to the door, thus giving Frank an opening to try to redeem himself.

'I'm sorry,' he whispered. 'I'm just not used to this side of the business. I've seen the light now. We're refuge collectors, not undertakers.'

Old Snape couldn't believe this last comment. '*Hellfire*, Eddowes, are you drunk? By thunder, man! Today of all days!'

'Alfred Briers, Harold Gadd and Perceval Proudfoot arrive!' suddenly announced Noddoes in his best Michael Hordern and Tessa began approaching the three very old men.

'Gentlemen!' welcomed Snape warmly. 'Three stalwarts of the industry!'

'The opposition, it seems to me!' thought Frank to himself, since Briers was a senior official of a main nationwide firm, whilst Gadd and Proudfoot's own company had for years rivalled the Old Firm for the heart and soul of Pendlesham's dead, scoring the occasional spectacular victory, but never coming close to affecting the total putsch.

Tessa led the visitors up to Mr Snape for the official handshake and then up to his terminally horizontal partner.

'Nice job,' nodded Mr Briers as he peered into the casket.

'Thank you,' said Peter and Tessa together.

'What? A girl embalmer, eh, Snape?' exclaimed Mr Proudfoot, smiling at Tessa. 'Whoever would have thought it! So what happened to that other chap, Foster? Did you get rid?'

'He's standing behind the coffin, granddad!' barked Frank suddenly, still with his head bowed.

Mr Proudfoot looked up and blinked. 'Oh, so he is, so he is! Sorry, Foster. Didn't see you there. And Briers is right. Damn good work!'

Peter Foster acknowledged.

'Mr Simon Plemster, nephew of dear Herbert arrives, representing the Woodcastle family!' announced Noddoes, switching effortlessly from Hordern to Gielgud.

'You must be Dolly's son,' said Snape, as the middle-aged man was 'ushered' up to him by Tessa.

'Yes, well remembered,' Simon said. 'Herbert was my mother's only brother, but they were never close. I think there was a falling out. Personally, I can't really remember having met him, if truth be told.'

'Come and meet him now!' sneered Frank, still with his head bowed; and as if this was a cue, Tessa smilingly indicated the casket, with the four sentries at each corner and Peter Foster standing behind it with a twist of a grin on his face.

'Oh my word, is he in there?' asked Simon, clearly uneasy at the prospect of eying a corpse.

'No, idiot, I'm standing over here!' rasped Frank, still with his head bowed.

Tessa started to giggle.

'Mr Ronald Willis, representative of the undertakers' guild arrives!' announced Lord Olivier.

Tessa walked over to receive him, now quite unable to control her laughter.

'Oh, hello there!' she gushed and then crumpled onto the floor in a heap.

'In the box! He's in the box!' shouted Frank helpfully, at the top of his voice, and then threw up a gargantuan helping of alcohol-rich vomit straight into the casket and all over Mr Woodcastle, who didn't seem to mind, bless his heart.

'Oh God. *Groovy!*' roared Tessa from the floor, her waterworks now having failed her completely. She howled with laughter as she splashed about, because she had spotted, not only the mortally wounded look on Peter Foster's face, but also the fact that the three other bearers had not moved an inch from their positions and instead remained head bowed at their respective corners, whilst Frank concluded his business with a splutter, coughing the last remaining lump of nausea safely into the conveniently open receptacle. Dignity was all.

There was a silence before old Snape exploded.

'Get him out! Get him out!' he commanded to nobody in particular. 'Eddowes. You're drunk!'

This ludicrously superfluous rider only made matters for poor Tessa worse. She was now thrashing away like a fish in the shallows, emitting a manic laugh which sounded synthetic but was only too real.

'Eddowes, your services are no longer required. Get out!' Snape then advised him, as the guests looked on disbelievingly.

Frank staggered unaided to the door *à la* Station Inn.

'Take that damn girl with you!' Snape demanded, throwing his arm towards the marine life on the floor.

Noddoes then stepped forward.

'Oh, Mr Snape. What a to do! What a to do!' he quivered. 'Are there any words… Is there any crumb of comfort that I may proffer you at this… at this *terrible* moment, a moment which has converted this beautiful, yet sombre celebration into the cruellest of comedies?'

Arthur Snape glared at him and at this most unlikely of moments, the penny dropped.

'Yes there damn well is, you pompous ass. Get out! You're dismissed as well!' Exit Noddoes stage right.

All fired then. The sick, the hysterical and the rumbled!

Chapter 7

Noddoes

THE CALAMITOUS GOINGS on at the Old Firm managed somehow to miraculously escape the attentions of the press, despite all the likely sources of correspondent who had been present and had witnessed the incredible scenes there. Perhaps it was the case that everyone had been so completely dumbfounded that they had simply been unable to believe their eyes and had therefore assumed that they had been dreaming. After Frank, Tessa and Noddoes had departed, the three remaining bearers had been snapped out of their trance by Snape and ordered to close the now less than fragrant casket. There had been clearly nothing else to do other than carry on with the funeral. To give old Woodcastle another wash and set was out of the question and, in any case, Peter Foster was in no fit condition to work. Inconsolable, he had sunk to his knees close to tears and had remained in this position even after the lid had been slid on. He was totally devastated. Mr Proudfoot offered him a swig of brandy from his hip flask, which was accepted with a sniff.

'It really was a frightfully good job, old boy,' he said comfortingly. 'I know it's difficult, but try to remember it as it was…'

Because of the sudden staff shortage, Foster should have been required to stiffen his upper lip and take up position as the fourth bearer. But he was obviously in no emotional state for this after what had happened and his condition was adjudged even less appropriate after he had taken more than a little advantage of kind Mr Proudfoot's goodness. This was when Simon Plemster, Mr Woodcastle's nephew, made the utterly decent offer to stand in, an offer gratefully accepted by the now strangely calm Mr Snape. The funeral passed without incident and the curtain came down on the most remarkable day in the Old Firm's history.

Whereas neither Frank nor Tessa returned to the Old Firm's offices, Noddoes decided to attempt a salvage operation on his career by appealing to Mr Snape's good nature. He turned up for duty as usual the very next day.

'I thought I had made it clear to you that you are dismissed,' old Snape told him. 'Now unless you have returned to claim any effects, leave the premises immediately!'

'But, Mr Snape!' quivered Noddoes. 'I really am unable to ascertain as to how I have transgressed so irreconcilably as to warrant summary dismissal. The unacceptable behaviour of Eddowes and Miss Sharma, for which they were so correctly ousted, had nothing to do with me, sir. I am at a loss to comprehend as to how I am implicated, as to why I too must accompany those sick jesters… those *traitors* onto the list of former employees of your noble and historical firm. Mr Snape, I appeal to you!'

The old man glared at him.

'I take it that you are asking me for an explanation as to why I have discontinued your employment. Is that right?' he then asked him.

'I consider my request of a nature nothing other than reasonable,' confirmed Noddoes loftily.

'You are right,' conceded Snape. 'And I have to say to you that the inexplicable behaviour of Eddowes and Sharma did indeed warrant instant dismissal. You are right about that too. But you, Noddoes, committed by far and away the gravest offence of all, one which, had it been revealed to Eddowes, may well have prompted legal action by him. Your unforgivable actions also in no insignificant measure triggered off the hysterical and astonishing performance displayed by Miss Sharma and can only be described as sabotage, for what reason I am at a loss to imagine, let alone comprehend.'

Noddoes suddenly went pale. 'I don't know what you mean, sir,' he stammered.

'Oh, I think that you do, my friend,' said Snape coldly. 'I also think that despite your constant obsequiousness, you take me and have always taken me for a complete buffoon; someone who is not only your intellectual inferior by some considerable margin, but a feeble, antiquated, vacuous old idiot; the total manipulation of whom would not tax the aptitude of a five-year-old child.'

'Oh, Mr Snape! How mistaken you are!'

The old man shook his head. 'Am I? I'm sorry to tell you, Noddoes, that your voice-throwing exercise, skilful though it was, admittedly, was severely flawed on account of the simple fact that Eddowes, whom you were endeavouring to implicate by its introduction, was unconscious on his feet due to intoxication before the first guests had even arrived, as you well know. He revived sufficiently only to do what he did to poor, dear Herbert. For this, Eddowes had to go. Miss Sharma had to go for her subsequent hysterical and astonishing display, the like of which I suspect has not been seen outside a lunatic asylum, or indeed in a third-rate repertory theatre, which brings me nicely on to you, Noddoes.' Here Mr Snape paused cruelly. 'You were right to consider it reasonable that I provide a reason to you as to why you also must go. I have now done so. Now I repeat, unless you have any personal effects remaining on these premises, get the devil off my property! If you have anything further to say, I suggest that you engage the services of a solicitor. That is all. Good day.'

Of course Noddoes denied everything. But he knew that it was useless to prolong his plea and he was too proud to beg. He therefore left, half-heartedly intent on revenge on the Old Firm and more particularly Frank Eddowes, but really far more worried about what in the world was left for a failed ham actor who had been fired from his position as an undertaker's bearer for impropriety.

Chapter 8

Pick Your Own Strawberries

O F THE THREE people dismissed by the Old Firm, Tessa Sharma would undoubtedly have had the best chance of lodging a successful appeal directly to Mr Snape had she chosen to do this. Noddoes had already tried his luck and had been sent away with a flea in his ear and Frank Eddowes had decided against even trying. He realised that what he had done had been a terrible thing and considered that dismissal was the least he could reasonably expect. Tessa, however, would have enjoyed the guaranteed support of Peter Foster, who might well have been able to influence Snape who, after all, had employed Tessa on his late partner's recommendation following an approach from Foster himself. Tessa had also been innocent of the initial outrage. She hadn't been drunk herself and had only reacted to the extraordinary events instigated by Frank and apparently Noddoes. True, her behaviour subsequently had been completely outrageous and worthy of her feline past, but mitigation could reasonably have been argued. Miss Sharma had decided that she did not want her job back. This, unlike with Frank, was not out of any shame she felt. She didn't feel any at all. She did however know that she could never return to the Old Firm, simply because she feared hysterics as soon as she encountered her first customer, another coffin, and more particularly Peter Foster, whose pitiful expression following Frank's rape of his masterwork she still couldn't get out of her mind.

Frank, meanwhile, had felt compelled to immediately break the devastating news to his mother. He had surprisingly remembered everything, particularly what he had done to the casket, but was quite unwilling to elaborate beyond the basic truth that he had been given his marching orders for being pissed on duty, adding the white lie that he had also fallen over for effect. He also omitted to mention the fate of his other two colleagues, but the names would not have meant anything to his mother anyway, and explaining that two others had been sacked over the same incident he felt could quite easily have fired his mother's curiosity for knowing what precisely did happen. The bizarre truth would have probably given her a heart attack. Frank, of course, didn't feel so great himself, as one of those dismissed had been a woman with whom he knew he was in love. As things stood, he might not ever see her again. The prospect of this made him more than a little miserable.

'This is all down to your drinking, Frank,' his mother emphasised, too upset to resort to nagging him at length. 'You're never out of that horrid dingy little place in the station. Drink has ruined many a good man and now it's ruined you.'

Hansel and Gretel sat glaring at their disgraced stepbrother and occasionally exchanged glances with each other. The sole wage earner in the house had been beheaded. Life might very well be a little difficult now.

'Well what in the world are you going to do then, Frank?' his mother continued, nearly in tears. 'Who's going to give you a job now? At your age? What are you going to do for a reference? Your firm won't give you one. You've been sacked. Frank, what are you going to do?'

'I'll pop down to the job centre tomorrow,' he said in a tone which suggested that this would be no more difficult than trotting down the road for a pint of milk and a loaf.

'Well, I think you should try to get your job back,' his mother advised him. 'I'm sure they'll give you one more chance, especially if you promise them that you'll give up drinking.'

This was a vain hope indeed.

'No, mother,' said Frank firmly, determined more than ever to protect her from the full story. 'I'll pop down to the job centre tomorrow. I'll be alright.'

He spent the evening of the 'bleak and beautiful day' doing precisely what he should have done the night before. He had a quiet night in with his mother and her 'babies', going to bed early and sober and catching a whole night of quality sleep. This was an extreme case of bolting the stable door after the horse had gone; but even more bizarre was what Frank did the following day. Instead of registering at the job centre, as he had so sanguinely assured his mother he would, he failed to arrive and for exactly the same reason that he failed to be home in time for the Nine o'clock News two nights before, Frank had got up at his leisure and taken a long bath. He had a mid-morning breakfast, rested up and then had walked out of the house to the job centre. He was on his regular stool in the Station Inn at five minutes past twelve. By a quarter past one he was completely hammered again and was telling the story of his sacking for the umpteenth time. Regulars and strangers alike had been trickling in gradually for the lunchtime session and not many of them had escaped copping an earful. Most were intrigued and amused; others dismissed his ramblings as those of a lying drunk, and everyone else couldn't give a flying fuck.

When Stephen Mauve came in, he made an immediate beeline for Frank and was more than a little delighted when Frank greeted him gushingly and then put his arm around him to make an announcement in what was intended to be a confidential whisper. Goodness knows why.

'I spewed up all over Mr Woodcastle as he lay at rest in his coffin. I've been fired,' he stammered.

'Bloody hell!' cried Stephen, never thinking for one moment that this could have been bullshit or a wind-up.

'Not only that,' continued Frank, 'but I also managed to get the girl of my dreams sacked for laughing at what I did to him.'

'Jesus, Frank!'

Frank paused. He raised his right index finger to indicate that the floor was still his, but then seemed to forget what came next.

'This is incredible, Frank,' began Stephen. 'I really don't know what –'

'NOT ONLY THAT!' roared Frank, nearly falling off his stool once more and slurring like a good 'un. 'Not only that… Not only… THAT, but I also succeeded in getting somebody else sacked too, somebody I don't like. I hate him and I got him the heave-ho. But I can't remember who and I'm blessed if I can remember why.'

'Would this be' –

'BUT I DON'T CARE!'

'Would this be that Noddoes guy that you were talking to me about?' just about managed Stephen.

Frank stared at him and seemed in that instant degrees more sober.

'Have we had this conversation before?' he asked.

'No, mate', Stephen assured him. 'But the night before all this happened, you were telling me about your undertakers.'

'Funeral directors,' corrected Frank with a belch.

'You told me all about how you hated Noddoes for taking your place, how much you loved Tessa and all about Mr Snape… and you were calling Mr Woodcastle a "doughnut", remember?'

'I remember! I remember! … No, I really don't think that I do.'

'Of course you do. You were at the drinks party over at my place,' prompted Stephen.

'Was I really? Oh, so I was!'

Frank had remembered now and both he and particularly Stephen Mauve were grateful, although for entirely different reasons. In fact, it was Stephen who was in the ascendancy now, as Eric Seebal had just entered the Inn and after the briefest of chats with Tom sat down on the other side of Frank, even acknowledging Stephen before taking his pew.

'Shit, Frankie. What can I say? Did you really retch up over the dead guy? Christ!'

'I didn't mean to,' Frank assured him. 'But it doesn't matter. It was only a doughnut. Just like you told me.'

Eric looked quickly over at Stephen and then back to Frank.

'Okay, okay,' he confessed. 'But I just said torch the old timer without all the regular bullshit. I never figured you'd give him breakfast first. Shit!'

'What will you do now?' asked Stephen.

'I'm going to the job centre in a minute,' said Frank. 'I'm sure that they can find me a job as a clerk somewhere.'

'You have a problem, Frankie,' Eric said. 'The guy at the job centre will want a reference from old man Snape. They'll want to know why you quit and shit. Maybe you can lie and hope that they don't get wise and check you out.'

Frank hadn't really considered this, even though his mother had mentioned it to him during her last outburst of nagging the day before. He reached for his drink.

'Bugger that!' snapped Stephen from the opposite flank, nearly causing Frank to drop his pint. 'Why don't you set up on your own? Why don't you find Tessa and bring her in as well? Your very own funeral directors. God knows there'll always be a market, especially in this town. Go for it, Frank. Go it alone. Do your own thing!'

'Say, that's a fucking excellent idea!' yelled Eric, jumping off his stool in excitement. 'Christ, that's *epic!*'

'Epic Eric!' added Stephen dryly.

Frank suddenly burst into laughter, a fit only punctuated with assurances that he would never call the young Canadian anything else. Eric, meanwhile, was now smiling himself.

'"*Epic!*",' he mused and then nodded. 'Yeah, that's cool!'

'Frank, you might want to call your firm *Doughnuts Are Us!*' suddenly added Stephen, now having a wonderful time.

This time, Frank did drop his pint as his hysteria heightened. Epic was laughing too and so was Tom from behind the bar.

'Do it! Do it!' shouted Epic when he had finally calmed down. 'Do it, Frankie!'

'No, I'm not sure that I can,' croaked Frank, getting up to leave, as if the crash of the glass had been his own personal bell calling time.

'What makes you say that?' challenged Epic. 'You're crazy! It's a great idea!'

'Come off, Frank! Course you can!' slipped in Tom. 'You must have a few quid stashed away. You'll have no trouble getting a loan for any more. And this is a golden opportunity to stick one over on the old sod who red-carded you. He's chucked down the gauntlet. Pick the frigger up!'

'And move in on Tessa,' added Stephen sweetly.

'You *know* you've gotta do it, Frankie!' Epic told him. 'Go for it! Power-play in Pendlesham, baby!'

Frank was way past merry, but was together enough to realise that the guys were not joking. He actually thought that Stephen's idea was superb but was not at all convinced that he would be able to do something like that. He had enough trouble boiling an egg. But running his own business? It was Stephen Mauve who again provided the prompt – this one changing the entire picture forever.

'Destiny awaits!' he said stoically.

In that instant, as the sage would have said, Frank Eddowes was enlightened. When he suddenly realised what he was going to do, his heart started to beat very quickly and he became incredibly excited and totally calm at the same time, to say nothing of degrees more sober. Nothing could deflect that boy now. He floated away, intent now on a visit to his bank to arrange an appointment with a business advisor, rather than to the job centre for a no-hope interview with a computer. After this, he would pursue Tessa relentlessly – for professional reasons, of course.

Epic turned to Stephen Mauve after Frank had left the Inn in the most upright way he had for ages.

'You did good, man!' he nodded.

'Thanks. I really think that he can do something for himself, given the opportunity. I really believe that.'

'I think you're right,' agreed Epic. 'I think Frankie's got the potential to torch this whole fucking town.'

Stephen was now at the centre of a mini cluster of other regulars – the blessed inner circle: The Inn Crowd, as Stephen himself had long since called them, though never *to* them. Epic had leapt over onto the stool vacated by Frank, and Thoad's newspaper had suddenly shifted a few degrees up the bar towards them too. Tom was at a touching distance behind the ramp; Kate, the tall, brunette, all-smiling, moon-faced barmaid with only a mild habit had also materialised. More interestingly, the stool on the other side of Stephen had all of a sudden been claimed by Amanda, the attractive punk girl who had added her own very personal mixer to Stephen's drink on an earlier occasion as a sign of contempt, but had now suddenly decided that the young man in the serious suit was perhaps rather more cool and attractive than she had previously thought. This consideration reached, having witnessed the merriment of the last few minutes, much of which had been down to Stephen Mauve.

Stephen was immediately conscious of her presence.

'Hiya!' he smiled.

'Hiya,' she said back, now wanting him.

Stephen chose this moment to leave. He acknowledged Tom, tapped Epic on the shoulder as he alighted from his stool and walked nonchalantly out. It had been his day by the length of the Pennines.

Chapter 9

Hansel And Gretel

FRANK'S APPOINTMENT AT the bank was arranged for the next morning at ten o'clock. He then went home and told his mother about what he had decided to do. He may not have been totally sober but he was also not the same man who had walked into the Inn at the beginning of the afternoon.

'I'm going to be the most successful funeral director in England,' he promised. 'Blow the job centre! Once I've got into the swing of things, the job centre will be sending people to me!'

'Frank, I can't believe this is you talking!' his mother said by way of a reply. Hansel and Gretel suddenly left the room together. Presumably neither could they.

'You don't approve?' inquired Frank curtly.

'It's not that I don't approve, dear –'

'You don't think I can do it,' he concluded for her.

'Oh, Frank, I really don't know what to think!' she admitted, which as far as Frank was concerned practically confirmed that she had zero faith.

He shrugged. 'I must admit, I can't blame you for thinking that way. I needed some convincing myself,' he told her. 'But destiny awaits.'

His mother stared at him.

'Don't worry, I can always submit myself to the tender mercies of the job centre if things don't work out,' Frank went on. 'I think employers would be impressed at someone who at least tried to make a go of it. But I'm going to make sure that things don't come to that.'

By this stage, Frank's mum had decided that drink was almost certainly to blame for all this nonsense, so she didn't say anything else. Instead she silently resolved to tackle her son again on the subject before he made his next trip to the Inn, rather than after it. It was then that it occurred to her that there was a whole evening of drinking time still left that day to supplement what Frank had already taken on board when he should have been at the job centre.

'Frank, I just want you to promise me that you will stop in tonight and rest. Promise me!'

Frank, however, saw through her. She was nagging him about his drinking once again. But then did she ever do anything other?

'Well, I'm not going to the Station Inn or any other pub if that's your fear!' he snapped, extremely cross that the inference seemed to be that he could not be trusted not to disgrace himself at the bank the next morning. 'But I'm going to have to go out again. Now.'

'Oh, Frank, *why?*' wailed his mother.

'I'm going to the library with your permission,' he said, walking away. 'I want to try to find one of those information packages on setting up businesses so that when I see the chap at the bank tomorrow, he won't think I'm a complete idiot.'

His mother dutifully felt an immediate twinge of regret now. It was clear that Frank had been serious and clear headed all along and not merely blurting out thoughts concocted by the demon drink; and when he returned less than an hour later carrying a fat folder marked *You And Your Own Business* and went straight up to his room with it, she took him up a bacon sandwich by means of a peace offering.

'The best of luck, Frank,' she said. 'It goes without saying that you have my blessing.'

Frank looked up and smiled. Hansel and Gretel had also appeared and were both sitting down grooming themselves and occasionally each other.

'Of course', he said. 'But I'm very grateful that you've said it.'

Chapter 10

Paris

TESSA HAD DISAPPOINTED her parents again. She had previously caused them a not inconsiderable amount of grief over her expulsion from medical school, and now after a lengthy, if unorthodox, period of stability, it appeared that she had gone off on one again. Tessa herself had told them that she had resigned, but Dinesh Sharma was no idiot. He just knew by instinct that his daughter had been dismissed. She had brought disgrace on him again. He didn't even want to hear the details. The less he knew about it the better, in fact.

Tessa herself had accepted her fate stoically. Having already ruled a plea to Mr Snape out of the question, she had decided on a short sabbatical in Paris before examining the job market again. She had enjoyed her work with Peter Foster and knew that she could rely on a reference from him without any interference from old Snape. If nothing came up and she ended up behind a shop counter somewhere, she promised herself that she would study pharmacy and see what happened there. Never say die.

While Miss Sharma was living it up on the Boulevard Saint-Michel, Frank Eddowes attempted to contact her at her flat back in Pendlesham. All he got for three days was her answering machine. He assumed quite rightly that she was on holiday and he didn't leave a message. He left it for a couple more days before trying again and she picked up the phone.

'Hello, Tessa. This is Frank.'

'Frank?'

'Frank Eddowes.'

'Oh, hello.'

'I was wondering… I was wondering how you were…'

'I'm fine.'

'...And if you've got another job yet.'

'I've just been in Paris actually,' said Tessa.

'Oh. Are you working in France now then?' Frank was instantly disappointed.

'No. I was just taking a break. How are you? Are you back at Mr Snape's now? Wasn't what happened just *wild*? I thought you were *brilliant!*'

Tessa started to giggle.

'Tessa, if you haven't got a job yet, I'd rather like to speak to you,' Frank said, trying his damndest to sound serious as he became ever more turned on by the girlish gurglings at the other end of the line.

'You're not asking me to support legal action or anything nutty like that, are you?' she chirped, as her giggling petered out.

'I want to make a proposition to you... Oh dear, I'm not very good at saying what I mean, am I? I want to offer you a job,' Frank told her.

There was a short pause before Tessa started to giggle again. 'What as?' she stammered. 'A cleaner-up of *sick?*'

Now she was laughing hysterically again in much the same way as at the ill-starred tribute to Mr Woodcastle. Frank waited for the fit to finish, or at least to stabilise sufficiently as to not render an interjection pointless.

'Doing what you were doing before,' he then finally answered. 'Except this time you'll be in charge.'

'What of?' howled Tessa, returning to hysteria immediately. 'Cleaning up the *sick?*'

The girl had lost any semblance of control now and Frank was beginning to understand just exactly why Mr Snape had sacked her also. Even so, it took her a little less time for her to get a grip this time, although she was still quite some distance from rationality.

'You liked being an embalmer, Tessa, didn't you?' Frank then said, deciding now on patronisation in an attempt to subsidise Tessa's puerile behaviour.

'Oh yes. It's great,' Tessa agreed.

'Would you like to do it again?'

'*Groovy!* Where?'

Frank had at last been given his chance. He had finally substantiated that Tessa might be interested. 'I'd like to outline it at length. Where would you like to meet? Perhaps we can have dinner.'

'How about my flat?' she suggested suddenly. 'You know where it is, don't you?'

Frank's composure snapped in that instant. 'Well… yes… if you really…'

'How about tonight?' she added helpfully.

'Yes… yes…' he stammered.

'I'll do dinner,' promised Tessa. 'Bring a bottle. A nice *full-bodied* red!' She giggled.

Frank found himself giggling back. He had turned to jelly, apart from his dick, which had turned to solid rock. Who had lost control now?

Chapter 11

Mr Craven

FRANK HAD VISITED his bank first and foremost for advice on how to start up in business. He was not necessarily looking for financial backing at that time, but such was the impression he made on the suit who interviewed him (who was already mindful of Frank's healthy personal balance and lifelong custom with the bank) that Frank swiftly found himself in the rather unusual but very happy position of being recommended for a substantial loan without having even applied for or requested one. From that moment, Frank had become his own boss.

His proposed business, Frank assured Mr Craven, casually leapt immediately over the first and in many ways the most vital hurdle, where others at a similarly embryonic stage had still yet to rise to the set position – that of targeting and securing a market. People would always die, especially in Pendlesham. Indeed, Mr Craven cheerfully assured Frank, on agreeing with this that, if anything, the town had an undertakers' shortage. 'It's not the sort of industry most new businessmen examine or even consider,' he told him wisely. 'The taboo surrounding it seems to constantly override the fact that the market is a very secure one and the returns generally very lucrative. The only cautionary note might be the reluctance of customers to use a newly founded firm. I need not tell someone of your experience in this industry that customers nearly always approach and seek out the services of an undertaker in a state of grief and shock. What these people are looking for is reassurance, and reassurance is not really conducive to trying something new and unfamiliar. They would therefore tend to gravitate towards an old and established norm and this means an old and established firm. Perhaps one their family have used before.'

'This I admit is the only thing that troubles me,' agreed Frank. 'Reluctance or refusal to change. This is something that not even cutting the costs of our services is unlikely to affect, especially in a well-healed town like this.'

The bank official smiled. 'I can see that you're a pragmatist, Mr Eddowes,' he said.

'Thank you. But I'm also determined to succeed. Destiny awaits. I know only too well that I'm competing against generations of tradition, something which has hitherto been a security blanket to hundreds of people who have been obliged to seek the services of our industry, relatives grieving a loved one, who decide without much thought that only a tried and trusted organisation could possibly be considered. Therefore, in order for me to get anything like a foothold in the business I have chosen, a run of the mill operation simply will not be good enough. Destiny awaits.'

Here the man from the bank raised his eyebrows.

'I'm going to have to do things a little differently,' explained Frank. 'And I intend to target a younger client too.'

'Aha!' exclaimed Mr Craven. 'The modern approach!'

'The modern approach!' nodded the new entrepreneur.

Chapter 12

Stephen

JUST BEFORE HE set off for his dinner appointment at Tessa's flat, Frank made a definite point of engaging in a lengthy and gratifying session of self-abuse, lest he should humiliate himself later at table. He anticipated that he would be carrying a log around in his trousers for much of the evening, as he had fancied Tessa insanely from the instant he had first set eyes on her, and this primeval lust (although Frank was pathetically convinced it was love) had, if anything, intensified since they had both been sacked and Tessa had fled abroad. Frank had always been the most enthusiastic of masturbators and had actioned such a vigorous and determined five-fingered shuffle this time because he reasoned and feared that the breaking of bread in Tessa's lair would be more than his stalk could stand. It would be particularly unfortunate if his cock exploded during dinner because he actually genuinely wanted to address Tessa on matters of business, even if this was only because if he succeeded in employing her, he was in the best position possible to try to shag her. It was a means to an end - *his* end, and Frank had therefore resolved that his pursuit of the girl, not that this had taken any form previously other than staring at her and then wanking himself daft later, must be temporarily deferred until Tessa had considered and responded to his job offer. Thus, the dirty water had to be rid of to prevent any cream rising to the top the second Tessa opened the door to him, and Frank set about his business with military precision, pulling his pud back and forth and from side to side to the accompanying and wholly appropriate imaginings of Tessa's endless, dusky legs. Having pleasured himself substantially, Frank showered down, freshened up and left the house a satisfied and nourished man, so that when Tessa did open the door to him, Frank's nevertheless inevitable stiffy was not one which otherwise would have matched the occasion and did not require first aid.

As the girl had requested, Frank had brought wine and had quite obviously not disgraced the sacred Bacchus. He had armed himself with a sufficiently potent blood-red potion from Hungary, hardly a cultured, nor indeed subtle choice of wine, but certainly 'full-bodied' enough not to dishonour any fare his lovely host was liable to present to him. In fact, Frank turned up expecting curry, and this was precisely what he got - lamb. Tessa had furnished the table with tumblers of spices and small dishes containing fresh chillies when there should have been a fire extinguisher instead. Making allowances for being alone with Tessa in her home, it was the finest food Frank had ever eaten and certainly the hottest. The wine was not remotely strong enough.

In an intriguing contrast to the superb main course, Tessa served up cheese (cheddar and stilton) and biscuits for dessert with a glass of port, followed by coffee and mints. The meal, Frank silently considered, mirrored the cook – Indian and English and very, very nice. He now knew for certain that he was in love and not merely in lust with this delightful young lady and he was extremely grateful that for once his cock agreed with him. It behaved like a gentleman.

After dinner, Frank put forward his proposal. He was starting his own funeral directors. He had the finance, he had the experience, he had ideas in abundance, but he didn't have any people. Would Tessa be interested in becoming his embalmer? If she was, the job was hers.

'When are you up and running?' Tessa asked.

'Well that's just it. I can't do anything until I appoint staff. At the moment I don't have anybody.'

Here Tessa smiled and then broke out into a giggle. 'You've obviously got your priorities right, Frank, haven't you? Getting the beautician first!'

'It's not the sort of position that's regularly advertised,' said Frank, neatly shielding the truth. 'But then I didn't feel a need to advertise because I thought of you immediately.'

'That's very sweet of you. When will you speak to Noddoes, the last of our disgraced trio? I suppose you'll be headhunting him too, won't you?'

This question came like a bolt from the blue, catching Frank uncomfortably off guard. He hadn't even given Maurice Noddoes a second thought since the day they had all been fired. Indeed, he still remained in contempt of him. As far as Frank was concerned, the failed Thesbian remained a mortal enemy, hardly deserving of being bracketed with himself and Tessa as hitherto trustworthy servants to the Old Firm, dismissed as the result of an indiscretion which had been a comic incident by anybody's standards. Frank had never been able to work out why Noddoes had also in fact been sacked, but what he did know was that Noddoes had been the one who had turned Mr Snape against him; the one who had secured Mr Snape's favours at Frank's expense; the one who had put the poison in and snatched away Frank's rightful position as Mr Snape's right-hand man at the tribute to Mr Woodcastle, and it was this, of course, that had been the catalyst for all that had happened to himself and Tessa, the trigger which had set everything off. If Noddoes had not been such a rotten creep, the disaster with the casket and its occupant wouldn't have happened, as Frank would have been precisely where he should have been – by Mr Snape's side instead of flanking the coffin. After all, where the devil else would a chap be expected to honk when such a convenient receptacle was available? They were going to set light to the bloody thing anyway. No, it might have been true that Frank was as excited as an infant on Christmas Eve about his plans for his new business, and it might have also been true that he would never have been alone with Tessa, drinking coffee in her flat, had the incidents at the Old Firm not taken place. Indeed, there would not have been any new business at all and Frank at this second would in all likelihood have been in the Inn getting blooted and fantasising tragically about having dinner in Tessa's flat, whilst offering her a dream job in order to save her from starvation. But the fact remained that Noddoes had been to blame, indirectly or otherwise, for Frank's humiliating dismissal and that of the woman he loved. Why the devil should he offer alms to a rat like this?

'He *is* a bit of an old fairy,' picked up Tessa, 'but I think he's super fun. He's almost a parody of himself with all that strutting around, pouting and posing. He reminds me of Mick Jagger sometimes. He's probably totally out of his gourd by now. You've *got* to give him a job, Frank. He's great for wind-ups!'

'My sentiments entirely,' nodded Frank. 'I'm going to hunt down the old luvvie relentlessly the first chance I get.'

'Groovy!' gushed Tessa.

Frank promised to contact Tessa as soon as things were finalised and then left, thanking her for a wonderful evening. The little twist at the end had been most unwelcome, but Frank was otherwise ecstatic. Tessa had said yes to him. The price to pay was Noddoes. But so what? Tessa had said yes. He went straight home and nearly ripped his cock off.

The next day he went to the Inn and set about getting hammered. It was a Saturday and everybody was there, including Stephen Mauve who had not only now become accepted in Inn society, but was now a confirmed member of the 'Inn Crowd', as Stephen himself now openly called them. In addition to this success in achieving a long held ambition, which had actually once bordered on an obsession, Stephen was now finding himself fending off the young punkettes and female scrotes, for which the Station Inn had long been a beacon, in very much the same way that Epic had found himself doing from day one. Chief amongst these new admirers was Amanda Plimmer, a young woman who had initially had nothing but contempt for Stephen and his suit and had even resented his very presence in the Inn, like so many of her ilk, but had now decided that he was the coolest guy in Pendlesham, a title which many outside the town would probably have considered a fairly meaningless accolade. Kate, the tall, brunette, all-smiling, moon-faced barmaid with only a mild habit whom Stephen had fancied forever, despite his bountiful relationship with his own fetching though disdainful girlfriend, Lucinda, was also more than willing to chat and flirt with him now. Amanda, the punkette though, had made up her mind to snare him, or at least to discover how things were hanging.

Stephen spent a lot of this increased time in the Inn chatting with other luminaries like Epic, Frank and Baz, as well as with Tom himself. But he became particularly friendly with Thoad, who although undoubtedly a pivotal member of the Inn Crowd, had nevertheless been a confirmed figure of monumental desolation up to that point. Amanda pitched in and threw herself at Stephen flagrantly and eventually he decided to grab her and give her a seeing to. He had learned that her boyfriend, for whom she had previously pined, had not returned, despite the assurances of Tom, and therefore Stephen saw fit to taking her back to his flat and losing a whole night's sleep. Amanda's immediate reaction was to tell Stephen that he was now hers and that her next step was going to be a conclusive assault on Lucinda with a Stanley knife as soon as she could track her down. Stephen saved her the trouble by informing his girlfriend that he had "found someone more intelligent" and was dumping her. It was a cruel way of putting it, but the wording did not lack truth, and from that moment, the shorthaired capitalist in the suit became an item with the volatile gothic punkette who wanted anarchy as well as death to everybody like Stephen Mauve. Whereas Lucinda had never set foot in the Inn and never would; something for which Stephen had never forgiven her, Amanda got extremely stroppy when she was obliged on occasion to set foot out of it. She was a Station Inn girlie beyond dispute and now she was Stephen Mauve's girlfriend. It was a match made in Pendlesham. The polar bear and the penguin get it on!

Frank, meanwhile, was dragging his feet. He recognised the need to trace Noddoes as the next step in furthering his ambitions, having been unexpectedly pressganged into this by Tessa, but was singularly reluctant to commit himself to the task and therefore confined his investigations to the Inn, a place in which he was as likely to encounter the old luvvie as he was his mother. And Frank knew it.

'What about a name for this business of yours, then?' asked Stephen. '*Doughnuts Are Us* is probably out.'

'That's easy,' said Epic. '*Frankie's!* He's gonna call it *Frankie's*. Ain't that right, Frankie?'

Frank smiled and shook his head. 'I was thinking of something more formal, really,' he told them. 'I fancied just having my initials and name followed by "Funeral Directors". Yes, that would do very well.'

'Get out of it, you boring old sod!' rasped Tom. 'What would be the point of that? Where's your sense of adventure?'

'I wasn't really looking at this as an adventure,' reflected Frank, not necessarily telling the truth. 'No, just my name will do nicely.'

'Say, what the hell *is* your name anyhow?' squawked Epic, lighting up again. 'Frankie *what*?'

'Eddowes,' Frank confirmed.

'Okay. So what we have here is "F. Eddowes. Funeral Director". You fucking geek, Frankie! Surely you can do better than that, man!'

This curt criticism fell some way short of amusing Frank who, from the very start, had envisaged his own name above the door; and even taking into account Epic's famed and sometimes endearing sledgehammer wit, such an outburst was difficult to take, even from him; someone whose business it quite literally wasn't. Commendably, Frank declined to show his annoyance and instead opted to irritate Epic further. 'I can *indeed* do better than that,' he replied, rather stuffily. 'I have *two* initials. My second name is Robert. So it will be "F R Eddowes. Funeral Directors". *Directors* plural.'

Epic smiled as if to acknowledge his mistake. But his own sledgehammer was only replaced by Stephen Mauve's more intuitive variety. '"Freddo's!"' he exploded, and Amanda squealed with delight and punched him on the arm. '"Freddo's Funeral Emporium"' Stephen concluded. 'How's about that, then?'

Everybody cheered heartily at this and Frank, forgetting how annoyed he had been with Epic, found himself just as dumbstruck as he had been when Stephen had initially suggested that Frank should start his own business in the first place and that "destiny awaits". Young Mauve's influence had certainly struck again. Only seconds before, Frank was genuinely ready to quit his stool for the day, wounded by Epic's tactless jibe. But now enlightenment had smashed him flush in the face one more time. He had begun his quest determined to found a traditional firm of Funeral Directors, but had felt obliged to assure the bank about his intention to "try to do things a little differently" just to demonstrate that his business would not just be run-of-the-mill but… different. But deep down, all he had really wanted was his own Old Firm. What Stephen Mauve had now done was to present Frank with the option, which supplied him with the apparent prerequisite that his own name should feature prominently, with the notion that his business was, after all, different from all the others and *particularly* the Old Firm, an idea which in that split second no longer seemed at all absurd and in fact appeared increasingly more appealing to him as the beer flowed subsequently. Stephen Mauve had indeed struck again.

'Freddo's!' roared everyone.

'Freddos's!' roared Frank in confirmation rather than resignation. All sorts of fantastic ideas were going through his head now. Perhaps it was incalculably wrong to attempt to create his company in the Old Firm's image. Perhaps he should have paid more mind to the reaction of the small business advisor who had interviewed him. "The modern approach". Would the public tolerate it? Would they tolerate a radical modernisation of what remained one of the great taboos? And if they did, how much could he get away with? How much would he *dare* try to get away with? Would the gamble cost him everything?

'FREDDO'S!' they all sang in chorus. 'Good old Freddo's!'

Frank now knew that it was vital that he found Noddoes as quickly as possible and bring him on board to supplement, and indeed secure, the services of Tessa whom he had already 'headhunted'. But he would need others too. People of like minds. He suddenly saw Epic cheering at him whilst clapping his hands above his head. 'Hey there, Frankie! Hey there!'

'Number three,' thought Frank to himself.

Next, Thoad, smiling broadly. A very rare sight. A very weird man.

'Number four,' decided Frank, who then turned to the Founder of the Feast, Stephen Mauve, arm around Amanda and both waving their drinks at him.

'Five, six,' counted Frank.

He acknowledged the continuing cheers and through the haze swore that he saw young Mauve mouth out the mantra, which Frank felt was responsible for everything that had so far happened and would thus be responsible for everything which would now follow, good or bad.

'Destiny awaits!'

Frank let loose an almighty roar, which he had only intended to be a reciprocal cheer, and fell off his stool once again. After that, blank!

Chapter 13

Peter Foster

THE OLD FIRM ENDURED.

Arthur Snape suspected that he would never recover psychologically from the terrible experience of his partner's funeral, but considered this of little consequence in comparison with the necessity of his company's survival and continued prosperity. But certainly not for his own sake. Pendlesham needed him.

Whereas both Frank and Noddoes had been replaced, Tessa hadn't been; something which hadn't troubled Peter Foster terribly; so fond had he been of his former assistant that he felt an acute (but rather silly) reluctance to work with anybody else in any case. In fact, Foster had been just, if not more, as devastated by what Frank Eddowes had done as Old Snape had been. Once Mr Woodcastle had died, the old man had become a raw material with which Foster had sculptured a work of almost faultless finery. That Frank had defiled such great beauty so spectacularly, obliterated it forever, had launched this most creative of men into such a state of devastation and depression that he had for a short while considered forsaking the art to which he had devoted his life and turning instead to a less taxing form of activity by which to earn his crust, one which would not have had the emotionally draining demand on his genius that he had suffered with such ignominy as the result of the Woodcastle tragedy.

Peter Foster, though, eventually pulled himself together, regained his appetite for his noble vocation and craft and started making dead bodies look good again. He knew that he could never erase the memory of what the drunk Eddowes had done to his masterwork, but as time went by and jobs came and went, the master embalmer slowly got his touch back.

Sometimes, after a particularly good job, Foster was touched by a curious feeling that the beastly incident had been nothing but a bad dream. Certainly the story of the outrage hadn't leaked. Could it be possible that it actually hadn't happened after all? Why yes! That was it! Eddowes, Tessa and Noddoes had merely resigned after Mr Woodcastle's funeral, which actually went off beautifully and without a hitch, with Peter's work as the crowning glory. From such a base, his art could only reach yet loftier heights of magnificence. Actually, the only reason he was feeling despondent at all was because he had lost the services of Tessa, a lovely girl and so eager to learn. Didn't she say something about accepting a position in the United States or something?...

Positive thinking by Peter Foster. The Old Firm endured and so did he. A testament to his fortitude.

Chapter 14

Classic Reggae

WHEN FRANK WOKE up, he discovered that he had been unconscious for nearly fifteen hours. He knew this because his mother told him that a 'nice American boy' had arrived in a taxi with Frank in such a state that she had immediately considered calling the doctor out. It was only when Frank recovered all of a sudden and started chuckling to himself, something about 'good old Freddo' that she accepted the young man's assurance that he just needed to sleep things off and would then be okay. This was at ten minutes to five and it was now twenty to eight on Sunday morning. It wasn't quite a record, but it was close. Hansel and Gretel were not impressed.

Frank devoured a breakfast of scrambled eggs and bacon, and was in a far more reflective mood when he reached the finale of the marmalade and toast. As usual, he had recovered brilliantly and was already intending to be on the back of his stool for twelve o'clock. This time he would really be fixing on doing some business. Stephen Mauve, he felt, had pushed him in the direction of revolution. Was this, though, to be the extent of Stephen's involvement, or would he join the struggle too, perhaps as Frank's adjutant? Would the girl, Amanda, come with him? And what of Epic, that insatiably enthusiastic and extrovert young Canadian? A sharp lad to be sure and one possessing a character perfect for what Frank now had in mind – the antithesis of the personality essential for any other funeral director. But would he be interested? Epic had never seemed to have had a job of any kind in all the time Frank had known him. Would he decline one now? Or would he join Frank in the crusade of a lifetime into spectacular glory or abject and total failure, and for Frank personally, total ruin? There could be no third option. No breaking even.

Thoad, Frank felt, would be the perfect front man; a tragic-looking, fat, bald man with no life, who would offer customers, through his own natural persona, a more traditional and recognisable face of the industry, that of abject misery, before lunatics like Epic and Noddoes took over and turned the whole shooting party on its head. Thoad would become the character formally known as Frank Eddowes, his portfolio being precisely that of Frank's at the Old Firm. For this role, Frank considered Thoad ideal. People who didn't know him, and even some who did, considered him a quiet, insular soul. But Thoad, once provoked into conversation, particularly about the one passion in his life outside the Station Inn – classic reggae - was far from being a mouse. He just required kick-starting sometimes. But there was no question about it; Thoad would be a choice signing. But what price Thoad? Could he possibly be tempted away into madness in tender middle age? Would any of the intended headhunted take the offer? Would indeed Noddoes when Frank finally got around to finding him?

Frank suddenly felt that everything hinged on that Sunday's lunchtime session at the Inn. If the euphoria of the previous afternoon's goings on had died down even a little bit, the offers of jobs would sound ridiculous. They might in any case appear just as ludicrous, due to there not being an actual company in existence yet. Frank would have to assure them that he realised that such offers were purely hypothetical, something he certainly had not made plain to Tessa. But then again, without the pegs hovering over the holes, he couldn't possibly hope to get started anyway. There was no other option – a hunting he would go. On reflection he had come to the conclusion that there was no other choice. The main quandary facing him was who he should speak to first.

Frank thus presently prepared to go out, negotiating with his usual skill his mother's perennial nagging pleas of not to spoil his Sunday roast by rolling up pissed. She had had the added ammunition this week of the little matter of the day before to use on her son. He had, after all, overstepped the mark even for him, even for a Saturday. Yet nothing could possibly have stopped Frank (now completely freshened up) from going to the Inn, equines wild or tame.

Gretel made a last minute bold attempt to halt him as he was about to leave by darting between his legs, not just once but twice, in an endeavour to trip him up, but Frank stayed up and walked on. Today was without question the most important day so far in the evolution of the New Firm and of Frank's new life. He strode through the door and off, knowing that notwithstanding the syntheticness of the statement, destiny really did await. Or perhaps nothing awaited at all.

Frank came to the Inn outrageously late (by ten minutes), opened the door and disappeared into the ganja smoke. Immediately a cheer and then a chant of 'good old Freddo!' was taken up and Frank saw everybody bunched up by the bar as if they hadn't moved from the last time he was in there. Was it possible that he had only gone to the toilet instead of home for bed and breakfast; indeed, being taken home after having drunk himself senseless, and that it was actually still Saturday afternoon?

Frank checked his watch.

'Hey, boss!' yelled Epic. 'How you doing? What you drinking?'

'Good old Freddo's!' roared the others.

'You piss artist!' cried Tom warmly, as he plonked a pint down in front of Frank's regular stool. 'I didn't even think you'd be here. Not after the session yesterday!'

Frank looked puzzled.

'I had to take you home, man!' explained Epic.

'I remember! I remember!' lied Frank. 'I was chanting "good old Freddo's!" and you met my mother. She thought you was very nice.'

'Get out of it!' sneered Tom. 'You fell off your stool *twice*! The second time you were out before you hit the ground, mate!'

'I remember Epic walking me up the road,' insisted Frank.

'It should have been a fucking paramedic!' laughed Tom.

'Whatever, whatever!' interrupted Epic. 'The main thing is that Frankie… I mean *Freddo* has got his team now. It's cool!'

'Good old Freddo's!' everybody sang.

This time Frank was very puzzled indeed. He generally remembered

Stephen Mauve christening him 'Freddo' and the subsequent merriment this had caused, but had no idea about anything else. He had thus assumed that he had tumbled off his stool, as he had done so many times before, and that Epic had taken him home, as reported by his mother. Unfortunately, this was only part of the story.

The clue was something which Tom had just said about Frank falling off his stool twice. It was only too true that Frank couldn't even remember his first journey to the floor, let alone the second. It now seemed clear that something significant had occurred between the two falls. Frank tried to reason it out. He must have climbed up off the floor the first time, plonked himself back on his stool and carried on drinking. What in the world had happened after that? What had happened before he hit the deck again and was obliged to accept Epic as an escort to his door? Frank didn't have long to find out. Actually, Epic had practically outlined the picture to him with his earlier remarks.

'When's our first staff meeting, then?' asked Stephen.

'Cool it, man!' butted in Epic. 'Frankie's gotta find this Noddoes guy first and then we can all get together, including this Tessa chick. I can't *wait* to meet *her* by the way.'

'You want to nob her already and you haven't even seen her!' sneered Tom from behind the bar. 'You carry on like that and Frank will give you the push before you even get started.'

Everybody laughed, including Frank, although he for one had no idea why.

'Good old Freddo's!' they all cheered, raising their glasses.

'I've already resigned,' suddenly contributed Thoad, most unexpectedly and totally out of character. 'After what you told me, I went round to the office and posted a note to my boss through the old door.'

'I didn't have a job in the first place,' admitted Amanda the punkette, 'so I was always going to be all yours.' She then turned to Stephen and grabbed his balls without mercy. 'And *they're* all *mine*,' she confirmed.

This clinched it for Frank. Oh, Christ! He had obviously already done what he had set off to the Inn that day in order to do! And now he knew exactly what had happened between his brace of tumbles off the barstool. He had thrown out job offers to all four of them… and all four had accepted. Silly drunken old sod!

Good old Freddo's!

Chapter 15

Noddoes' Agent

IT WAS NO good. Frank could clearly put it off no longer. Nor did he now want to. It was imperative to find Maurice Noddoes. This task wasn't difficult. He was in the 'phone book --- in bold. Frank decided to try to reach him in the morning rather than any other time of day. This, Frank reasoned, would be the best chance of catching the old luvvie at home. The real reason was that any other time of day would almost certainly see Frank atop a familiar wooden pedestal and in no fit state to call anyone, let alone negotiate with them.

He had initially toyed with the idea of writing to his quarry instead of hitting him cold with a call as he had done Tessa. After all, he had historically found it very difficult to communicate with Noddoes, a man who had taken narcissism to new heights and was certainly someone whom Frank had always disliked and mistrusted and now loathed. He eventually dismissed the approach by letter for these very good reasons, and that he doubted that Noddoes' colossal ego would permit even a reply, let alone an acceptance of an offer of employment from someone Frank assumed he clearly considered beneath him. The need to secure an early answer came into the equation now too. The Inn Crowd were baying for an early start – the bank, having granted a decent loan, would soon be wondering when kick-off time was, and most importantly of all, the lovely Tessa might well be snatched from Frank's fevered grasp if he didn't get a move on and it was Tessa who had practically demanded employing Noddoes in the first place. If the old luvvie didn't make the line-up, Frank was sure that she would not hesitate in asking why not.

Frank dialled the number at just after ten o'clock. It rang and rang and then the receiver was picked up and a loud, exaggerated yawn flew down the wire and straight into Frank's ear. It petered out but did not give way to a voice, not indeed to any other sound at all.

'Maurice Noddoes, please,' ventured Frank after a few more seconds of silence.

'It is I,' confirmed Noddoes sleepily.

'Noddoes, it's Frank Eddowes speaking,' said Frank.

'Frank Eddowes? Frank Eddowes? Is this by way of some ruse? Are you aware of the tenderness of the hour?'

'It's ten past ten,' Frank told him.

'Ten past ten?'

'Correct.'

'Are you certain of this?'

'Of course.'

'My word, I do believe I may have overslept,' explained Noddoes, most unconvincingly, yawning again. 'I have an appointment with my agent at noon, you know. The telephone simply hasn't stopped ringing since I departed from that dreadful place. Considering all the consequent offers has got me into quite a tizz, I must say. One must have sought a more pro-tracted service from the tender arms of Morpheus than is usual due to the conundrum of having to disappoint someone, a director, perhaps, who is also a friend. Very vexing. What do you want?'

This was all raving bollocks, of course and Frank could quite easily have got Noddoes off his back forever by congratulating him on this appar-ent deluge of job offers in the profession he loved, informing him that he knew now that Noddoes could not in that case possibly be interested in a job offer which would involve returning to his previous loathed profession and putting the 'phone down. Indeed Frank was dangerously tempted to do just that, but held back for two reasons. The first, of course, was Tessa. He figured that if he went to Tessa and told her that Noddoes was una-vailable to join them because of a dramatic renaissance of his acting career, the girl would either tell him that he had been ridiculous to believe the yarn Noddoes had spun him, or even, heaven forefend, accuse him of not approaching the ham actor at all, which might have put a question mark over Tessa's own participation in the new organisation. Frank knew that Noddoes' acceptance would be a major plus, even taking into account how Frank thought about him personally. The second reason for Frank persisting with the call was for pure entertainment value.

'Well actually, Noddoes, I wish to widen your options and thereby vex you further,' he said.

Noddoes coughed uneasily. 'Are you claiming that you are somehow in a position to offer me… employment?' he then said.

'Most definitely,' replied Frank stridently. 'And only you, Noddoes, could do the job.'

There was another uneasy cough. 'What… What is it?'

'I'll be honest with you. It's much the same as you were doing before.'

'Oh! So Mr Snape has asked me back! Oh, wonderful man!'

'No, no, that's not it at all. I'm talking about *my* company.'

Noddoes was wide-awake now. 'Are you telling me that you have, by fair means or foul, affected a takeover of the very firm from which you were recently dismissed? I don't believe it. I *won't* believe it! You have returned only to mock me, you cur!'

'Noddoes, you're not listening! Arthur Snape would see hell freeze over before relinquishing the reins of the Old Firm. As far as I'm concerned, the wretched place is still going and will continue still going until old Snape becomes a doughnut. I am talking about my *own* company. A brand new, modern approach firm of funeral directors!'

'Goodness!'

'I want to headhunt you, Noddoes. You were always far too talented for the Old Firm anyway. You knew this yourself but were far too much of a gentleman ever to let it show, even though it must have tormented some-one of your intellect. Everybody else saw it too.'

'Oh how kind!'

'Come with me to the future. Together we'll *bury* the Old Firm!'

'Oh, I say, that's jolly good!'

Frank wound down now. He was amazing himself at how brilliantly he was doing, but then he did even better to bag his bird. 'All I ask, Noddoes, is that you bless my offer with the sparsest of considerations amidst the orchard of rosier apples, which have inevitably fallen onto your lap since your bold resignation from that nineteenth century hovel.'

'Bugger that, dear boy!' roared Noddoes. 'When do you want me to start?'

Chapter 16

Tessa

THE FIRST MEETING of the staff of Freddo's Funeral Emporium was held at Tessa Sharma's flat on the same day that Frank secured a select premises for his parlour in the centre of town. This would be promptly converted according to a plan Frank had drawn up, based largely on the setup at the Old Firm, and once that had been sorted out, in would go the furniture. Everything was securely in hand.

The Inn Crowd descended upon Tessa's abode on foot, picking up Noddoes on the way, who was waiting outside a bank in a purple cape worn over a dinner suit and holding a cane. On his head was a flat tweed cap and between the fingers of his outstretched left hand was a cigarette holder of a quite ludicrous length. When Frank first caught sight of him, he immediately feared the others would laugh him out of court before they had even met him and that this would have a mortally wounding effect on Noddoes, who was not exactly famed for his modesty and certainly took himself most seriously at all times. But Frank shouldn't have worried, as in actual fact the ridiculous buffoon was hailed immediately as an icon by the Inn Crowd from the second they clapped eyes on him. Epic was particularly moved: 'Hey, man, that get up is wild. *Wild!*' he raved.

The others shuffled in and greeted him, Amanda completing proceedings in a singularly over the top but somehow only too fitting fashion by flinging her arms around the old luvvie's neck and planting a kiss on his cheek. 'My beautiful daddy!' she assured him.

Noddoes, shaken but not stirred, reached into his cape, removed a cigarette from a silver box, inserted it into his holder and lit up. He took a long drag and then pulled the imbecilic contraption dramatically from his mouth and emitted a groan of satisfaction, which couldn't have been more false had he repeated it continually until Christmas.

'Onwards then to the abode of the fair, dusky maid!' he then commanded, getting his adjectives involved in a terrible head-on collision, and with that he swung his cape about him and strode off, not possibly knowing where he was going, but as it happened in the right direction.

'Frankie, this guy is fantastic!' marvelled Epic, practically genuflecting towards the rapidly disappearing phantom.

'My beautiful daddy!' repeated Amanda softly, staring almost tearfully after him.

Noddoes started to vanish from view and it seemed sensible that the others ran after him and caught him up. The ham actor, ever in a dream world, had no idea that he had been an instant hit, but Frank did, and having initially been relieved that Noddoes had not been held to ridicule as he had feared, he now felt a slight twinge of irritation because the man he disliked so intensely had gone down such a storm with the folk from the Inn first time out of the cannon, despite all the negative things Frank had told them all about Noddoes from his stool during previous binges. Only Stephen Mauve offered a smidgen of sustenance: 'I think this boy is completely full of shit, but I can't help thinking he'll be perfect if you're really serious about revolutionising undertaking,' he said, as they all trotted after the caped figure, who was periodically thrusting his cane forwards to indicate the way, which he still didn't know was the right one.

'He's my beautiful daddy!' reiterated Amanda, who had clearly been partaking of stimulants other than cider recently.

'It would be great if he really was your old man!' beamed Epic, as he ran up alongside them. 'He's quite a guy. But I can't help feeling that he might be pitching for the other team. Know what I'm saying?'

'I suppose that you thought that about me once upon a time!' said Frank with the slightest hint of a sneer.

'Frankie. Never!' Epic assured him.

They had all caught up with Noddoes now and the old luvvie, having made his point, relinquished his role as the group's pathfinder to Frank, who knew the way to Tessa's flat like the back of his hand and had known it long before he had actually gone there for super-hot curried lamb and blue stilton. Presently they came by their destination and the door opened to reveal a beautiful barefoot woman, jet-black hair flowing free and a smell of food nearly as heavenly as the girl.

'Oh hello there!' gushed Teresa and then to Noddoes: 'Oh, hi! You made it!'

Frank was immediately stricken with a trouser problem, but he wasn't the only one. Thoad had the horn too and Stephen, who knew class when he saw it, regarded Tessa as mesmerizingly beautiful and could scarcely peel his eyes off her. It was just as well that Amanda was still away with the fairies at this point or he could have been in a lot of trouble. But it was Epic who was affected most of all. Too often had he had his ear bent by Frank with talk of Tessa and of how stupendously lovely she was, to the point in fact that Epic had set out determined that she would be a dog. Now before him was a gorgeous, exotic, leggy, sexy brunette who could quite easily have just wiggled off a 'Bollywood' movie set. The pure fact was that Frank had not been complimentary enough and for once the sharp, brash, loquacious Canadian was entirely lost for words or deed other than to stand there with an award-winning hard-on and salivate like the other three.

The staff had convened and after Frank had formally introduced everyone to Tessa, the hostess passed around some nibbles that she had just happened to rustle up (it was practically a meal) and then everybody with drinks in hand settled down to listen to the opening remarks of their new boss:

'I would like to begin by expressing my immense gratitude to you all for having the courage to embark with me on a trip to goodness knows where,' he said. 'I would be a liar if I claimed that I know exactly what I have in mind for Freddo's Funeral Emporium and I'd therefore like to make it as clear as possible from this early stage that I am not only encouraging ideas from all of you, but that without such feedback, we are well and truly dead in the water here. Even those of you who have no experience at all in the world you are now entering should not be backwards in coming forwards. On the contrary, the principle of the modern approach concept, the very foundation on which we are poised to build our organisation, can only be realised when those for whom this world is alien freely submit ideas which run contrary to those practices which they in their understand-able ignorance have hitherto considered must be sacrosanct. Similarly, you, Noddoes and you, Tessa, like me, late of the oldest firm in this town must be mindful of the need for change to bring this company up through a new counter-culture, something which would have triggered our even earlier departure had such things been suggested to Arthur Snape during our time there. You too must both be prepared to offer your own suggestions for the way we must go, lest we fall into the age-old trap and produce by default and through lack of courage and imagination a facsimile of the traditional funeral directors' mentality and critique, something which not even the astonishing events of the sixties made an impression on.

'We are refuge collectors, nothing more. People cease to become people as soon as they become corpses. A funeral is in practical terms merely a disposal of something which is of no further use. I want to emphasise this point most empathically. It's a case I intend to take to the country. Death is the last stage, the very *last* stage of that person being a person. After that, I consider it not inappropriate and certainly not improper to dispose of the tai-lor's dummy which remains in a manner void of the insincere, obsequious and, above all, costly ceremony which has been encrusted into the traditions of this business and is still extant. It is time to exchange our outlook, and by associa-tion, our industry. Respect the dead, but never respect a corpse. A corpse is not a person. A corpse is a doughnut. How the fuck can you respect that?'

Frank paused here to look quickly at Epic, from whom he had com-mitted a quite mercenary theft of that quote, never mind the idea. Epic remained silent. Everybody else, even Noddoes, were similarly spellbound. Nobody had expected a speech like this.

'I want to make dying more available to the ordinary man,' continued Frank. 'I want to cut the price of funerals on the understanding that corpses are doughnuts. People can hold their own tributes to their dead elsewhere.

They will not get any of that from us. Any tributes need not have to have the corpse present and this is my point. One might just as well have an empty bottle or a doughnut on display. Do you all understand what I'm getting at? I'm getting at not using coffins. Just chuck the doughnuts in the ground, or tip 'em down the chute. Okay?'

'We'll never get away with it!' bleated Stephen Mauve, finding his tongue at last.

'Get away with what, exactly?' hit back Frank.

'Well, really! From what you're saying, we might just as well get a horse and drag the body through the streets and then tie it to a stake and set fire to it!'

'Fire daddy!' added Amanda.

'Is that a suggestion, Stephen?' asked Frank.

'I infer the scenario from what you've just said,' Stephen replied.

'In that case I must write it down.' Frank assured him. 'But that was your imagination and not mine.'

'In that case, I think it *is* a suggestion,' conceded Stephen.

'So where's the goddam horse?' Epic wanted to know, coming storming in after a silence lasting some centuries and seemingly addressing Stephen. 'You want to go get a fucking horse? Okay! Is your stoned woman gonna act as Lady Godiva? Huh? Where's the fucking horse?'

'Horse daddy!' chipped in Amanda, pulling at Noddoes' cape.

'Calm down, now!' interjected Frank, imagining that Epic was feeling just a little phased at having just met the beauteous Tessa, when he had obviously set his dick on a lady some degrees plainer and was thus turning on Stephen to compensate for a rare miscalculation which had let him know that he shouldn't always be the wise guy he had been all his life.

'The point of all this,' continued Frank, 'is just what I said at the start. To put forward views and ideas that will help us.'

'So why do you still want me?' asked Tessa. 'A beautician for something you have likened to an empty bottle. I can't understand what my function will be. What do you want me for?'

Everybody had the answer to this except Tessa and possibly Noddoes. But Frank prattled on about legal requirements which had to be adhered to regarding hygiene regulations before anything could be done to a dead body, and that revolutionary though he certainly intended to be, he had no intention of transgressing the boundary of the law, at least until he was certain that he had run out of alternatives and reasons for adhering to unreasonable regulations. Also, Frank insisted, relatives would be expected to exercise their right to view their loved-one before the funeral. Tessa's role was to be very vital indeed.

Nobody bought it. Frank had doubled back on himself with the most monstrous crock of bullshit imaginable. One minute he had been talking about 'doughnuts', now he was referring to 'loved-ones'. One second he had insisted that the staff of the new firm were going to be 'refuge collectors', seconds later he had uttered the unutterable curse, 'funeral', a word which surely had no place in Frank's awaiting destiny. The pure fact was that Tessa's berth on the team was due totally to the fact that Frank wanted to sleep with her. His earlier address had made the case for an embalmer as obsolete as a doughnut. If he now tried to justify it, which he certainly had, it could only mean that he wanted sex with the embalmer, which he certainly did.

Chapter 17

Danny

N O HORSES, BUT perhaps cars. Saloons, thought Frank. An ordinary estate car, which would be just big enough to cater for a corpse in a zip-up black body bag. Just chuck the thing in the back, close the hatch and away you go. And flowers would definitely be discouraged from the coffin car --- the coffin car with no coffin. They would stink to high heaven and would, in any case, only serve to impede the work of his staff. The sole task of the 'doughnut car' would be to transfer the corpse to the crematorium or burial site and nothing else. The last thing his people wanted was to do battle with Interflora in order to reach the client. Any flowers which were unfortunately delivered contrary to Freddo advice would be thrown into the back of Frank's own vehicle, a bright yellow 1962 Ford Anglia, which had actually been bought second-hand by Frank's father just after Kennedy got twatted, and driven on to the funeral site separately. You certainly didn't need anything special for this, and besides, the thirty-year-old car was still in remarkable working order. Frank bought two estate cars in the end, both Cortinas and both second-hand. In addition to this, two Rovers were snapped up to act as escort vehicles in lieu of Limousines, again second-hand but slightly newer, and after the briefest of excursions through the slime of the used car market, the funeral fleet had been secured at a bargain basement price.

Things really started moving after this. The Emporium's new premises, bang in the centre of town, was soon primed and furnished and then stationery was ordered, accounts opened and links with credit card companies established as well as with the local coroner, Klaus Butsch. This and that. That and this. Frank then summoned his troops together again. This time, they convened for the first time at their HQ. Everyone was bubbling with excitement and expectation. They were actually on the threshold of kicking the whole thing off now.

One of the matters still outstanding was the new organisation's relationship with the Church, something which could not be ignored, indeed had to be addressed. Frank's fear was that the holy ones would boycott them. It could not be assumed that even the trendies, who had such a stranglehold on the Anglican order now, would be quite ready for something like Freddo's. Weddings, yes; bog-standard Sunday services, always; but funerals and the 'updating' of them would become right-on at the peril of even the most modern-thinking clergyperson. This was the worry. Frank, in fact, envisaged a problem.

The solution came from a most unexpected quarter. It was Amanda, who told the meeting (she wasn't stoned this time) that she knew of a young Church of England minister who would, she promised, be not only receptive, but enthusiastic to what their new organisation wanted to do: 'His name is Danny and he's really nice,' she insisted.

'Where do you know him from?' asked Stephen in cross-examination.

'Drying out, man!' sneered Epic, ironically from behind his reefer.

'I met him at a party, I think it was last year,' said Amanda, taking no notice other than to proffer a vertical middle finger in Epic's direction. 'Somebody I knew from college had a party and I was there with a couple of mates. This really nice looking bloke was there, wearing a dog collar. We thought he must have been a stripagram, but when he didn't get his kit off, we found out he was a real vicar with a wife and everything and we had been taking the piss out of him! We felt terrible but he *was* nice. He didn't even talk posh. He just kept talking about old rock music all the time and about how Jesus was really this bloke out of some band called Medicine Head.'

Frank squealed and clapped his hands. 'This chap wears an earring and has long, unkempt, wavy hair, doesn't he?' he asked. 'Mid thirties.'

Amanda looked at him amazed: 'Yes. But how do you know?'

'I don't,' chuckled Frank. 'Or should I say, I didn't. But he sounds bloody marvellous!'

'Okay, okay. So he might look the part,' interjected Epic, for some reason sounding agitated again. 'But what makes you say that he's going to be good for us? Huh? I say we have more chance of getting through to some fruity old relic type of guy who still thinks that Churchill's your Prime Minister, rather than some cool young guy who feels that he's some kind of latter-day John The Baptist or whatever.'

'Oh I say, young man. I do rather hope that you're wrong!' argued Noddoes, standing up for some obscure reason (not so obscure for him, perhaps). 'No matter how nutty an elderly English cleric becomes, I can assure you that any dwindling faculties which remain, and I concede that this is never much, would be utilised in putting down most fiercely anything at all that our fledgling company has thus far mooted. And even if he were to be persuaded, I must tell you now that the fearsome hags who sadly but nevertheless inevitably predominate in the parishes of this town would respond by putting him right in double quick time. It's all tea and Jerusalem here, my boy. It's clear that we should seek out someone… well, someone like you, for example!'

'No, but Amanda said that this Danny guy was nice looking!' whimsically slipped in Stephen.

Everybody roared.

'Smark punk!' muttered Epic, now seemingly more crabby than ever.

'I think Noddoes is correct,' continued Frank. 'I hear what you're saying, Epic, but I really can't see any of the old traditionalists going for this. This doesn't mean to say that this young chap would either, of course, but I have to say to you that he must be the better chance.'

Epic put his hands up in resignation. 'Okay, Frankie, you win. It's your party and you cry if you want to!' he announced, inducing a rare smile from Thoad for this Lesley Gore-related comment.

Frank, having missed the joke, turned back to Amanda again. 'Would you actually be able to find this vicar, do you think? Or, should I say, would you know where I could find him?'

'IN…A…CHURCH!' sang out Tessa suddenly, and off she went into one of her fits of giggles again. She wasn't stoned, as Amanda had certainly been at the first meeting, but she might just as well have been.

Epic lit up immediately. 'Way to go, princess!' he shouted and then joined in the laughter, which had been triggered off by Tessa and was now affecting everybody else except Frank who, in all honesty, didn't really need any of this.

Chapter 18

Barefoot Sally

T HE REVEREND DANNY Hare was married with no children. His wife
Sally had much in common with Amanda Plimmer. Both had been
wayward young women (Amanda really still was and Sally had at one time
been a habitual shoplifter and had served a spell in a youth detention centre
for it) and both were strikingly attractive although, unlike Sally, Amanda,
realising her pretty, girly looks, had tried to nullify them with her punk get-
up, thereby, alas, only succeeding in transforming herself into something far
more seductive rather than just girly.

Sally, meanwhile, had blossomed into a gorgeous young woman with
long, dark brown hair, fantastic legs and a pert little arse. She was now
twenty-seven with a fondness for going barefoot and certainly did not look
like a vicar's wife. Here was a very horny woman.

Danny and Sally, married for four years, had been trying for children
for the last three with not even a sniff of a false alarm. But such had been
their obsession with starting a family that their consequent sleepless nights
together had enriched the physical side of their relationship and turned it
into something almost sordid. Poetry recitals and games of scrabble were
hardly their passion. Sex became it for the best of reasons.

Surprisingly, they had met at a church fete in Pendlesham, which Sally
had decided to attend only because a friend of hers had told her that she
was working on one of the stalls selling cakes and Sally wanted to take the
piss out of her. The friend didn't turn up (it had been a wind-up) but the
vicar certainly did, a mutual physical attraction was recognised instantaneously, and that very evening, Danny bestowed a very special all-night
blessing on Sally at his own home after 'communion' had been celebrated at

Luigi's, acknowledged by many as being the best restaurant in Pendlesham. Then a very odd thing happened. The couple genuinely fell in love and then got married. Most uncool!

Sally's parents were overjoyed. Their daughter had been a bit of a handful over the years. Her little stint of kiddy stir had almost destroyed her mother, yet here she was now a pillar of the community --- a vicar's wife. Praise the Lord!

Sadly, no. The Reverend Danny Hare then went bonkers, or more properly was finally seen to have gone bonkers, since he always had been. Unlike Sally, he had never gone wrong in the law-breaking sense, but had always been a worry mentally. Never into drugs either (the contents of his imagination had provided plenty enough to keep him firmly round the twist) and practically teetotal as well, Danny, now thirty-four, had never been anything other than a clean living fit young man, but also somebody who was permanently off the wall, never quite grasping the principles of reality. He had been born in Suffolk, the son of a senior metrological researcher, but had been brought up and educated in London. He went to College in Brighton where he distinguished himself as a popular DJ both on and off campus and had set his heart on record production. Danny's big love was rock and roll. His knowledge of this subject was truly astonishing, was much admired and respected and no other career was going to do for him. Undoubtedly, his most astounding gift was his ability to memorise lyrics. He knew quite literally hundreds of songs and could recite by heart complete songbooks: The Stones, The Beatles, The Doors, Hendrix, Bowie, Queen, Jacques Brel, Lulu. The list was endless.

He began by oddjobbing it, spinning discs in clubs and sidelining this with work as a teacher (his degree was History) whilst he waited for his chance to pilot a major new band. It was at this point that God came to call. Danny remembered the moment explicitly. He had been lying in the bath one evening listening to a radio station playing a selection of tracks by Cream when the signal appeared to fade. Mindful of the perils of adjusting an electrical device whilst being submerged in water (French songwriter

Claude François had famously frazzled himself into non-existence when he rose from his tub to replace a light bulb), Danny contented himself with continuing the record in his head, determined that when the signal returned, the radio and his brain would be in precise tandem with each other. About thirty seconds later, the signal did indeed return, but not so Jack Bruce; because blaring out of the radio/cassette player now were the Edwin Hawkins Singers with *O Happy Day!* And the Almighty had secured another convert. Religious training followed and subsequently the vicarage. But in all this time Danny remained bonkers and a disciple of rock and pop. The Lord provided the day job, but 'Dazza's' music was with him all the time. He was certainly never one to force religion upon anyone.

Danny's madness naturally rubbed off on his wife, who already had antecedents for nutty behaviour, and Danny and Sally quickly became a very strange and silly couple indeed. The elderly parishioners (ancient, actually) who had initially been bowled over by the young minister before Sally had come along, because they hadn't cottoned on to the fact that he was a lunatic, now gradually drifted away from services, although some just went the whole hog and drifted away from life. They were replaced by a small but much younger and trendier set, not far removed, but perhaps just a tad farther up the evolutionary scale from most of the folk in the Station Inn, only older. Some of his flock remained but were comfortably in the minority. The real turning point came when Sally began appearing at her husband's side in church barefoot and tapping and shaking a tambourine to the traditional hymn, which still surprisingly predominated at Danny's services (he and Sally called them 'gigs'): 'The words are all meaningless but the tunes are wonderful,' he once explained. 'Some of those melodies could have been composed by Bobby Dylan or Paul Simon.' A choir was certainly not part of the set-up.

The 'encore', even more surprisingly, was always the chronically banal sing-a-long number, *Kumbaya* for which Danny picked up an acoustic guitar and dispatched his organist, a hairy, tobacco-stained forty-something called Keith Tate, out amongst the pews so that he could pass through the congregation creaming them of all their cash. Keith would always return to his instrument before the final chorus in order to pick up a saxophone for a quick burst which interjected on the last note of the hymn (as Barefoot Sally slithered to the floor, tambourine in full shake), thus bringing the hymn and the gig to a conclusion in a crescendo of grooviness.

Not at all surprisingly, the congregation dwindled even further. Danny, in fact, was paying the price for trying to please everybody, always a fool-hardy venture. His outlook to his ministry was modern, far too modern for most churchgoers in the town, yet paradoxically he was a traditionalist at heart and this was reflected in his services. The result was that the more previously typical parishioners in his flock (the old steamers) had left immediately, being reminded perhaps, on observation of the pouting, barefooted lovely who had married their vicar, of the madcap hippy days of the sixties when they themselves were in middle age and shaking their heads and tutting at the rebellion being enacted all around them by youth and their champions throughout the free world. But also, the younger element had begun to stay away too, smelling a rat by considering that even the trendy get-up could not disguise the fact that the 'gig' was still after everything just half an hour of the same old thing followed by the passing around of the plate.

Danny Hare thus had a choice: either he and Barefoot Sally calmed down in the hope that some of the older worshippers would return (obviously at the expense of the younger sheep), or else he could turn even nuttier and thereby preside over an even crazier parish ultimately. There was no middle ground. No compromise. He had tried this and it had proved to be an entirely flawed doctrine. It was either one or the other. Therefore, Danny Hare made the same decision that was subsequently reached by Frank Eddowes in respect of the not entirely unconnected world of undertaking. He decided that he might have to try to do things a little differently. The modern approach. Freddo's type of modern. He and Barefoot Sally started gigging for real.

Danny, in effect, became a freelance vicar, separated from the established Church of England but still retaining the cassock (which he did not wear), style and dignity of his ministry, if not his church building.

'Are you still a real vicar, then?' one young man asked him.

'Preachers are appointed by God, alligator!' was Danny's reply.

He and Sally obtained permission to shift their base to one of the town's crematoriums, not an entirely whacky move really, since the building contained a rather plush and compact little chapel with a cloakroom in which Keith Tate was able to set up a more than adequate sound station. The one thing they couldn't take with them (nor did they want it) was the church organ. Everything was provided by CDs.

It certainly wasn't long before Danny's 'church' began to realise the best attendances he had enjoyed since he got married. Nearly all of the 'parishioners' were under forty, though one or two of the oldies remained as faithful to him as they were to their Lord. The chapel was at no time ever full, but its relatively small size always meant that a parochial ambience exuded from it in greater abundance, and it was this which went such a way to lending the 'gigs' much more charm and, in fact, sincerity, than Danny had ever received back in the main church.

It was against this pleasant backdrop that Frank and Amanda took themselves off to Sunday worship. Amanda was particularly keen to see Danny again and Frank was particularly keen to see if he was as off-piste as he had hoped. Neither were to be disappointed, although the opportunity to speak to the vicar was not to come until after the service, which had been Frank's intention anyway, if not Amanda's.

The situation in which they found themselves reminded Frank from experience and Amanda from old videos of a sixties' 'love-in'.

'Jesus died for all of us and he also died for rock and roll!' Danny reminded the congregation. 'Praise him!'

The congregation howled and applauded.

'Let's shake!' panted Barefoot Sally, doing just that to her tambourine as well as to her bum.

The Reverend then continued: 'Okay. The Lord died for Elvis! He died for John Lennon! Our Saviour perished for Janis Joplin! He was nailed up for the two Jimmies – Morrison and Hendrix! Tim Buckley! Alex Harvey! Marvin Gaye – don't forget Marvin, now! Jesus was the first hippy! The first blues singer! The first jazz player! The first soul-man! The first folkie! The first classical composer! Shake if you know where I'm coming from. Let's shake!'

'Shake it all over!' encouraged Barefoot Sally.

'Oh yeah, Johnny Kidd! He's another one Jesus died for!' quickly added Danny, his extraordinary knowledge of his subject allowing him the chance to nip in again with a funny.

The congregation shook and then launched into a CD backing track of *Message In A Bottle.* The Lord's Prayer was followed by more shaking and *Ticket To Ride.* After this, a reader entered the 'pulpit' in order to compare 'the first hippy' with characters as diverse as Yuri Gagarin and Top Cat. Barefoot Sally shook.

The service concluded with an actual bible reading by Danny from Luke's Gospel, and finally, a raucous delivery from the 'pews' of *Kumbaya* with Danny on guitar and with the regulation saxophone finale from Keith before everybody dispersed behind Danny and Sally to a soft instrumental version of *Nights In White Satin,* which went by unmolested by either voice or shake. A bucket for cash was by the door.

Frank was mesmerised by the whole performance and knew immediately that the matter of Church acceptance for his project was no longer an obstacle. Danny and Barefoot Sally were either both basket cases or merely pragmatists. Either way they were of apparent immeasurable value to Freddo's. He and Amanda waited for the final member of the congregation to give 'Dazza' a 'big hug' outside before walking up to him. As they did this, Danny caught sight of Amanda and recognised her: 'Hey, there! How you doing!'

Amanda's pretty face brightened up. She hadn't really thought that he would remember her. 'Hiya!' she said.

Frank introduced himself and without wasting any time outlined the purpose of his company: 'Having watched and enjoyed every minute of your service today, I have no doubt at all that you would be more than equipped; indeed are in the best possible position, to officiate over the funerals in which my company intends to specialise.'

'Sounds good!' beamed Danny. 'You guys rock and rollers?'

'I should say so!' confirmed Frank. 'Those dead people you mentioned in your sermon, I love them all! Amanda here – she's a punk!'

'That's great! So your funerals are all going to have a rock theme, are they?'

Frank, who was now full of wonderful new ideas, answered immediately: 'What I saw today is what I want!'

'My man, as long as you can bring all your clients to me here and nowhere else, you have your minister!' Danny said.

The two men shook hands and then unexpectedly fell into a 'big hug' as Amanda looked on with some amusement.

'Now we've agreed in principle to establish a link,' Frank said, 'perhaps I can send you some details.'

'In your own time,' Danny assured him.

'*"In my own time"?* That was Family, wasn't it?' snapped back Frank with lightning speed.

This quip provided Danny with the final proof, had it been needed, that Frank was on his wavelength. Family, fronted by Roger Chapman, was to be sure one of the Reverend's favourite progressive bands – Keith Tate's too. And Frank's!

There was another embrace and then Barefoot Sally came up to say hello to Frank and Amanda and it all ended up with tea and biscuits with Keith too in a side building which had been set aside as a vestry.

Chapter 19

Sheba

FRANK HAD SET a date for the big opening and everyone in the organisation were poised like coiled springs.

Advertisements had been restricted to half a page in *The Pendlesham Gazette*, which gave the company's new name, "Freddo's Funeral Emporium" and location, plus the slogan "Freddo's – For The Modern Approach". He expected word of mouth to do the rest.

With less than a week to go before kick-off, Frank held a final staff meeting, during which he reminded everybody of their briefs – their respective positions in the great scheme of things. It was roughly along these lines:

Noddoes: Deputy Manager / Chief Bearer / Head Driver / Chief Collector.

Stephen: Financial Director / Bearer / Driver.

Thoad: Director of Administration / Greeter.

Epic: Director of Public Relations / Bearer / Driver / Collector.

Amanda: Secretary / Administrative Assistant / Greeter.

Tessa: Embalmer.

Frank himself was Managing Director and would actually be overseeing much of the administration of the company himself with Thoad as his number two. Thoad, however, would be left solely responsible for greeting the customers, as Frank himself had been at the Old Firm – a thankless task, whilst Amanda, Thoad's deputy, would be in charge of the 'switchboard', remaining also in the office to add to the 'caring face' of things.

Frank had been very careful to ensure that each of his staff had been given (or more precisely had been seen to have been given) proper jobs with associated responsibilities. He felt that it was vital that everybody knew that they were actually doing something, not only worthwhile, but important. Epic, for example, by far and away the sharpest and most loquacious of the band, was ideal for the task of making and maintaining contacts with the assortment of organisations with whom Freddo's would have to deal. In addition, the young Canadian would be encouraged to liaise with Stephen with regards the financial side, whilst Stephen reciprocated by assisting with Epic's brief of PR. Frank had come to the conclusion that the pair showed more than a little promise and suspected that they would work better and very well together, but was also sensible enough to realise that they would both appreciate being given their own specific specialisms and that the financial brief was always going to fall to Stephen anyway because of his accountancy and computer skills. He nevertheless hoped that a partnership would develop. Both men would be drivers and bearers during actual funerals.

Frank had been particularly astute in his delegation of named duties to Noddoes. His loathing for the old luvvie had diminished slightly since the founding of the Emporium, but he still disliked him intensely and had of course only hired him in the first place because of Tessa. The titles Frank had bestowed on him, "*Deputy Manager, Chief Bearer, Head Driver* and *Chief Collector*" were meaningless monickers designed purely to fortify Noddoes' colossal over-estimation of his own worth, which in Frank's opinion was negligible. The basic fact of the matter was that Noddoes would be merely a bearer and a driver and that was all. Indeed, the intention was that it would actually be Epic who would act as the driver on the pick-up, even though it was reluctantly acknowledged that Noddoes' experience in "collection" would, at least initially, be valuable. But the ruse of the dummy titles worked admirably. Noddoes considered himself a very important person indeed – a heartbeat away from the presidency and, as an unexpected bonus, Tessa actually indicated her approval of the apparent elevation of Noddoes, taking it as a sign of the bonding between the former employees of the Old Firm. Naturally, the truth could not have been more wide of the mark.

The two female members of the team had long since been aware of what was expected of them. Tessa's position was uncontested. As for Amanda, she owed her berth on the squad entirely to her relationship with Stephen Mauve and the young woman was only too conscious of this. She was thus happy to assume the junior role of "Secretary" and assistant to Thoad. The girl was, after all, significantly younger than everybody else.

A dispute arose over dress code. This was something which had not been discussed before and was an issue that had actually been overlooked entirely by Frank. It was on the agenda now:

'I am torn between two opinions on this,' Frank told them at the final gathering of the cast before its momentous opening curtain. 'Notwithstanding "The Modern Approach", I shall still insist on everybody being clean and presentable. What I am less sure of is not so much whether sombre suits should be dispensed with as to what should replace them.'

Here an incredulous Noddoes interjected: 'My dear Eddowes, I do rather hope that you are not expecting us to wound our clientele by donning the garb of fools? If that is your intention, I must tell you now that you will not avoid objection!'

Frank glared at him angrily: 'No, I am not saying that at all, Noddoes. Don't be silly!' he snapped. 'I thought that I've just explained to everyone that I'm merely disposing of regulation funeral dress. Neatness, however, will not be compromised. Dressing as fools is certainly not what I have in mind. I don't want any more talk like that. It is in no way helpful. Instead, I should like to hear some constructive alternatives.'

'I think we have to ask ourselves whether we all adopt similar dress to each other,' said Stephen. 'If we do not, which is certainly my suggestion, our problem multiplies and becomes more subjective.'

'Good. Thanks for that,' nodded Frank. 'Anybody else?'

Thoad put his hand up and then put it down again. Tessa crossed her legs, which was just as attention-bringing as raising her hand. 'Can I dress up as a cat?' she asked.

Everybody stared at her.

'It won't matter, will it? Dressing up as a cat, I mean? I'll be in the

background beautifying the patient. Please let me be a cat! You can call be Sheba. *Purrrr!'*

She re-crossed her legs.

'I don't really think that you're in the equation, Tessa', Frank confirmed. 'Just as you say. Dress as you please.'

'*Purrrr!'*

'You're one hell of a wild woman, Sheba!' plonked in Epic, who now fancied and wanted Tessa just as much as Frank and scoring an outrageous brownie point with an instant recognition of her feline state (actually a renaissance, of course, but he wasn't to know that).

At this point, Amanda found her tongue. It had only recently been down Stephen Mauve's throat: 'Well, I'm not cutting my hair and brushing it so that I look like some kid out of *The Little House On The Prairie*. I like myself like this!' she said stridently.

'And I want you to stay that way too, Amanda,' Frank insisted. 'But I don't suppose that you have anything other than an affinity towards good clothes, do you? Neatness is the only stipulation, my dear. And manner. Manner even more so. Are you reassured?'

Amanda smiled and crushed Stephen's bollocks between her hand. 'Am I reassured?' she chirped to him, still not letting go. Stephen indicated without speech that she did seem to be.

Noddoes rose. He prefaced his address with a shake of the head and a protracted sigh: 'This can only be described as a tragedy!' he begun, wiping no sweat at all from his brow. 'Here we are on the threshold of founding a new company in the most dignified of professions and the items currently being discussed are whether we permit our embalmer to take the appearance of a domestic animal and to confirm that our secretary need not alter her appearance, lest she no longer resembled something which would otherwise be tended to by the aforementioned embalmer. I have to tell you that I find this all fantastic!'

'Fuck off, you old poof!' spat Amanda, squeezing poor Stephen's balls again as if they were a stress comforter. Stephen recoiled in pain.

'Now then, now then!' Frank said, immediately regretting sounding like Jimmy Saville. 'I want to instigate debate, not insults.'

'Well, you tell him over there!' demanded Amanda, squeezing only air this time, as Stephen had at last escaped. 'The old wanker called me a doughnut!'

'Now, that's enough!' snapped Frank. 'Look, has anybody got anything to add without slagging off somebody else? Come on now. Speak!'

Noddoes rose.

'Not you. Sit down!' roared Frank.

Noddoes sat down.

'I have come to a decision,' Frank summed up. 'One of the only contributions from any of you that was worth spit was when Stephen hinted that we did not adopt a formalised dress code. Peas in a pod. I have to say that I am happy with this, with the stipulation that I have made more than once that each member of staff is responsible for their own neatness. Okay?'

Stephen, now practically recovered, put his hand up. 'Does this also mean that we are all open to our own interpretation of what is neat?' he asked.

Frank smiled. This was a good question. Only a straight answer would do. 'Yes', he said. 'But don't let me down. Don't let yourselves down. That's the main thing. It really is.'

'We know and we won't,' Stephen assured him.

It was at this point that Epic got to his feet. He had been very quiet up until then. Sheba again was purring. 'I'm gonna dress all in black, man!' he announced. 'Just like Johnny Cash! For me, that's gonna be wild!'

'For you, that's gonna be different,' Frank pointed out.

'Absolutely, Frankie!'

'*Purrrr!*'

'And we're going to *bury* the Old Firm!' Stephen promised, unknowingly quoting Frank and receiving chuckled acknowledgements from the others.

'The Old Firm?' spluttered Frank. 'I'm finished with the Old Firm. As far as I'm concerned, they can go and fuck themselves!'

'They probably will,' nodded Stephen.

Chapter 20

Doctor Preston

MONDAY 31ST JANUARY 1994 was when it all began. At nine o'clock. Everybody was in position, with Thoad and Amanda ready in reception to receive the first client. Thoad had plumped for the conservative look, a dark suit and black tie; whilst Amanda, still a gothic punk, had turned up in a very smart dark blue top and matching skirt. Frank told her she looked fine, whilst really thinking that she didn't but realising that it was too late now. All they were waiting for now was for someone to die and, in Pendlesham, this never took long. Indeed, the new organisation's debut was secured when two young men walked in at five minutes to ten. Thoad activated a button from under his desk and suddenly there was Stevie Wonder singing *Don't You Worry 'bout A Thing*, albeit at a low volume. The music was shut off just as the young guys reached the desk. Amanda was perched on a stool a little farther back tapping away on a computer. Goodness knows what. Thoad smiled weakly at the chaps and then, suddenly remembering that it was certainly up to him to inaugurate the exchange but forgetting his line, blurted out the first thing that came into his head: 'Hello. Who's dead,' he asked.

'Our father,' replied one of the lads gloomily.

'Has the doctor written out the old death certificate?' asked Thoad.

'The doctor's with him and our mother now. Dad died at home about half an hour ago. It was cancer. Doctor Preston told us to come directly to you.'

'Us in particular?' asked Thoad.

'Just an undertaker,' admitted the boy.

'Fair enough! Fair enough!' said Thoad, reaching for a pen. 'What's the old address?'

'Fifty-one Cable Parade.'

'Righty-ho! Righty-ho!' nodded Thoad, writing this down. He pressed a second button on his concealed intercom, this one marked "Doughnut Alert" and this in turn lit up a corresponding unit in Frank's office. Frank immediately hit a switch: 'DOUGHNUT!' he roared, and within a split second, a screech of tyres saw an estate car driven by Epic with Noddoes riding shotgun bombing it out of its parking bay as if it were a fire engine and off up the road towards the roundabout at the town centre. The trouble was, of course, they didn't have a clue where they were going.

'Say, Frankie! Where's the doughnut, baby?'

'Yes, yes. Wait one!' Frank said and then requested this information from Thoad. It actually wasn't an oversight. Any point in Pendlesham could be reached from an exit off the main roundabout. The most important thing, Frank felt, was to hit the road running, and he had specifically told Thoad this and had instructed the driver to go straight to the roundabout in the first instance, by which time the details of the pick-up would have been known (usually the main hospital, it was anticipated) and could be relayed to them. Thoad had not forgotten. Epic, as usual, was being impetuous.

'Cable Parade. Number fifty-one,' Frank said. 'Over.'

There was a few seconds silence before Epic radioed in again. Something else important had most certainly been forgotten.

'Shit, Frankie! You wanna give me this dead guy's name here?'

'Oh, bugger, yes. Sorry!' came back Frank. He buzzed Thoad again. 'Thoad, what's the name of the doughnut?'

This was naturally overheard by the two sons, who looked at each other in horror.

'Before your dad died, what was his name?' asked Thoad, pen poised.

'What are you saying?' the older boy demanded. 'And why did that man on the radio call our father a "doughnut"?'

'Don't answer that for Christ's sake!' screeched Frank's voice, floating as clear as a bell out of the intercom.

Thoad looked horrified. 'It's code, it's code! We have to use code over the old radio,' Thoad assured them urgently, telling the truth first and then a lie.

The boys glared at him and Thoad, who had done so well up to that point, went back into his shell again and Frank wasn't about to say anything else either, even though radio contact was maintained between these two drips. The vital information was still at large. Meanwhile, the firm's estate car had just overtaken a young man and his girl in a two-seated sports. It was now but a matter of seconds from Cable Parade and still they didn't have the name. This was when Amanda came of age. Walking quickly up to Thoad's desk, she addressed the two boys directly as Thoad himself sat slumped like a sack of potatoes, eyes bulging.

'We really need to take your dad's name, guys,' she said. 'What you've been hearing is just radio talk. Nobody means any offence by it. We have to talk in code. Would you like to just give us his name?'

'Terry Cutler,' one of them said.

'Thanks. What age was he?'

'Fifty-six. Nearly fifty-seven.'

'Right. Thank you. Did you get that, Frank?'

'Yes, I did. Jolly fine job, Amanda!' Frank replied. 'Bloody Thoad!' He switched off and contacted the pick-up vehicle. Amanda put her hand on Thoad's shoulder. 'You can take down the rest of the details now, can't you?' she said to him and walked away. Thoad did. He found his tongue and got on with it.

Epic and Noddoes soon screeched to a halt outside 51 Cable Parade. Epic, dressed in a black tank top, baggy cream trousers (which Johnny Cash wouldn't have been seen dead in), black running shoes and carrying a folded-up black body bag under his arm, leapt out and dashed up to the door, vaulting the small garden gate, rang the bell and rattled the letterbox at the same time. 'Freddo's!' he yelled. 'Good old Freddo's!' He rammed the door with his fist and then kicked it for good measure. 'Open the goddam door! FREDDO'S!'

Noddoes, in traditional funeral dress, appeared next to him just as the door was opened by a middle-aged woman who had clearly been crying lots. Epic greeted her with a wink and a Grand Canyon smile. 'Good morning, ma'am. How you doing? Freddo's. We're here to pick up the dead guy,' he said, holding up the bag. 'Tommy… Tony… Christ! What was that goddam doughnut's name again? I've clear forgotten. Shoot!'

'Would you be Mrs Cutler, madam?' asked Noddoes, removing his hat and pushing Epic firmly to one side and thus out of sight.

The widow nodded and crumpled a well-used tissue into an even further state of disrepair.

'Terry Cutler!' came a transatlantic voice from the wings. 'Of course! Boy, was that embarrassing!'

Noddoes attempted a discreet cough. 'Madam, we are the undertakers engaged by your son.'

'Frankie said that there were two of them, man!' sneered the voice.

'By your *sons*, yes,' corrected Noddoes. 'Please accept our sincere condolences for your great loss.'

'Way to go!' cheered Epic.

Mrs Cutler's eyes widened. 'You were very… you were very… quick,' she sniffed, standing aside.

'Our task is never a pleasant one, dear lady,' said Noddoes as he entered. 'But experience has shown that the bereaved desire we come and go with the swiftest possible turn of speed.'

'My husband has been dead for less than an hour,' Mrs Cutler told them. 'And already you're… already you're…'

'Please be reassured, dear lady, that there will be ample provision laid by to enable you and your sons to visit your dear one on more than one occasion before the funeral,' Noddoes kindly informed her.

'You can bet your sweet ass on that one, darlin'!' confirmed Epic cheerfully, poking his head suddenly round the door. 'Your old man's gonna look just great!'

Mrs Cutler sniffed again into what was left of her tissue. They had entered the lounge now and therein was a man lying motionless in a sofa bed and a mature man in a suit in attendance, who turned to face them as they came in.

'Good morning, Doctor Preston,' Noddoes said to him.

'Good morning,' returned the doctor, who then looked at Epic and frowned at him in disapproval and surprise.

'Woodcastle and Snape?' he then asked.

'Er... no,' began Noddoes.

'You've got it wrong, doc!' Epic advised him. 'We're from Freddo's, man! Freddo's Funeral Emporium. Trust ol' Freddo to deal with your deado! Can you dig it?'

Doctor Preston's mouth shot open in utter astonishment.

'It's my young colleague's first... shall we say... *assignment*,' Noddoes explained, clearly embarrassed. 'I'm afraid the boy's a trifle nervous.'

'Nervous! Horseshit!' rasped Epic.

'Doctor Preston, do you think you would be so kind as to accompany Mrs Cutler through to the kitchen, or perhaps upstairs?' asked Noddoes, ignoring Epic completely and hoping to goodness that the doctor would do the same. 'The initial removal of the patient, as you are well aware, can fairly be adjudged to be a ceremony which somewhat lacks dignity, no matter how discreetly and professionally it is performed.'

'Certainly,' said Doctor Preston, and with one final unfavourable frown at Epic, he led the grizzling widow away.

After they had left the room, Noddoes turned to Epic. 'Alright, my boy. Are you ready for your inaugural patient?'

'Let's do it,' nodded Epic. 'Can you feel the force?'

'Then kindly follow my lead.'

'No, no, daddy-o!' sneered Epic, striding up to Cutler's remains. 'All wrong! Now, the whole point of what we're trying to do here is turn this industry on its head. Am I right? Frankie told us never to respect a dough-nut, 'cause the person ain't there any longer. Now, you've been creeping and bowing like a fucking English butler ever since we got in here. And for what? Huh? Because you figure you're back in that old Charles Dickens place with those two old pappy guys and Frankie. Well you're not, man, and that's the point. Here what I'm saying?'

'Oh dear!' said Noddoes.

'Maybe I'd better do the leading, pal!' Epic told him, putting the body bag down and lifting the corpse up by the shoulders and then pulling so that it was now sitting up.

'No, wait,' Noddoes said. 'There's a technique to this, I promise.' He marched up to the sofa and Epic shrugged and let go. Terry Cutler (1937-1994) slid back onto the surface of the bed with a dull thud.

'Let's have that black zip-up bag,' signalled Noddoes.

Epic picked this up again. 'One doughnut holder!' he said, holding it up.

'Right, now unzip it all the way down,' instructed Noddoes.

'All the way down! All the way down!' repeated Epic, unfolding the bag and then pulling the zip back as far as it would go.

'What we need to do, my boy, is to roll the patient carefully into the bag and then zip it back up. It's really quite easy. These bags are jolly user-friendly. Much better than the ones of old. Squeezing patients into those was like trying to stuff a turkey, especially if the patient was on the portly side. Very cumbersome.'

'Hey, Mac. I sure wish you would quit with this "patient" crap! The word is "doughnut". Frankie said so and Frankie's the boss!'

Epic held the open bag taut and Noddoes expertly rolled the body into the middle of it before flinging the side nearest to him back over to Epic. 'Zip it back up as far as it will go, my boy, and there you have it.'

Epic sealed the package. 'Well, that was easy!' he said, slapping the bag with satisfaction. 'Okay, let's get it out of here!'

'Oh my, where's the stretcher!' suddenly blurted out Noddoes.

'Asshole! We don't have a goddam stretcher! What the fuck do we want with a stretcher? This man ain't hurt. This man is a doughnut.'

'But we can't simply walk out into the street carrying this poor devil as if he were a carpet!' wailed Noddoes.

'You still don't get it, do you?' rasped Epic, generally annoyed now. 'Frankie just wants us to collect the doughnuts and drag them back to HQ. And that's all we do. The only one who gets to pet any of these deados is Tessa. We're just the garbage men, know what I'm talking about? Now, let's get going while this thing's still fresh!'

He thrust one end of the giant black pudding under his shoulder and angrily gestured that Noddoes did the same with his. Noddoes, stung and surprised by Epic's reprimand, nevertheless complied and the two men headed for the door.

'We're up, up and away with the doughnut now, ma'am!' Epic yelled up the stairs. 'We'll be in touch! Catch you later, doc!'

A sudden burst of sobbing was returned from above as the undertakers left with Terry Cutler's body. Epic, who had driven the estate car and thus had the keys to it, unlocked the back and pulled the door open. In almost the same motion, he hurled the long black bag into the vehicle. Noddoes had relaxed his hold on his own end in preparation for tenderly placing the deceased inside, as had been the custom at the Old Firm, but Epic's sudden thrust was more than enough to relieve Noddoes of his part of the burden and the corpse flew straight into the estate car, slid with speed up to the front and thundered into the back of the driver and passenger seat. Epic slammed the door, locked it and then ran along to the driver's door, opened this and jumped inside. Next second, the engine was running.

'What are you waiting for, Hamlet?' he yelled, revving the engine angrily without even giving himself a chance to draw breath, let alone Noddoes a chance to reach the passenger door. Noddoes put his hand on the door handle, but a spectacularly impatient Epic flicked the knob from inside and pushed the door open. 'Come on, now. Let's move it!' he barked, revving the engine again.

Noddoes climbed in and closed the door, and by that time Epic was on his way to sixty, with Cutler's body smashing against the back door and Noddoes thrown back against his seat before he even had time to contemplate his seatbelt. 'Oh, dear me!' he gasped. He still hadn't belted himself in as Epic broke a red light, not outrageously, but by enough and, in any case, his infringement would have been more than enough to interest plod had they been around.

'You know something, man?' Epic sneered, putting his foot down still farther. 'I figure that before today you actually felt that what Frankie had told the guys was all bullshit and something which would be put right by some good old fashioned English manners. Shit, man! You were never with us at all, were you? You still can't see the difference between the dead and a doughnut. We were told: the first you respect, the second you treat like shit. This is Frankie's policy. This is *Freddo's* policy. But it ain't yours. I've got you all figured out, pal!'

'Stop this car immediately, you snivelling transatlantic little twerp!' demanded Noddoes.

'You wanna get out?' sneered Epic, swinging the car across and pulling up on the kerb.

'Never!' Noddoes assured him defiantly. 'On the contrary. I want *you* to get out and lend me your services. I'll soon teach you who's figured out whom!'

'What you gonna do?'

'Just get out!'

'Okay, okay! Take it easy!'

Epic got out of the car.

'Open the boot!' ordered Noddoes.

'The what?'

'You know damn well what I mean. Just get on with it!'

Epic unlocked the back door and opened it out. 'Now what?'

'You know "now what"!' snapped Noddoes. 'Unzip this doughnut of yours. Let's see how he's enjoying the trip!'

'You're crazy!'

'There's a rope in there somewhere, isn't there?'

'Sure there is. It's a towrope. So what?'

'I was just thinking,' mused Noddoes. 'Since the doctrine of that idiot

Eddowes, something by which you seem irretrievably captivated, my boy, states that a corpse is merely a piece of refuge, I rather feel that being dragged by rope behind our vehicle is certainly the most fitting mode of transport for it. Indeed the only one. What do you think boy?'

Epic's eyes lit up. 'I think we should quit with the black bag and tie the doughnut to the fender!' he declared, as if it was his idea all along and beaming all over his face.

'Or perhaps just to the bumper,' corrected Noddoes, now smiling himself.

'Let's do it!' Epic cried.

They did it. Noddoes' probation was surely over. And so was Epic's too.

Chapter 21

Julian And Derek

JULIAN AND DEREK Cutler, Terry's boys, had only just begun discussing financial terms with Thoad when the corpse in question was being removed by Epic and Noddoes from the home of widow Barbara; and as the Cutler boys were signing the papers, Freddo's estate car was already roaring around the corner towards its parking bay with Cutler *pere* safely in tow in the purest sense.

Because of the liveliness of their exchange of views, Epic and Noddoes had failed to contact Frank after making the pick-up, contrary to instructions. The first that the boss learned of the car's departure from the Cutler house was when he actually heard it screeching around the corner and looked out of the window to see the return of the gladiators. Stephen Mauve was with him.

'Here they come!' Frank said. 'Aren't they naughty for not calling?'

'What's wrong with the car?' asked Stephen, pointing. 'They're pulling something along behind them. What the devil is it?'

Both men stared hard. Frank then snapped his finger. 'Good heavens above. It's Cutler!' he laughed. 'They've tied him to the bumper. How original!'

'*Very* original indeed!' nodded Stephen approvingly, and he and Frank trotted down the stairs to meet them. 'Although I seem to recall a similar ploy using a horse.'

The vehicle needed to back into its space now, but could hardly do this with Cutler in the way. Frank though, by now, had arrived. He marvelled at the treatment of the corpse. 'Now, this is fantastic. *Remarkable!*' he exclaimed, eying the road-worn, bruised and severely twatted cadaver and smiling as if he had just had a whole segment of melon rammed in his gob. 'What a capital idea. Well done, Epic!'

'Not so fast, Frankie!' Epic said. 'Don't thank me. This is all down to my man, Hamlet, here!'

'*Noddoes!*' roared Frank incredulously. 'Good heavens, man. It's brilliant!'

'I'm glad you approve!' sniffed Noddoes with wonderfully disguised sarcasm.

'*Approve?* Noddoes, you're a genius! I always thought so, and now I know it. Bravo! Bravo!'

This major slap on the back ignited Noddoes' vanity all of a sudden, which had undergone a rare spell of dormancy of late. He had already received similar plaudits rich in obsequiousness from Frank as an incitement to join the Emporium in the first place. Frank had now gone for a win-double and had surprisingly succeeded, although at least this time there was a smidgen of sincerity tied up with Frank's genuine delight at what they had done to Cutler, even if calling Noddoes a 'genius' was unquestionably a bridge too far.

'It was rather an obvious course of action to take, you know,' Noddoes said airily, swallowing the bait nicely. 'It was the corollary of our decision to eliminate the importance of the actual presence of the corpse due to its having nothing whatsoever to do with a tribute to the deceased. Placing this shell of a person in a black bag and carrying it out like a carpet didn't somehow seem disparaging enough for such a useless article. I therefore instructed our young colleague to assist me in assuring that we discard said black bag and tow in the corpse like a dredger draws fish in a net and submit the remains to our lady embalmer for further ill treatment. It would appear that I have not made the wrong decision.'

'Indeed you have not!' Frank assured him. 'Good heavens, Noddoes, you've opened all sorts of doors!'

Frank may have genuinely been cheered by this new development, but he, along with everyone else it seemed, had quite forgotten the Cutler boys, who were still on the premises finalising things with Thoad. Neither

Thoad nor Amanda had any inkling that Terry had already arrived at this point, and had the lads departed at this moment, they would have bumped straight into their father. Their reaction to the treatment meted out to his body was unlikely to have been the same as Frank's, it was fair to say. Fortunately, Cutler was quickly bundled into the Emporium just before the paying customers withdrew and was taken straight to Tessa so that she could take a look at what was left of the carcass.

As for the bill, Julian and Derek had considered Thoad's quote most satisfactory. Everyone made a great play in slagging off undertakers, always seeming to accept the line that the cost of dying was prohibitive, but here was a company that was able to do the necessary for a song, plus small change.

'We think that mourning shouldn't be part of the old funeral at all,' Thoad had explained to them, remembering his script almost word for word. 'We believe that funerals should be over in minutes with the absence of ceremony being the order of the day. We think funerals should purely involve the incineration of the old corpse, not a tribute to a loved one. That is something which we believe is a matter for the people left over. It has nothing to do with us. It is not proper for us to intervene, we argue. The only proper function for us, as far as we can see, is to dispose of the old corpse and that's basically us.'

'But we *loved* our father!' quivered Derek.

'Then let us take care of the old corpse!' pleaded Thoad. 'You can deal with all the sobbing and grizzling yourselves, but we *must* have that corpse. Memories? We're not interested. You'll be quids in if you deal with us.'

'We'll do it!' agreed Julian, probably still too grief stricken to realise what he was letting his family in for, to say nothing of his dead dad.

As this conversation was taking place, Terry had taken matters into his own hands by arriving at the Emporium in any case, and as his sons were leaving, his remains were already being examined by Tessa in this her inaugural effort as the head (indeed sole) 'beautician' after such a long time as assistant to the excellent Peter Foster. Julian and Derek had not seen a thing. It had been a tight squeeze though.

'Has this man been killed in a road accident?' asked Tessa, eying the carcass on the slab. 'If he has, this is a matter for the coroner.'

'It's cancer, Tess,' explained Epic cheerfully. 'The road got him later.'

'And what's this rope doing tied around his ankle?' Tessa wanted to know.

'How else were we gonna get him here, sweetheart? The doc told us that he figured the guy was gonna have a bit of trouble jogging upside of us, you dig?'

Tessa gave Epic a quizzical look before glancing down to examine Cutler more closely. Seconds later, enlightenment.

'Oh right! Yes! *Groovy!*' she laughed. 'So the death certificate's already sorted?'

'Why, certainly!'

'And it *definitely* mentions cancer?'

'It sure does!'

'*Groovy!*'

So Tessa got down to work beautifying the now quite seriously damaged corpse. It was mentioned to her that Cutler's widow had made it perfectly plain that she intended to view her husband at least once before the funeral. This was something which seemingly flew spectacularly in the face of the entire Freddo critique, since it was an acknowledgement that the carcass was indeed of some consequence and needed to be treated with a surfeit of care and respect for the benefit of loved ones left behind, rather than having as much to do with the person as a doughnut. It of course endured because it allowed Tessa a spot on the team on the pretence that embalming or 'beautifying' the corpse was, in fact, much more of an insult to it than an instrument of preservation governed by solemn respect. A doughnut was certainly not worthy of such pampering by Frank's own rulebook and Tessa's services were thus superfluous. Yet she remained in place for the one reason which everybody understood except Tessa herself, the one person who could still not grasp that Frank was obsessed with her.

Tessa, it had to be remarked, had at least not received her first client in her lunatic guise of 'Sheba, the Imperial Cat of Doom', but the result of this, her inaugural work, might just as well have been, because when she declared her task completed, the wretched Cutler was lying on the slab looking for all the world like the grotesquely smiling pale-faced clown who came to world prominence hanging around hamburger bars with little kids. Her 'beautifying' had indeed been an indisputable insult to the Cutler memory, and despite Frank's claims about her role being nothing but 'insulting', on the basis of what she had just produced, it was now quite clear that Tessa and her services were certainly not out of place there.

Chapter 22

Barbara And Terry

TERRY CUTLER'S WIDOW, Barbara, went around to the Emporium with Julian and Derek for a viewing of their beloved husband and father. They were greeted (as the sons had been before) by Thoad and followed this spectre of abject misery down a corridor, with small tables of flowers dotted down both sides and arrows with the word 'DOUGH-NUT' painted on them every few feet along the walls, until they reached the viewing room. Terry was sat in an armchair, looking better than he had done for days in a smart blue dressing gown and Panama hat. A bedside-style table was next to him on which a cup of coffee had been placed with steam rising from it. Cutler's clown face had been tempered slightly, at Frank's 'suggestion'; the painted smile not nearly as predominant as before, but he still looked a very jolly fellow indeed, as if he were about to burst into song. Stephen Mauve had hit the nail squarely on the head when he had first seen Cutler: 'He looks fucking pissed'. Hence the coffee, probably.

Barbara took one look at the display and burst into tears. 'That ain't my Terry!' she howled miserably.

'Quite so, dear lady,' confirmed Noddoes, walking in just at that moment. 'I am *so* glad you concur.'

'Where's my Terry?' sobbed the woman.

'Dead,' said Noddoes benignly, raising his hands to the ceiling. 'Gone.'

'She's asking if that's his body,' Julian explained, pointing at the dummy on the chair.

'Indeed yes, young man,' Noddoes beamed. 'Very well observed!'

'He looks brilliant!' Julian said. 'He would have loved it!'

'But that's never your father!' insisted Barbara. 'What have you done with my Terry! *Terry!* she blubbed.

'I beg your pardon, madam!' rasped Noddoes crossly. 'We have done nothing whatsoever to your husband. You really must try to understand that he was dead when we arrived. Quite dead. Doctor Preston was most insistent on that. Indeed, one would have been astonished to have encountered him in any other state than that of a corpse. And as you've just confirmed yourself, for the second time now, quite correctly, what you see here is certainly not him.'

'Oh, Ju, what's happening? Is this really your father? What's this man talking about?' Mrs Cutler grizzled.

'Dead! Dead! Dead! Dead! Dead! Dead!' stamped Noddoes.

'What you see is just the old corpse,' clarified Thoad, as Noddoes swept out of the room rather hurt. 'Doughnut.'

'I think you're right, Ju,' Derek said as he tried to steady his mother who had nearly fainted. 'I think dad would have loved all this old caper! Fancy calling him a "doughnut"! Marvo!'

'Terry!' pleaded Barbara faintly. 'What have they done with my Terry?'

Cutler continued to look jolly even though his coffee was getting cold.

'Perhaps things will become plainer on the day of the old disposal,' Thoad advised her softly, as he placed a comforting hand on her shoulder to lead her away. As far as the poor woman was concerned, she had arrived for a viewing, but had viewed nothing too much beyond the inside of her own handkerchief, which now resembled a dishcloth. Her sons understood and accepted everything. She understood nothing.

She departed the Emporium still pining for a glimpse of her husband at rest, not knowing that she had already been admirably accommodated, and could now only look ahead to what she believed would be a funeral. She had no inkling that her Terry had actually been funeralised at the instance of his death as far as the Freddo organisation was concerned, and that what awaited would be a less than generous tribute to his memory, and particularly his corpse.

Things indeed would become plainer when the 'doughnut' faced its 'sell by date', which was the day of the disposal of the property which had recently housed Terry Cutler as leaseholder.

Naturally the disposal of Cutler's corpse a matter of days later was a defining moment in the evolution of Freddo's Funeral Emporium. Some thirty 'leftovers' had been advised that they should report to the Eastgate Crematorium for 'a brief ceremony followed by cremation' at eleven o'clock that Friday. It would be presided over by the Reverend Danny Hare with his wife Sally in attendance, for it was their headquarters. Any floral tributes should be sent directly to Freddo's. These, of course, had not been encouraged. Barbara Cutler and her sons, Julian and Derek, would be going straight to the Emporium at ten o'clock where Terry would be retrieved from the comfort of his chair and, unknown to his immediate family, tied to the bumper of the Cortina estate, once more driven by Epic, with Noddoes alongside him, the vehicle being modified to allow Barbara, Julian and Derek plenty of space. The flowers would be hurled into Frank's yellow Ford Anglia, containing Frank and Stephen Mauve, and the two vehicles would then hurtle around to Eastgate Crematorium to roast the carcass.

Thoad gloomily greeted wife and sons for the final time. Barbara still harboured a frail ambition to view her man before he was dragged off to be torched.

'It's a bit difficult,' murmured Thoad. 'They're getting him ready.'

As a matter of fact, this was a lie. Cutler was still lauding it up in his armchair, smiling away, at this point in the game, but Thoad assumed quite rightly that had Barbara been taken in to see Terry again, she would have only missed the point one more time and got herself all worked up. The best thing would be to bundle the widow into the estate and then craftily bring Terry out afterwards. This policy had been rubber-stamped by Frank.

Julian and Derek calmed their mother down: 'We're going to have a gigantic piss-up for dad after the service,' Julian said. 'That will be when all the tributes will come out. That will be the real funeral.'

This was indeed excellent. The boy was feeding his mother good Freddo food here. He and brother Derek had been enlightened extremely quickly in the doctrine of this pioneering funeral company. Similarly, Terry himself had proved to be a model debutant. Not a peep of a complaint had come from him throughout the whole business. A more willing and courteously compliant guinea pig could not have been wished for. Even when Epic and Noddoes came for him, he appeared to be enjoying himself enormously. Most people would perhaps have lodged a complaint against being tied by a rope to the bumper of a car and dragged off to a crematorium. But not Terry Cutler. Full to the brim with the renowned English spirit which had seen so many of his countrymen through the appalling carnage of Hitler's Blitz to ultimate victory over the cancer of Fascism, Terry Cutler kept smiling through, his upper lip no less stiff than any other part of him. He undertook his duties with Churchillian fortitude and with the fearlessness of a Tommy in a foxhole. This man obviously refused to recognise fear. To him, everything appeared a music hall amusement, his joviality trumping his terror and his resignation of the worst. Men had been given the George Cross for less. It was such heroes whom Her Majesty Queen Elizabeth, the Queen Mother, when still regent to George VI, had in mind when the decision was taken not to flee the Palace when Adolf was doing his worst to the capital. The ordinary man. The sort of people who would surely eventually win that beastly war and thereby restore decency, dignity and democracy to England, Europe and the world --- Terry Cutler.

Terry was moved off in triumph to Eastgate Crematorium, modestly smiling off any plaudit to gallantry as he was dragged away. For the brothers, meanwhile, the penny now had well and truly dropped.

'I didn't see your dad's coffin,' Barbara said when the tiny convoy was safely on the road, although going a tad too fast for her liking really.

'Don't look back, mum, but he's right behind us,' Julian assured her. Barbara did look around though. All she saw was a silly little yellow car with two men inside waving at her frantically.

'He's never in there!' she wailed, bursting into tears immediately.

Julian peered over his shoulder, saw Frank and Stephen and waved back, grinning.

'No, no, not in there,' he corrected. 'All the flowers are in there. Not dad!'

'You told me he was right behind us!' blubbered his mum. 'Oh God. I'm so confused!'

Bumpity-Bump!

'But he *is*, mum!' Derek insisted. 'Come on, now. Don't be such a *drag*!'

Julian laughed out loud at this excellent pun. Epic exploded too. Barbara sobbed loudly. Frank and Stephen waved frantically. Epic caught them in his mirror and waved back. Only Noddoes remained dignified. He sat straight-faced, staring straight ahead. Terry kept smiling though. What a capital bloke!

Bumpity-Bump!

Try as she might, Barbara still couldn't see Terry behind her. Small wonder, actually. He was bouncing along quite nicely between the two vehicles, but completely invisible to anyone travelling in the one in front. Crafty Terry was loving his game of peek-a-boo!

Bumpity-Bump!

The tiny cortège soon came by Eastgate Crematorium. Upon immediate arrival, Frank and Stephen leapt out of the van and dashed up to untie Cutler. Epic and Noddoes made sure that Barbara remained inside the estate, whilst Terry was cut loose and bundled inside. Barefoot Sally and Keith Tate, the organist, were already inside. This time, Keith's musical talents would not be needed. He was there solely to operate the equipment which would spout forth the recorded music the Cutler boys had asked for to see their dad's corpse away to the flames.

Frank and Stephen hurled Terry onto the catafalque. Still not a single whinge came from this giant of a man. A bright multi-coloured duvet was flung over him to add further cheer to the happy scene. Frank and Stephen then ran like hares back out to officially greet the leftovers. Julian and Derek Cutler were in fine spirits, despite what was suggested by their sombre black suits. Their mother, Barbara, alas had 'party pooper' written all over her miserable face. What was wrong with the wretched woman was anybody's guess.

'Come and meet the Reverend Hare and his enchanting wife,' beamed Frank at the trio.

'Where's my Terry?' blubbered Barbara, looking all around her, having failed to see him in the second vehicle.

'Dead!' at least three people reminded her.

'Gone!' added Noddoes for emphasis.

Sally Hare suddenly appeared in a Hawaiian grass skirt at the door of the crematorium. 'Welcome to Danny's Bar and Grill!' she chirped. 'Shake your booties this way!' And she wiggled back inside.

'Oh my God! Who the hell was that?' wailed Barbara.

'Well fit, whoever she is!' observed Julian.

Barbara broke down again, rather more noisily this time, unfortunately.

'Oh really, mum. *Must* you?' scolded Derek, irritated at her performance.

The Cutlers were escorted inside. There they were introduced to Danny Hare. Barbara, on seeing the vicar in a 'psychedelic' cassock and with a massive flat wooden cross around his neck, immediately flung her arms around the young man's neck. She had clearly seen the crucifix and not much else. 'Oh God, Father!' she rasped, sobbing still.

'Steady!' Darren warned her. 'Don't malign the Man!'

She was led to her seat by her sons. The other guests were arriving now. Barbara, at this time, noticed the duvet-covered lump on the podium. She went cold and pointed.

'Terry... *Terry!*' she stammered. She screamed and sobbed back into tears.

'That's *not* dad. Will you please calm down!' hissed Julian.

'Dear lady,' said Noddoes softly, suddenly appearing at Mrs Cutler's shoulder. 'I must warn you. If you will not, or are unable to compose yourself, I'm afraid we must ask you to leave the crematorium.'

'Oh, sweet Jesus, please make this a nightmare!' bawled Babs.

'It's okay. We'll shut her up,' promised Derek.

'Thank-you kindly, gentlemen,' smiled Noddoes, and he withdrew satisfied.

Derek turned sharply to his mum. 'Now, belt up you old bint! You can blub all you like when we finish here, but not now. You're spoiling everything! Stop your childish sobbing! Shut the fuck up!'

The little chapel-type building started filling up - family and a goodly number of Terrys' mates. Most of Danny's regular congregation were also present, unsolicited guests, quite frankly.

At precisely eleven o'clock, Danny picked up a microphone and roared into it at the top of his voice: 'SHOWTIME! READY TO RRRUMMMMMMMBLE!!!'

The congregation cheered. Immediately *Glad All Over* by the Dave Clark Five came blasting out of some overhead speakers erected by Keith Tate and everybody (well, *nearly* everybody) started grooving and stomping to that great old track. Danny Hare bellowed out the lyric through the mic, stomping like a maniac at the appropriate moment during the chorus. Barefoot Sally spun around the floor like a top, her Hawaiian skirt spinning around also providing anyone who was watching (and most men were!) with a prolonged and very pleasant sighting of her excellent legs. The Freddo people were jumping up and down too, as were the guests and the Cutler boys. Even the wretched Barbara took time off howling to raise a part smile. *Glad All Over* had been at the top of the charts when she and Terry had first met. It was one of *their* songs.

When the record had finished, Danny addressed the assembly again: 'You feeling ALLLRRRIGHT?' he bawled.

There was a roar of affirmation.

'Get the moozic back on, guvnor!' spewed one of Terry's mates, who looked and sounded as if he had slopped out once or twice or, if not, certainly someone who had escaped prison on a technicality. Pondlife, in any case. His suggestion was greeted by cheers too.

'Later, groover!' Darren told him. 'First we're gonna square things with the Lord. Let us pray, here.'

The congregation reluctantly settled down. Dazza cleared his throat before beginning: 'Okay, Father, we're gonna thank-you for the life of Terry Cutler. You've got him now and so it's now down to us to clear up the mess you in your wisdom left behind, namely the doughnut...' The Reverend then led everyone into the Lord's Prayer, after which he bellowed: 'Okay, people. Shall we do it?'

'Yes!' shouted the Freddo people and Barefoot Sally, as well as a small selection of Terry's chums who were desperate to get to the pub.

'The preacher can't *hear* you cats!' chided Danny in a sarcastic singsong voice. 'I said... shall we do it?' he spat through the mic, adding echo for effect.

The congregation roared and the thirsty blokes were beginning to lose it a bit. They would have to wait a little longer.

'One more time, because I'm *so* deaf!' thundered Danny. 'SHALL... WE... DOOOO... IT??'

This time, the roof nearly came off the building.

'THEN LET'S SHAKE!!!' he concluded, and he spun around to give Keith the signal, and the track chosen for the committal, *Telstar* by the Tornados, began its deceptively lethargic intro before exploding into the melody which made it a monumental hit all over the world in 1962, indeed providing a British group with its first number one hit in the United States.

The gathering rose again, humming, and in many instances growling along, and nobody seemed to notice Stephen and Epic, both whistling away, walking up the aisle to the catafalque, at least not until the moment when they jumped up onto it. The duvet of such bright colours was whipped off by Epic, and he and Stephen yanked Terry up by the shoulders so that he could say hi and join in the mass jive to Joe Meek's old smash.

The introduction of the doughnut, bloodied and battered though it was, brought the crowd to the point of frenzy. Such was the roar that Danny was obliged to signal now to Keith to turn the music up. In fact *Telstar* was just entering its final triumphant finale at this point, and quite frankly folk were going berserk. Terry was tripping the light fantastic brilliantly, and as the track came to its end, Stephen began waving Cutler's arm at the revellers and the cheering became deafening as everyone waved back.

'ROCK AND ROLL, TERRY!' thundered Danny through the mic. 'GIVE OUR LOVE TO THE KING!' And with that, both Stephen and Epic let go of the excellent Cutler and jumped down. Terry fell awkwardly (but still smiling) and the catafalque rose suddenly quickly to allow the corpse to slide effortlessly through a hatch which had just opened, down a chute and straight into the waiting, crackling furnace. *Telstar* came to a stop in that instant. The timing was simply marvellous. It was a track that was impossible to follow up. *Kumbaya* was summarily abandoned. The congregation had gone bananas in any case. That sickly-sweet hymn was never to be heard again.

Danny's Bar and Grill had cooked its first doughnut and Freddo's had begun life in fine style. The only debris seemed to be an utterly exhausted Barefoot Sally, who seemed to have fainted as a result of a particularly vigorous dancing accompaniment to *Telstar*, and Barbara Cutler, who also seemed to have fainted as a result of not sharing entirely the otherwise universal appreciation of Terry's adieu, humourless old bat.

But after this debut, there was to be no turning back for the Freddo organisation. Things really began hotting up, and not just at Danny's Bar and Grill. But before our story moves on, let us pay tribute one more time to the undoubted star of Freddo's inaugural matinee – to wit, that prime example of the fearless, indefatigable, yet incurably cheerful bulldog breed - indeed, of everything good that leaps out to proudly proclaim that one is English: Terry Cutler! Heroes like that mould a nation. Heroes like that mould a funeral company.

Chapter 23

Three Babes

THE NEXT DAY was a Saturday, and that evening all of the Freddo people including Station Inn debutantes, Noddoes and Tessa rolled into the group's principal place of recreation and set about getting down to serious business drinkie-wise. Because Tessa happened to arrive with her personality at least halfway towards that of her alter ego, Sheba the Imperial Cat of Doom, her entry saw her fall immediately in love with that sleazy shithole and it with her.

Instantaneously she became an indispensable member of the Inn Crowd, with Tom the proprietor hopelessly added to her growing list of panting admirers. If this was nothing of a surprise, the unforeseen event was provided by Noddoes, who also felt far from uncomfortable, although this was helped by a stoned Amanda being all over him and telling all the kids how wonderful her 'daddy' was. Everyone got totally shot to pieces.

During the course of the evening, it was just about possible for Frank to make certain points to everyone about how he thought things had gone with their first doughnut and on how they could be improved for their next visit to Danny's Bar and Grill. 'I thought Sally Hare looked absolutely charming,' he told Noddoes early on in proceedings.

'Horny!' added Stephen out of Amanda's earshot, which actually didn't matter, as she was far too gone anyway.

'Oh yes, I do so agree!' gushed the old luvvie. 'Just as lovely as our own dear Tessa.'

'Say, Frankie!' said Epic, barging in from seemingly nowhere with a fresh pint of ale in one hand and a reefer the size of a rolled-up newspaper in the other. 'How 'bout using Sheba next time as well as the Sally chick up front with the pastor? Two major babes on either side of the preacher man. Now, that scene's gonna blast the people into orbit!'

Frank suddenly looked horrified.

'No, no. I don't think that's a very good idea,' he said.

'Hell, *sure* it is!' Epic insisted.

'Oh, my dear boy, I think it's a splendid suggestion. Simply *splendid*!' argued Noddoes.

'Yo! Splendid' barked Epic. 'Listen to the man, Frankie!'

'No, no, no. It's out of the question. Quite out of the question,' Frank said. 'And anyway, Tessa wouldn't want to do it.'

'What makes you say that?'

'*Purrr!* Tessa wouldn't want to do *what?*' enquired a silky feline voice from behind.

'*Sheeba,* baby!' cooed Epic. 'What's new, pussycat? Have we got news for *you!*'

'No, we haven't. Do be quiet, Epic!' snapped Frank urgently.

'Sure we have! Do you wanna do some jiving at the next burning, baby? You and the preacher's lady?'

'Tessa, perhaps we can discuss this at another time,' insisted Frank. 'Another *quieter* time.'

'You can't keep her all to yourself, Frankie!' Epic warned him with a knowing grin.

'What are you saying?'

'Perhaps, dear boy, we should ask the young lady how she feels about it?'

'Well, I---'

'*Purrr!*'

Frank was desperate to kill this thing dead in the water if he could. Secretly he knew only too well that Tessa would be a perfect and exotic addition to the husband and wife act of Danny and Barefoot Sally at the pulpit. She was eye-catchingly beautiful and graceful, and as Sheba would add, a touch of class (and an erotic class at that), providing she wasn't too stoned to perform, to what had already proved to be a mouth-watering display from Sally at the inaugural doughnut disposal. The problem was, Frank still imagined that he had other plans for Tessa (he was an eternal optimist if not a sad fool), and to allow her to cavort around with the delicious Mrs Hare for the gratification of an entire congregation was not acceptable. He didn't admit this, of course. Instead he neatly came up with another potential obstacle which, to be fair to him, sounded quite feasible, even though Frank knew that it was actually a crock of old shit.

'I really don't think that the Reverend Hare would be terribly happy if we tried to impose this on him,' he claimed, trying to cover up his growing discomfort with a glance at his watch.

'You must ask him, dear boy!'

'Right! Go ahead and check him out!'

'*Purrr!*'

'No, no, no. I mean that we're the undertakers, aren't we? Tessa's the embalmer. The Reverend Hare and his wife are… well, the vicar and his wife! We wouldn't expect them to get mixed up in our side of things, would we? And they certainly wouldn't expect us to get involved in theirs. Right?'

'No. Wrong, man. All wrong!' came back Epic, who had seen through Frank immediately and was now intent on making mischief. 'If you really wanna make this thing wild, I mean *really* wild, you've just gotta bring in Sheba, Frankie. The preacher ain't gonna be a problem. Hell, he's just gonna love it! Anyone can see that Sheba's a natural!'

'Epic's right, Frank,' chipped in Stephen who, having taken the cue from Epic, was now desperately trying not to laugh.

'Frankie, tell me something,' chipped in Epic. 'This reluctance of yours. It wouldn't have anything to do with your fondness for cats, now would it?'

Frank went scarlet. 'I don't know what you mean,' he stammered pathetically.

'*Purrrr!*'

'Is that a fact?'

'Look, Frank,' Stephen added. 'I know that you're the boss and this is your show, and if you don't want to use Tessa for some reason, then she stays just an embalmer and that's it, but---'

'I think you're being frightfully unfair, dear boy,' opined Noddoes. 'We all thought you cared for our dear Tessa. The least you could do is to give this suggestion a modicum of thought. I'm sure that the girl would love to do it, wouldn't you, my dear?'

'*Purrrr!*'

'But---'

'Frankie, Frankie,' cut back in Epic. 'Here's the deal. We contact the preacher, okay! We let him speak to his chick. If they're hip, then every-thing's cool! Just talk with the preacher!'

Frank made a grab for his last straw: 'Ah, yes. But what about Amanda?' he asked hopefully, indicating the burbling spaced-out punkette, who was smiling stupidly into space and practically swinging off Noddoe's left arm. 'I would suggest that if I were to offer such an additional duty to Tessa, I would be failing as a manager if I did not offer the same opportunity to the other female member of my team...'

There was a split second of silence, followed by an explosion of laugh-ter and purring. Frank had patently gone too far this time. Everyone had happily gone along with him whilst he had put a seemingly credible but nevertheless still ludicrous obstacle in the way of Epic's excellent sugges-tion to bring their gorgeous embalmer into the forefront of things. But to now attempt to employ the excuse that such a move should be stifled because it was unfair on Amanda was such blatant bollocks as well as such a monstrous exploitation of Amanda's apparent unsuitability for any other duty than the one to which she had been allocated (to say nothing of the young woman's current condition), that nobody was going to pretend any-more. They were all laughing, but the reaction was certainly one of derision rather than amusement. Stephen was actually rather angry to say the least and was ready to savage Frank for being such a bullshitting and mercenary liar and using his little girlfriend as a tool.

He was spared the chance, beaten to the punch by the ever-sharp Epic; and the Canadian's blow was far more effective than anything Stephen had

had in mind (which was merely a volley of expletives woven around a loud proclamation of the real reason Frank didn't want Tessa to join Sally Hare on the dance floor). Its delivery did nothing other than put Frank in his place in the most spectacular of ways. It also meant that he not only didn't get what he wanted, but in fact ended up getting something he most decidedly did not want: 'Frankie, baby!' beamed Epic. 'That's a fucking excellent idea! Three babes and the preacher all jiving together! Boy, have you struck gold or *what*, darlin'?'

Frank's bluff had been well and truly called and Stephen, realising straight away what Epic was doing, then gleefully stuck the knife in even further: 'I think Amanda will be overjoyed at this chance you're giving her when she gets back down,' he said, pretending to be delighted on her behalf. 'She may well overindulge too much on the old wacky backy occasionally and she's done a bit of snorting, but then so has Tessa here. And Amanda's a very fit kid. She'll look super alongside Tessa and Mrs Hare, especially in the right horny togs! This idea of yours is fantastic, boy! *Fantastic!*'

'Well, I...' began Frank.

'*Purrrr!*'

Noddoes, alas, always slow at grasping the point, had failed to come in on this one too. He looked down at the now virtually comatose girl suspended from his arm like a stationary yoyo and shook his head sadly. 'Oh, no,' he said. 'I should have to say that I do not consider that to be a very adequate exchange at all. Dear Tessa, a most admirable choice. But never *this* poor child!'

Frank had inadvertently been given a quite undeserved last chance of survival, but before he was able to even contemplate snatching it, Epic concluded matters: 'Don't argue with the boss-man, daddy-o!' he snapped, addressing Noddoes. 'Frankie wants all three chicks in on the action and that's the way it's gonna be. Right, Frankie?'

'*Purrrr!*'

'Thanks again, Frank. Nice one!' added Stephen.

'Yes, but I ---'

'You're a fair man!'

Stephen walked quickly away. Epic took the cue and sprang a leak too. The discussion about the go-go girls was over.

Frank was left looking at Noddoes and they both stared at Amanda, who was stoned, pissed and out.

'You will forgive me, dear boy, if I suggest that you have just made a mistake,' Noddoes told him, as he allowed the girl to slowly slip to the comfort of the floor.

Frank certainly knew that he had. Noddoes was correct. But the old luvvie didn't know the half of it. Epic and Stephen did. And Frank knew that they did.

Chapter 24

The Hut

THE OVERWORKED PENDLESHAM branch of the Lifejoys was headed by a man called Reg Doorman, who was admirably suited for the post on account of having once attempted suicide himself for the piss-weak reason that his wife, Doreen, ran off with his brother, Roland. All three participants were already of mature age when this had happened, which gave the event such a ludicrous spin that the trauma which Reg clearly suffered as a result should really have been emersed by the comic irony of it all, especially since the reverse was made even greater by the unfaithful pair also managing to sell Reg's house without him knowing anything about it and bagging the profit as well as everything else of value, including the contents of all bank accounts etc., before pissing off to Zimbabwe. It came to light that Reg's missus had actually made arrangements for prospective buyers to view the property while Reg was at work and then drafted in Roland to pose as her husband. The poor bastard knew nothing right up to the day when the new owners arrived to move in and told him to fuck off. Reg wouldn't, called the Old Bill, documents were produced and Reg suddenly saw reality and was driven off in a piggy car. He later discovered that his wife and brother had been traced to a suburb of Harare and were not on Safari. Reg was suddenly alone, potless, homeless and nicked. Not exactly gigglesville, really.

He considered a solicitor, but opted instead to make use of just about the only thing that the fleeing pair hadn't been able to take with them --- the car. He thought he'd try the old exhaust pipe and hose routine. But first he made the mistake of calling the Lifejoys to let them know what he was going to do, lest he was not discovered for days, and some bastard came round and saved him. After that, the psychiatrists had a go at him and then

Reg went all religious and silly. The Lifejoys, most of whom were Jesus nut-ters anyway, then came back to see how he was getting on, and in a fit of pique and lunacy, Reg, who was now living in a one-bedroom rented flat in the toilet area of the town, pledged himself to saving the souls of other poor wretches. He chucked his job as a double-glazing salesman (a sad profession in any case) and took up the mantle of a full-time Lifejoys advi-sor. Within eighteen months, he had become chairman of the town branch after his predecessor, Elsie Arnold, topped herself because of the pressures of work. After all, to whom does the voice at the other end of the phone turn when things become hopeless? To whom does God pray?

Elsie's suicide was made even more hilarious by the manner of its exe-cution. The Lifejoys' main office was in the centre of town, but the more visible and far more appropriate base was the small cabin-like building on top of Rocky Point, which was supposed to monitor, intercept and thereby prevent people intent on jumping to their certain doom from carrying it out. It was this office (which was known by staff as 'The Hut') which Elsie was occupying when she suddenly became so depressed at dealing with so many depressed people, that she decided to close the book on herself in the very manner which her own presence in the Hut was supposed to preclude with regards other people. She slammed the door, galloped towards the cliff edge sobbing, vaulting those wretched scripture plaques erected by her own organisation, which were only there to offer desperate people like her a last gasp of hope, and plunged howling over the side without so much as a by your leave. This demonstration of gross petulance was hardly the greatest advert for the workings of the organisation. Charitable contributions dipped that month.

Chief coroner Klaus Butsch delivered his verdict in his distinctive Swiss-German accent from his bench, flanked by two milkmaids who, like him, were in traditional alpine costume. Behind him on the wall hung a large Swiss flag, and on the bench itself a sturdy-looking cowbell sat with a much smaller Swiss flag threaded through the loop at the top.

The verdict was, of course, a foregone conclusion: 'I am not hesitating. Actually, I mean, it's not choice. It is a verdict of suicide, self-killink, when the mind was of temporary unbalance on this old lady. Her life she did not want. She said no to it. This is understood. She came out of her cabin run-nink and then this lady, she goes crazy! Oh no! Somebody save her! The old lady jump… and like all who fall from Rocky Point, survival is impossible. *Bumpity-Bump!* There is nothinks to say extra. This ist strange dyink when one thinks of her profession. But my verdict I cannot alter. I must not. Nein. I must think always of my duty. She brings this to herself. Nothings else is possible. Ja, alles ist klar. She did it. Poor lady! That is all, thank-you. That is all. Grüß Gott!'

Herr Butsch rose, as did the milkmaids on either side of him, and as he did so, he raised the cowbell up and swung it back and forth with both hands. The noise was deafening and signified more empathetically that the court was no longer in session.

The usual scramble for the corpse saw the Old Firm snatch Elsie's funeral from right under the nose of rivals Proudfoot and Gadd, which was a particularly spectacular piece of work, since the old lady and Percy Proud-foot had been bridge partners for nearly thirty years down at the rotary club. The junior firm were livid at having been mugged yet again, but although the funeral had escaped Proudfoot and Gadd, it did not escape the atten-tions of the press, who made much of the priceless irony of the business. By this time, Reg Doorman had already taken up position as chairman of the lucrative Pendlesham branch of the Lifejoys. The keys to the main town office and to the Hut were now his.

His impact was immediate. Within two weeks, five people had killed themselves. One of these was a silly teenaged boy who hung himself in imi-tation of a similarly pubescent actor in the United States, but the other four were all off Rocky Point. Comically, three of these had taken the plunge together (a student trio who had failed their exams) at the precise moment that Reg was counseling another candidate in the Hut, a recently declared bankrupt called Barry Clive whom Reg had intercepted after becoming suspicious of his movements up on the cliff, whereupon somebody burst in and delivered a line which, when one considers it, was perhaps the most pungent mix of the pointless and the inadvertently hilarious: 'Come quickly! They've just jumped!'

Even more remarkably, Reg responded to it by flying out of the door and racing over to the cliff edge like a hare. By the time he got there, the camcorders were already whirling and it was only then that it suddenly dawned on the idiot Doorman that his presence was entirely fucking useless. He therefore turned and walked mournfully back to the Hut in order to notify the coastguard of the tragedy. On the way, he passed by Barry Clive (totally unnoticed by Reg), who was determinedly on his way to the edge to fling himself off, having assumed that Reg had forgotten all about him and therefore couldn't give a toss whether he totaled himself or not, only the first half of which was true. At the moment Reg was on the phone, the camcorders were trained firmly on Mr Clive as he approached the point favoured by most jumpers, proffering as it did the sheerest drop. The failed businessman sat solemnly down on the edge with his legs dangling over the side before leaning forward and tumbling off, as if he were a deep sea diver entering the water from a boat. One member of the camera crew responded by cursing his ill fortune that he had by mistake switched his device off at the vital moment. He had missed the student threesome too and threw his camcorder down in disgust.

'Fuck!' he spat.

The other Camcorders (there were about six in total), immediately swung around, hoping that this act of peevishness would be a prelude to a fifth suicide. But all they picked up was the man looking to the heavens, shaking his fist violently and screaming 'You bastard!' presumably to whoever or whatever was supposed to be up there. There was no chance of him jumping, however.

'Fuck!' the other Camcorders all muttered, before turning their instruments on the Hut again to see if they could pick up Reg.

'You bastard!' they added, shaking their fists skywards.

One of them rammed his ankle into one of the stone plaques. 'Aaggh! *FUCK!*' he screamed.

The others all suddenly swooped on him urgently, as if he were royalty, and he, once recovered, trained his on them. Nothing else happened.

'Fuck!' they all said, before glaring hatefully up to the clouds together and concluding matters with a communal reprimand of 'You bastard!'

Reg Doorman's call to the coastguard saw what was left of four corpses, rather than the three Reg had reported, being peeled off the jagged rocks. When this was finished, the Camcorders walked away to view their treasured videos over tea and cakes. As for Reg, he only got around to remembering Barry Clive when he saw Clive's name listed alongside those of the three students in a local rag a couple of days later. Needless to say, he felt a bit of a drip.

At the inquest, Swiss coroner Klaus Butsch requested clarification from the Lifejoy's chief: 'Bitte. Why did this poor man slip through your fingers? You are a kind man who has a job to prevent such tragedies. How did this man jump *bumpity-bump* if you are there on duty telling him that life is precious for a man with no money and business so crashed? I understand no. You must answer, please.'

Reg got himself off the hook by convincing Herr Butsch that he had been summoned to the cliff edge during his counseling of Clive by someone telling him that the three students were at that time threatening to jump, which wasn't true, of course. It was a good job that the chap who had alerted him wasn't called to give evidence.

'When I got there, it was too late,' testified Reg, head bowed.

'Too late, yes. Zu spät, ja. *Bumpity-bump!*' agreed Klaus.

'On my return, Mr Clive, the deceased, had absconded,' Reg concluded.

'Bitte?'

'He was gone. He was not there.'

'He went for *bumpity-bump?*'

'Yes, sir.'

'Danke. Now I see the light. Step down, kind man. Now the puzzle is over. Grüß Gott!'

The well-endowed milkmaids stood up as the alpine coroner reached for his cowbell and a relieved Reg Doorman resolved to do a little better next time.

Chapter 25

Salty Sid

FRANK WAS ONLY too aware of the succulent wild fruit which grew up at Rocky Point. Ripe and ready for picking, all seasons. Hitherto, the Old Firm had secured a virtual monopoly on either the funeral itself of any Rocky Point suicide jockey, or otherwise as acting as a paid intermediary for other selected firms up country. For example, in the case of the three students who had jumped together just prior to Barry Clive (they were not overseas students as first had been suspected), one of them had come from Glasgow, and it was quickly established that the boy's body would be taken back north for burial. Arthur Snape simply alerted Maxwell McCluskie, a company from the Hillhead area of the city, and left them to deal with contacting the boy's family with the line that they had been made aware of the tragedy 'by the authorities'.

'We're already in contact with undertakers in Pendlesham,' a representative from Maxwell McCluskie told the dead student's mother. 'We can deal with everything, unless, of course, you wish to make your own arrangements...'

More often than not, the business was settled there and then. Arthur Snape then simply watched the post for the arrival of his retainer.

Proudfoot and Gadd had long since abandoned any hope of competing for Rocky Point suicides. It had for some time been suspected, if never substantiated, that Snape enjoyed a particularly civilised understanding with certain members of the coastguard. It was far too much of a coincidence that news of any action on the cliff top should regularly reach the Old Firm with such rapidity. The celebrated 'theft' of Elsie Arnold was in the eyes of Percy Proudfoot conclusive evidence that something was going on. But nothing could be proved and nothing to be done other than the waving of the white flag. Instead, Proudfoot and Gadd developed the trawling of the countless hospices in the town for advanced bookings into a fine art. Occasionally, the Old Firm picked their pocket here too. The junior firm was thus constantly on a hiding to nothing.

Frank Eddowes, despite having worked for the Old Firm for years, had no solid evidence that Arthur Snape and the coastguard were cohorts, although rumours had continued to persist during his time there. The official line had been that the Old Firm had managed to corner the Rocky Point market simply because they were the better team. With the blinkers having been removed, Frank now had absolutely no doubt that insider dealing had been afoot. He resolved to provide far stiffer opposition for contesting the vital Rocky Point crown.

'People tumble off there like lemmings. It's great!' Frank reminded his troops at the next staff meeting at HQ, following the celebration of their inaugural job down at the Inn. 'Up until now, old Snape has had a virtual monopoly on Rocky Point leapers. I had to ask myself how he managed to do that. Any ideas? Come on, Noddoes!'

'Clearly somebody tells him when somebody jumps,' Stephen said.

'Quite right,' smiled Frank. 'Good. Who?'

'It could be anyone,' Stephen continued. 'Perhaps he has a guy up there all the time who keeps his eyes open.'

'Perhaps.'

'Or maybe he has a direct line with the Lifejoys!'

Everyone laughed.

'Okay,' chuckled Frank. 'Anyone else?'

'Whenever I go walking up there, I always see some chaps with the old video cameras,' Thoad told them. 'It could be them.'

'Possible, possible,' Frank agreed. 'But then again, those chaps haven't been up there very long, have they? Old Snape's spy has been in place long before they came along.'

'Hey, Frankie, I sure hope you're not gonna say that these people contact pappy Snape themselves and then jump, 'cause that's just bullshit!' contributed Epic.

'I'm not, and it certainly is,' Frank told him.

Everyone looked at Frank in suspense.

'In the absence of any evidence, I am drawn to one of two conclusions,' Frank summed up. 'Either old Snape does indeed have a permanent presence up on the cliff top, which would be impractical to say the least, or else he is being alerted directly by those who retrieve the doughnuts from the rocks.'

'Oh, really, Eddows, that is a *monstrous* allegation!' whined Noddoes. 'I don't believe it!'

'I never used to believe it either,' admitted Frank. 'And, as I say, I have absolutely no evidence to substantiate an accusation as serious as this. It therefore must remain a suggestion.'

'So what are we gonna do, man?' asked Epic. 'You can't fight City Hall!'

'Oh yes you can,' Frank said.

'I am simply not going to sit here whilst you malign the integrity of Her Majesty's coastguard!' sniffed Noddoes loftily. 'I suppose you're going to suggest that the police are involved in this conspiracy with Mr Snape too, are you?'

'I bet they're all in the same lodge!' slipped in Stephen.

Everyone except Noddoes laughed.

'Say, I've heard about those wackos!' then added Epic. 'They're the guys who dress up as wizards and dance around stars drawn in chalk and kiss skulls and whatever else!'

'That's them!' confirmed Stephen.

'That sounds brilliant!' enthused Amanda. 'Do the pigs really get up to all that?'

'Constantly!' nodded Stephen.

'It sounds *brilliant!*' said Amanda again. 'Where do they do it? I'm going to gatecrash!'

Frank clapped his hands twice. 'As I was saying,' he said in a raised voice, looking first at Amanda and then at Stephen, 'I am *suggesting* that old Snape is alerted from at the bottom of the cliff rather than the top. And the reason, Epic, that I say that we *can* fight City Hall is because all we need to do is employ an agent at the foot of Rocky Point ourselves. And I do *not* mean bribing the coastguard, Noddoes!'

With this, Frank walked to the door, opened it and beckoned to someone to come inside. In walked a tall strong-looking man who looked about sixty-five. He was spectacularly bearded and was sporting a thick pale green woollen roller-necked jumper and had a pipe clamped firmly between his teeth. The rich tobacco smoke immediately enveloped the emissions of the reefer which Epic was attending to. He was a very impressive looking figure indeed and could have only been one thing – a man of the sea.

'Say hello to Salty Sid!' Frank smiled, indicating the newcomer.

The old man grunted a greeting and sat down in Frank's chair.

'What the fuck's going on here, Frankie?' Epic demanded. 'Who *is* this old pappy guy anyhow? He looks like that Cuban guy that Hemmingway wrote about, for Christ's sake!'

'You've just answered your own question, Epic,' Frank told him. 'Salty Sid is a boatman. He's spent a lifetime as a fisherman, but for the last ten years or so he's been plying his trade here in Pendlesham providing trips from just past the pier to people who wish to view the foot of Rocky Point. Sid is acquainted with these waters better than anybody else afloat. He has seen many things, many harrowing things, some of which have nearly landed on him. Need I go on?'

Everyone looked at each other.

'Frankie. This is perfect!' enthused Epic. 'So you're gonna get this Salty guy to ---'

'*EXACTLY!*'

'Cool!'

'The instant a jumper hits the rocks, Sid will be there,' said Frank. 'Because Sid is *always* there. He will scoop up what remains of the doughnut and immediately contact HQ. We shall then notify the coastguard and also the coroner's office in order to comply with the law and the job will then officially be ours. We shall need someone erudite to be the intermediary between Sid and the authorities to ensure that old Snape is warded off at every juncture. With Klaus Butsch's office already having been notified by ourselves, it would be in any case highly unlikely that our business is snatched from us, even if the coastguard *is* bent.'

'Unless, of course, the coroner is taking backhanders from Snape too,' added Stephen.

'Impossible!' Frank assured him. 'No matter how many times one reminded old Snape that Herr Butsch is in fact Swiss and not German, he still persisted in referring to him as "that bloody kraut"! I can't imagine any liaison there at all. Old Snape, and indeed Herbert Woodcastle, were affronted that Butsch was even in this town at all, let alone as a distinguished legal officer. When he first arrived, old Snape rattled off a letter to Simon Wisenthal. No, you don't have to worry there, Stephen. And once Herr Butsch has confirmed that the verdict is suicide, the doughnut will be handed over straight away to Tessa for beautification. In short, from the instant that that carcass smashes onto those jagged rocks, it becomes the property of Freddo's. Sid will see to it. First come, first served. That's the brief I've given him. In a sentence, folks, we're going to seize Rocky Point away from Mr Snape! We're going to liberate it. Its sovereignty will be ours!'

Noddoes rose: 'Er… this… this… *"erudite"* chap you have in mind to be the intermediary…'

'Could only possibly be you, Noddoes,' smiled Frank. 'If you'd care to do it, of course.'

'Delighted, old boy. Delighted!' beamed the old luvvie, feeling frightfully important again.

Epic turned his attention back to the rustic-looking old man, puffing contentedly at his pipe and then addressed him: 'You okay with all this, Hemmingway?' he enquired rather rudely. 'You may be in over your head, man!'

Salty Sid leaned forward and removed his pipe from his mouth for the first time. 'I don't knows nothing about that,' he said in a growly, salty sort of way. 'Ever been in a boat, son?'

'Sure!' Epic said. 'For fish. Just like you. Back in Canada.'

'Fancy being ship's mate, son?' Salty added.

'Hell, no!' Epic fired back, as if a wasp had just stung him.

Salty Sid relaxed back into his chair and stuck his pipe back into his mouth again.

Epic in turn looked more than a little confused. 'What's going on?' he asked the audience, who were sitting silently and smiling at the scene. He then suddenly realised that he had been put in his place and smiled himself in resignation of it. 'Excuse me, sir,' he then said, looking back at Salty Sid. '*I* may be the one in over my head here!'

This apology was accepted by Sid, who did not reply verbally. Instead he merely nodded. He then produced a flask of rum from his front trouser pocket, no mean feat since he was sitting down, and swapped this for his pipe. This little trick won him a round of applause from everyone and the mantra of 'Respect! Respect!...' from a now thoroughly bedazzled young Canadian.

Chapter 26

Auntie Audrey

A FTER HAVING MADE such a monumental debut, Frank and his band
had to wait a full ten days before their groove machine could boogie
on into action again. The doughnut was that of Audrey Shackleton, a sixty-
three-year old maiden aunt, who apart from two stuffy nephews who were
not much younger than she was, had no family but who had been a keen
parishioner of Danny Hare's; indeed the senior member of his regular congregation. She had stayed loyal to Danny even when he and Barefoot Sally
went bonkers that time. This was hardly surprising; Auntie Audrey was also
completely bananas.

It was Sally herself who had contacted Thoad on the expiry of the old
woman. Audrey had always told Danny that she wanted him to conduct
the service 'when the Lord pulls my number out of the hat' and had actually attended Terry Cutler's funeral in reasonably good health. 'I'd like to
be able to do what Mr Cutler did,' she told the vicar afterwards. 'Dance
at my own funeral.' Thus Freddo's was able to book Audrey in advance, as
well as four much younger members of Danny's parish, and almost the day
that the arrangements were confirmed, Auntie Audrey suffered a massive
heart seizure in church, whilst the choir were singing *We've Gotta Get Out
Of This Place* and obligingly rolled over within an hour of reaching hospital
with Sally sitting close by softly humming snatches of old Connie Francis
numbers to ease the croaking Aud over the River Styx. Epic and Noddoes
were at the hospital almost at the instant of the flatline and accompanying
continuous bleep registering on Auntie's life-support unit. The Old Firm
didn't get a sniff and there was no need for any milkmaids or cowbells. The
death certificate came fluttering in...

Audrey was dragged off to HQ and Tessa gave her a bit of a scrub and brush up before embalming the carcass and leaving it to set. The embalmer girl was overwhelmed with excited anticipation at the prospect of starring alongside Barefoot Sally at the torching, and it was probably because of this that her job on Audrey was fairly routine and certainly not as creative as her work on Cutler. She had been so warm and gushing towards Frank when he had grumpily offered her the chance to perform, that for a fleeting moment Frank had decided that the whole thing had been a fine idea after all.

Amanda, meanwhile, had been told by Stephen precisely why the offer had been extended to her also. She was thus torn between being very excited at the prospect and being incandescent with rage at Frank for only offering involving her in order to force the rest of the staff to abandon their collected suggestion to involve only Tessa. The scheming Frank may have fallen flat on his face (as Tessa was doing it anyway) but Amanda felt certainly slighted and so she should have been. She nevertheless had every intention now of taking the chance she had been given, even though it had arrived in a less than gracious, indeed absolutely false, wrapping. She may well have wanted to get back at Frank, but she even more wanted to jive – to get down and get with it. This was an opportunity far too good to ignore and Amanda was much too sensible not to realize this.

As Epic had said, 'squaring things with the preacher' had been all that was needed to set up the new dance troupe. It had been no more difficult than that. Indeed, as Frank had initially feared when the prospect of Tessa joining Barefoot Sally was mischievously risen by Epic, Danny was full to the brim with enthusiasm with the idea.

'This is great!' he said. 'Three girlies grooving in a row! Hey, this is going to be like gigging with the Supremes! This is great! I'm really going to have to give serious thought as to what we're going to call this band! *Wow!* I can't wait!'

By the time Audrey Shackleton was oven-ready the vicar had not only named his backing group, they had also had their first rehearsal. Danny had decided, after much thought, to call his girls The Exotics, having been much taken, understandably so, by Tessa at the group's first convening. No woman could ever replace Sally, but Danny was as red-bloodied as the next man and Tessa was sex on legs, right enough.

Certainly all three were appealing in their own ways and arguably represented three distinctly different periods of rock/pop erotica. Undoubtedly, different styles. Sally Hare was a pretty hippy peace child, full of love and Joni Mitchell; Tessa (or rather Sheba) represented the true *exotic* side to The Exotics – a dark, leggy, mysterious feline temptress, a fly-bursting blend of Diana Ross and Diana Rigg; and Amanda stood for the vibrancy of the mid-to-late seventies, the punk rockers, many of whom far from impoverished and who had rebelled more against boredom than the social climate and adopted grotesque appearances as an emphasis more to the raucous music itself, which when intelligible, was far more tongue-in-cheek than most sworn critics (and some disciples) had thought. As a pretty suburban girl in an unpretty get-up, Amanda represented the girl-next-door gone wrong. But only for show. Her sexual attraction was obvious.

The Exotics' first rehearsal had been over at the Bar and Grill, where soundman and former church organist Keith Tate spun a few discs for no-one but themselves. The repertoire ranged from The Mamas And The Papas to Sham 69 via Tina Charles. Danny boomed out each number from the mic and The Exotics got down, much to the gratification of Keith in his control box, who viewed the spectacle through some ballet binoculars which he had nicked and with a tea towel draped across his boxer shorts to cater for the consequences. Sheba (Tessa was stoned) purred her way through the set, whilst Barefoot Sally's tambourine, which she had purloined from her school music department years ago (it still had the sticky label inside it with the school's name and address upon it), almost came apart with her incessant shaking. As usual this wasn't the only thing she shook, which the now decidedly sinful Keith Tate saw only too clearly.

Amanda, although certainly too young to have been involved in the punk movement the first time around, was well versed in its protocol. Thus she 'pogoed' her way through the entire set, a strictly punk dance involving springing up and down wildly on the spot, whilst staring moronically around at nothing in particular. This may have been all fine and groovy as an accompaniment to The Clash, for example, but it looked rather out of place when Keith slapped a Barry White track on. In addition, Amanda began 'gobbing', that is to say spitting into the air, something which was supposed to represent a tribute in punk terms, but whilst understanding its intended significance, it wasn't exactly something which the vicar wanted to see. Amanda was quickly told to cut this out. And she did.

Danny and The Exotics were only given the chance of this one rehearsal before Frank and his band had to deal with the doughnut of Auntie Audrey. The day of the torching arrived and everybody piled into their motors. Audrey was tied to the bumper of the estate, the out of place floral tributes were hurled into the back of Frank's yellow Ford Anglia and off they all sped.

As with the noble Terry Cutler, all leftovers but those deemed closest to the corpse had already been advised to go straight to the Bar and Grill at a pre-set time. For Audrey, an impressive total of three neighbours would be joining Danny's regular congregation of loonies, misfits and scrotes. This left the two stuffy fifty-something nephews to ride with Epic and Noddoes in the lead vehicle. They, of course, had no idea that Auntie had been tied to the bumper, and indeed one of them asked the stock question once the cortege had thundered off, as to where the deceased was at that time, only to receive the stock reply from Epic, which was only too truthful. 'She's right behind us, Mac!'

Both stuffy nephews immediately looked behind, only to see a silly yellow car with two men inside waving at them frantically.

Bumpity-Bump!!

Whereas the disposal of the excellent Cutler had proved to be a dream debut, Audrey Shackleton was nothing but trouble from the start. The whole business was to have very profound consequences for the future path Freddo's would take with regard to doughnuts on the day of disposal.

Things started going wrong from the moment the two Freddo cars arrived at the Bar and Grill after a super charged high-speed journey from HQ. As before, Frank and Stephen jumped out of the Anglia, intending to untie the doughnut and race inside with it. But as soon as they arrived at corpseside, they knew they faced problems. The carcass had been ripped to threads, looking for all the world as if it had been half-cremated already, or indeed exhumed after having been buried for a month. In addition, Audrey was leaking and smelt like shit.

'Jesus. What a whiff!' recoiled Stephen, backing away immediately. 'God. That's fucking rancid!'

'Oh dear, she doesn't smell very jolly, does she?' agreed Frank, as both men peered at her from a distance.

'And just look at her!' howled Stephen. 'She's totally torn to shreds! Fuck me! We can't use *this!* The state of it! It's completely shot to pieces! Christ!'

Frank and Stephen grimaced at the prospect of what faced them, both reluctant to even start untying Aud, let alone pick her up. Epic, as pin sharp as ever, arrived seconds later, having seen from his driver's seat mirror that things were not good. The smell hit him first and then he spotted Audrey and it wasn't exactly love at first sight.

'Jesus shit! What have you guys done!' he managed, which helped not a lot.

'We've got no choice, Frank,' Stephen conceded reluctantly. 'We've got to get her inside. Now!'

'Yeah, you guys do that!' agreed Epic. 'Me and Hamlet will stall the two jokers in the back!' And off he scampered before risking another intake of breath.

Stephen finally took out his sheaf knife and cut the rope. 'Fucking horrendous, but come on Frank. We're going to have to do it!'

'Oh my! I wonder what happened!' Frank said, reluctantly picking up the cadaver's shoulders after Stephen had grabbed the ankles.

'It's that bloody embalming fluid, I think!' diagnosed Stephen, as the two of them finally trotted off towards the door of the crematorium. 'The bastard stuff's seeping out of all the cracks!'

'Oh dear!'

'I think you might want to review the wisdom of dragging the dough-nut along the road *after* it's been with Tessa, Frank. You might want to consider chucking it in with us. In the back with all the flowers. We can't be doing with this sort of old carry on!'

'Well, yes, I certainly shall!' Frank nodded, now on the point of throw-ing up.

'Dragging it from the pick-up point to HQ is fine and no more than it deserves,' Stephen added. 'But after that, I have my doubts. Just look at the state of this bloody woman. Cop that whiff! Fucking revolting!'

They were at last inside and hurled Audrey onto the catafalque and covered her remains with the duvet, which had been laundered since Terry Cutler had used it in accordance with basic health regulations. It would certainly need to be vigorously cleaned again after the unhygienic Audrey had finished with it, but at least the foul stench had been masked for the time being.

'I've got to get to a bog,' Stephen said immediately. 'I can't eat my sarn-ies with *these* fucking hands!'

Frank followed him into a little side room inside the chapel, which contained a single toilet with a washbasin alongside. Stephen immediately started to scrub away the pus. 'I didn't expect something like this after the smooth ride we had with Cutler,' he said. 'I don't for a moment think that Tessa didn't do a good job on this old bag. I just suspect that some dough-nuts are not as resilient as others. This is why it is vital that we review our policy.'

Frank agreed with this, especially since Stephen had exonerated Tessa from any blame, something that Frank had been preparing to do himself anyway as soon as he became accustomed to inhaling fresh air again. 'I'm afraid that dead bodies are not what they used to be,' he mourned. 'I shall definitely be reviewing my policy on this. You're quite right, Stephen.'

Danny and The Exotics, meanwhile, had appeared from the vestry at the opposite end of the chapel along with Keith Tate, carrying his case full of compact discs which he took across to his control box and then began setting up his sound equipment. As he stepped up, Danny was approached by Frank and immediately cautioned as to the little problem with Audrey.

'She's being a bit petulant', Frank whispered.

Danny walked across, glanced under the duvet and promptly agreed. He consulted Tessa but she could only recommend a liberal spray with a regular air freshener before cremating the old woman as soon as possible.

It wasn't exactly panic stations, but it certainly wasn't without some anxiety either that the leftovers were finally allowed into the building. The two stuffy nephews had been kept waiting in the car by Epic, who had eventually managed to convey the message to Noddoes that it wasn't yet all clear, whilst Frank and Stephen were recoiling from the whiff and state of the corpse, by saying in low tones that there was 'a doughnut problem' at least three times before it finally sank in. He then turned to the two stuffy nephews and gave them some rubbish about having to wait for the vicar to turn up, who had been delayed in traffic and that they might as well wait in the comfort of the car.

Noddoes in the passenger's seat pulled down the sun visor and looked into the mirror fixed into it, wondering what the devil was causing the delay. 'I do wish that they would buck up!' he said aloud without thinking. 'This is so dreadfully unprofessional. Typical Eddowes! Ah! At last they have her!'

The two stuffy nephews, having heard this, began to turn around, which would have been fatal. Epic, once more, saved the situation by shouting; 'No. They're over there!' and pointing straight ahead of him, thus re-diverting the attentions of the two stuffy nephews to a safe direction, but paying for this by causing maximum confusion to, not only them, but also to Noddoes, as all three men glanced furtively around at an empty area.

Noddoes was about to open his mouth again in protest, but by this time Epic, who had kept his wits about him all the time, especially when he knew that he now had Noddoes to contend with too, had noticed that

Audrey had been safely bundled inside the Bar and Grill and that the coast was now clear. He quickly jumped in before the old luvvie could dig himself in any deeper: 'Okay, gentlemen. Maybe we can get out of the car now,' he said, turning to the two stuffy nephews and leaping out himself. The panic was finally over, it seemed.

The two stuffy nephews found themselves mingling with the three neighbours of their aunt, as well as with the remainder of Danny's congregation, none of whom they knew, of course. Their faces did not show signs of wishing to remedy this. It was moments after this that Danny himself came out and greeted them and then led them and everybody else inside. The two stuffy nephews, having taken their pews, quite literally, stared with more than a little suspicion at the catafalque with the multi-coloured, duvet-covered lump resting upon it, much in the same way that Barbara Cutler had done at the same stage of the game last time.

It only seemed a second before: 'SHOWTIME! READY TO RRRUMMMBLE!'

The congregation, much smaller than the Cutler party, cheered. The two stuffy nephews looked at each other astonished. A split second later, James Taylor came on singing *You've Got A Friend*, a song particularly loved by Audrey and not particularly out of place for a conventional funeral in most people's eyes, due to the melodious nature of the acoustic backtrack and Taylor's gentle delivery of the lyric. This docility was extended to this, the inaugural public appearance of The Exotics, who harmonised nicely with Danny on this Carole King composition, which probably took the two stuffy nephews' attentions away from how the girls were dressed. This somewhat eccentric character of their late aunt, about which both stuffy nephews had long since become aware, had also prepared them for a degree of peculiarity at her funeral service and, in any case, they just wanted the wretched thing over as quickly as possible, as, if truth be told, do most unholy people who wind up in church for marriages, christenings, or deaths once in a blue moon.

If the opening had been to the two stuffy nephews an acceptable display of the unconventional, in fitting with their aunt's character and thus memory, what happened next was unfortunately viewed as falling a tad short of good taste. It was a demonstration which was alas set to displease them considerably. Frank had been adamant that despite the appalling state that Auntie Audrey had got herself into, this was no sufficient excuse for her to scratch from her own shebang. Therefore, after Danny had finished his short sermon, reminding everyone what a 'major groovy old chick' Aud had been and how she had been there 'when the King had been crowned' (and he certainly didn't mean anyone from the House of Windsor), Miss Shackleton was produced from underneath the duvet and courtesy of Epic and Stephen, began dancing on the catafalque to Stevie Wonder's *I Just Called To Say I Love You*, another passionate favourite of hers. But things did not go well.

'Holy shit, man! I don't think I'm gonna be able to hold onto this much longer!' Epic warned. 'She's breaking up! She's breaking up! She needs the flames and like now!'

'You're fucking right, mate!' gasped Stephen, as they operated her as best they could by arms and waist. 'She's disintegrating! And that whiff! Judas Priest, that *Whiff!*'

The congregation, meanwhile, were on their feet and Danny and The Exotics were in full swing, everyone unaware of the increasing problems on the dais. The man to save the day, or at least part of it, was Keith Tate. Noticing the problems Epic and Stephen were having in bringing the increasingly stroppy Audrey to heal and realising why this was, he cut short Stevie and banged on a totally unscheduled track, *Don't Stand So Close To Me* by The Police, and segueing this with *Let Me Go, Lover* by Kathy Kirby in order to give the clearest possible message to the rapidly ailing Epic and Stephen to write Audrey off as a loss. They did so gladly and jumped down. Keith Tate hit another switch and Auntie Audrey slid, obligingly for once, down the chute. The congregation went nuts.

Because the problems suffered by the Freddo couple had not been known to Danny and The Exotics, they had been caught off-guard totally by Keith's salvage operation. They had been expecting Stevie Wonder to be followed by Elvis Costello's *I Can't Stand Up For Falling Down* and the intervention of Sting and Miss Kirby had left them all flatfooted. These hadn't been on the schedule at all.

'What's he playing this crap for?' Amanda had demanded, turning to Sally. Nobody knew. As a matter of fact, only Danny had recognised what the Kirby track was and whom it was by.

The committal may have indeed been a monumental cock-up, but this was nothing compared to the reactions to it of the two stuffy nephews, about whom everybody seemed to have forgotten. They both slowly stood up just as Danny's congregation were slowly filing out of the Bar and Grill, most lobbing coins into a box by the door marked 'TO THE GLORY OF ROCK AND ROLL!' Danny, still confused, walked off to find Keith Tate to ask him what had gone wrong. The stuffy nephews remained standing, staring open-mouthed ahead of them and blinking heavily. And then one of them turned around to Danny and screamed after him. 'You there!'

Danny turned around.

'Yes, you! YOU!' roared the stuffy nephew, pointing.

'Steady!' warned Danny.

'What have you done?' he demanded.

Stephen Mauve, who was only just recovering from his own trauma, stepped forward. 'Please try to have some respect, gentlemen!' he pleaded. 'Some decorum, okay?'

'*Respect?*' howled the stuffy nephew, glaring at him. 'How *dare* you! Was this some kind of grotesque joke? Who the blazes are you lunatics anyway?'

'Now, *steady!*' snapped Danny, pointing back. 'Let's chill out, okay?'

'YOU, THERE!' continued to thunder the stuffy nephew, not only glaring at Danny, but now advancing towards him. 'You're not a *real* clergyman, are you?! So what the devil are you? Some kind of bloody actor? Some television prankster? You will explain this charade *immediately!*'

At this, Noddoes stepped up, which was probably the least helpful thing that could have happened at this point. It was unclear whether he had been upset more by the stuffy nephew's bad mouthing in a holy place, or by the associated derogatory comment about his former and still much loved former profession. In any event, the old luvvie went into one: 'Oh, you blasphemous knave!' he howled, hand to tilted forehead. 'Oh, how could you even *countenance* demonstrating such appalling theatre? You should be ashamed of yourself for your wicked cursing at a man of the Lord! And at your beloved aunt's funeral too! Oh, you toad, sir! You dastardly exponent of evil buffoonery!' And maintaining his renowned 'distressed' pose magnificently, Noddoes exited, leaving the stuffy nephew to stare in disbelief after him.

This particular stuffy nephew had been alone in challenging the tastefulness of the occasion. Indeed he had been the only one of the two who had so much as uttered a word. There was a very good reason for this. His brother had in fact been even more appalled than he had been, but so much so that his over-excitement had brought him to the advanced stages of a fatal heart attack. He had long since slipped to the floor and now had only seconds left to live.

Sheba spotted him first. 'Oh, look!' she purred. 'That man is going to die! Groovy!'

Everyone crowded around the prostrate stuffy nephew 2. Danny reacted admirably. He walked across and grabbed his microphone again. 'Yo! Keith! Some guy is passing away down here! He looks the sort of easy-listening kind of guy. Do you have any Perry Como up there, or Andy Williams, maybe?'

Within a touch of a button or two, the most inappropriate *Magic Moments* (one of Perry's biggest) came on and to this, stuffy nephew 2 soon breathed his last. There was clearly nothing that could have been done to save him. Not that anyone was falling over themselves to try, of course. First Stephen and then Epic confirmed that he had gone.

'Dead. This bloke's definitely played on! Off stump out of the ground!' nodded Stephen.

'This thing on the floor is a doughnut for sure!' agreed Epic. He looked at the hitherto voluble, but now stupefied brother of the deceased. 'Since we're here, Mac, we might as well cook him now. Are you cool with that?' he said to him.

Frank, who had suddenly and finally appeared, withdrew this prospect of a special offer immediately. 'Yes, thank you, Epic, but I rather fancy that we need to get a doctor in here and wait to get the go-ahead from Klaus Butsch if necessary,' he said.

'And I'll need to book the old doughnut in and take some money off this fellow,' added Thoad, waving his hand at the stuffy nephew who was still alive.

'Good thinking, mate,' Frank said. 'My other point entirely. We're certainly not going to start doling out freebies!' He too turned to the surviving stuffy nephew.

'Come into our office tomorrow. We'll soon straighten this nonsense out!' he said comfortingly.

'And I'll go and check on my embalming fluids,' added Sheba helpfully. '*Purrrr!*'

At this point, the stuffy nephew who had survived sank to the floor in an obvious attempt to join his brother, but was unable to imitate him. Perry Como was singing *It's Impossible*. His heart attack was genuine enough but it was certainly not fatal, which was just as well really, or else there would have been nobody left to pay the bill for the first bugger.

Chapter 27

The Stuffy Nephew Who Survived

THE HOSPITAL DOCTOR was happy to sign the death certificate for a heart attack, but Klaus Butsch took more convincing this time and the surviving stuffy nephew (now fully recovered) went off into one during the inquest and had to be brought to order by the bench.

'Achtung! Be silent, bitte, dead man's bruder!' spat the coroner. 'This is serious times. No room for argument is available! I am the man to decide the answer to this puzzle and not you, bitte! You must sit down mit no more inbutting. That is all!'

Herr Butsch was pondering over whether he should record a verdict of death by misadventure, rather than by natural causes. The stuffy nephew who survived, who was clearly not acquainted with the vernacular of a coroner's court, had initially hoped that a verdict of 'murder' would be retained, but quickly realised that things would not be going his way in this regard.

'What I must consider ist diese,' summed up Klaus. 'Did this man perish because he liked not the funeral of his auntie? Did this alone make his heart attack him? Even if I said yes to this, do I then say to myself "Ja, this ist ein unlawful killink"? Since I must eliminate the verdict of accidental dyink from this inquirinks, I come to decide between natural or maybe unnatural dyinks. Or maybe an open verdict, ja? I wonder, which must I choose? The answer to this, of course, is death by natural dyink. Nobody can be blamed for the passink away of this poor man. And the verdict must not be open, because the death for me is not a mystery. His heart just attacked him like *Boom!* And this was the answer to his doom. This ist what I must decide. Ja!'

The cowbell and the milkmaids confirmed it.

But once again, drama. As Herr Butsch strode off with fräuleinen and goats to snatch a fondue break before hearing the next case, the malcontent stuffy nephew who had survived attempted his second take in the great movie of emulating his brother's fatal heart attack, and this time it was a print. Jolly alpine music was chirping away in the background as a junior court official in a suit crouched down to examine the man and then quickly waved away any assistance as useless. On the piped music at this point, some guy suddenly latched onto the music and started yodelling manically.

'Herr Butsch. Wait, please! Warten Sie, bitte!' shouted the official. 'This man is dead, sir!'

Klaus stopped and walked back. 'Did you say *dead?*'

'Yes, sir.'

'Are you certain that he has died? Please examine him!'

'I'm sorry, sir.'

'It can't be true! Try please with mouth against the mouth. Then he revives!'

'I'm sorry, sir. There's nothing anybody can do. He is gone. Er wird gegangen,' confirmed the man with the corpse.

'You all saw it!' wailed Klaus rabidly, successfully drowning out the ridiculous Swiss music at least and waving his arms like a traffic cop gone bananas. 'This angry man ist eine kopiekatze of his dead bruder. He also has accidental dyink! Such is true. Where is undertaker?'

'Ich bin hier, mein herr!' announced Frank with a smart click of the heals.

'Danke. Very well. Sehr gut. Please let your staff take away this man who has just had the accidental dyink. Do it now. I will add the answer of his doom to that of his bruder in same way.' Klaus then addressed the court again. Pointing at the corpse, he reiterated his verdict with a thunderous roar: 'THIS IS BUT EINE KOPIEKATZE!' He then turned to Frank again. 'Remove him!' he demanded.

So the cowbell was brought into play again.

'Game on!' Stephen said, waving Epic and Noddoes forward. 'We've been given the nod. Let's get going!'

'It is necessary to remove him!' Klaus Butsch said again. 'He has passed away. Bring doctor to sign for his doom!'

Not for the first time, only the young Canadian kept his head. 'Hey, wait a second. Wait a second, sir! What's to stop us torching the doughnut right now? Nothing, right? But then who's gonna pick up the tab on *this* joker, know what I mean? This whole frigging family is now dust, you dig? So who's gonna pick up the cheque on either of these two bozos? Seems to me we're working for nothing here, Frankie!'

'I say. That's a thought!' Frank said.

'I understand, no,' came back Klaus.

'Check for a credit card,' Stephen suggested. 'We're unlikely to get a claim of forgery from this lad. And he's obviously got plenty of wedge, especially as he was the last in his family to slip away. He must be quids in. There might even be enough cash in his wallet just now.'

'Smart move. I'll take a look,' Epic said and he began frisking the corpse.

'What are you boys doing with this dead body?' Klaus Butsch squealed.

'Hey, sir. Just remember that this turkey hit the snooze button in your courthouse, you dig?' Epic reminded him, helpfully. 'Now, all we want is the money, honey and we're out of here and over the Alps like Julie Andrews. Okay?'

'You are talking like a boy from out of this country. I understand nothing from you,' Klaus informed him.

'Oh, Good Lord!' Epic sneered, and at the same time produced a wallet from the inside pocket of the dead man and started going through it. 'Okay. This man has sixty-five pounds and a Visa card,' he declared. 'Crap signature on the card. We can charge the full amount and then tip him down the chute along with his bro'. There's zero problem, guys. It's cool!'

'Then that's what we'll go for,' decided Frank. 'He'll get nothing from us until he pays his bill. Damned cheek!'

'Hey, but Frankie, we have to move on this now, man! We ain't gonna be able to cash in on the credit card if the receipt is dated later than the guy's dead certificate. It's gonna bounce for sure! Frankie, listen to me!'

'Herr Butsch!' Frank said, turning to the coroner. 'If you are happy with us contacting Doctor Preston, you can instruct him to issue a death certificate citing a heart attack. After this, nach diese, es ist alles uber. It is all over. Good for everyone. Heart attack, bitte.'

Klaus had already decided that this was the way out. He had even said as much. Frank's request for something on which Klaus had already ruled was less designed to seek confirmation than to suffocate the actions of his organisation in respect of achieving remuneration for the impromptu and unscheduled torching.

'Very well,' nodded Klaus. 'I accept. You go for Herr Doctor. But remove this dead person now, bitte. I tell you this not again. He is no good here. You must agree that he has passed away. Doctor will come to you to certify corpse. That is all.'

'Cool!' Epic beamed, turning to Frank. 'Now all we need to do is predate his account for yesterday and we can get this baby on!'

'No,' said Frank. 'I'm going to date it a week ago, just to be on the safe side. The inference will be that he had decided, after the sudden and untimely death of his brother, that he would make provisions for himself whilst settling his brother's account at the same time. That scenario sounds entirely credible, it seems to me.'

'Smart move, again, Frankie!'

'Perhaps we could knock a few quid off to make it look like a special offer for doing the two of them,' suggested Stephen. 'That would make it look even more convincing and would also be sound business sense for the future if any of this gets outs.'

'I'm going to agree to that reluctantly,' Frank said. 'This man did try to cheat us by going for a freebie. But as you rightly say, Stephen, we have to look at the future in a business perspective and enticing deals of this nature might well be the way forward.'

'Remove him immediately!' screeched Klaus Butsch. 'I say this for the last time! It is not allowed to leave corpses piling up in my court. He makes milkmaids run away!'

'We're outta here!' acknowledged Epic.

Under these strange circumstances, Doctor Preston's authorisation of a death certificate was a formality and everyone steamed around to Danny's Bar and Grill, both stuffy nephews travelling in the back of Frank's little yellow car, and the troublesome pair were tipped down the chute. The 23rd Psalm and The Lord's Prayer only. Nothing else. No rock and roll and The Exotics had a day off. Ten minutes max.

Chapter 28

The Camcorders

THE NEXT MONTH to six weeks saw a procession of jumpers tumbling off Rocky Point like lemmings, which meant bumper business for Freddo's, whilst sending Reg Doorman into a spin, poor man. The introduction of Salty Sid to the staff had proved to be as inspired as it had been spectacularly prophetic. This season of abundance had indeed provided the old boatman with ample opportunities to demonstrate his remarkable maritime talents to the glory of the Freddo cause and he rose to the occasion magnificently. The earlier edict from Frank that Freddo's would be specialising in suicides henceforth had immediately earmarked Sid's role as pivotal, and as he cast his heavy net into the waters at the foot of the cliffs and began trawling in corpse after corpse, his very indispensability was revealed. Frank had also ruled that doughnuts would no longer be dragged by rope en-route to the Bar and Grill. The lessons that had arisen from the incident with Auntie Audrey had been learned. It was, though, made abundantly clear that the policy of dragging would still apply with regard to the journey from Rocky Point to HQ and everyone was happy with this decision. Sid would net the corpse and deliver it to the boat station at the other side of the pier, a doctor would be at hand to certify death and the matter would then be reported to Klaus Butsch at the coroner's office.

Everybody was frightfully busy as the doughnuts rolled in, from Salty to Klaus, through to Tessa and eventually on to Danny and The Exotics. Whenever plenty of work is generated, one will always find contented people, and there was nothing but smiling faces at the Emporium and the Bar and Grill during this boom time. Klaus Butsch too was a happy man.

At the top of the cliffs, the Camcorders were in clover. Accomplished now to a man, they secured excellent footage of many suicides; and having enjoyed a perfectly lovely evening playing their tapes to each other, depicting the self-twatting from a variety of angles during cocktails and cheese, they submitted their work to the coroner, thereby providing Klaus with incontestable evidence that the deceased had taken their own life. Some of the videos were fabulous, showing Reg Doorman sprinting over from the Hut waving and shouting to try to save the person who was there to jump before the cameras were again trained onto the only true star and encouraging shouts of 'Quick, you bastard. Fucking jump!' were picked up.

Present at most of these delightful little soirees was none other than Thoad, who had initially come across the Camcorders quite by chance during a routine stroll on the top of Rocky Point and had become immensely impressed with these charming people, to say nothing of understanding immediately that they might be of immeasurable value to Freddo's. Most of the Camcorders were, in reality, sad and weird and Thoad was thus able to befriend them at the drop of a hat. He had decided to do this quite off his own bat without any prompting from Frank, displaying for the first time an acuteness of mind nobody knew he possessed: some of Stephen Mauve's stardust had obviously rubbed off on him. The Camcorders quickly accepted 'Tom' as one of their own and a valuable union was established as a result.

At one particular function, the subject of Reg Doorman and the Lifejoys came up. Doorman was, of course, the *bête noire* who was endeavouring to spoil the Camcorders' innocent fun and at the same time cordon off a vital market to the Freddo company. Clearly Doorman had to be stopped. The discussion about the nemesis was not friendly:

'I think we should fire the bastard's hut!' one of the Camcorders sneered, as he placed a video in the machine, which depicted a poor young girlish-looking boy, who had been taunted and bullied at school, cycling off the Point at full pelt.

'Or at least superglue the old door,' agreed Thoad. 'That might be enough to drive him to the old edge when he finally gets out again.'

'Good old Tom!' the Camcorders all roared.

'He goes all soppy when they jump,' another one of them complained. 'I've seen him crying like a fucking baby. I've *taped* him crying like a fucking baby, the lightweight bastard! I'd give anything to get a video of *him* galloping over the edge. He's such a righteous fucker. I can't be doing with him. He does my head in!'

'Perhaps there *is* something you chaps can do to put a stop to old Reg's little game and let you get on with your hobby in peace,' Thoad said mysteriously. 'It might even be the thing which forces him over the old edge.'

'Really, Tom? What's that, then?'

'Well, I was just thinking. Reg has a cabin up here, which he uses as an office, a consulting room for people he tries to stop jumping, doesn't he?'

'THE BASTARD!' the Camcorders all shouted together.

'Well, what if you start up a rival club, which, err...'

'Presents the other side?' interrupted one.

'Encourages people to jump?' added another.

'... doesn't *discourage* them from jumping,' completed Thoad.

Such a cheer of affirmation went up! 'Good old Tom!'

'The Rocky Point Suicide Appreciation Society,' slipped in Thoad, after everyone had calmed down again. 'ROPSAS!'

Everyone joyously roared approval. 'Brilliant! Fucking brilliant!' they all enthused. 'Doorman might as well jump now, the miserable dirty rotten bastard! Good old Tom! Long live ROPSAS!'

'And perhaps you would tip us the old wink?' Tom asked innocently.

'Of course, dear fellow! Of course!' sang all the Camcorders. 'Good old Tom!'

The last video of the night was ready for presentation now. It showed a middle-aged man peering curiously over the edge and then stepping away again like a coy maiden to safety. A voice off camera, not the cameraman's, was heard to hiss quickly 'Bollocks! Here comes Doorman!' and the camera swung around to bring into focus Reg, who was indeed running up, waving at the man and shouting 'No!'

'Fucking jump! Jump now! Go on, you selfish bastard! Don't listen to him! Get over there!' the Camcorder roared at the man, who then turned around and stared into the camera lens like a startled rabbit. Reg Doorman was making ground.

'What are you fucking doing, you idiot?' the Camcorder rasped and his left hand was seen to violently wave backwards towards the edge. 'Back! … Fucking back!'

The man stood rooted to the spot, burning holes into the lens. Reg was almost upon him.

'Fuck!' spat the Camcorder. 'Shite and bollocks! We're going to lose this fucker!'

In the next second, Reg Doorman arrived and was heard to roar 'No!' at the top of his voice, thereby giving the man such a fright that he disappeared over the edge instantaneously. Surprisingly, perhaps, the Camcorder didn't make a sound, but trained his steed on a similarly stupefied Doorman, staring open-mouthed into the empty space. Ten further seconds of this scene and nothing but the sound of the camera whirling past and then the camera cut out.

There might have been silence between Reg and the Camcorder on the video, but the gathering watching the recording of the spectacle was not so reticent. They all pissed themselves, some, quite literally.

In a matter of days they were all back on top of Rocky Point in the mist of an early morning, camcorders at the ready, all sporting blue blazers with white badges with "ROPSAS" displayed in bold red lettering. The Rocky Point Suicide Appreciation Society had been born with Thoad as their president. They were committed to destroying Reg Doorman and the Lifejoys forever.

Chapter 29

Epic

SALTY SID WAS remarkably matter of fact about his new line of work. He had spent his entire life in boats. Not just his working life, but a good deal of his childhood too. He was a hardy old bugger who didn't get easily flustered. Trawling in bits of body might have been a novel experience for him, but that's all it was. All he asked was for a full flask of dark rum and a pipe packed tight with his favourite aromatic backy and he was more than content. He would have clashed with Moby Dick for less. Dredging up a few shredded cadavers was certainly not going to faze *this* old lad. If anything, the work actually lacked the sharp element of challenge, which had hitherto made Sid's life afloat so remarkable. Fish could always swim away to avoid being netted, whereas the sole respite for a Rocky Point corpse concerned only a temporary liberty in the event of one catching the tide and bobbing around a bit against the rocks. Even this irritation was nothing a heavy hook couldn't bring under terminal control. Sid was one step ahead of the Coastguard every time.

The work became even more boring when Salty failed to bring home a catch at all, something which was of course no smear on Sid's boatmanship. It was inevitably the case most of the time in the early days before the suicide bug began to take hold. The old boy would sweep the area at the foot of the rocks, maintain his patrol and would then take a break by floating farther out to sea, or else treat himself to a trip around the pier before returning to the rocks for his afternoon watch. His days of providing pleasure trips for tourists (a profession which had never really matched his insular temperament) were well and truly at a close.

Sid was even more unique in the sense that he was the only one of the

Freddo staff not to be a Station Inn disciple. He had grudgingly gone there once for a 'staff meeting' and had left after ten minutes. He was certainly not going to park himself on a hard wooden stool for hours on end, surrounded by piss-taking teenagers, most of whom persistently attempting to shove something other than St Bruno in his pipe, whilst an offensive cacophony as far removed as possible from sea shanties or The Seekers ripped his eardrums to buggery. He thus repaired to his regular hostelry, The Galleon, a microscopic pub a stone's throw from the foot of Rocky Point, where half a dozen salty old lads sat around playing cards or shove ha'penny over tumblers of rum or scotch, whilst a bloke even older and saltier sat slumped in a corner cuddling an accordion, playing six notes to every belch or fart.

Even though on Sid's many fruitless trips (and indeed on trips when he made a trawl) his rum and pipe provided him with all the companionship he required, the old man welcomed with curious open arms a surprising and sudden request from Epic to go with him on a patrol. Epic had already declined Sid's mocking offer of making him 'ship's mate' and Sid had not expected a change of heart. In addition, despite Epic's flippancy at that first meeting, Sid had taken quite a shine to the brash young man, thus joining a long list of people who had felt exactly the same way at their first contact with him. It was, however, certainly true that Epic was no stranger to boats and particularly trawlers. He had first boarded one as part of a school project he had been assigned to on the importance to Canada of her fishing industry. The Young Seebal had enjoyed the experience, and after he had completed the project, he wangled more trips with local fishermen on the premise that he intended to make it a career as soon as he had quit school. It was only when having been invited to take part in some of the actual work of the industry that he discovered just how arduous a life it was, and if any genuine interest in that sort of future had ever existed at all, it certainly evaporated after his first encounter with a heavy net. These men were rock hard. Eric was not. He promptly locked himself back up in the pipe-dream he had only just relinquished, a dream shared with just about every other kid of his age – to form a rock band and become a superstar, even an icon. He saw it all now. A kid had set his heart on a career as a fisherman – a man's job. But then, all of a sudden, creativity called and he was reluctantly kidnapped from a life on the ocean by the avaricious clutches of the rock business. There were times when the press were hounding him that he wished he'd remained a fisherman. *Perfect!*

Epic's assurance to Sid that he had trawled for fish was thus partly true and his subsequent curt dismissal of Sid's offer to him was a direct consequence of it. Now, however, he thought that it would be cool. He certainly didn't figure that the work would be that tough. He was older now and Sid would be doing most of the heavy stuff anyway. He convinced himself that he would actually be taking part in a management capacity, but naturally did not reveal this notion to anybody else, least of all Salty Sid. As a matter of fact, he felt that floating around with the old man, whom he now considered a 'respect magnate' would be 'most excellent' and in any event a respite from merely riding shotgun with Noddoes, especially since their 'doughnutmobile' wasn't dragging the doughnut any longer en-route to the torching.

The first time the unlikely partnership set sail together, land ahoy! A customer! It was a teenage boy this time, who had decided to jump after being dumped by his girlfriend. The kid helpfully left a note in his bedroom to further satisfy Klaus, as if film of the wretched event wasn't evidence enough. ROPSAS had, after all, captured every second of this early morning drama with poor Reg Doorman, not only too late this time, but *in absentia*. The bungling Lifejoys' chief was still tucking away into a marvellous full English breakfast at his favourite seaside café at this time. When he eventually got to the top of the cliff in order to open up the Hut at still quite a respectably early hour, ROPSAS were already at home watching their videos over coffee and croissants, having put in the promised call to Thoad (which this time had proved to be quite unnecessary) and Sid and Epic, having long since dredged in the main trunk of the boy's remains, had already delivered this to shore and seen it dragged off to HQ in the doughnutmobile driven by Stephen, who had taken Epic's place on this occasion. Just as Reg was altering his date-stamp, Tessa was already busy at work salvaging what she could. The idiot had no idea that he had failed again until Head Office called him two days later and bollocked him. His credibility farther down the chute, Reg felt pretty miserable about the whole shooting party. Freddo's and ROPSAS were elated and nothing else.

The dead boy was called John-Paul Brisley, a local kid and therefore a natural Freddo client. As expected, Klaus Butsch did not delay matters in issuing his verdict in his usual faltering English: 'Diese lovesick junge jumped as we see on film. All these *bumpity-bumps!* When he lands, it is the finish for him. One can do nothing. Many older persons do self-killink because of love not returned. Here comes a story of likewise mit this boy.'

At his funeral, John-Paul danced to Bon Jovi and Iron Maiden before being committed to the flames to the strains of New York City singing *I'm Doing Fine Now Without You Baby*, a disco smash from the seventies, which was naturally John-Paul's own personal swipe at the little minx who had jilted him. Danny and The Exotics were very much in attendance and John-Paul, dressed defiantly in bikers' leathers, gave the impression of having enjoyed himself immensely.

Freddo's' style of funerals had now begun to take off spectacularly, as news of the great new phenomenon spread. The most satisfying consequence of this was that potential suicide jockeys began to make provisions for their special funerals *before* careering off Rocky Point, usually by making an appointment with Thoad at the Emporium, who then notified his friends at ROPSAS in order to secure video evidence to put before Klaus. This, of course, was a curious turnabout. Whereas Thoad had initially requested that ROPSAS informed Freddo's about potential business, the situation had now been reversed. 'Good old Tom!'

More significant was the knock-on effect of the dramatic rate in the suicide rate itself *vis-à-vis* Rocky Point. Whereas before, depressed people would previously have merely disappeared for a few days, or at best taken a fistful of tablets or cut their wrists just to show off, people were now forsaking the statutory 'cry for help' by heading to Rocky Point via Freddo's, something which could not possibly be a cry for help in anybody's books. Most of these customers were, naturally enough, impressionable young people, desperate to cash in on the Freddo groove, mindful that missing out would mean a significant loss of street cred. Some clients though, were older, and it was for these for whom the classic rock cuts were more likely to be requested, as opposed to the uninspired drivel of the day hoovered up by the uncultured teenagers and twenty-nothings. Eventually Danny began suiting himself with these kids. The vicar would announce the commencement of 'Showtime!', play a record which had been genuinely requested by the dead scrote and then surprise the leftovers by completing the service with a couple of unsolicited tracks from the sixties or seventies, on which he and The Exotics had been working a routine. The track chosen for the committal was more often than not wonderfully ironic, so that one seventeen-year-old girl called Jackie Shepherd, who did away with herself because of her obesity and the associated non-stop trauma she had suffered at the evil hands of those contemporaries who pretended to be her friends as a result of it, and whom had requested a trio of appallingly contrived dance hits by the latest superstar 'boy band' whose love she could never hope to win, found herself with the aid of no less than four Freddo staff and extra sturdy ropes dancing instead to Love Sculpture's rendition of Khachaturian's *Sabre Dance*, one of Rock's most undoubted masterworks and a piece which The Exotics had turned into something of a spectacular under Danny's tutorage. She then flew down the chute to the cruel strains of Joe Tex's superb *Ain't Gonna Bump No More (With No Big Fat Woman)*, which had been arbitrarily chosen for the committal at the last moment to replace the previously rehearsed *Get Off Of My Cloud*, the Stones' track. Middle of the Road's sugary singalong *Chirpy Chirpy Cheep Cheep* completed the unsolicited trilogy for poor Jackie.

In fact, although the hijacking of all three choices of track was extremely rare, the committal number (the most important of all) was hardly ever the choice of the punter at all. It was instead the choice of the

Rev Danny Hare, or occasionally Barefoot Sally and was designed to match as broadly as possible a facet of the doughnut, either its former character, or the reason it decided to make itself a doughnut. With Jackie Shepherd, one was talking fat, which was why the excellent Joe Tex was given a spin. It would have been far too easy and not at all original to play Van Halen's *Jump* all the time.

Frank Eddowes had failed to take over Pendlesham's funeral industry totally, nor was he winning the battle piecemeal. The Old Firm was still alive and well, but Freddo's had nevertheless made enormous strides in seizing a sizeable business from it for itself. What was ironic, of course, was the fact that Freddo's remarkable success had been a major, perhaps decisive, contributory factor towards a spiralling increase in the town's death rate and thus the number of available customers, although since nearly all of these were suicides, just about every one of them were either snapped up or else directly bequeathed to the trendy newcomers. There was already a clear dichotomy between the Freddo clients and those of the venerable Old Firm, the establishment which Frank had set his heart on systematically destroying. The Old Firm clung on with all its might (which was still considerable) to the town's natural wastage and practically all of the non-suicide quota, whereas Freddo's was rapidly becoming a suicide-only service and indeed was not merely the beneficiary of the suicide craze encroaching upon the town, but also the creator of it, although this initially had been inadvertent. The fact that the company secured an even split of total clients with the Old Firm (with other companies like Proudfoot and Gadd being forced to pick at the bones of the carcass, so to speak), served only as a testament to what dizzy heights of popularity suicide had now risen, with the guarantee of a 'Rock and Roll Funeral' at the end of the rainbow.

The focal point of everything was irresistibly the Station Inn, where Tom Beck was forced to engage extra staff to cope with the increase of business brought on by being the recreactionary meeting point of Freddo staff and thus, not only the home hostelry of the most renowned band of pissheads in Pendlesham, but also a shrine for those fans of the rock and roll suicide culture, who were not quite committed enough to go the whole hog themselves but wished to be in the presence of the coolest, most happening guys on the south coast.

The wooden stools alongside Tom's bar were the preserve of the Freddo people. Any regular customer who took a spare one knew straight away that his custody of it would only last as long as it took for Frank, Epic, Thoad or Stephen and Amanda to stroll in, generally to cheering and whooping from the youngsters, to claim it. Noddoes too was a firm Station Inn fixture by now, as was the eternally lovely Tessa who, not surprisingly, spent most of her time in there as Sheba, due to the wondrously varied choice of happy pills and powders she was able to acquire in front of the bar just as easily as she could acquire a glass of dry white wine behind it. Frank's manic lust for her had not diminished with time and familiarity and she still provided practically the exclusive rights to the inspiration for his twice-daily wanking sessions. Frank, though, now had a couple of teenage groupies all to himself and had long since quit paying for it. These two were bollock-busting little madams, turned on by the fact that he was the top guy of the whole Freddo empire. Tessa Sharma was still the one he wanted, but the frustration over not having her was clearly nowhere near as desperate as it had been in the gloomy days when he used to monk up with alarming frequency thinking of her, whilst rarely having a proper fuck, even if he had hired a woman for just such a purpose.

Pursuers of Miss Sharma, meanwhile, were not merely confined to her boss. Not only did Epic consider her 'a knockout, if not a little weird', although out of respect to Frank, whom he knew worshipped her, he did nothing about it despite how hard the contents of his pants tried to persuade him otherwise, but most of the boys (for this was nothing but a fair description of them) who hung around the Inn were also agog, conscious that they were confronted by a lively, sexy, grown woman and thus sensibly realising that she was totally out of their scummy reach. The main nuisance by far, though, was Tom Beck who, recognising class when he saw it, had been struck dumb from the moment the dark, leggy beauty had glided into his bar for the first time. He had been flirting with her quite pathetically ever since and had been rewarded quite deservedly by getting absolutely nowhere at all. In fact, Tessa's recent sexual history remained a mystery to everyone. When she was just 'plain Tessa', she was a charming, sexy piece of fluff with almost an air of innocence about her and whose top-drawer qualities kept all the scrotes and saddoes (in other words, all the guys in the Inn) firmly at bay, these lads knowing that she was a ridiculous target and almost certainly spoken for anyway. When she transformed into Sheba, however, the girl was so far out of her gourd, she actually frightened everyone off; and those who chose to hang around bravely hoping for a shag, were confronted by a repetitive, giggling, irrational diatribe from the loveliest loony tune in town. But that was it. This situation, needless to say, provided Frank with the most fragile of straws on which to clutch. Since Tessa was apparently celibate at that time, there remained the faintest of hopes, he thought, that she would at last return the 'love' he had for her. The fact that Tessa remained clueless of his feelings about her, due to the fact that Frank had still not mustered up enough moxy to tell her even after all this time, did not occur to this most pitiful of would-be suitors as even remotely consequential to his lack of success hitherto. Even more remarkably, he still lived in hope.

Noddoes too had his fan club, although these were not clients of the Station Inn necessarily. He had been interviewed by a local hackette who had been so taken with him that she had persuaded him to attend functions as after-dinner speaker, entertaining the sort of old dears who liked Tom Jones, Engleburt Humpledink and Tony Bennett. At the first of these he was listened to with polite curiosity. The second night he did it, he was mobbed by the more mobile of the late middle-aged hens and interfered with in the bollock area. He reasoned that it would be better to avoid that sort of circuit forthwith, return to the Inn and take his chance with not being inconvenienced by the spaced-out advances of the teenies, which he had already experienced when he had first encountered Amanda, a situation he handled with consummate ease. Noddoes was never more attracted to anyone more than he was to himself. And that was the rub.

Danny and Barefoot Sally occasionally put their heads around the door of the Inn, if only to catch a word with the other two Exotics in order to discuss gigging arrangements. In spite of the unquestioned rock and roll theme of the Inn, the place wasn't really the vicar's scene and he was never much of an imbiber anyway, being one of those unfortunate men who gets helplessly hammered midway through their second pint. He was more bonkers than a regular drunk and he and Sally spent all of their time, waking and sleeping, together anyway. So that was the finish of that.

Chapter 30

The Lifejoys

WHAT HAD BEGUN as a war of nerves between the Lifejoys and ROPSAS had degenerated into a pitiful massacre of the innocents with the waving of the white flag surely now only days away. The pious suicide preventers, led by the idiotic Reg Doorman, had been out-manoeuvred at every station and ROPSAS as a consequence had so gorged themselves on everlasting banquets of suicide tapes, thanks principally to Thoad's excellent counsel as an admirable exchange for allowing those tapes to be entered into evidence for the benefit of Klaus Butsch, that one Camcorder had actually become totally disinterested with the hobby, which had hitherto been his passion, and had turned it in to follow another pursuit. The others had desperately tried to change his mind, pleading with him that it was only a question of time before Reg himself jumped, which would signal the final victory for ROPSAS and then all of them would finish.

'A couple of weeks. Just a couple of fucking weeks and the bastard's going to do it! Come on, son. Don't pack up now!' one of them had begged him.

The disaffected member would not be convinced: 'No. Reg is no match for us. Game over. I even feel a little sorry for him.'

'You're fucking joking!'

'I'm going to take up bookbinding now. It's great!'

'You horrible bastard!'

Happily, this was to be the only defector.

Reg Doorman was indeed very close to the edge in every sense. He had, during the few short months of his tenure as chairman of the Pendlesham branch of the Lifejoys, seen a summary self-destruction of a number of young people in the area he was supposed to patrol. His organisation had been of no use at all to them. They had spurned him completely. They had not even bothered contacting him. Not only this, but they had actually travelled to the top of the cliffs in order to kill themselves yards from his hut. They had defied him. Vilified him. Ignored him. Were not even aware of him. They had been totally taken over by the insatiable desire to make full use of the excellent Freddo facilities and had cheerfully and premeditatedly done away with themselves right under the nose of the ill-starred Doorman. Suicide was the in-thing for the smart set that summer. Death leaps and cool funerals. To remain groovy, these kids simply had to book their ceremonies and the jump.

The Lifejoys had lost. ROPSAS maintained a twenty-four hour presence at Rocky Point, poised excitedly for the inevitability of Reg Doorman's final desperate bumpy curtain. It surely wouldn't be long now.

Chapter 31

Thriving Acorns

FRANK EDDOWES' REMARKABLE success had catapulted him to the summit of Pendlesham's affluent business community and the consequence of this was that he felt it was his duty to attend seminars appertaining to the world of commerce to which he now found himself invited by various sources. One of these was put straight into his diary as being of particular importance. It was entitled 'Thriving Acorns' and was designed to bring together representatives from over one-hundred recently founded companies from fields across the board, which had recorded initial profits the organisers described as being 'above reasonable expectations'. This national seminar was by invitation only and the gathering at the National Exhibition Centre in Birmingham would see delegates from all over the UK descending on the county's second city in order to pick up a parchment, quaff a couple of glasses of moderately palatable wine, hear a meaningless address from some bloke equally as meaningless, filled to the brim with sickly platitudes telling them how wonderful they all were and how even more wonderful the organisers were, and then wandering aimlessly around the NEC, shaking hands and chatting with folk they would never see again. Frank recognised it as the tub-thumping crock of shit that it was, but overridingly it had potential for being of immense long term value to him, introducing Freddo's to the UK-wide commercial network. The invitation itself had also been wonderful for Frank's ego and it all sounded a good crack, so he acknowledged the invitation by return of post and said that he, the 'Managing Director', plus a 'senior director' would be delighted to attend, thank-you very much indeed.

The choice of who he would take with him provided Frank with something of a headache. It had been made clear from the start that there was no designated second-in-command to him and that Frank himself was barely the head man, although the others all acknowledged Frank as their boss. This state of affairs meant that technically any one of them qualified to make the trip. Stephen and Epic thus braced themselves for what they saw as the inevitable announcement that Tessa would be going. Frank had of course immediately thought of his gorgeous embalmer as the ideal companion, but for the first time, as far as Tessa was concerned, had been struck down by a virulent strain of pragmatism. Since Tessa spent at least an equal amount of time these days as Sheba, Frank conceded that he could scarcely attend what he saw in part as an important meeting (in as much as he regarded the invitation itself as nothing less than a reward for his company's achievements and excellence thus far – and this was absolutely right) with 'The Imperial Cat of Doom' in tow. For a similar reason, Noddoes also missed the cut.

Despite the mellowing of Frank's attitude towards the old luvvie, to the point where he was now nearly rather fond of the idiot, he still recognised that Noddoes remained an incurable fraud and that, not only was he eminently unsuitable as a companion to a seminar on the grounds that he would ham things up incredibly and make them both look like arse-holes, but that his selection would almost certainly send the same false signals to Noddoes as had been received when Mr Snape had unwisely appointed him as a 'master of ceremonies' at the ill-fated tribute to his late partner over Frank's head, a decision which had taken Frank a lot of time to get over. Noddoes had interpreted this as a promotion and had acted even more insufferably as a result of this totally false assumption. Frank, in all honesty had no reason to believe that this particular leopard had, or indeed could, change its spots and therefore was able to exclude Noddoes on an entirely sound and reasonable basis.

The third staff member who was struck off the list immediately was Salty Sid. The old boatman was quite clearly never in the running and would never have wanted any part of it anyhow. Frank and guest were to spend the night in Birmingham before returning to Pendlesham, which would have meant two whole days for Salty trapped in a massive city miles from any coastline. This would have been more than purgatory for Sid. Even half an hour without the whiff o' brine brought him abject misery. To not be in a position to immediately clamber aboard a boat and feel the waves beneath him would, as sure as eggs were eggs, driven him nuts. Even more nuts.

The most painful decision Frank thought he would have to make was to knock Thoad out of the reckoning and then tell him that he wasn't going simply because this most pitiful of men clearly wasn't seminar material. 'I can't take you. You look like one of our doughnuts' would have summed things up tidily enough. Instead of this, Frank went for fudge and utilised the old 'I need you here' chestnut, reminding Thoad that ROPSAS remained dependant on his proven counsel and that he was 'probably the only member of the team who is indispensable… apart, of course, from Tessa', a tribute which like any sentence containing the word 'probably' meant absolutely squat.

Kicking the otherwise superb Thoad into touch, who when told did not exactly show signs of being any more mortified than he always was, thus allaying Frank's fears, left either Stephen or Epic as Frank's adjutant for Birmingham. Frank's own choice was Stephen Mauve, as he considered that in Epic, as sharp as a pin though he undoubtedly was, there remained an element of the Noddoes factor, in as much as Epic was rarely serious and also an element of the Sheba factor, in as much as Epic was frequently stoned. The clear difference though between Noddoes and Stephen was that whereas Noddoes was never taken seriously by anyone else and thus ended up looking like a prat, Epic never took anyone else seriously, and the consequence of that was that *they* ended up looking like prats, a situation which Frank had found himself in more than once and had no intention of having replicated at the seminar. Epic had far too much of the tinderbox about him. Stephen was a far safer pair of hands, unexcitable, whilst being witty, intelligent, smart and well mannered. He would be the ideal lieutenant for a gathering where making an impression and not a fool of oneself was decidedly the order of the day. There, it was settled then. Stephen would be going to the seminar.

Only, no. By a supreme irony, the one member of his staff Frank had not even considered in order to rule out ended up deciding matters. The second of the two days of the seminars was Amanda Plimmer's birthday and Stephen had arranged a trip to Paris as a present. It had all been arranged and there was no prospect (even less an inclination) that Stephen would cancel it now. He had even already cleared the dates with Frank, something that had not seemed important to Frank at the time and thus had been easily forgotten. The fact of the matter was Stephen was not going to be able to make the seminar.

'I quite understand, Stephen,' Frank assured him, rather pissed off none the less. 'If it were me given the choice of the Champs-Élysées or Spaghetti Junction, I can't really say that the choice would be a difficult one.'

Stephen offered his own mitigation: 'She'd have my balls off if I went with you,' he said.

This unexpected disappointment told Frank that it would after all have to be Epic making the trip. Frank broke the good news to the Canadian over a beer at the Inn. Epic was delighted: 'Hey, cool, Frankie! I've been up at Birmingham one time before. Toilet city, man! It's nearly as bad as Detroit!'

'Yes, well I'm pleased to say that most of our time will be spent in the world class exhibition hall they have there,' Frank told him. 'Straight off the train and straight in.'

'Sure. That's okay.'

'But afterwards, and bearing in mind that we'll be staying overnight in a hotel in the city, I'm sure we'd both like to unwind, if you know what I mean,' Frank assured him.

Epic's face lit up. '*Perfect*, Frankie! That's most excellent!'

'As long as we don't go too mad.'

'Sure… sure.'

Chapter 32

Ropsas

N O SOONER HAD Frank decided on who the other delegate for the Birmingham seminar would be, then all attention switched to the fervid excitement of a message received from Thoad from one of the Camcorders that Reg Doorman had at last fulfilled his shit-hot potential as a suicide candidate and had jumped off Rocky Point. Sid had already bagged the spoils. This ironically removed the main obstacle Frank had stated was the reason Thoad had not been selected for Birmingham. Now that Doorman was dead, there would no longer be any ROPSAS for Thoad to remain in contact with. They had all agreed that once Doorman was beaten, that would be it. He was, and so it would be.

In describing Doorman's demise, the emotional Camcorder, almost sobbing with joy, outlined how the entire force of ROPSAS had been present on the cliff top with their instruments primed, when at approximately 10.57 and in perfect conditions, Reg had opened the door to the Hut and closed and locked it deliberately behind him.

'When he turned around, he looked up at the sky and then down to the ground,' explained the Camcorder to Thoad quakely. 'Weather-wise it was a perfect day to be on the Point. The sun was just getting up and there was a delightful little breeze. We all homed our cameras on him and many of us were sure that this might be it. It was too early for a lunch break, nobody else was near the edge and the only time that Reg ever locked the door was when he fucked off for the day. We all looked at each other.

'Doorman remained rooted to the spot for a while at first, then looked up to the sky again before starting to walk very slowly indeed towards the edge of the cliff. We knew now that this had to be it because the bastard always used to run like a hare towards the edge whenever he twigged that there was a job on, and this confirmed that not only was there no-one threatening to jump, but that no-one was anticipated. Except, of course, Reg. All the lads started to get really excited now. We had initially been rather excited about a guy in a woolly jumper, who had looked a good bet, but he had disappeared into the tourist office and now the landscape had changed entirely. That bastard Doorman had a definite death walk on, shaking his head and looking to the floor, also occasionally gesturing to the sky. I zoomed in and saw that he was fucking crying. That was the final confirmation we needed and we were now all very excited indeed. We now had only one thing left to worry about – whether the tosser had enough bottle to go through with it.

'Reg stopped about ten feet away from the edge and then clasped his hands together. I suppose he was praying, which I suppose was fair enough. So we waited until his arms dropped down by his side to signify that he had finished and then we all started to cheer him on. Reg turned around when he heard this support. Normally, whenever he appeared, we all booed him and called out "cunt!" and stuff like that and then ripped the piss out of him whenever he lost a job. This time we wanted to show him that what he was doing commanded the greatest respect. *Our* fucking respect, the prat! We were screaming out things like "Go on, Reg! Over you go, you old fucker!" I zoomed in on him again and he was sobbing like a girl. I think he'd really been moved by our tribute to him.

'The last thing he did was to look straight out to sea with his fists clenched and it was as we were all screaming "Jump, Reg! Jump, Reg! Jump, Reg!" that the bastard galloped up and fucking swan dived off the edge. Fucking beautiful it was! One of our blokes thought that he might have picked up a faint scream on his cammy. Doorman somehow managed to maintain the arc of his dive almost all the way to the bottom, and at one point I thought that he had done enough to go straight down, which doesn't happen very often. But he lost it with about a hundred feet left and the trajectory drew him back in to crash against the cliff and bounce straight off again. He went straight down like a fucking stone after that. It was, in all honesty, Tom, a fucking ace jump. Nine point nine dive. He certainly knew what he was doing, the bastard! The last thing we filmed was your old boat bloke sailing off with the wanker wrapped up in his net...'

As the Camcorder had intimated, he and his ROPSAS brethren were not the only guys who had been all set for Reg's death leap at the precise moment that Doorman had decided that enough was enough. Salty Sid had also been firmly in position at the vital moment, having set sail on patrol on a glorious morning from the boat station farther along the coast on the other side of the pier, where his vessel was routinely moored. Sid had been floating around by the Rocky Point lighthouse when his binoculars fell upon Reg Doorman and his superb Olympic class dive. He immediately set a course to go and reel in the doughnut and then radioed in to Thoad: 'Some bugger's just come over,' he reported. 'I'll go and net him up and bring him in after I've had me dinner.'

'Righty-ho, Sid...'

Soon after this, Thoad got the call from ROPSAS confirming that Reg Doorman was the guy.

As had always been agreed amongst the members themselves, ROPSAS now intended to disband. They had for some weeks now been a single issue party and now that the one pertinent objective had been achieved, everyone was more than happy to wind the group up with the most merry of parties, during which dinner would be eaten and members' tapes of their late, defeated adversary's suicide would be presented and compared, followed by showings of each member's personal favourite jump from his copious collection of self-destructions, most of which, of course, would again feature Reg *in excelsis*. The guest of honour for this joyous festival was Thoad, 'Tom, our founding father', a tribute which, had Thoad cared a flying fuck about not being picked for Birmingham by Frank (which of course he didn't), would have compensated him for it several times over, since it came straight from the heart from guys who had always thought he was wonderful, instead of just weird, lonely and sad.

In all honesty, it had indeed been Thoad who had, if not actually founded ROPSAS (there had for some time, even before Freddo's founding and Reg Doorman's arrival, a hardcore presence of Camcorders on top of Rocky point), had at least given them a name, an identity, and had overall instilled in them an understanding of the absolute imperativeness of the success of their crusade to triumph over the despised Doorman. This had now been accomplished in spades and Tom Hoad was indisputably the star. As soon as he arrived at the large comfortable house of the ROPSAS member holding the party, he was presented with a bottle of champagne by the host and a standing ovation by all the other Camcorders present. Inside the dining room, a long mahogany table covered with a cream silk cloth was bulging under the weight of a prepared four-course feast, many dishes balancing on hot plates: cream of mushroom soup for starter, roast silverside of beef with seasonable vegetables and roast potatoes for the main dish, served with claret, homemade rice pudding for dessert and then Stilton and biscuits to follow with vintage port ahead of the coffee and mints.

After the company had repaired to the lounge for brandy and cigars, the host proudly slipped his own tape of the Doorman suicide into the video recorder and switched on the TV. How those guys all roared with laughter (not Thoad) when the image of Reg appeared stumbling, sobbing towards the edge! How they toasted the excellent Doorman as tape after tape subsequently depicted his demise and its hilarious preliminaries from every different vantage point around the cliff top! Indeed, the viewers got so carried away with the show that the host, pissing himself more than most, staggered off, laughing in a helplessly slurring stupor in a fair to middling (but entirely inadvertent) impersonation of Norman Wisdom to the bathroom to fetch indigestion tablets for those who needed them.

When the Doorman tapes were finished, it was the turn of each member to present his favourite memory from his own personal archive – the most popular being undoubtedly a failed rugby tackle by Reg on a Portuguese student intent on terminal glory. Reg scrambled to his feet and wouldn't give up, but the boy staggered on. Reg somehow caught up with him and was next seen to frantically point at one of the stone plaques displaying a glowing tribute to life from the scriptures which, being biblical gobbledygook, was unreadable enough for the natives, let alone a foreign kid with minimal English, and had in any case been significantly defaced by someone from ROPSAS who had scratched 'JUMP NOW!' clearly onto it.

The teenaged scruff from Lisbon, distraught at being kicked into touch by his girlfriend, and having taken appropriate action by downing a couple of large plastic bottles of supermarket cider in Pendlesham town centre, responded by throwing his hands up in the classic continental gesture of professed confusion and then high-kicking Reg in the bollocks, flooring him immediately. The picture on the screen then moved manically up and down as the filmmaker heaved with laughter before recovering to record the lad exiting most spectacularly off the Point with what looked like a kung fu kick, whilst Reg still writhed around on the ground holding his wounded tackle after his kick in the plums. One tape went on to show the kid being splattered all over the bottom of the cliff. After that, the abuse started from the Camcorders:

'How was it for *you*, Reg, you useless old bastard!' rasped one, as he zoomed in on Doorman, who attempted to rise, but was forced down again by the pain to his cock and stomach.

'Fancy a cup of coffee now, do you, you fucking tosser?' growled another. 'So how do you want your eggs, boy – scrambled? Like your bollocks?'

'Might as well jump, Doorman!' spat a third prophetically. 'You're a failure! You're a fucking *murderer*, son!'

All the Camcorders on the films were heard to be pissing themselves heartily. Back in the 'cinema', the viewers could really have done with a doctor with a respirator in attendance. The last scene of this wondrous event, which any of the Camcorders picked up, was one of Reg Doorman practically crawling back to the Hut, beaten and hurt, to the accompaniment of catcalls and curses from all the lads. The show now being over, the host, barely recovered himself, scrambled unsteadily to his feet to deliver his closing remarks.

'Gentlemen. To borrow a line from The Beatles, we have reached the end of the long and winding road,' he began.

'So the fuck has Reg!' interrupted someone. And everybody laughed (not Thoad).

'I'm sure that I speak for everyone when I say that we have had nothing but good times with our cammies,' the host continued. 'Naturally there were some fruitless days, but these became progressively rarer after we were fortunate enough to run into good old Tom...'

'Hear, Hear!' affirmed everyone. 'Good old Tom!'

'... Tom's organisation has, not only made jumping off Rocky Point fashionable, they have converted it into an artform, a cult, ignored by right-on youngsters at their peril. The bounty of jumpers this has produced has been fucking overwhelming, and it was this glut which finally made Reg Doorman's position as chief bottle washer of the Lifejoys completely untenable, as we all knew that eventually it must...' More cheering and whooping. '... Realising that his defeat was absolute, our opponent signalled his surrender by offering himself to us for study, and by doing so presented us with our last subject as laid down in our constitution.

'Gentlemen, The Rocky Point Suicide Appreciation Society has run its course. We disband now on the most agreeable of terms and in the knowledge that our just cause has been met beyond dispute. God bless our membership and let us part, not only friends and colleagues, but comrades, indelibly linked by the fortitude, steadfastness and dignity that we have brought upon our society and upon ourselves.'

The party finally came to a conclusion with the singing of *Auld Lang Syne* and then three cheers for 'good old Tom', who was only really interested in getting back to the Inn for some sort of session before last orders.

Chapter 33

Reg

RICHARD SIMMS, NOT being Reg Doorman's doctor, reported his death to coroner Klaus Butsch, who did not waste much time in reaching for his cowbell. A copy of a ROPSAS tape had, as usual, been produced as evidence for his benign consideration.

'One more *bumpity-bump* self-killink!' confirmed Klaus. 'But wait! This man had a job for to stop others from overjumpink. Yet he stops nothink. And now this man he sees the red. We have the film and it cannot be ignored. In his job he has failed, and here we see him when he speaks to his guardian angel before he jumps to his fate. I hesitate nicht in my findink. Nein. After all, check out the film for those who don't believe. My decision is that Herr Doorman takes away from himself his own life with no balance of the mind. It's understood.'

A sound decision, clearly.

Later, back at Freddo's, Doorman's carcass was being slapped into shape by Tessa.

'Are any of your friends going to the torching?' she asked Thoad, after he had strolled in for a quick peek. She meant ROPSAS.

'Oh no,' Thoad said. 'Funerals were never really their bag. Only jumping. They were only ever interested in jumping.'

'*Were*? Aren't they doing it anymore?' Tessa asked, kneading away.

'No. They decided to wind the old society up. We had a goodbye party yesterday.'

'Oh, how sad!'

'They all departed with fond memories, though. They were great lads!'

'Whatever prompted them to finish if they enjoyed it so much?'

wondered Tessa, chopping away pison-like with the outside of her hands.

'Well, to be honest, it's old Reg,' admitted Thoad, indicating the doughnut.

'You mean that it's *this* man's fault that your friends don't have a hobby anymore?' Tessa asked, beginning in that instant to become more catlike.

'Well, I suppose it was really, yes,' nodded Thoad, and then added a rider to complete an absolute truth. 'If old Reg hadn't jumped, all the lads would still be up there,' he admitted mournfully. 'Up there... enjoying their hobby...'

Sheba looked hatefully down at the corpse. 'The beast!' she hissed. 'The absolute *beast!*'

She began to slap Reg sharply across the face back and forth: 'In *that* case, mister!' she chided. 'In *that* case, mister!...'

Thoad gloomily nodded approval as Sheba then began to claw away. It was an irrefutable fact that had Reg not been so selfish as to kill himself, the ROPSAS boys would have all still been up on the cliff top, merry as ever. That excellent society was now lost forever and it was all down to bloody Reg Doorman and his bloody-minded cult of self.

Sheba, though, had retribution on her mind and was in full flow now. 'I see nothing but darkness for you now!' Sheba cautioned Reg bleakly, as she slapped him with one paw and scratched him with another. 'When I finish with you, mister, you are going to look ridiculous. *Ridiculous!*'

Thoad showed no expression, but looked on satisfied.

'I'm going to turn you into something special, mister!' continued Sheba. 'I'll soon teach you the meaning of fun, you horrid little man. But first, I disfigure your face. *Hissss!*'

Sheba then began to claw away freely at her prey with both paws and poor Reg was quite unable to do anything to escape the butchery.

'This is what happens when you displease Sheba, mister!' she told him. '*Doom!*'

The next second saw her immediately starting to patch up the damage to Reg's face, first stroking his head and then rubbing cream lovingly into the wounds. Thoad didn't have a clue what was happening to Reg and was looking on in forlorn astonishment. To confuse matters totally, the Imperial Cat was now purring loudly, even though her mantra remained familiar: 'Something special, mister!' Something *special*! Ridiculous! *Ridiculous! Purrrr!*'

There was no getting away from it. Reg was in deep poop this time around!

Chapter 34

The Exotics

REG DOORMAN'S FUNERAL was a five-star windup from start to finish. This tormented man was summarily given the entire works and the event was Freddo's finest hour hitherto.

Despite Sheba's savagery and her promises made in curses to make Reg look 'ridiculous', Doorman's corpse ended up, in fact, looking rather splendid. First up, he had appeared to have lost weight, which to be honest, wasn't terribly surprising, bearing in mind that much of him remained at the foot of Rocky Point in any case. As far as his face was concerned, Sheba had started out with every intention of turning Reg into a completely misshapen, discoloured, disjointed, bug-eyed freak. The thing was, since by this time she was totally caned on her most recent line of coke, her usually masterful work ended up being crap, which of course meant that the intentional bad job unintentionally wound up being an extremely good one.

In fact, Reg looked pukka. He gave the impression of a much younger man, bore a proud, dignified but unobtrusive smile and had even developed a cute little dimple from somewhere. Sheba's addition of a panama hat gave Reg instant super cool, and by the time he had been plonked into a safari suit, the guy looked just great.

Later, at the funeral, The Exotics lent the occasion the appropriate dignity by appearing as Serengeti animals, dressed (but only just) in fake but realistic looking skins. Amanda had just enough black and white stripes around her to inform people that she was a zebra; Barefoot Sally presented perhaps the least convincing image but still looked very fetching, clung precariously to part of a monkey suit, a sight which left very little indeed to the imagination and a curly tail tied to her bum; the least surprising sight, but a glorious one all the same, was Sheba appearing as a 'leopard cub', which meant a furry covering so ludicrously inadequate she needn't have bothered really. When the girls were lined up ready to rock it was a very pleasing spectacle indeed, and this was even before they started strutting their stuff.

What made Doorman's funeral more remarkable than any which had preceded it was the pioneering tactic of The Exotics actually performing with the doughnut up on the dais with Danny standing off it to one side. This of course meant a heavy job for Stephen and Epic who needed to operate Reg by ropes off stage for a change, since there was no longer any room for them to stand. These were attached to both arms and legs, with an extra fine one around the cadaver's neck. Naturally this new routine would mean a more realistic dance performance from the doughnut, but this would be at the cost of the considerable increase in the degree of difficulty for the puppeteers, who were now crouched down out of sight. The height of the catafalque was risen to accommodate this, but it was always going to be tough going. As it turned out, Epic, Stephen and Thoad, who was back there in reserve, performed magnificently.

Because Reg had died a sad and lonely twat there was nobody to come to the funeral except the Freddo people (sans Sid), one or two interlopers from the Inn and an old bat from the Lifejoys, whom the Reverend Hare soon neutralised by swiftly dispatching her to an adjoining room with a bottle of sherry so that she would not be in any position of either place or mind to witness everyone ripping the piss out of Reg. After this aged lush had been dealt with, all hell broke loose. It was one of those wonderful occasions when everything went swimmingly. It was the best, most raucous, most successful and certainly most sexy torching they had ever delivered. Hot stuff!

The steamy session started with Danny's usual introductory scream 'Ready to Rumble!' and then from behind a cloud of blue smoke (a new, exciting special effect, courtesy of Keith Tate) The Exotics were revealed all lolling erotically over Reg, who in full safari regalia was sitting in a wicker chair with his arms folded looking well wicked.

Everybody cheered and whistled. Applause broke out. Within five seconds, the first track came blasting through the speakers. It was the girls' own special tribute to Reg, who remained in his seat whilst they all wrapped themselves around him and pampered him terribly to the sound of *Lady Marmalade* by La Belle, the pioneering feminist soul classic which screamed female sexuality from the rooftops. Reg waited politely for the girls to finish molesting him before leaping to his feet to accompany them on the second number, *The Witch Queen Of New Orleans*, the brilliant Redbone single from 1971, which had long been requested by Keith Tate 'for sheer fucking excellence' and had finally been choreographed by Danny and The Exotics with Danny himself overdubbing on lead vocal. Neither he or any of the girls had told Keith that they were going to do the number until immediately before the ceremony when he was presented with the final playlist, so that halfway through the track, Keith got so carried away that he abandoned his sound station and rushed towards the 'stage' so that he could really get wild. Much later, after the funeral, in a reflective moment back in the Inn, Epic announced that this single performance of *Witch Queen* was probably the finest work that Danny and The Exotics had ever produced: 'It blew me away, man!' he enthused, nursing his joint lovingly. 'Gasville, baby!'

There were no dissenters.

Keith went berserk at the end of the number and it took some moments for him to remember that he needed to get his arse back to the controls to put on the third track. This unscheduled delay allowed Danny to offer Reg a breather before 'handing him over to the Big Guy'.

The element of prayer in the rock and roll funeral culture had always varied. Some kids who had opted for Freddo's services had done so in order to avoid any ecclesiastic involvement in their service at all, something which was always honoured by Freddo's unlike, of course, the customer's choice of tracks. Perhaps surprisingly, there were a number of others who made requests for a firm, albeit short religious content betwixt the secular rock and roll, which Danny was only too pleased to deliver. The initial intention with Reg was simply to do a four track set this time and then tip him down the chute with Danny blessing the doughnut with the sign of the cross as it disappeared into the flames as the final number was finishing. However, Keith Tate's almost orgasmic enthusiasm over the *Witch Queen* routine had forced Danny into saying a few words about Doorman, as the man himself sat smilingly only a few feet away, nodding his thanks.

'Hey Lord! It may be said that this guy was bad for business… for both of us,' Danny prayed. 'It may be said that this guy interfered with those who would enter your House. But Lord, we want you to give this guy a break, okay?'

'Amen!' slipped in Epic. 'Tell it as it is, Dazza!'

'Brother Doorman was basically a good man, who became misguided through crass fucking stupidity. We pray, Father, that in your mercy you will see fit to accept this sinner into your glory, through Jesus Christ, our Lord…'

'Amen!' affirmed the congregation.

'Cool eulogy, Father!' approved Epic. 'Never mind the guy was a geek!'

'And now, Lord, we're gonna hit you with the prayer which you yourself taught us, Okay. "Our Father…"'

'"Who art in heaven…" joined in everybody.

Keith Tate managed to scramble back into place by the time The Lord's Prayer had been completed and the instant the reverend gave the signal, he hit the switch for the third and penultimate track, Patti Smith's seminal Punk ballad *Because The Night* from 1978. For this superb piece, Reg once again enjoyed the attentions of the girls, whilst he and Danny remained redundant until the chorus when they both exploded into action, Danny on the mic and Reg jumping up and punching the air. The congregation went bananas.

The final number - the committal track - stayed faithful to the critique of a personalised track for the particular subject concerned. Several options had been mooted: KC And The Sunshine Band's *Please Don't Go* had been in the frame, since it seemed to mirror exactly what Reg Doorman was all about and also had irony value, taking into account that Reg had eventually done exactly the same thing which he had spent all his working hours trying to prevent others doing. Thunderclap Newman's 1969 chart-topper, *Something In The Air*, one of the classics of Pop history had been suggested, but was bounced because it was considered too general - not personal enough. For the very same reason, seemingly ideal choices like Van Halen's *Jump* and The Stones' *Jumping Jack Flash*, another truly great one, were excluded also, as was Streisand's *Stony Ground* and Presley's *Way Down*, the last single the King ever recorded. The eventual choice was given the nod on account of it being entirely appropriate, not only for Reg but also for all the guys and gals who had managed to turn themselves over, despite Doorman's desperate, unsolicited attempts to stop them from going ahead with it. It was McFadden and Whitehead's Disco anthem from 1979, *Ain't No Stopping Us Now.* Big sound!

While this track was on full blast, everybody in the Bar and Grill got down and grooved it up. The Exotics, meanwhile, now realising that Reg would soon be saying adieu, were now flinging themselves all over each other rather than him. Whilst they were in the midst of this provocative routine, Reg finally bowed like a kung fu master and then waved frantically, before collapsing onto the catafalque. The girls then jumped down to wild cheers from their admirers and Keith Tate, barely recovered himself, hit the switch which raised the dais on one side causing Reg, who must have been all in by now, to slide effortlessly through the now open hatch and into the furnace.

'Go and be with Christ, matey!' roared Danny to cheers from everyone.

With the usual impeccable timing, the track faded just as the furnace doors closed again. The torching was finished, so patently was Reg, the old Lifejoys' woman had finished her bottle of sherry and was unconscious in the vestry, so everyone fucked off and went up the bar.

Chapter 35

Mr Parfitt

FRANK'S MUM WAS a bit worried about him going to Birmingham without her, even though he was fast approaching fifty. 'What about your washing, Frank?'

'I'm only spending a night there, mother, for goodness sake,' he reminded her wearily.

'Well make sure you wrap up and don't be going and getting pickled, Frank!'

Hansel and Gretel were not impressed. Those cats knew that drink was on the agenda, which it was, of course. Lots.

Frank hadn't often gone away without his mother, and no matter how much he tried to emphasise to her that it was a business trip, which it was, he could never really hope to escape the inference, without so much as a word, that he was deserting her. He packed himself a medium-sized night bag containing two changes of underwear, an extra suit, a pair of pyjamas, his razor and his toothbrush and left it in the hall. When Frank came to collect it on the morning of his departure, it had been replaced by a gigantic suitcase crammed full of just about every item of clothing Frank owned, including three pairs of pyjamas, twelve Beatrice Potter hankies, a Winnie The Pooh water bottle and an extra blanket and bath towel. His mother had also slipped in a framed photograph of herself into the case too. Frank could barely pick it up. There was enough in there for a month's holiday in Alaska, rather than just a one-night stop-off in The Midlands. Frank was livid but knew that it was far too late to throw any of the crap out as he had to go and meet Epic at the station in less than quarter of an hour. In addition to the huge suitcase, Frank also had his attaché case containing the conference papers and hotel documents. He picked both of them up and hobbled off to the station, Hansel and Gretel monitoring his departure very closely. When he spotted Epic outside the Inn, just yards from the railway platform, waiting with just one small sports bag and nothing else, he felt a right prick.

'Travelling light, huh Frankie?' Epic quipped.

'I was silly enough to let mother do the packing, I'm afraid,' Frank gasped, almost telling the truth. 'I've got my whole life in this case. And it's so darned heavy!'

'That's too bad.'

They boarded the London train and on arrival they went across on the Underground to Euston where they picked up the fast train to Birmingham NEC. This had been the first time that Epic had been back to London since he had arrived by accident in Pendlesham and the first time Frank had been there for goodness knows how long. When he went away with his mother it was usually to either somewhere else along the south coast, or else the West Country. The cats always went too.

It was still early, but neither had any inclination to hang around London for the sake of it. Euston and the neighbouring area of Kings Cross held painful memories for Epic. He had become very close to a girl from New Zealand called Anne-Marie who worked in one of the pubs as a lunchtime waitress. He had met her at a gig. She was backpacking around Europe, like so many kids from her part of the world, picking up jobs where she could. The couple, both lively and intelligent, became inseparable and for a while, Epic was considering asking Anne-Marie to come back to Canada with him (or at least to Seattle where he was still claiming residency at that time).

Epic himself had been experimenting with a variety of controlled drugs, but had always fallen short of injecting anything. One night at a party when both he and Anne-Marie were stoned, some tosser was handing out syringes which he had lifted from a hospital, spinning the line that since they were individually wrapped, heavier stuff could be enjoyed without any risk. Epic took one just for show and so did his girlfriend. But whilst Epic's went straight into the bin the second a chink of sense was able to penetrate his dope-infected brain, Anne-Marie held on to hers, having convinced Epic, and indeed herself, that she had actually thrown it out. Two nights after this, she and Epic were at a nightclub, and once again both of them overdid it on the puff. An associate of the lad who had given Anne-Marie the syringe, somehow managed to farm off some heroin to her, telling her that 'It will give you a high you will never believe.' Anne-Marie, suddenly remembering the syringe she still had with her and out of her brain already, went to the toilet and fired the whole lot into her arm. There is never any good smack, only bad smack and Anne-Marie, nowhere near down from the weed, promptly collapsed. She was found and tended to quickly, but by the time the ambulance came, her heart had already failed. The crash team at the hospital worked feverishly, but the young woman's cause was hopeless and everybody knew it. The consultant in attendance waved it all off.

Epic actually didn't find out about the tragedy until the day after it happened. Not having been privy to her being removed to hospital via a side entrance, he had immediately become fearful that Anne-Marie had left the club with someone else. The thought of this distressed him more than anything else he could imagine until a friend, who had not been at the club, suggested 'Have you tried the cop shop, or the hospital?' and he did. Once the police had satisfied themselves that Epic was, not only an innocent party but a bereaved one, he was asked to identify his girlfriend's body, and this he did too. It was an event which almost certainly triggered off Epic's 'doughnut' doctrine under which Freddo's was now governed. When he saw Anne-Marie lying on the slab bereft of life, he immediately nodded the required confirmation that it was her, whilst at the same time knowing that it really wasn't. The girl he had seen himself marrying somewhere along the line had gone completely, and this thing stretched out stiffly on the slab certainly wasn't her. It was a doughnut. Burn the shell and let it be.

The loss of somebody he thought he loved precipitated Epic's flight from London and his random choice of the south coast as a refuge. A misunderstanding of the workings of the rail network had seen him deposited to Pendlesham rather than to Brighton, his intended destination, and this was the point when he had wandered off the train, rather than attempting to double back and entered the Station Inn for the first time. He had been in the town ever since, mostly in that same pub.

Frank's own most recent trip to the capital had been far less traumatic. It had involved taking his mother on a day trip to Earl's Court for the Ideal Home Exhibition. This was three or four years ago. It was perhaps a rather peculiar coincidence that on that occasion too he had gone off a train straight into an exhibition hall, as would be the case in Birmingham, only this time with a hotel booking having been confirmed, the *après ski* was likely to be quite different.

It was still the morning side of noon when the train pulled into the station serving the National Exhibition Centre. Frank immediately called the hotel to inform them of their arrival and then he and Epic secured their luggage in two separate lockers before walking on towards the exhibition hall. Banners and flags with the 'Thriving Acorns' symbol were all over the place and people in suits were running around trying to look important. Frank was convinced that most of them probably were. He and Epic walked up to the entrance and Frank theatrically produced the invitation from the inside pocket of his jacket to where he had transferred it from the safety of his attaché case.

'Mr Frank Eddowes and Mr Eric Seebal, Freddo's Funeral Emporium, Pendlesham!' he announced, quite unnecessarily to the NEC official on the gate. The man silently perused the invitation and handed it back over.

'Thanks. That's fine, gentlemen. Straight through for registration,' he said.

'Hey Frankie, how 'bout that? We're gonna get registrated, baby!' Epic remarked, before turning to the official. 'You're doing a great job, pal!'

The two men passed on through and were immediately leapt on by a smiley middle-aged woman in a green blazer, which had the organisers' symbol on a patch on the left breast pocket.

'Hello!' she gushed. 'Welcome to Thriving Acorns. We're so pleased you could make it. Follow me to registration, please!'

'Thank-you,' Frank said. 'It's lovely to be here.'

'They said it again!' enthused Epic, enjoying himself already. 'Man! I just can't *wait* to registrate! No representation without registration, darlin'!'

Frank looked at him uneasily as they followed the lady to the registration point, a circular desk, behind which other smiley middle-aged women in green blazers were busily booking people in.

'Present your card at the desk, please gentlemen,' their escort beamed. 'Please don't hesitate to ask any of the green goddesses if you have any questions about Thriving Acorns. Thanks for coming.'

With that, she turned sharply on her heels and walked away.

'Nice lady,' Frank said, watching her go. 'Green goddess.'

'Come back twenty years ago, sweetheart!' sneered Epic most ungraciously, well out of the lady's earshot at least.

'You'll appreciate older women one day,' Frank promised him, shaking his head.

'Only when I can't get younger ones no more, Mac,' rasped Epic as another smiley green goddess addressed them:

'Hello! Welcome to Thriving Acorns. We're so pleased you could make it!' she chirped, following her script. 'Can I see your registration card, please gentlemen?'

'Hey, Frankie!' gasped Epic. 'This is it! She's ready to registrate. *Registrate!*'

'Certainly,' Frank said, handing it over. 'Here it is.'

'She's gonna registrate us for sure, Frankie,' panted Epic. 'She's really getting ready to registrate. I can sense it! Wow! What a doll!'

The green goddess swiped their card over a panel and received a bleep as a reward.

'Mr Eddowes of Freddo's Funeral Emporium, Pendlesham, plus one,' she read.

'Indubitably!' confirmed Frank.

'In *what?*' squawked Epic, looking at him.

The lady dropped the card into what looked like a ballot box and handed Frank two green clip-on plastic labels with the single word 'DELEGATE' printed on them in bold, black lettering.

'Thank you, gentlemen. Enjoy the conference,' she concluded.

'Thank you very much for inviting us,' Frank said, taken as much by this woman as he had been with the first.

'Have we been registered now, ma'am?' Epic asked her.

'Yes, sir. Go along through.'

'Through right here?'

'Yes, sir.'

Frank blinked heavily and walked on. He was beginning to wish he had taken Thoad with him now.

'How was that for you, Frankie?' Epic asked, catching him up.

Frank shook his head.

'Okay, Frankie. I'll quit kidding. So we're in the place. So what happens now?'

'We mingle and make contacts,' Frank replied, relieved that Epic has passed a sensible comment for once after all the carry-on he had made over the formality of getting into the conference.

'Cool. Catch you later!' nodded Epic, turning away to leave.

Frank was incredulous. 'What do you mean, catch me later? We're supposed to be working, you silly boy. Where are you going?'

'Cool it, Frankie! You know as well as I do that all this is nothing but a piss-up and a babe hunt.'

'*What?*'

'Those greenie grandmas are all yours, pal. Me? I'm gonna find me a girlie who can't remember Woodstock. I'll catch up with you at the registrating desk when school's out. Okay? Sure! Catch you later!'

Epic bombed it, and this time he was away and gone – on the pull and on the piss. If Frank had been silly enough to have taken anything at all about the conference seriously, he was most certainly by himself now.

He was livid, but he also quickly decided that he was going to pursue his intended agenda in any event. He was going to mingle and make contacts. To have missed an opportunity like this would have been unforgivable, he felt. It was fine to go and get bladdered and to take everything that the Thriving Acorns' people were content to drop on people's laps gratis. The whole thing was a crack and Frank knew this more than anybody. But he wanted to exploit the conference beyond its more obviously baser elements. Frank wanted to have a go at establishing some connections. He was going to mingle and make contacts. Even false ones.

The first contact he made was with another green goddess; this one with a tray of glasses of champagne.

'Courtesy of Thriving Acorns, sir!' she smiled, thrusting it along with her ample breast into Frank's face.

'Thank you kindly,' he said, tentatively accepting a glass of bubbly and then stepping back. He was feeling a little stiff downstairs now. His rescuer was another clearly marked 'DELEGATE', a tall impressive looking fifty-something man, who looked like a senior civil servant. He already held a glass of champers.

'Jolly nice, all of this,' he said to break the ice.

Frank hesitated before smiling back. 'It's wonderful,' he finally managed. 'I feel privileged to have been invited…'

This wasn't exactly the best thing he could have said when he was out to impress strangers. It distinctly put Frank in the diminutive before any introductions had even been made. And this wasn't supposed to happen.

'Donald Rawlinson, Managing Director of the O'Connell Group,' the man announced grandly, offering his hand.

'Computers!' wildly guessed Frank.

He was saved by pure luck. The O'Connell Group was indeed concerned in computers, although through their sale between other companies, rather than their direct manufacture.

'Good news does travel fast!' Mr Rawlinson said, looking entirely delighted.

'The whole of this seminar is about good news, isn't it?' Frank said. 'My own company is about good news too.'

He presented his card and announced himself. 'Frank Eddowes, Managing Director of Freddo's Funeral Emporium.'

'*Funeral* Emporium?' asked Mr Rawlinson, with raised eyebrow. 'Do you mean you bury people?'

'Cremate,' corrected Frank.

'How fascinating!'

'Incinerating!' corrected Frank again. 'We serenade them to the flames to the soothing sounds of rock and roll classics. Cremations are cool. Well… bloody hot, really!'

'Good gracious!'

'Who are your favourites, I wonder… Lonnie Donegan, perhaps? Herb Alpert?'

'You're being disingenuous, Mr Eddowes.'

'*Frank*, please.'

'I'm not that bloody old! My type of people were The Who, The Small Faces and The Troggs.'

'Oh gosh, mine too! Mine too!' gasped Frank, getting quite excited.

'You were a Mod, then, Frank. So was I. Isn't that funny!' smiled Donald.

'*Was?*' enquired Frank.

'Oh, well, you know. Times move on, don't they,' Donald said, addressing his glass.

'So you feel that you've outgrown the music that you loved during the best times of your life? I find that terribly sad, Donald, terribly sad.'

'People mature, Frank. It's the way of the world. And I'd like to think that the best times of my life are the ones I'm having just now.'

'But does everyone "mature" with regard to musical preferences, I wonder?' Frank wanted to know.

'I think they probably do, yes,' nodded Donald.

'You think they probably do? But what about children who were brought up on Wagner, for example? This represents the music of their youth. Their *immaturity*. Are you suggesting that it is perfectly fine to jettison, when they get older, their understandable passion for Wagner in favour of a new found love of The Sex Pistols? If this is what you are saying, I have to say that I do not agree with you. Musical flavour is governed by choice, by circumstance, by memory, by the indelible linking of one piece or one type of music with a golden period in one's life. Surely it can't be governed by a synthetic "maturity", which insists that one follows a cosy pattern of nursery rhymes on to Pop, on to Rock, on to Blues and Jazz, on to Easy Listening, on to Classical and finishing with Opera, heaven forbid. My suggestion is that to claim that one has grown out of something which has given them so much pleasure is merely an admittance that they have grown out of that pleasure…'

'I'm afraid I don't agree with you, Frank,' Donald said. 'You mentioned nursery rhymes. Indeed, I was brought up on Uncle Mac. I had a very happy childhood. Blissfully happy, in fact. But I am nevertheless, in middle age, quite adept at preventing myself from singing *Here We Go, Looby-Lou* out loud in honour of its memory. It's much the same with the music of the sixties. Naturally I feel nostalgic whenever I hear *My Generation*, but to start singing it outside a Karaoke would seem to me ridiculous now. I might make the suggestion that, whilst I agree with you that musical taste is very subjective indeed, and based quite significantly on how that music assimilates with certain periods in one's life, I would also contend that the rejection of classical music, especially by young people, is based on an ignorance of it, together with a peer pressure requirement to dislike it because it's seen to be the taste of the elite, which is poppycock. I still like the sixties' pop, Frank, much for the reasons you've outlined. But at university, I also developed a taste for classical music. And yes, I like opera too!'

'Oh, I have nothing at all against opera,' Frank urgently lied. 'I suppose what I'm really saying is that I feel that it is a great pity that people dismiss, or should I say, leave behind, music which enveloped the best years of their lives. My argument is that the music is not the only thing which is left by the wayside.'

Donald smiled again. 'There you go again, Frank. "The best years of your life"! I honestly think I'm living mine now. And naturally I'd like to think that even more golden years lay ahead, in which case, Mozart will end up being more wonderful than I'd ever imagined him!'

Frank laughed nervously.

'You know what I find particularly sad though, Frank?' Donald added. 'Chaps of our age turning up in clubs or pubs full of kids and trying with appalling desperation to blend in with what these folk half our age are up to. It's tragic!'

Donald Rawlinson couldn't have possibly known, but this was a bull-seye! An inadvertent personal dig at Frank, whom he didn't know from Adam. Despite the total absence of any malice aforethought, Donald had succeeded in hitting the rawest of nerves. The 'chap' Rawlinson had just described was none other than Frank Eddowes himself, the lonely, 'tragic' barfly sitting unsteadily on his stool in the Station Inn.

'As you say,' Donald concluded, totally ignorant of Frank's acute discomfort now. 'Musical preference is not just about musical taste. And if this preference is attached to, or even determined by a link with salad days long past, then that's perfectly alright. There's no right or wrong answer. Only opinion.'

This apparent concurrence failed to heal the damage. Frank had been sussed as a pathetic, sad, middle-aged drunk, whose life clock had stopped in about 1971, his best years gone forever, and was now reduced to going into a kiddie pub and reminiscing about the days when music was really music with other tragic figures, one of whom (Tom Beck) even more pitifully attempting to engross himself in contemporary pop too just so that he could impress people who may or may not have been children.

Frank had started off gently ribbing Donald for no longer putting rock and pop at the top of his preference list, thus turning his back on the happy and carefree days of his past and had ended up being told, albeit inadvertently, that he himself was a tragic old anorak, who lived in, and indeed, exclusively for the past, solely because he had neither a present, nor a future.

He thereby had no option left other than to keep his humiliation down to the barest of minimums and creep away, promising himself ludicrously that he would grab Rawlinson the second he had popped his cork and throw him down the chute to the strains of *Wild Thing* (preferably Hendrix's version) as the most ironic of punishments.

Frank had swapped cards with Rawlinson, but this bauble had come at a grim cost. Three things would cheer him up: an introduction to a top London businessman who would live and die for the glory of rock and roll; a successful wooing of a choice green goddess and the acquisition of her hotel key; and a goodly sample of the local beer before anything else, since Frank had decided that the champagne wasn't quite chilled enough. He also decided that he would make a sweep for Epic, an objective which he felt would surely run in close tandem in achieving the third of these, or at least start the ball rolling.

He looked around for a green goddess to hand his empty champagne glass to (and to ogle pathetically at) and immediately saw one close by. But before he had even had a chance to hesitate as to whether or not to go to her, another middle-aged male delegate intercepted him and offered his hand.

'Hello. I'm Stanley Parfitt, Financial Director of Longhorn Furnishings, Northampton.'

Frank took Mr Parfitt's hand without looking at him. The green goddess had got away and for once, the loss of a female had nothing to do with Frank.

'Er… Frank Eddowes…' began Frank before finally conceding defeat and turning and smiling weakly at the man whose hand he still held. '… Freddo's Funeral Emporium, Pendlesham.'

'Funerals? Well I really don't suppose *you'll* ever be short of customers, will you?' Mr Parfitt quipped, as Frank stared at another green goddess who was particularly glamorous, he thought.

'I suppose you're going to tell me that Val Doonican's your sort of thing!' suggested Frank, turning to face him again.

'I beg your pardon?'

'We're specialists, you see, Mr Parker.'

'Parfitt.'

'Oh, I am sorry. But we're still specialists. You see, what we do is serenade people to the incinerator to the strains of the greats of rock and roll!'

'Oh, right. I understand now.' Mr Parfitt said. 'Novelty funerals!'

'Well I suppose they must be a novelty for the client, yes!' Frank nodded.

Mr Parfitt unexpectedly belly-laughed. Frank smiled back.

'What could we tempt you with then, Mr Parfitt? Perhaps not Val Doonican. You look more like a Searchers man to me.'

'I shall have to be honest and say that my taste was always a bit more raucous than Merseybeat,' Mr Parfitt countered. 'Creedence Clearwater is more my sort of thing. I used to drive my father up the wall with Creedence and Canned Heat and all that kind of stuff.'

Frank's eyes widened. Parfitt may have used the dreaded past tense initially, but he had amended his error immediately. Frank was sure he had found a kindred spirit this time.

'I'll put you down for *Bad Moon Rising* and double it up with *On The Road Again* then, shall I?' Frank beamed, taking out a notebook.

'Ha Ha! An excellent suggestion. Add *Proud Mary* to the playlist and you've definitely got the contract!'

Both men laughed.

'Perhaps I can make the coffins for you,' Parfitt slipped in.

'We don't use coffins, but do let me take your card,' Frank said.

Parfitt's mouth shot open in total astonishment. 'No coffins?' he finally managed. 'So how do you... What do you use for the...'

'Nothing, nothing. We just tip the doughnut down the chute. But only after it's taken a full and proper part in the torching.'

'I'm afraid you've lost me completely now,' Parfitt said, shaking his head.

'Yes, well here's my card. Call my office for an information pack. It will explain everything. Goodbye, now!'

Frank walked quickly away.

The reason for this sudden and apparently curt dismissal was that Frank had spotted a bar alongside one of the far walls. Perhaps the errant Epic was there, and if he wasn't, certainly beer was. Just because Frank had encountered a trader with whom he had immediately clicked, didn't mean he had to spend the remainder of the seminar with the bloke. He had established contact and that was enough. It was time to mingle again. Mingling at the bar was just as good as mingling anywhere else. Where better?

He still had the empty champagne glass in his hand, but deposited this at the bar at the same instant he ordered his pint. Having received this, he looked around him. No Epic. No green goddess. Two delegates talking to each other rather loudly just alongside him.

'I think that we must always remember to get our perspectives into focus,' one said. 'People tend to forget about things like that. Very important.'

'You're talking sense, Mr Chadwick,' the other guy said as Frank tipped half his pint down a thirsty throat. 'In my business the customer is king.'

Frank walked past them to the other end of the bar. 'In my business the customer is dead,' he said. And there was no answer to that.

Epic remained elusive. Frank irrationally imagined the jammy young man already in a hotel room shagging the arse off a continuous chain of ripe green goddesses, which would have explained why he hadn't seen any of these handsome women for a while. Whenever Frank had seen Epic in action in the Inn, he had always tried to convince himself that he himself never wanted fifty women at his feet. 'Just one by my side.' It was a good line and gave him plenty of scope for self-indulgent misery when that one didn't appear. Epic had enjoyed more than his fair share of successes within his natural habitat. If it now proved to be the case that he was servicing any number of goddesses, having dismissed them so cruelly earlier, Frank rather fancied that he would have blown his stack. Nobody deserved that much luck, even making the necessary allowances for Epic's youthful, attractive, physical appearance, insatiable vibrance, magnetic personality, unbridled confidence, priceless wit and bewitching charm. *Nobody* deserved *that* much luck…

'How are you enjoying the seminar, sir?' a pretty green goddess suddenly asked Frank.

At that point, Frank would have given anything not to have been holding a pint of bitter (his third). But there he was.

But then, a brainwave: 'It's all splendid!' he pretended to enthuse. 'I know this may sound awfully pompous, but it's actually rather comforting to realise that it's not just myself who's made his first million recently. I feel very much like small fry in comparison to some of these chaps. And if that wasn't enough, my assistant seems to have disappeared, leaving me holding his beer. I'll end up drinking it if he doesn't return soon.'

'Would you prefer some complimentary champagne, sir?' the woman asked, smiling like a housewife in the last throes of a washing powder commercial.

'Some champagne would be delightful, miss. Thank you.'

The resplendent mature lady rewarded this syrupy flattery with an even broader smile. 'Please don't go away,' she said, and off she went.

'Never, leggy!' Frank softly returned.

The goddess returned in a matter of moments with the champagne. Frank had it in his mind that the apparent special attention he was receiving was due to his mention of the magic six-figure word and that he had definitely pulled.

'What brought you to Thriving Acorns?' the lady asked.

'That's a strange thing to say,' Frank said, his confidence fortified by the beers he had supped. 'Your invitation did, of course.'

'I think they like successful men,' the goddess said.

'*They*?' Frank enquired. 'Doesn't that go against your script a bit?'

'Yes, I should really say *we*, shouldn't I. We're actually all agency girls.'

'Yes, I thought that you must be models. I must say that this little shindig is rather nice, but there's still something not quite right about it. Perhaps it's got government backing.'

The woman laughed. 'I wouldn't be surprised.'

Frank then noticed a name badge clipped onto the green blazer and leaned over to look at it. 'Angela Stockley,' he read out loud. 'I'm Frank Eddowes from Pendlesham. Have you had far to come for this job?'

'Well, I'm staying here this evening, but I live in Gloucester…' she said.

Angela Stockley was a very fine looking woman indeed. With her fiftieth birthday probably behind her, she was tall enough to be able to display superb legs and was immaculately turned out within the confines of her prosaic green uniform, her shoulder length fair hair fixed well enough to allow a genuinely engaging smiley face to emerge. And she smelt delightful. It was more than likely that she would have appealed to many younger men, even the very choosy Epic, but to Frank, who was of a similar age, she was everything he could ever hope for and was seemingly his for the taking, if only for the night. The last thing he needed now was for his 'assistant' to appear.

'So you've already joined the millionaires club, have you?' Angela asked (it was her turn to fish now). 'What is your business? Pendlesham is always depicted as such a quaint little place, isn't it? A lot of retired people dozing on the sea front…'

'And lots of young people leaping off Rocky Point,' Frank added.

'Oh, yes,' Angela sighed. 'That's such a desperate shame. And I read somewhere that it's getting worse too.'

'The suicide rate is increasing,' Frank nodded, not of course agreeing that it was a bad thing.

Angela paused, still waiting for Frank to explain by what means he had made his 'million'. Frank suddenly realised this. 'I'm the principal funeral director in the town,' he finally claimed.

'Oh, golly. I had no idea!' Angela blushed.

'I do hope that you don't think ill of me,' Frank continued. 'There are plenty of people who do not regard people in my profession favourably. They think we are callous vultures. The truth is I am a businessman who recognised a healthy market… I haven't put that terribly well, have I? I do hope that *you* don't consider me callous.'

'No, no. Of course not. I suppose that…'

'Somebody's got to do it, yes. The funeral director's best defence! I know only too well that the profession carries all sorts of taboos, but I will never apologise for the way I have become a success, and the bottom line is that I refuse to consider it as exploitation. It is merely a service, just like anything else. Selling doughnuts, for example. If one does not like doughnuts, one does not buy doughnuts. And similarly, if one does not take to the service I offer, they go elsewhere. It's as uncomplicated as that.'

'I don't think you're callous, but you are sounding rather technical,' Angela said. 'I've never heard of people going shopping for funerals before.'

'Well that's exactly how we've broken ground,' Frank said. 'Angela, tell me. Who was your pin-up? David Essex? Donny Osmond?'

Angela's smile widened. 'Bless you. You've just knocked ten years off me!' she beamed. 'I was a little too old for David Essex. My idol was Elvis, just like every other girl then. But I also liked Adam Faith and was also rather keen on Anthony Newley, though why I ever fancied *him*, heaven alone knows!'

'I ask that because the feature of our funerals is that they have a rock and roll theme to them. That's what makes us different.'

'Oh, right!' Angela nodded, understanding now. 'I've heard about this sort of thing. People having jazz bands following their cortege or having somebody play their favourite song in church. Is that what you do?'

'With certain modifications, that's it precisely,' Frank said.

'Well in that case, I don't think that you're callous at all,' she told him warmly. 'I don't think funerals should be morbid. I think that they should be celebrations.'

Frank had the bit well and truly between his teeth now. 'This is exactly the argument which we are winning and shall continue to win,' he assured her. 'This is why I can point to so much success in the face of what I must admit is very strong competition in the town.'

'It must be a nice place to live, though,' Angela said, skipping neatly off the subject. 'Isn't Pendlesham supposed to be one of the sunniest towns in England?'

'Quite so... Quite so,' Frank confirmed. 'Perhaps you might consider working your considerable charm around your husband and persuade him to come and visit us.'

Angela looked away. 'I'd like to move there and leave him in Gloucester,' she said.

Frank's pulse began to quicken. 'I'm sorry to hear that,' he lied.

'He's probably with that little secretary of his as we speak. He's old enough to be... well... you know the story. I'm sorry. I shouldn't have bored you with it.'

'The man must be insane. What the devil is he doing drinking Ribena when he owns one of the great clarets?'

This was truly a grim line, but all the hard work had been done now, Frank felt. All that was required now was the pounce – or at least an attempt at one: 'So did these Thriving Acorns' bods book you into somewhere nice for the night?' he asked, as to his horror his cock started to stiffen.

'They've given some of us rooms here at the NEC, but I was booked into a hotel about twenty minutes away. It was more convenient for me to get back home afterwards.'

'Of course,' Frank said. 'As for me, I have the dubious pleasure of a night in the Birmingham International for my sins. My assistant has a room too, but he's since learned that he needs to get back to Pendlesham to take care of a private matter. So he'll be straight onto the London train. Come to think of it, I'm beginning to wonder whether or not he's already on it. I haven't seen him for ages!'

'The International? Gosh!'

'A bit ostentatious, I know. I'm not generally one for such opulence. But I considered this conference a bit of a special occasion, its invitation to which is something of a reward for my company's success. So I decided to reward myself further...'

With Frank so close to the goal now, it was extremely annoying that at this moment they were interrupted by a young man who asked Angela how he went about paging someone. Angela smilingly deposited the information and the guy walked off. She turned back to Frank.

This break in momentum could very easily have been fatal to Frank. But this time, for the first time in his life, he was not going to botch his chance with a woman. His opening gambit (that of being a millionaire) may have been a mercenary lie, but everything else about his business had been perfectly true and Angela had been impressed. Her sudden revelation about her own personal unhappiness had also swung the drawbridge in Frank's favour. Why else would she have brought it up if not to signify interest? It looked like a firm green light and even if it wasn't, Frank had absolutely nothing to lose, and to give him further encouragement, he no longer had the horn.

'Angela. Would you care to join me for a drink in my hotel later this evening after the fun and games here are over?' he asked, not fearing a rebuttal at all.

'Aren't you really asking me to spend the night with you?' Angela said.

Frank nodded. 'I am. Yes,' amazed with himself as to how calm and rapidly he had answered that momentous question.

Angela lowered her voice. 'I'd be being unfaithful to my husband, which he fully deserves, but who would *you* be cheating on, and does she really deserve it?'

'Absolutely nobody,' answered Frank truthfully.

'Are you sure you haven't got a wife or a girlfriend somewhere?'

'Nowhere. I give you my solemn word.'

'I find it difficult to accept that there's no-one special. A man like you.'

'Less than a year ago, a man like me was working for somebody else for a pittance and there was certainly no-one special then. Since breaking away and going it alone I have done nothing other than to work my fingers to the bone to become an entirely new man like me. And there is still no-one special. I haven't had time for someone special. I have now.'

Angela smiled weakly. 'I don't know how you think that could apply to me. You don't even know me.'

'Philandering is not in my nature,' Frank claimed. 'And I'm certainly not in the business of waving my money around, hoping that I will be pursued relentlessly by a posse of females. One could get sex anywhere. I'd like to get involved with someone warm and mature on a serious basis. And if correspondingly you are really unhappy with your husband, if I won't be jeopardising a stable marriage, I'd like to be involved with you. Indeed I do not know you. I do, however, find you utterly charming.'

This time Angela blushed and Frank had his girl.

'Do you think you could find yourself to the lobby of the International?' Frank asked her, still maintaining his composure and the length of his dick magnificently. 'For all sorts of reasons I think that would be wise.'

'Yes... yes,' Angela said. 'I can get there. I get off here at eight... This is so sudden. So immediate. Didn't you... Didn't you have any other plans for this evening?'

'I've just cancelled them,' Frank assured her. 'I'll be in the lobby at eight for eight thirty. Dinner will be waiting for us. And the champagne will be on ice. So this will be my last glass of *this* stuff!'

Angela affected another smile. There lingered in her a tenseness about which Frank was acutely aware and this was the signal to close the conversation quickly. He did so by making the perhaps precarious decision of offering Angela a get-out clause:

'If you have second thoughts and go back to your own hotel and then back to your husband, back to your life, I shall quite understand. My disappointment would be enormous, but it is I after all who is propositioning you. If you choose to resist my advances, this can only be a matter for you. Destiny awaits and so shall I.'

With that, the rekindling of his entire doctrine in two words, Frank bowed courteously and walked smartly off to the toilet, where in privacy of the farthest cubicle from the door, he wanked himself daft.

Jubilant though he was, Frank now had a whole sequence of problems which had to be tended to bloody quickly. The most immediate of these concerned his boarding arrangements. He and Epic had already arranged their reservation in a modest but comfortable hotel. Separate rooms, of course. Frank would now have to forfeit his own room and almost certainly the fee which went with it. Before he did this, he would have to secure himself in the Birmingham International, or at least attempt to. Failure would mean all his hard work accounting for nothing and a very pleasant dream would be in tatters. A silent prayer was thus uttered as the call was made with a request for a double room en-suite for that night.

'When would you expect to arrive, sir?' the receptionist wanted to know.

Frank's gasp of utter relief was not exactly well concealed. 'I can get to you at six o'clock,' he recovered.

'That will be fine, sir.'

'I trust I'll be able to order dinner direct to my room for later in the evening?' pressed home Frank.

'Certainly, sir.'

Frank passed on his particulars to the girl and told her to expect one item of luggage, which would arrive by taxi within the hour. He was so beside himself with joy and anticipation, he did not even suitably react when told how much he would be paying even before any extras would be considered. He always assumed that it would be through the roof in any case.

With Frank so much in the ascendancy now, it was with something approaching contempt that he next contacted his original hotel to cancel his booking. 'If it is indeed the case that I must forfeit the fee, either in part or in full, you have the option to either invoice my office, or else bill directly my associate, Mr Seebal, whose own reservation remains extant to my knowledge,' he explained coldly, secretly hoping upon hope that Epic would be saddled with the tab.

The last thing Frank did was to obtain an exit pass from another green goddess so that he could retrieve his suitcase from the left luggage locker in the railway station. He then wheeled it out to the taxi rank.

'I'm not going anywhere,' he told the cabbie. '*This* is your passenger.' He indicated the heavy case sitting on the trolley. 'Its destination is the

International Hotel, where I have a reservation. They're expecting it. Here is my card.'

The driver eyed the battered suitcase suspiciously. Frank understood immediately and nodded. 'Perhaps *this* might reassure you,' he said, and dropping the case onto its side, he jumped on it three times, on each occasion with an accompanying 'Ha!' The driver looked at him in amazement.

'Yeah, alright, mate. I'll take it,' he said.

Frank then produced a ten-pound note. 'Is this enough?' he asked.

The driver's face lit up like a lantern. He was looking at a sizeable tip there. 'Yeah, great, mate. Cheers!'

Frank nodded again. 'Just make sure somebody at reception takes it from you and give them the card as well, please.'

'Yeah, alright, pal, no bother.'

Frank had never been as assertive, at least not when a woman had been involved. Just about everything had gone his way from the moment he had walked through the gate that morning. Even his uncomfortable exchange with Donald Rawlinson had been forgotten, and whereas Epic's blatant desertion had initially been regarded as impertinence, it was now being seen as the most judicious thing the Canadian had ever done – the consequence of destiny, of course. As Frank walked back into the conference centre, only one thing remained for him to do. This was to find Epic and gleefully explain the position to him. Frank was half expecting to discover that Epic too had also made alternative nighttime arrangements by this time. He had, after all, abandoned Frank just for that purpose. But when Frank finally found him, inevitably at one of the bars, he was, to Frank's great delight, unaccompanied. Frank knew that this was where he would get back at the boy for all the little joshings he had received from him down at the Inn. Custard pies, one after another. Good natured, of course. Epic could be nothing other. But the sheer volume would have tested the patience of Job. It had certainly tested the patience of Frank. Here was now an excellent opportunity for a long overdue volte-face. Frank was serving with advantage in his favour for once.

'Hello,' Frank said to him cheerfully. 'How has your mingling been going?'

'Hey, Frankie! This ain't exactly Babesville, man!' Epic complained. 'Just lots of dorky types in dorky clothes waving diaries at each other. Most uncool. I've given up the chase and stayed right here. What you drinking?'

'Well, I think the whole day's gone swimmingly,' Frank countered, barely able to contain his delight.

'Yeah, well I figure that this scene's gonna get more *swimmingly* when we quit this joint and hit the city. So let's get going.' He started to drink up.

Frank's smile widened. 'Oh, I'm sorry you haven't enjoyed yourself,' he said. 'I've had a marvellous time. And productive too.'

Epic scowled at him. 'Time to split,' he then said, slapping his glass down on the bar and signalling to the barman his thanks and his adieu.

'This is true,' Frank agreed. 'But I need to inform you of a change of arrangements first…'

Frank then outlined what had happened, trying to sound as matter of fact as possible, and concluding with reminding Epic that this meant that he would have to make his way alone, not just to the hotel, but also back to Pendlesham the following morning. Naturally the night on the piss, which they had planned together for that night, and to which Frank had actually been fervently looking forward, had been knocked on the head.

'Jesus, shit, Frankie. You can't *do* this to me!' Epic wailed, when he realised that this wasn't a joke.

'I'd be the first to admit that this is a discourtesy to you,' Frank said. 'But having said that, it is merely a reciprocation of your own actions towards me earlier.'

'What makes you say that?' howled Epic, missing the point entirely, or perhaps just choosing to ignore it. 'Shit, man. This is *so* uncool!'

'I'll make it up to you,' Frank promised him.

Epic suddenly smiled. 'Okay, okay, Frankie, but just have one beer with me first. Okay? *One* beer and then go and get your green lady. One beer and it's on me, pal. It's on me. Hey, bartender!'

Frank had no leeway at all to escape this. The time it took for his beer to arrive was simply too brief a period for him - nowhere near enough - to come up with a good enough reason to decline. Three-quarters of the way down his pint was enough to send his euphoria, already high enough, sky-rocketing into the stratosphere.

'I really think that I've struck gold this time, my boy. Or should I say struck *green*!' he gushed, as he handed Epic a fresh pint of a new round moments later. 'So what if I might have exaggerated a tad with regards the company's worth? Angela's scarcely going to examine the books, is she, hum? And, in any case, it's not going to be long before we actually *are* a million pound concern. Am I right?'

'Hell yes, Frankie!'

'Yes, and Angela's no gold digger, boy! She's a classy lady. A classy lady, who's been lumbered with an unfaithful pig of a husband. She simply wants somebody to be good to her. To look after her. She's not interested in my money...'

'Hell no, Frankie!'

Less than ten minutes after this, Frank took two giant gulps out of his third plastic pint glass and released an exaggeratedly satisfied out-take of breath. 'This is the one! She's going to be the one, my lad! I've struck gold this time. Or, should I say, struck *green*...'

For Frank, of course, the dream was already over. He was half-cut, beginning to slur and would not be going anywhere now unless it was to another bar. He might well be prattling on about Angela all night, but he was never going to do anything as productive as keep his appointment with her. Wasn't she going to call him anyway after he got back to Pendlesham?

Epic, naturally, did nothing at all to dissuade Frank from continuing to imbibe and the two chronic drunks ended up going on their mega beano after all, hitting nine of the city's drinking establishments and finishing up in a curry house in one of Birmingham's lesser quarters. Both of them got shot to absolute fuck. When it was time to kiss goodnight at half-past midnight, Epic walked off with the small sports bag he had carried with him all night in search of a cab. He had been walking for about a hundred yards when he sensed someone at his shoulder. He swung round and it was Frank.

'Shit, Frankie! You nearly scared the crap out of me! What ya doing, man? It's time to go home, baby!'

Frank started to blink heavily through the haze, his brain threshing away in a whirlpool of alcohol, desperately trying to catch his breath. Finally, he took a gasp of air.

'Am I supposed to be somewhere?' was the consequent ridiculous question.

Epic looked at him. 'Sure! Sure you are, Frankie! You're going to your high class joint with your high class broad. Don't you remember, Frankie? You booked yourself out of our fleapit and left me right there. Nice guy!'

Frank shook his head. 'I don't know… I don't know where I'm going' he stammered.

'You called it "The International" or some shit,' Epic reminded him helpfully.

Frank's jaw dropped. 'Oh, God! Oh no' he gasped. 'Oh, God!'

'Wasn't that the name of it?' enquired Epic innocently.

'Oh, my God! Please, *no!*' Frank spluttered.

'Well you're sure as hell ain't having *my* room, pal!' rubbed in Epic cruelly. '*You* made this scene!'

A minicab with a dim red light on top of it came rolling up to them at a snail's pace in anticipation of being hailed, which of course it was. Epic spoke to the driver: 'Okay. We're gonna take this guy to the International Hotel here in Birmingham. Then I need to get across town to someplace else.'

The driver looked up at Frank, who was urgently whispering sweet nothings to himself, and then back at Epic, who gave him a semi-pleading shrug. The driver nodded and gestured them both to get in. By the time they arrived at the Birmingham International Hotel, Frank was no longer conscious. Epic shook him and slapped his face and got a lot of snorting and grunting as a response. Satisfied with this, he then jumped out of the cab.

'Wait there, driver,' he said, jumping out. 'Don't go away now!'

'I'm not going anywhere until you've paid, mate,' the taxi driver said.

'Right. Good.'

Epic attempted to pull Frank out of his seat, but Frank was out cold again. The driver, realising that the delay was not going to do anyone any good, suddenly appeared and the two men managed to extricate Frank from the cab and drag him into the lobby.

'This here is Mr Eddowes,' Epic told the receptionist. 'He has a reservation with you guys. He is sorry that he is a little late. Mr Eddowes apologises.'

'Ah, Mr Eddowes! We didn't think that we were going to see you, sir,' the receptionist smiled. 'I take it that you will not now be requiring dinner?'

'Mr Eddowes just needs to go to his room at this time,' Epic replied. 'Can we get the bellboy to go with Mr Eddowes in the elevator? Mr Eddowes has had a big day.'

The receptionist nodded an acknowledgement at Epic for his diplomacy and then picked up the phone. 'Oh, there was one message, sir,' he said, courteously continuing to address Frank, even though he knew he might just as well have been talking to the flower arrangement on the desk. 'I have it here.' He then turned back to Epic. 'Perhaps you would care to sign Mr Eddows in, sir.'

'Sure I will. No problem. Just make sure that your guy leaves the message by the side of Frankie's bed, please.' Epic stipulated, dropping the formalities for the first time.

He quickly scrawled Frank's details in the ledger and then nodded his own thanks to the receptionist before walking across to join the taxi driver at the door.

'Okay, man, I guess it's my turn now.' And with that, they were gone.

The hotel porter, summoned to tend to Frank, appeared, and not anticipating a tip, guided the piss-head to the lift and ultimately to his room. By this time, Frank was a little more with it and was able to undress himself and then, from out of nowhere, phone down to the lobby to arrange an alarm call for eight o'clock. The tipless bellboy had, as requested, placed the envelope containing the message on the beside table along with the key. The room was fabulous, but for all Frank knew it could have been a Salvation Army hostel for all the difference it was going to make to him. He went out like a light. His usual dreamless, drunken oblivion.

Frank Eddowes, great recoverer, woke up with a jolt at five thirty-six. Instantaneously he knew what he had done - or rather, hadn't done. Paradoxically, oblivion had refreshed his memory. He slapped on the bedside lamp and noticed immediately a small envelope with his name and a number written on it - the same number as on a crimson flat piece of plastic resting nearby. His room key.

The message was handwritten on a cream embossed leaf of hotel paper:

'*Perhaps it was always going to be a mistake after all. Thank you for being so nice to me.*'

And that was it. No signature. No need for one.

Frank turned the light off and lay back. He felt like crying, but instead began slowly and silently to pull himself off, imagining what almost certainly would have happened had he kept the appointment as fuel. His frustration was absolute. He had come undone by drink again, but this time the penalty had been incalculably severe. He had managed to set himself up with a lovely desirable woman in what had been the social performance of his sad little life, but when the crunch came, he had abandoned her without a second thought because pissing it up with Epic was always going to be more attractive.

In his misery, Frank felt that it was unlikely that he would be presented with a chance quite like this again and that the only way he was going to survive this devastation would be to forget Angela as soon as possible. He resolved that he would fortify each future intensified bout of self-abuse exclusively with fantasies of Tessa, with whom Frank remained obsessed. He may have recovered from being drunk, as he always did – better than any of the Inn Crowd, in fact - but recovering from Angela was going to be monumentally difficult. Tessa, he felt, would be the only acceptable nurse-maid, even though she remained only in his thoughts and not in his bed; the problem of remedying this ancient condition appearing just as insur-mountable as it had always been.

Chapter 36

Angela

FRANK SETTLED HIS considerable account with the Birmingham International Hotel and then went and got the London train. Across town he went by Underground to Victoria station and from there he boarded the southbound service to Pendlesham. He sat practically motionless on each stage of the journey and time flew for him. He got back at just after ten minutes past three that afternoon and it was only as he handed his ticket over to the inspector at the barrier did he get around to deciding where he would go now. Would it be straight home, on to the Emporium, or straight into the Inn? The fact he had the luggage with him (the suitcase seemingly heavier than ever) ruled out an instant visit to the Inn in Frank's view, although it was to the Inn where Frank desperately wanted to go. Home, he felt, was out of the question, so in order to dump his luggage in advance of returning to the Inn, Frank climbed into a cab and set off for the Emporium where he was met by Thoad.

'Where's Epic?' Frank demanded. 'Over at the Inn, I suppose?'

Thoad looked confused. 'Not with you?' he asked pointlessly. 'We all assumed you were coming back together. I haven't seen him since he got back. That's if he *is* back. He must be over at the old Inn, as you say.'

Frank indicated his cases. 'Can you get someone to take these back to my house, please? I'll call Mother to let her know to expect them. I've got some paperwork to finish and then I'm going to pop over to the Inn to see if I can find that idiot boy. I'll probably see you in there, won't I?'

'Yes. Probably.'

'Where are the others?'

'Well, Stephen and Amanda are in Paris, as you know, and Tess and

Noddoes are out the back.'

'Good. Had any bookings?'

'Loads. People have been tumbling off the old Point in their droves.'

'Well that's something positive, at least,' muttered Frank to himself.

'How did the conference go?' asked Thoad.

'I think I'll go straight over to the Inn, actually' Frank told him. 'I'll call Mother from there. Would you see to my luggage, please?'

'I'll take it in about half an hour. That will give you a chance to call your mother first,' Thoad suggested.

'That's a thought,' Frank nodded. 'Thank you.'

Within fifteen minutes, Frank was atop a certain stool and Epic was in the Inn too, just as Thoad had supposed. He was busying himself trying to charm himself into a new girl's knickers in a dark corner of the bar. His bullshit trans-Atlantic brogue was unmistakable. Frank decided to have a beer before confronting him. He had suddenly got it into his head that Epic had conspired to keep him away from Angela, which if the truth be told, did not fall short of the way it was.

Epic, however, had made amends, as Frank discovered as soon as Tom served him: 'The boy tells me you've been playing hide the sausage, mate. You're a bit of a dark horse, Frank. No offence, mate, but we all thought that if anyone was going to get their rocks off up there, it would be the boy. But he tells me that you got off with a right piece of quality. Nice one!'

Frank suddenly looked horrified. 'What *exactly* did he say?'

'Was this a wind-up, then?'

'What *exactly* did he say?' Frank repeated.

'Well... it's probably a piss-take,' Tom confessed.

'No, no... no, it isn't,' Frank assured him. 'Epic is right. I... I met someone.'

'You *met* someone?'

'I...'

'Did you poke it?'

'Oh God! Why is that always so important?'

Tom smiled broadly. 'Well, mate, it was obviously important to you from what I've picked up, you old devil. Apparently you had this sort in the sack before she could say "I've got a headache". That's what the boy's been putting about. What would your old dear say? She probably thinks you've never had a bonk in your life. Tell me it wasn't a wind-up. I think it's great.'

Frank was in no situation other than to "confirm" everything. It was quite clear that Epic had been telling everyone that he, Frank, had succeeded in bedding Angela. Frank even thought that he knew the reason for this. It was in actual fact a payback for causing Frank to lose her when he hoodwinked him into a session Frank most certainly did not want. Epic had indeed made mischief, but this of course was only part of the story and Frank would not have been inhabiting the real world had he claimed that none of it had been his own fault. The fact was he had nobody to blame but himself, as he could have left for the Birmingham International Hotel at any time and his failure not to do so was his own spectacular error. Epic's part had been significant but ultimately peripheral.

Even though this was all true, Frank had been spot on about why Epic had introduced the flattering but totally false rumours about him. This was confirmed when he finally got to speak with Epic alone.

'It would appear that I'm Don Juan all of a sudden,' he began, not smiling.

'Hey, it was the least I could do, Frankie,' shrugged Epic. 'Say, I'm real sorry you got to miss your date with your lady. I guess I was sore that I didn't score myself and wanted company to go piss it up so badly and I guess I led you astray. Man, I'm nothing but a drunken bum!'

Frank shook his head sadly but still couldn't suppress the slightest of smiles. 'You're no more wretched than me,' he confessed. 'We're both as bad as each other. Both drunks. Angela would have found out about my drinking sooner or later and she would have never put up with it in a month of Sundays, especially after what had happened with her husband. What *was* I thinking? I was bloody deluding myself. I'm a fool.'

'Sure you're not,' Epic comforted him. 'And not so loud, Frankie. I don't want Tommy hearing us. He's been telling all the kids how excellent you are. Nothing but respect from here on in!'

'I've decided to declare myself to Tessa,' Frank said.

'Say what, now?'

'You know. Tell her how I feel about her.'

'Say, that's great!'

'I was mortified about losing Angela. I might as well get Tessa's rejection over and done with while I'm still miserable. That way I can recover from both blows at the same time.'

'You don't know for sure that she's going to turn you down, Frankie,' Epic suggested. 'Sheba's far more on your wavelength than your green granny. It ain't as if she's ever complained about your drinking, that's for damn sure.'

'No, I don't suppose she will,' acknowledged Frank, smiling for the first time.

'And you've always been kinda cute on her, Frankie.'

'I'm in love with her.'

'Okay, okay. So here's the punchline, Frankie. Sheba was in this bar on her lunch hour. She knows all about your Warren Beatty act up in Birmingham… She started purring, man!'

'Oh my giddy aunt!'

'Hey, but Frankie, that's cool. Because *now* she figures that you're a wild man. She just purred and purred, Frankie. You ain't ever had a better chance of moving in. You gotta believe me!'

'Oh God! Do you really think so?' panted Frank.

Why, certainly!' Epic assured him. 'It's a different ball game now, bud. That cat was purring so sexily, I figure that she might just come and get you, Frankie. But don't quote me though.'

'Oh God!'

Epic looked at him. 'You don't want that, Frankie? You don't like that?'

'Well of *course* I bloody want that!' dribbled Frank, his dick throbbing away quite manically already. 'Epic, you're not winding me up again, are you? I'd never bloody forgive you!'

Epic shook his head deliberately. 'Frankie, let me tell you this, at least. Now, I've personally gotta tell you that you're way off base if you figure you can move in on Tessa. Absolutely no offence but it's gonna take a major dude to ride off into the sunset with *that* babe, know what I'm saying? But, hey, *Sheba*, you know? Well, she's a different saucer of cream! She's just purring to be put out for the night… By *you*, Frankie!'

'Oh, really, I've never heard such nonsense!' gasped Frank, thrusting his arm away in an obvious sign of annoyance and dissent.

'Hey, Frankie, don't shoot the messenger, okay?'

Frank turned away. 'You're talking absolute tosh!' he hissed. 'Everything's always a joke to you. You're never off duty, are you? Leave me alone!'

Epic was genuinely hurt by this, although he disguised it well. 'Frankie, please don't get mad at me. This ain't no wind up, I swear. I'm not kidding. I'm just telling you what went down with the cat-girl. It definitely ain't no wind up, Frankie. I wouldn't do that to you, man. Not over Sheba. You gotta believe me!'

Frank shook his head and then looked to the floor.

'You gotta believe me, Frankie!' Epic repeated.

'Alright,' Frank conceded eventually. 'I don't really suppose you would lie so speciously about Tessa, knowing how I feel about her.' He turned back to face Epic.

'Thank you, Frankie.'

'I suppose even if I can only interest Tessa when she's in her other state, so to speak, this would be better than no Tessa at all!'

'Sure, Frankie. Now you've got it!' agreed Epic. 'Half of heaven is better than nothing. Am I right?'

Frank picked up his glass again. 'Half of Tessa would be better than most things,' he proffered. 'But *all* of Tessa would be better than everything,' he said. 'Even heaven.'

Chapter 37

Frank Ifield

BUSINESS WAS STILL brisk as young people continued to tumble off Rocky Point like lemmings, most in search of the rock and roll funeral culture which had taken such a grip on the imagination of everyone and which had shown no signs yet of giving way to the next fad. Frank's seemingly outrageous and unsupportable boast to Angela about the financial worth of his company was no longer the gross exaggeration it had been when he had delivered it.

But life (or destiny) has a way of kicking certain people in the bollocks just as everything seems all set, and this happened to Frank a matter of hours after Sheba, stoned to fuck, had told him directly in the Inn that unless he submitted to her immediately, she would 'as ordered by the Cat Mistress, claw all (his) reproductive parts savagely until they are rendered forever useless to you and any future lovers.' Frank pondered this for a moment and considered whether this 'punishment' might in fact be worth the risk and then decided that submission would probably be the best option. It was thus that following the conclusion of the drinking session, he woke up to a suitably repulsed Tessa, who in the sweetest possible way under the circumstances, banished Frank summarily from her bed and begged him to swear that he would never mention to anyone that she had given him a shag. Frank naturally agreed and promptly left her lair without the traditional benefit of breakfast to await for Tessa to become Sheba again. The kick in the bollocks was that he had quite literally not remembered a fucking thing. There was further grief when the understandably confused and mortified Frank returned to his mother. Arriving home that morning, he let himself in, only to find his mother sitting down on the sofa sobbing uncontrollably with a young policewoman in attendance.

'Oh, Frank!' blubbered his mum. 'There's been some tragic news! Thank goodness you're here! Where have you *been* all night? Something… something terrible has happened!…' She was then overcome by sobbing again.

Frank swiftly moved in and sat down next to her: 'What is it, Mother? What is it?'

His mother was trembling and she gripped Frank's wrist and held it in a sustained pinch, which was painful enough to Frank and heightened even more, Frank surmised, the gravity of what must have happened.

'It's my babies!' she howled. 'The *babies*!… Both… Both dead!'

'*What?*'

'They've been *killed*!' she wailed. '*Killed!*'

'*Killed?* The cats?' enquired Frank, amazed but not apparently distraught.

'The *babies!*' corrected a spluttering Mrs Eddowes, pinching Frank even harder. 'They're *dead*! *Killed*!'

Frank shook his head in confusion: 'Well I'm blowed!'

'*Killed*!'

'Well, what the devil happened?'

His mother was causing such a carry on now and she sounded as though she was yodeling – loudly and badly.

The young WPC, not before time, picked up the story: 'A local man, whose identity we've yet to release, was found dead in a car in a locked garage,' she told Frank gravely. 'We do not at this moment consider that the circumstances are suspicious.'

'He poisoned himself with car fumes, I suppose?' Frank enquired.

'First reports do point towards suicide being the most likely answer,' the officer admitted, 'but I am in no position to confirm this, other than to say that the deceased was found dead in his vehicle and that a hosepipe was linked from the exhaust through the window to the front seat.'

'Yes, well that's suicide, isn't it?' Frank nodded. 'Klaus won't be spending too much time mulling over this one, I don't expect.'

The girl looked at him strangely: 'I'm sorry, sir?'

'Oh my word! The cats were in there, weren't they?' he then said suddenly.

'My *babies*!' yodelled his mother, now seriously rivaling Frank Ifield.

The officer nodded: 'I'm afraid that the bodies of a male and a female cat were recovered at the scene,' she confirmed. 'They were both wearing identity pendants, confirming their names and the address of their owner. I'm extremely sorry. Hansel and Gretel must have already been in the garage before the incident occurred and were overcome. It's a tragedy, but death would have been utterly painless, if that's any comfort to you.'

'Who the devil was this chap, anyway?' Frank demanded.

The WPC shook her head. Frank then snapped his fingers: 'Wait a minute! I *know* who it was! It's bloody Evans again, isn't it? I bet it's that old Welsh queer, Harry Evans! He was always a lonely, gloomy old so and so! And now he's assassinated our cats! Oh, the selfish old bender!'

'We haven't released the name yet, Mr Eddowes,' the officer reminded him.

'Thornhill Road!' Frank growled. 'I don't recall the number, but I know where his house is. Hansel and Gretel were often over there. Evans used to give them titbits. I bet that's where the house is, isn't it? Thornhill Road?'

The officer stood up, put her hat back on and walked to the door: 'The garage is that of a house in Thornhill Road,' she admitted.

'*Evans*!' hissed Frank to himself.

'We took Hansel and Gretel to the veterinary surgeons in Kings Avenue,' she said. 'You can't believe how sorry I am about this. I'm a cat lover myself.'

'Harry Evans hasn't heard the last of this. Not by a long chalk!' Frank warned, opening the door. 'He'll pay dearly for this. He'll soon atone for this most savage slaughter of innocents. Oh yes!'

The girl officer smiled meekly and left. She was genuinely sorry about the dead cats, but as she walked towards her car and away from a household featuring a man promising appraisals against a suicide victim and a woman who would clearly triumph in a Howlin' Wolf impersonation contest, she couldn't help thinking that Hansel and Gretel's visit to chez Harry Evans had not worked out that badly for them after all.

Meanwhile, Frank had suddenly found himself revising the principal doctrine of Freddo's for Harry's specific benefit. For the first time in his remarkable new career, Frank had viewed a corpse as something other than a doughnut as he vowed retribution against the perceived slayer of the family cats. As distinct from "burning the shell and getting it out of there", with Harry Evans it was to be anything other.

It was to be a turning point in the history of the Emporium.

Chapter 38

Dead Cats

FRANK TOOK STEPHEN with him and went round to the vets mid morning of the next day to pick up the bodies of Hansel and Gretel. The cats both looked peaceful enough and Frank delivered them straight to Tessa, who ironically, and inappropriately on this occasion, was nowhere near her cat state and therefore greeted her latest clients with a somewhat indifferent and irreverent air.

'I don't want too much doing to them,' Frank told her. 'That would upset Mother too much. Just tidy them up a bit. Give their fur a clip, alright?'

'Aren't we going to give them a proper Freddo funeral, then?' Tessa asked, rustling the fur on the top of Hansel's head.

'But naturally!' Frank said, sounding surprised at the question. 'And I'd like you, Tessa, to orchestrate it, please. Who better with your catty background?'

'They're very cute,' Tessa admitted, now sliding her fingers through the length of Gretel's tail. But they're not really *my* kind of cats. They're just regular house cats, aren't they? They're not even pedigree. They're hardly cats of doom, are they?'

Frank poked Gretel firmly with his forefinger: 'By God, girl, they're *dead* aren't they? How much more "doom" do you want in cats?'

Tessa giggled: 'I know! But I don't think that they're terribly *imperial*, though, are they?'

Frank drew an exaggeratedly heavy breath and shook his head: 'Look, Tessa. These animals have been executed by a drunken old Welsh homosexual. Now, if you can't empathize with that, my dear, I rather fancy that your own "imperial" credentials might be reasonably brought into question.

What do you think?'

'Oh, gosh! I think you're telling me off!' she said.

Frank disagreed: 'I just want things to be right for Mother,' he assured her. 'She worshipped those creatures. They were her "babies". She would have breast-fed them had she been able to.'

'Isn't that sweet?' smiled Tessa.

'They may not be imperial to you, or indeed to me, but I'm afraid that these dead cats must be anything and everything Mother wants them to be. And it falls to you, Tessa, to make sure that they are.'

'I think that's lovely,' sighed Tessa. 'You just leave them with me.' And without further ado, she seized Gretel by the tail, swung her around and slapped her onto the slab. She then started to chop away at the animal carcass piston-like with the outside of both hands until she had a flat even mass across the marble surface with which to work.

Frank looked on lovingly.

'I hope I get a chance to get hold of the man who killed them,' Tessa then said, now reaching for her oils.

Frank's benign expression turned dramatically on a sixpence as once again he was reminded of the murderous Harry Evans: 'My dear girl, I give you my solemn word here and now that you will. You most *definitely* will!'

Tessa smiled, worked some more oil into Gretel's fur and then flipped her over and started chopping again. 'I'm going to make him look *so* sorry,' she promised.

Frank allowed a smile to redevelop as he surveyed the caring scene. He was then struck with another thought. Whilst he had initially considered it unthinkable, if only for his mother's sake, to attempt to arrange a double-header featuring the cats and Evans with Hansel and Gretel exacting full revenge for what Harry had done to them, Frank now felt that it would not only be acceptable, but perhaps a fitting tribute to Hansel and Gretel, and one which his mother would recognize as just that, if the late mogs were to be given the full Freddo treatment as decreed by Imperial Mother Sheba. The ceremony might well prove to be a tad too gothic for his mother's taste, but this could easily be explained away by telling her that in death Hansel and Gretel had deservedly attained a higher plain and that this needed to be demonstrated, especially to her, the person who had been the closest to them during their lives as housecats *before* they became imperial. In any case, as soon as Frank had his hands on Evans, there was nothing to stop the cats from taking a full and appropriate part in Harry's torching, an event which would have to precede their own ceremony and one which would also have to go ahead immediately behind closed doors without Danny and Sally, since Harry's body had to be 'acquired' first.

The more Frank considered this regime, the more he became convinced that he could get away with it. Naturally he was not interested in paying tribute to the memories of his mother's cats (he had never got on with either of them and they in turn had hated him for the drunk that he was), nor was he (and this was unusual) thinking about the feelings of his mother. The only two things on his mind were to have some harmless fun with Harry Evans, who had been a notoriously slimy creep, who 'liked' young boys and, much more importantly, something else which had suddenly occurred to him, to persuade Tessa that in order for her to do proper justice to Hansel and Gretel, she would have to become Sheba again. Sheba's last appearance, of course had ended up with Frank waking up next to her in her own kitty basket. The evil catch to this still remained that Frank had remembered nothing about the night itself.

'I think before you get started properly on Gretel, we can both get some lunch,' Frank said. 'Let's pop over to the Inn.'

Tessa stopped kneading away and looked at Frank doubtfully: 'That would be groovy, but I'd probably end up eating nothing and getting stoned.'

'I can't really recommend that,' Frank remarked, most untruthfully, 'but it might provide some inspiration to your art, if you see what I mean.'

Tessa looked down at Gretel: 'If you are really talking about the full imperial treatment, I am going to have to have a completely free hand to alter them to Mother Sheba's own required specifications. I shall change them beyond recognition and I will change their names.'

Frank nodded: 'I realise now that what these drab little cats need is a special touch. Indeed an exotic one. An *imperial* touch.'

Tessa looked straight at him: 'Mother Sheba *is* imperial,' she confirmed. 'But Mother Sheba is also about doom. She is not to be messed with. Nor can she be summoned like a genie from a bottle. She will punish severely anyone who tries to exploit her. That ought to be completely understood.'

This warning couldn't have been any clearer to Frank, who was particularly brought to attention by the bit about genies coming out of bottles. 'Perhaps you ought to stop back here and carry on,' he conceded. 'I'll arrange sandwiches.'

Tessa recognised her little victory and smiled again. She then reached for a sheet and gently covered Gretel before doing the same with the as yet untreated Hansel. 'It's cool enough in here,' she said, as she began to scrub up. 'They'll be fine for a couple of hours.'

Frank looked confused. 'You don't want sandwiches then?'

Tessa's face blossomed into the renowned girlish smile. 'If you want to go to the sandwich bar, I'll see you back here later,' she said, walking past him. 'I'm going to grab *my* bite at the Inn.'

Chapter 39

Harry Evans

THE MOST IMMEDIATE problem now facing Frank was the thorny conundrum set by Harry Evans. The Welshman's body had been swiftly claimed by the Old Firm pending confirmation from Klaus Butsch of suicide, which was quite rightly passed as a formality.

'This crazy man. He turned on the gas pipe himself!' Herr Butsch had summed up. 'He closes the door of his garage, turns on engine of car and *Hissssss*! until he passes away. It is said that this man likes not the ladies. Only guys. I think so, ja. No doubt that this killink is homemade.'

The Swiss milkmaids on either side of the dais wiggled appetizingly as the cowbell rang out signaling, not only the rubber-stamping of Klaus' suicide verdict, but also the desperate race now facing Freddo's to apprehend Harry's corpse before the Old Firm could take any action with it.

'I have to make this as clear as I possibly can that we will not benefit financially from this torching,' Frank briefed his staff. 'It is simply an act of revenge. And I also have to say that the fact that it will mean stealing business away from the Old Firm is entirely coincidental, and indeed irrelevant. Our quarrel, or should I say *my* quarrel is not for once with Mr Snape. It has everything to do with Harry Evans, the Welsh gay. That monster slew my mother's babies and must now be brought to book. We shall therefore enter the viewing room at the Old Firm under the cover of lonely darkness and invite Harry to come with us. Tonight! After teaching him the error of his ways, subjecting him to unrivalled humiliation, we shall then dispose of the carcass immediately. Tessa has assured me that she will do her utmost to make this hateful murderer look nothing short of ludicrous. Evans can expect no mercy and shall receive none. He must, and will pay dearly. Oh yes!'

Everyone looked at each other as they suddenly saw the entire ethos of Freddo's disintegrate before them.

Epic was the first to point this out: 'I guess you don't consider this guy Evans is a doughnut, Frankie. Am I right?'

'Evans *is* Evans!' hissed Frank in confirmation.

'In that case, my dear fellow,' slipped in Noddoes, 'I would suggest that any treatment of subsequent clients under the policy which you for this occasion have disavowed would be disingenuous. We must be free to concede that the doughnut policy has been discontinued.'

'I guess what Hamlet means is that if the Evans guy ain't no doughnut, then there ain't no more doughnuts!' translated Epic.

'It's taken a lot of thought,' nodded Frank wistfully. 'I had always thought that my belief in the doughnut theory was unshakeable, that when one dies, one becomes a lifeless lump, as far removed from that person as a doughnut. It has taken the unspeakable evil of Harry Evans to show me that a corpse is still, if not a person, at least something we can, and indeed must use as the ultimate testament to that person. We've been such fools! This has been jumping out at us from day one, ever since Terry Cutler. None of the families of our clients would possibly have regarded their loved-ones as doughnuts! Why the devil have we? The mask slipped farther with Reg Doorman. From now on we shall be treating our carcasses like live people. Who are we to discriminate? And our trial run will be with Harry Evans. EVANS!'

'This is going to open up all sorts of new prospects,' suggested Stephen.

'Only as far as we ourselves are concerned,' Frank said. 'I honestly believe that we have only just caught up with the mood of our customers. I don't really think we need change anything except our own attitude.'

'I think things will never be the same again,' Stephen predicted. 'Anything can happen now.'

'I want to get back to Evans,' Frank informed them. 'It's time we discussed how we're going to capture him.'

'Most excellent!' Epic enthused. 'Give us the low down, Frankie. Are we going in through the window? Down through the roof like *Mission Impossible*? What?'

'Nothing as dramatic,' Frank said. 'I still hold a copy key to the front door of the old place. I'm sure old Snape doesn't know that I still have it, and even if he did know, I strongly doubt, knowing his tendency towards, shall we say, frugality, that he would have gone to the expense of changing the locks. No, we'll simply open the door, walk in, scoop up Evans and stroll out.'

'Bad move, man,' warned Epic. 'If we're gonna lift the stiff, we're gonna have to make this look like a heist. If we just walk in without making it look like a break-in, the cops are just gonna figure that they're looking for a guy with a key. And that's you, Frankie.'

Frank allayed all fears. 'No, if we force our way in, then everybody will know for certain that the corpse has been snatched. Suspicion will fall on us immediately, especially after the somewhat injudicious remarks I made to the police on first learning of Evans' butchery. But if we just go in and out again using the key that nobody knows I have, the smart money, if I know old Snape, will be on him not reporting the matter at all. Just think! If word got out that somebody can just waltz in and out of his premises with impunity, to say nothing of with one of his clients, Mr Snape's reputation, something which I must tell you means everything to him, would be damaged, perhaps irrevocably. No, I believe that Arthur Snape, who's a shrewd old bugger, if truth be told, will take stock of the fact that he almost certainly holds a fee from whomever is paying. He simply then only needs to craftily deny a viewing to any of Harry's friends or family, the few who probably exist and would wish to clock him, on the grounds that the corpse has gone bad, or some technical nonsense like that and then go ahead with an empty casket because the real corpse of Harry Evans will be with us, as old Snape would have guessed. We keep Harry and old Snape keeps his fee and his dignity, which is all. It's superb!'

Noddoes, meanwhile, who had been present, but apparently in body only, suddenly jolted and then sprang to his feet. 'Harry Evans? *Harry*

Evans? I think I know this man! I worked with the fop! *Ghastly!* The gossip was that he was a fairy!'

'I thought *all* you actor guys were faggots!' stated Epic. '*You* ain't exactly Schwarzenegger for a start, bud!'

'Harry Evans *acted?*' Frank asked, amazed. 'I didn't know that! I knew that he was a florist. I had no idea that he dabbled in the arts too!'

'Oh, he was *ghastly!*' Noddoes repeated. 'I did one season with him in Brighton. He came directly from rep in Swansea or somewhere beastly. His diction was simply *terrible.* That horrible, common Welsh accent! *Ghastly!*'

'Well, that's Evans to a T, certainly' nodded Frank.

'He finished each and every sentence with "my flower", no matter to whom he was talking,' Noddoes added. 'I've never *heard* such pretentious nonsense. Oh my!'

Muffled laughter from everyone else at this last comment.

From out of nowhere Noddoes then exploded into a soliloquy in a terrifying brogue quarried from the depths of the South Wales valleys, but with definite effeminate undertones and punctuating every fifth word with 'my flower'; and everybody, none of whom apart from Frank knowing Harry Evans from Gareth Edwards, dissolved into hoots of delirium, all except Frank himself, whose mouth shot open in absolute astonishment and remained open almost perfectly rounded like the entrance to a tunnel. 'Noddoes... That's *brilliant!*' he then stammered. 'It's him! It's *him!...*'

Noddoes was nothing short of ecstatic at the ovation he had been given, but only Frank could have known how well deserved it was. As if to maintain momentum, Noddoes then pulled off an even more impressive stunt. Harking back to what he ludicrously considered to be his salad days when he made his meager living as a voice-throwing artist as a warm-up act for more distinguished players, he began his Harry Evans repertoire again, only this time the dialogue appeared to spring forth from the mouth of Stephen Mauve, who was seated at the other end of the room. Everybody stared at Stephen and then back up at Noddoes. Back and forth, back and forth, like spectators at a tennis match.

'Say, how the hell did you do that?' Epic demanded, who like everybody else was far too flabbergasted to pay proper tribute to Noddoes with either laughter or applause.

'My goodness, that's truly amazing!' spluttered Frank, who in that second realised that Harry's funeral was now bound for absolute glory, an occasion to eclipse entirely any of the triumphs that had gone before. This giant leap forward, conceived as a result of what Noddoes had just done, was to be the formulation of the purest type of self-participating funerals, of which that of Harry Evans was to be the first. If this pioneering effort, which was to be held in camera, went well (and there was no reason to suppose that it wouldn't), a brand new package could then be offered to an increasingly ravenous clientele. In this fleeting moment, Frank could see potential customers being interviewed by perhaps himself and/or Stephen on videotape, which would then be viewed by Noddoes so that voice and verbal mannerisms could be studied and learned. The customer, if accepted, would then flutter off Rocky Point, have his remains collected by Salty Sid before the coastguard could get their grubbies on it, patched up by Tessa/Sheba and then handed over to Danny and Barefoot Sally for the torching, during which the requested music (or *some* of the requested music plus a few extras from Freddo's) would be played to accompany a narration and performance of dance from the client himself, courtesy of Noddoes. It might even be arranged for the corpse to read his own lesson in certain circumstances, as long as this was cleared with the Reverend Hare. This, in fact, did have a precedent. In Roman funeral processions, a 'chief buffoon or jester' was employed to imitate the gait, gestures and speech of the deceased. This performer was known as an 'archimime' and Noddoes would now be resurrecting this most peculiar of entertainments. Self-participating funerals in their purest form! Self-participating funerals! The requirement to capture the guinea pig, which was Harry Evans, had suddenly taken on a new and greatly intensified urgency.

Chapter 40

As-Salih And
Shagar Ad-Durr

HANSEL AND GRETEL looked stylish and magnificent and had been renamed by Sheba, As-Salih and Shagar Ad-Durr after a mid-thirteenth century Egyptian sultan couple. They had thus ceased to be brother and sister in life, and in death had become an imperial husband and wife. Both of them had a gleaming green stud in their head just above the nose and their drab tabby coats had been spectacularly treated with a sparkling multi-coloured stardust. On top of their heads were embedded an amuletic scarab, the ancient Egyptian beetle jewel designed to give protection and symbolizing the intimacy between the cat and the sun god. They were also both adorned by a silver breastplate, decorated with the protective eye of Horus, an Egyptian deity represented in art by the head of a hawk. The faces themselves were pale white and a deep ruby-red dye covered the length of their mouths, whilst gold crosses pierced both ears, their noses and the tips of their tails. It was indeed quite impossible to say which was which – two indistinguishable but glorious bookends. Frank took one look at them and pronounced the work as a masterpiece: 'What fabulous beasts!' he declared chokily.

'They are ready to avenge themselves on the man who destroyed them!' Sheba purred. 'No longer house pets. They are the servants of doom!'

As-Salih and Shagar Ad-Durr were not very furry to touch but amply compensated for this by smelling agreeably sweet. Sheba had unquestionably excelled herself this time. Harry Evans was for the high jump.

For it was Evans who had to be fetched now and Frank, Epic, Stephen and Noddoes set about their early hours' task with gusto. Amanda had wanted to go too and had become rather petulant when told that she could not. She was stoned, as usual, but even had she not been, Frank reasoned that she would only have been a hindrance had she been given a berth on the lifting operation. The appropriation of Harry's body was a serious business and it required a campaign which was both clean, and above all, swift. If everything went to plan, Frank felt that the snatch could quite easily be accomplished within three minutes. Eventually, when Amanda's procrastinations became too intense, Stephen solved the problem by telling her that she was needed 'to keep an eye on Sheba'.

'What the fuck for?' Amanda spluttered, stoned.

'She's stoned,' Stephen told her.

'So fucking what? I'm not her fucking mother!'

'We need to make sure that she *stays* stoned,' explained Stephen. 'We need you to make sure that she stays as Sheba. Okay?'

Amanda stared at him in an 'I'm just about to combust' sort of way. Stephen held his hand up: 'If she starts to sober up, Frank worries that she'll not do such a hot job on Harry Evans after we've grabbed him. This whole Evans business means a great deal to Frank, love. You know that. Come on, sweetheart, we're relying on you.'

Amanda nodded slowly as she attempted to digest this explanation, which in fact had an element of truth to it, if having very little to do with why Amanda had been banned from the raid. Frank, of course, had a second reason why he wanted Tessa to remain as Sheba…

'You're all bastards!' Amanda finally hissed and stormed off.

At three o'clock the next morning, four men all dressed in black woolens, trundled off in their battered pre-Great Train Robbery Ford Anglia Estate and pulled up outside the offices of the Old Firm. Frank got out, having told the others to stay inside, and walked quickly to the front door. He took the key from his pocket, slipped it into the lock, turned it and pushed the door open. He then turned quickly to the others and beckoned them forwards.

'Okay, chaps, this is it!' announced Noddoes, far too loudly, and Epic tumbled out of the back, leaving the doors open, whilst Stephen sprang fourth from the passenger seat like a Jack-In-The-Box. By the time the three men had entered the hall, Frank had already found his way down the corridor to the small viewing room as he began his hunt for Harry Evans. He had suspected that he could find his way around the old place in the dark and he certainly wasn't wrong. It struck him immediately how little had changed, particularly the aroma, which transported Frank in a trice back to his working days there in that most Dickensian of workplaces.

Two caskets were on display in the chilly viewing room and Frank whipped out a maglite torch just as Epic, the next to arrive, hit the main light switch and Frank started: 'Damn it! Kill that bloody light!' he responded in an angry whisper, reeling backwards.

'Shit, Frankie!' Epic barked. 'We can't see! Nobody knows this joint!' This of course was not true, as Noddoes by now was standing right behind him, a man who, like Frank, was also late of that parish.

Frank wasn't going to waste any time arguing: 'Come ahead! Come ahead!'

One of the coffins contained an old woman, the other a slightly younger man. Everybody gathered around this one and peered curiously in at the occupant.

'This the guy?' asked Epic.

'Oh yes indeed, my flower!' replied Harry from the Valleys.

Only Stephen chuckled.

Frank stared without emotion at the pale dead face of the gay Welshman: 'It's been a long time, Harry,' he pronounced, shielding his bitterness, but only just. He then addressed the others: 'Okay. Grab him!' and walked towards the door to make a path for them.

'Alright, Harry. You're coming with us, son!' hissed Stephen. 'Don't give us a hard time!'

Harry Evans was bundled out and hurled into the back of the Anglia. Frank, the last to leave, made sure that any light switches had been knocked out and then locked the door behind him. He hopped into the driver's seat and set off at an unremarkable speed back to headquarters. The raid had been successful. It had taken longer than the projected three minutes, but a lot less than ten. Harry Evans would not escape justice now. His comeuppance was now only a few hours away and there was nothing whatsoever that he could do to help himself. The only thing that faced him now was justice…

Sheba, once she had possession of Evans, worked feverishly throughout the remainder of the night to complete the job on him. She pronounced it finished at five minutes to eight and then stretched herself out on a mat and went to sleep. Frank was the first to arrive later that morning and was thus the first to see what was what. Indeed, Evans looked grotesque. It was clear straight away that Sheba had modeled the work on Edvard Munch's *Scream*. Harry's face, that of absolute terror, vacant but lamentable eyes, mouth shot open, long bony hands held to the side of an oval, skull-like bald head, and most noticeable of all, the paleness of his hopelessly bleak visage peering out of a shroud of the blackest of blacks. Instead of making Harry look '*so* sorry', as Sheba had promised, she had instead transformed him into a work of genius, for the genius could not be denied. The display was in fact so breathtaking, Frank believed that Sheba was now finished as an artist. For clearly she would never be able to create its equal again. Far from churning out something which would signal humiliation for the murderer of Frank's own fur and blood, Evans had instead been rewarded by being transformed into a work of art of unparalleled brilliance and haunting beauty. It was nothing short of the most sycophantic of tributes, albeit entirely inadvertent. Yet somehow, Frank understood and accepted this contradiction. He understood and accepted the consequent injustice, this unfair madness. And somehow, he applauded it. Somehow… somehow, he *loved* Harry Evans!

By noon, everyone else had clocked Harry also. They dealt with Harry's torching immediately over at the Bar and Grill, sans Danny and Barefoot Sally, of course, but with the indispensable aid of Keith Tate, both as sound

man and stoker of the furnace. Frank had previously had everything organ-
ised: Harry was to suffer. Nothing else was acceptable. The cats would have
their day in court…

No longer. Harry Evans had now been moved to another plain as a
direct result of the brilliance of Sheba's feline creativity. It was so fitting
that Harry was to be the first client to be tended to under the new Freddo
critique, the critique which no longer had room for The Exotics, the critique which disavowed entirely the doctrine of the doughnut – 'It ain't him.
Just burn the shell and let it be.' Only it *was* Harry Evans and now revenge
was not sought. Instead, all of a sudden, the emphasis was solely on respect
– from the cats too!

Harry's funeral was thereby a magnificent spectacle of puppetry and
Welsh song. He began by rising to his feet, flanked by As-Salih and Shagar
Ad-Durr, one on either side and blasting out *The Green, Green Grass Of
Home* in an accent sounding more like Richard Burton than Tom Jones.
Evans, of course, defiled the original lyric by slipping in 'my flower' as a
punctuation for just about every line.

The cats looked on admiringly and offered even more support when
Harry launched into a second Tom Jones number, *Delilah*, perhaps the sta-
pliest of diets for any crap pub crooner, and his adieu was a superb rendition
of the ultra-Welsh *We'll Keep A Welcome In The Hillsides* (My Flower) and as
Harry was tipped down the chute, As-Salih and Shagar Ad-Durr, who had
performed with daffodils tied to their tails throughout the ceremony, stared
desperately at the departing Evans in a passionate expression of love for an
imminent irrevocable loss, the prevention of which they could do nothing.

Harry himself manfully maintained his composure when he could quite
easily have cracked under the weight of the emotion which had enveloped
the proceedings entirely, creating a pressure cooker atmosphere, a boundless
extremity of feeling, the only remedy for which was tears, or else the danger
of an irreversible lapse into the oblivion that is insanity. The cats too kept
calm at this pivotal point, despite that impending harrowing loss. At the
conclusion of this secular ceremony, human and feline eyes were pumping

out enough water to baptise a newborn. The Evans funeral was nothing short of a catharsis, a gluttonous feast of undeniable magnificence. Harry had been hunted as a hated slaughterer of innocents and had emerged as a Welsh icon, no less than Dylon Thomas or Barry John, his departure now mourned as acute as that of the Son of Man himself.

Harry Evans had died. Nobody could really take it in. Harry was lost. Gone. The cats, those poor deprived creatures, could only hope now to join their idol in eternity via a manner equally as dignified; a wait which understandably was almost unbearable for these noble beasts, for whom the loss of Harry was an all-consuming torment.

This bleakness was extended to everybody else present, in whom emotion was completely drained, and morale was crawling around on its belly like a dying snake. But for the sake of the cats they had to act fast. In order to preclude the tragic drama of animal psychosis, they were obliged to move instantaneously.

Ten past one.

'I'm going to fetch Mother now,' Frank grizzled, finding it almost impossible to make himself heard over Amanda's wails. She was being cradled by a trembling Stephen, who had only just avoided tears himself by the combination of a miracle and a dogged determination to uphold chivalry and take care of his girl. Epic's remark 'Now I know how everybody felt when the president got iced' put things into perspective just about perfectly. The puppeteers themselves had thus been greatly struck by the performance in which they had also played such a significant part. The show over, now they were free to reflect. Even Thoad looked infinitely more miserable – a remarkable feat indeed. He too had been knocked sideways by the emotion of the committal, whilst Tessa only avoided tears courtesy of a line of coke she had snorted just before the ceremony. In fact the only member of staff who remained unaffected was Noddoes, whose show it essentially had been. He surveyed the landscape containing the wreckage of his grieving colleagues and knew then that he had, after so many years of failure and self-delusion, finally arrived as a Thespian – a Thespian who could move his audience to any emotion which arbitrarily took his fancy. Epic, Stephen and now Thoad were mere puppeteers. He, on the other hand (Noddoes reasoned) was the puppet master. And he most certainly was that!

At this time, Nellie Eddowes was brought forth swiftly by her son. She had already been briefed by him as to what to basically expect ('They are not Hansel and Gretel anymore. They have adopted magical, somewhat orbital guises. They have reached a higher plain. Do not be alarmed. Marvel at their beauty') and then shown into the crematorium where she encountered Amanda, a tear-stained zombie, sitting next to Stephen who had also clearly succumbed and was now blowing his nose into a large blue hankie. Nellie was grateful for this apparent empathy, but her gratitude was of course misplaced. Nellie was mourning her 'babies'. But for the young couple, dear Harry's departure had totally overwhelmed them, controlling their emotions now like an expert angler does his rod and line.

As-Salih and Shagar Ad-Durr's funeral was consequently a suitably solemn affair, lacking much of the good-naturedness of all previous Freddo torchings; the Harry Evans' affair notwithstanding. It started when Keith put on the first record. Naturally it was a recorded track this time with the vocal left on, unlike with Harry. Noddoes may have proved his undeniable talent of voice-throw and impersonation, but not even he would have claimed to have known how to go about pulling the same trick with these latest brace of clients. The chosen number, *What's New Pussycat*, would have been ideal had it not been for the singer. For it was, of course, Tom Jones: and the immediate introduction of this otherwise brilliant Welsh exponent of voice provoked such an immediate outburst of emotion amongst staff that by the second verse, and despite the commendable enthusiasm of the dancing cats, a frenzy of wailing ensued, cumulating very nearly in panic.

'Oh, Harry!' everyone howled, all except Nellie, who had no idea what anyone was talking about. She nevertheless believed she knew why they were crying and promptly burst into tears too.

The second record thankfully stabilised matters. It was the jolly 'glam-rock' track, *The Cat Crept In* by Mud from 1974. Perhaps Nellie could have been happier with the choice, but unbeknownst to her consideration of her own feelings was now peripheral, as emotional breakdowns were certainly on the menu for everyone else and even under normal circumstances, the Mud record would have been generally well-received in any case.

The committal went ahead to the bizarre strains of Tony Hatch and Jackie Trent singing *The Two Of Us*, a truly awful record from a less than revered couple, but a choice which did not lack irony admittedly, after which Frank's mum was whisked back home without even the offer of a glass of Bristol Cream and Frank then returned, locked up the Bar and Grill and then everybody, having naturally finished the Bristol Cream, steamed round to the Inn and drunk themselves into a state which was several degrees beyond unacceptable.

Chapter 41

Dave And Ansel Collins

HE NEXT INTERVIEW held with a potential punter took place a few days later and was conducted, not by Frank or Stephen, but by Thoad. A hidden video camera recorded the proceedings in order to provide Noddoes with the necessary base on which to learn his act. The applicant was a youngish-looking black guy called Peter Nash, who had a broad London accent.

'I've had enough, chief!' he told Thoad. 'I want to end this bollocks now. Know what I mean?'

'Excellent,' Thoad said. 'This really is excellent. How old are you?'

'Thirty-two, chief.'

'Have you come down here specifically to put yourself out the door?' Thoad enquired.

'Yeah. Out the door. That's it,' Peter nodded.

'Very wise,' applauded Thoad. 'Well, once you've dived off the old Point, you'll have as much chance of surviving as I have of winning Wimbledon.'

'Fucking ace!'

'What sort of music do you want, Pete? Tell me.'

'Reggae, man!' enthused Peter. 'Give me reggae! I want to go out to my roots! I'm a ragga! My old man and old lady are from Jamaica, yeah? Yeah, fucking reggae! The reggae beat!'

Here Thoad allowed the unthinkable to happen. He smiled. Reggae was his bag too, of course: 'It gives me great pleasure to tell you that your application has been successful,' he announced immediately.

'Oh cheers, mate!' brightened up Peter. 'I'm well chuffed! You're a diamond geezer!'

'And I trust that you, Pete, will soon be a dead one!' Thoad inserted encouragingly.

'Fucking right, chief! Yeah!' chuckled Nash.

'You shall have your reggae funeral, Peter!' Thoad promised. 'I personally guarantee it. Your old folk are going to be knocked for six!'

'No more than me, guy!' Peter gushed, now in the highest of spirits.

Both men laughed and then embraced warmly.

'You'll soon be killed!' Thoad then assured him, patting Peter comfortingly on the shoulder. 'If you hit the old rocks at the right place, we may even be able to give you *two* funerals!'

Peter lit up like a lantern at the thought of his confirmed doom and they both embraced again before Peter added: 'I ain't fucking paying twice though, chief. Know what I mean?'

Thoad had never laughed so much. Indeed, Thoad had never laughed at all as far as anyone could remember, this including his mother who was now dead and therefore was clearly in no position to remember whether he ever had or not.

Thoad took Peter's credit card and fed it through. The machine kept him waiting whilst it thought about it, like a spoilt child who, having opened a Christmas present given in love, was now considering its uses and whether it was worthy of acceptance, irrespective of who had given it to him. However, to everyone's benefit, the card eventually lethargically spluttered out the confirmation of its worth and Peter Nash signed on the line to verify the end of his life. Two days later, he jumped and was dead on impact.

Meanwhile, Noddoes was attempting to master a black London accent, as well as familiarising himself with Peter's own foibles – his lapses between sentences, his tone and pitch and the use of words like 'chief', 'boss' and 'matey' as regular punctuation points. As he was doing this, Salty Sid fished Peter out, Tessa applied the plasters and Peter Nash, a freeborn Englishman and a free-determining self-destructor was ready to orchestrate his own funeral to the accompaniment of the native music of his immediate forebears. The Exotics' 'split' meanwhile had been announced in the local paper. 'Musical differences' was given as the reason. Twas ever thus.

The Peter Nash Show started, after a welcoming address from Peter himself, with Desmond Dekker singing *You Can Get It If You Really Want*: 'I got it, so there ain't no problem, know what I mean?' narrated Peter; and then lest he should disastrously be accused of impersonating Frank Bruno, he added, complimenting Desmond's original lyric, 'I succeed at last, chief!'

Peter's parents, Neville and Dezna, gave their dead son every encouragement as he danced away, singing along with Desmond: 'Always a good boy!' smiled Dezna. 'Always a good boy!'

Not everyone in the predominantly black congregation, however, was impressed:

'Rass Clat!' some unhelpful unanglicised youth yelled out.

'Don't say that to me, darkie!' rasped Peter, incandescent with rage, pointing at the heckler and fixing him with a hateful glare. *I'm* the fucking daddy here! And if you have a problem with that, you can come and fucking discuss it with me now, you black fool! Cum na! You're nothing, son! *Fucking nothing!...*'

The mildly chastised interjector slunk off into the sidelines. Botty man!

The second piece of music was a bit of a cheat really, specially formulated by Thoad, for whom reggae was a passion. It was a montage of hits by Judge Dread, an aged white skinhead and former minder for the Rolling Stones, who had enjoyed a string of chart hits in the mid-seventies, risqué verses sung to the accompaniment of a reggae backtrack. These records nobly reminded those who later called themselves 'skinheads' but were a different kind of animal (inexplicably and unacceptably ingratiating themselves four square behind the swastika and the laughable but at the same time menacing and massed forces of the British National Front) that the pioneers such as Dread had lapped up and were still lapping up the music of the Caribbean out of solidarity and love for the musicians and their people and had no truck whatsoever with their disgusting young imitators who waved the Union Jack around for the most nefarious of purposes.

The Judge Dread collection, whilst it might not have met with Peter's own approval (he remained silent throughout the montage) and certainly caused more than a little puzzlement to the congregation, was even so well-received, as it indubitably presented itself unchallenged as a reverse microcosm of Peter Nash's life. Dread, a white skinhead absorbing black culture and Nash, a black Englishman absorbing white London culture simply because he had had little choice and because colour to all decent people never matters, is never challenged and because the advent of a black cockney is often applauded, perhaps for the wrong reason – that of it being quaint instead of being genuine, which it most certainly is – and imitated to the point of a parody which is entirely undeserved.

The committal of Peter Nash was serenaded, as Peter had requested, to the strains of *Double Barrel* by Dave and Ansel Collins, a seminal reggae hit of such magnitude that it had topped the main UK singles chart in 1971, removing T-Rex, no less, off the top of what was then still called the Hit Parade. This time Neville and Dezna reacted favourably, even joining their dead son in a serious boogie and lending him every encouragement as he slipped down the chute yelling 'I AM THE *MAGNIFICENT!*' The young heckler from earlier remained stilled in a mesmerized cloud of wonder. This was the music of his forefathers also.

When *Double Barrel* came to a finish, nobody present considered that they had been denied or cheated out of their money's worth. It was a blinding little episode. Peter Nash had gone out just as he had hoped and paid for.

'Everything's well sorted, Pops!' he had assured his father in the viewing room on the day before the funeral. 'That jump off that poxy cliff was nothing, chief! Fucking nothing! As soon as I'd dived off, it was all over, just like when Hursty scored the hat-trick in Sixty-six! All over, chief! It *is* now! Know what I mean?'

Peter was getting very excited, but that was about the size of it really, and he had every right.

'All fucking over, Pops!' he repeated at the top of his form. 'It *is* now!'

And indeed it was.

Chapter 42

James And Sophie

MUCH TO HIS own supreme delight, if not to his surprise, Nod-does had become the most indispensable member of the Freddo team. His ego had never been so well fortified. His handling of the Peter Nash job had won him countless admirers, quite rightly so, and Freddo's had consequently become the most exclusive funeral service nationwide. No longer was it now acceptable for instructions to be merely left with Thoad for a Rock and Roll funeral in an arrogant assumption that everything would be tended to as soon as the punter had plunged to his death. It was now necessary to undergo a vetting interview, a pass or fail event, which assured that the dice was loaded almost hopelessly against the applicant. Scores of wannabees were sent away desperately disappointed, some so utterly distraught that they chose to dispense with any plans for suicide entirely and carry on living, a tragic consequence to be sure. Those who made the shortlist had an agonising wait whilst a further sift then took place. Normal practice now saw six applicants, who had emerged from an initial block of anything between twenty-five and forty, halved so that three finalists were invited back to face a three-man panel of Thoad, Stephen and Epic in a decisive interview. It had been decided that because of the volume and irrepressible flow of applicants, even in the case of three superb and seemingly inseparable candidates appearing before the jury, it was imperative on the grounds of ease of administration, if for nothing else, that one was rejected outright, thus leaving the triumphant applicant on the one hand and on the other, a candidate who was either placed on a 'reserve list' or else offered immediate qualification for the next round of considerations, although this meant applying from scratch at a preliminary interview again. The 'reserve list' sounded good but actually meant nothing at all. It was a hopeless state of limbo and nothing more – hopeless because for in order for a 'reserve' to have any chance, a gap would have to be created by someone who had either beaten him or had triumphed in an earlier or subsequent round pulling out, and anyone who had succeeded in coming through from an oversized classroom to be selected was hardly likely to withdraw, save perhaps through illness or a bereavement. It all meant that the chance of acceptance was monumentally against any, indeed every candidate, and this naturally meant that the exclusiveness of acceptance attracted certain individuals who came forward thinking that they could jump the queue. One of these was sent away by Thoad within thirty seconds of arrival. It was none other than Curtis Morgan, a national radio DJ, who had made his name presenting the breakfast show but had since moved on to presenting pop shows on television. Morgan was a crass, foul-mouthed, obnoxious, inarticulate, narcissistic, belligerent, but above all talentless 'man of the people' who associated with fat drunken footballers and other associated pond life and enjoyed all the manners and courtesy of a Belsen gas chamber operator along with a summarily lack of charm and intellect, which always guaranteed that he was despised by those with a brain in their head and worshipped by those who could only dream of a brain in their head and therefore were hampered because you need a brain in your head to be able to dream about anything in the first place.

'Hey, rock and roll!' Morgan announced as he took his seat opposite Thoad.

'What's your name please, sir?' Thoad asked.

'Wow! Cool!' the tosser enthused. 'Cool dude! I like it! "What's your name please, sir"! Cool piss-taking old dude! I like it!'

'What's your name please, sir?' Thoad asked again.

'Hey!' snapped Morgan, snapping his fingers and pointing at Thoad. 'Not a second time with the gag, cool fucker! Now listen. Here's my list of groovy sounds! I'm not really jumping. That's for losers. This is just a wind-up for my show. For my fans, okay? My agent will settle the account. Just bill him. Okay? See you, cool dude!'

Curtis Morgan got up to leave. But Thoad, who hadn't listened to the national pop radio station since Peters and Lee were having hits and Roger Taylor was still a minor threat at Wimbledon, had some bad news: 'I have to tell you that your application has not been successful,' he said.

'Fucking *what?*'

'I'm sorry. We have a strict sifting policy here at Freddo's and you've just been sifted out.'

'Fucking *what?*' repeated Curtis. 'Do you fucking know who I fucking am?'

Thoad, who honestly *didn't* fucking know who Morgan fucking was, didn't bat an eyelid: 'No, sir. I'm sorry but the decision has been made. I'm afraid that you're a candidate who's failed. It's best now that you leave.'

'Fucking *what?*'

'Goodbye now.'

Curtis Morgan was going ballistic now, threatening Thoad with litigation as well as with a visit from 'my mates in the East End.'

Thoad outlined the situation once more: 'I have no more time to offer you. Your old application has failed. You are welcome to reapply at a later date. Until then, cheerio.'

This placated precisely nothing. Morgan's ridiculously oversized glasses were steaming up and the confirmed lack of recognition from Thoad was causing him an inordinate amount of humiliation, if not genuine pain. But before he could open his mouth again, Amanda, the pretty punk girl, who just for a change was shot to pieces, entered the room, having heard and recognised the voice of the failed applicant and flew at him, clawing and biting. She wrenched his spectacles off and destroyed them with the heal of her shoe, and whilst Morgan was struggling with the consequent impaired vision, Amanda highkicked him in the knackers and then began clawing his face to friggery, spitting into his face every few seconds, as if this was necessary to lubricate the butchery of her talons, which did not relent. The little girl beat him up totally and conclusively and finished the 'fight' by kicking him twice in the head whilst he was crawling around on the carpet trying to get away. To Thoad, the man was simply a failed applicant. To Amanda, he was a nob who was shit and was paid too much. She would have gleefully put him to death had she been given the opportunity to continue, but Thoad finally stepped up between her and the badly twatted celeb and Amanda granted her prey mercy and walked away.

The next morning saw Curtis Morgan back at his controls on the breakfast show as arrogant as ever with not one word about how he had been rejected by an undertakers and then smashed up by a girlie. Many of his listeners loathed him and would have dearly loved to been privy to what had happened to Curtis over at Freddo's, but the DJ said nothing and not a sound was made by his agent either. Equally, Frank remained ignorant of the episode featuring the self-important player of records who had been forced to creep away cowering, humiliated and battered with no further reference to his own beauty. It was probably just as well.

Things were not always this dramatic. One finalist was actually a double-act, a young couple who had met at university and were now intent on a suicide pact. Noddoes, when he viewed their tapes, was particularly taken with the pair: 'The girl has such a fragile, delicate beauty about her,' he sighed. 'She reminds me of someone, but infuriatingly I can't quite remember who. Most annoying. And the young man has a passionate love for her which is undeniable but at the same time indeterminate. They are a fascinating study and could, I think, quite easily provide a showcase and in any event a totally original funeral.'

The panel agreed and James Brayburn and Sophie Lutz were given the good news personally by Frank. The couple hugged each other joyously and Tessa handed Sophie a bouquet, which complemented perfectly the smile which would simply not leave her pretty face.

They immediately discussed their music: 'I'd like to sing to James *The Power Of Love*', requested Sophie.

'You want to sing Frankie Goes To Hollywood?' enquired Epic, amazed.

'I'm sure Sophie means the Jennifer Rush song,' corrected Frank.

'Yes. Jennifer Rush,' confirmed Sophie. 'Mummy bought it for Daddy and I bought it for James.'

'Of course,' Frank said. 'It's a beautiful song. And how would James like to respond, I wonder?'

James took Sophie's hand, looked at her lovingly and started singing *You Are The Sunshine Of My Life* softly in a light tuneful voice.

'Hey, that's *Stevie!*' beamed Epic. 'Great number, Jimbo! Way to go!'

'Yes, that's a delightful choice too, James,' agreed Frank, writing it down. 'Now, the last number we'd like you to sing together. Any thoughts?'

The loving couple consulted each other with their eyes.

'*To You I'm Born Again* would be nice,' James suggested as Sophie nodded.

Frank wrote this down also. 'Yes, well perhaps you'll leave that with me for the time being. What you need to do now is sort your affairs out and then come in on Thursday, please and settle your account. Your funeral will be held three working days following the coroner's verdict and you'll actually be jumping this Friday at 8am. We like to ask for a morning leap. It makes things easier for our boatman, okay?'

James and Sophie hugged each other again.

'I can pay with my Visa now if you like,' Sophie then offered.

'No, no. That's perfectly alright, my dear,' Frank said. 'Thursday's fine.'

'Thursday it is then,' James confirmed.

Stephen showed the happy couple to the door.

'Thank you so much for accepting us,' James beamed, as they all shook hands.

'It's our pleasure,' replied Frank warmly. 'You were a delightful couple.'

'And thanks awfully for the flowers. They're really lovely,' added Sophie, sniffing the bouquet for the umpteenth time.

'Yes, well just make sure that you trim the stems and put them in a vase as soon as you get home, my dear,' Frank advised. 'They'll last twice as long that way.'

'I shall,' said Sophie. 'And thanks again for everything.'

'Take care.'

'We will. Goodbye.'

'Good day!'

Chapter 43

Beverley Thornton

S OPHIE, SURE ENOUGH, dropped by on Thursday and settled the account by herself, leaving James to tie up a few loose ends with a solicitor in the town. The young woman seemed as bright as a button, full of enthusiasm and expectation. The big moment was imminent.

Noddoes, meantime, had been preparing himself for what promised to be the performance of his career. Not only had he the difficulty of having to familarise himself with the voices and mannerisms of two people this time, but one of course was a girl and this fell well outside anything he had attempted before. Whether it would be beyond him would soon be proved. For the fact was ever since the advent of self-participating funerals, each of the successful applicants had been male, the arbitrating panel (of which Noddoes was not a member) deciding who would succeed with the extent as to how Noddoes would perform firmly in mind. Added to this had been the fact that there had been precious few female candidates in any case. Indeed, female clients had been disappointingly thin on the ground prior to self-participation, something which the Freddo company had been keen to remedy. Eventually, Frank had asked Amanda to produce a written opinion to examine the problem for later discussion by a special 'steering committee.'

'The terms of reference for this report will be as broad as you choose to make them,' Frank told her. 'But basically, the objectives are two-fold. Firstly, we need to examine not so much the extent of this phenomenon of lack of female applicants, because we know this already, which is precisely why I am commissioning this report, but rather the reasons *behind* the phenomenon, okay? We need to try to discover why there has been a singular lack of interest from women consumers in our product, especially when one takes into account a female's renowned feel for and susceptibility to a real bargain. And secondly, Amanda, I want you to discuss a forward plan, a reasoned outlook of opinions and ideas which will produce suggestions to the steering committee for the best way ahead for remedying this worrying problem. Now, nobody, least of all me, my dear, can expect your report to produce a magic formula, but in the month I am giving you to publish it, it would be expected that this matter would have been comprehensively discussed so that the consequent committee under my chairmanship can debate its findings at length and thereby arrive at a pragmatic decision as to where we go from here, okay? Do you have any questions, Amanda?'

The punk girl stared wildly at Frank and then blinked twice. She was pissed this time, rather than stoned and thus wasn't too far removed from sensibility.

'You want this in a month?' she asked.

'Six weeks at a push,' conceded Frank.

'I really think I can manage it in rather *less* than a month,' she claimed boldly.

Frank looked satisfied. 'A commendable attitude, my dear,' he smiled. 'I have no reason to doubt that your study will be not only refreshing and far-reaching, but perhaps even decisive.'

'So it's okay if I turn this thing in less than a month?' pressed Amanda, just to make sure.

'My dear, the sooner the better!'

Amanda smiled and scurried off. In three minutes, forty-one seconds, she had 'published' her opinion. She waited for Frank to leave his office for a second and then slipped in and placed it on his desk. It was a single sheet of notepaper, displaying a few scribbled lines written in a green felt tip:

There are fewer women customers at Freddo's because fewer women jump off Rocky Point than men.

We are in no position to change this situation because the only way to even things out would be to attempt to force more women into a mood which makes them more likely to want to kill themselves. This falls outside the extent of our influence, unless we consider offering financial inducements, and might even represent a criminal offence.

CONCLUSION: There's nothing we can do. So we might as well stop trying.
Submitted:
A. Plimmer (Ms)

Needless to say, Frank did not present the report to his steering committee. The truth was, he had overstretched himself this time. In a fit of pique, he had again attempted to play the psychologist when there was no patient. Business was booming. Everyone in the company was thriving. What more did Frank want?

In any event, Frank had ended up with the report he totally deserved. Amanda, who despite her many shortcomings was actually lively and intelligent, had actually summed everything up perfectly adequately. There was absolutely nothing that could be done to increase the female client rate aside from offering discounts for women. Because there were so fewer women killing themselves than men, this naturally meant that fewer women jumped off Rocky Point and thus there were a sparser number of Freddo clients for consideration. It really was as simple and uncomplicated as that. As for the prospect of any 'remedy', this was clearly preposterous. Amanda's 'conclusion' had said everything. There was nothing they could do, so they might as well stop trying; and Frank, despite his earlier pompous airy hopes for his foolish 'committee', realised just what an idiot he had made himself look and how even more ridiculous he would risk appearing if he decided to persist with this particular madcap project. He therefore did the best thing possible and binned Amanda's report and said nothing more about it to either her, nor anyone else. He hoped Amanda would do the same, which she did. Ironically, Amanda quite admired him for this capitulation.

What was even more ironic was something which happened less than a week later. A woman called Beverley Thornton presented herself to Thoad to book an appointment for a funeral. This, of course, being before the sift system had been introduced, indeed even before Frank had gone to Birmingham, meant that she was guaranteed a place immediately. On the face of it, Beverley was something of a trophy client, even having taken into account that she was a woman. She was an attractive, smartly dressed, articulate, fair-haired advertising executive of forty-one with a university degree and a love and broad knowledge of classical literature. She also formally had a love for her husband, who had tried to ditch their childless marriage by leaving Beverley for a younger woman he had succeeded in impregnating. Beverley had responded to this minor irritation by helpfully placing a bread knife in him just as he was closing his suitcase. His body was still lying on the floor of their bedroom.

Thoad had began the consultation by pragmatically insisting on a written confession from Beverley for her husband's murder. 'It will make things easier for the old coroner,' he explained.

'I don't really need to,' Beverley said. 'My fingerprints are all over the knife and the fact that I'm killing myself should tell even the densest of police who killed Tony.'

'Yes, but if you scribble down a note admitting to sticking the old knife in Tony's back in advance of your own well-documented suicide, the police, as well as the coroner, will be suitably accommodated,' insisted Thoad. 'Everything will be cleared up nice and tidily. One murder, one suicide. This will also mean that we can guarantee that there will not be any delay with regards to your own funeral.'

'Oh yes,' nodded Beverley. 'I can see that that makes sense.'

'You're actually our very first murderer,' Thoad informed her, handing Beverley a sheet of writing paper.

'As far as you know,' Beverley suggested.

'As far as we know,' Thoad admitted. 'But you're a very nice lady.'

'Thank you.'

Beverley jotted down her confession to her husband's murder and just for good measure, her own forthcoming suicide. She named someone called Michelle Tucker as being the woman her husband, a freelance financial adviser, was leaving her for before Beverley struck with the knife. Miss Tucker was the assistant of a client of Tony Thornton's and Beverley had been long suspicious of the liaison and had obtained the necessary confirmation of her fears after a modicum of amateur sleuthing, during which she had posed first as her husband's secretary over the telephone and subsequently as a 'market research analyst'. Here she managed without too much persuasion to extract a detailed outline from Michelle (not the most complicated of creatures) about what was going on in her love life. The confession that 'Tony is leaving his frigid wife for me' seemed to be fairly conclusive, as indeed was the consequent revelation '*I'm* not frigid. *I'm* pregnant!'

'I even feel a little sorry for the poor little girl,' Beverley said, as she handed her written cough back to Thoad. 'She's entirely inarticulate and could only have dreamt of somebody like Tony, and now she's going to end up as a single mother. I suspect that she'll be perfectly miserable now.'

This contrition didn't make Thoad any less uncomfortable. He was actually quite disturbed by what he saw as an entirely cold-hearted killer. But Beverley was not gloating. Her pity for Michelle and her unborn baby was quite genuine. Certainly the manner in which she had dispatched her cheating husband had been very icy indeed and calculated too, but what was also true was that Beverley felt utterly indifferent to what she had done. Plunging a bread knife into Tony had been of no greater significance to her than giving a troublesome fly a dose of spray. It had been simply something which needed to be done. And she had done it.

Beverley's record requests for her torching turned out to be rather whimsical and amusing, contrary certainly to Thoad's perceived impression of her. What wasn't surprising, Thoad thought, was her choice of three female singers and indeed also her first track. Carly Simon's *You're So Vain*, an excellent and celebrated swipe at an unfaithful lover, which Simon had allegedly composed for the benefit of a notorious womanising lover, who had famously jumped the singer and then dropped her.

The second request was an ironic masterstroke. It was Karen Carpenter's love song, *Close To You*, the Hal David lyric full to the brim with favourite reactions from birds, stars and angels to whenever the object of Miss Carpenter's love (the subject of the song) was close to them, the very proximity of which was ardently desired by the delightful lamented Karen, naturally enough. The choice was comical because if one imagined Beverley as Karen, then one was left with the surreal picture of a girl paying a starry-eyed, loving tribute to a man she had just brutally slain by assuring him constantly that the most important thing in the world to her was to be 'close' to him, which technically speaking with Tony, Beverley soon would be.

The final number requested by Mrs Thornton was designed to add even more hilarity to an already fun-filled picture. It was Connie Francis singing *Who's Sorry Now*, certainly one of the most popular pop songs ever recorded by a female artiste and in Beverley's (and indeed Tony's) circumstances, a choice which complemented undoubted irony with a surfeit of piquancy, with Beverley taunting her victim sweetly but firmly.

Thoad had nothing but admiration for Beverley's list and he emphasised to Frank just how ideal her choices were, which was as far as he would go in pleading for no changes to be made. Fortunately, Frank too agreed that the choices were excellent ('we could have employed this woman as musical editor') and he promptly instructed Danny that no mischief was to be made. The Exotics could suit themselves, but Beverley's musical list was a tablet of stone and that was an end to it.

Mrs Thornton jumped to her death and her corpse was soon the property of Freddo's. Her torching went ahead with Carly and Karen opening the show and Connie closing it, just as she had requested. Beverley ran a truly great show and this very feminine event ran even more successfully than even Thoad dared think it would. It was a celebration of women and a stark and deadly warning to philandering males everywhere.

Beverley was also the last female client before Sophie Lutz came along with her boyfriend James. But this funeral would be different. This funeral was of the new order of 'self-participating' ceremonies with the excellent Noddoes at the forefront. This funeral would be seeing two young people making a loving commitment to each other in song and in death. Every available Freddo hand would have to be put to use, with even Frank himself picking up a role as a rookie puppeteer. They had thought about asking Salty Sid to help, but didn't think about it very long. Noddoes was certainly going to earn his corn this time. His show without a doubt.

Sophie and James took the early bus up to Rocky Point to arrive at a quarter past eight of a fresh and misty morning and walked hand in hand across the grassy edge, chatting happily, past Reg Doorman's derelict, boarded-up Hut, daubed all over in paint and marked with such tributes as 'Dead Twat!' and 'Flying Goody Goody Tosser!' and then hugged each other for the last time in life. With that they hopped over the edge proferring the sheerest drop of all as casually as if they were boarding a train and dropped like stones to the bottom. They had leapt hand in hand, but became detached almost the instant they were in the air and Sid recovered their remains several feet apart. He hoisted first Sophie and then James up with his heavy net, hurled the corpses into the hull of his boat and flung a tarpaulin over them. The little boat then chugged off into the morning mist, which had begun ever so slightly to lift as the sun slowly eased its way through it. It was still chilly though, and Sid was already addressing his hip flask of rum. He had, after all, been on the water since six. His ragged heavy pale green woolen jumper provided the only other warmth he needed. Such a garment he always donned in any case, weather fine or fowl.

The boat's transistor was chattering away to itself, but at such a lower volume as to render the instrument practically worthless, since it emitted only an inaudible hiss, which would have probably been unbearably irritating to anyone other than Sid. The salty one was not musical. He paid no mind to current affairs, religion, or sport. Nor did he care for comedy, drama, or variety programmes. The radio was for picking up weather and shipping forecasts and nothing else whatsoever. Apart from the collection of this information, Sid's remaining concerns were for his flask and his pipe, his only leanings towards luxury. Even food was of little importance to him and he never ate at all when he was afloat. He took solid sustenance only at home, or more likely in his favourite tavern after he had moored his boat. Sid had spent his life as an early morning person. He had never slept late, even in ill health or on days he did not sail, occasions which brought him nothing but misery and exasperation. He had never owned or needed an alarm clock because his head *was* one. He was in bed every night by nine o'clock, woke up a little over three hours later for the main weather forecast and shipping synopsis, picked up on a second radio (his only extravagance – he had never owned a television set), then went back to sleep and got up at five. He had never been burdened by marriage, not even close to it. He had lived and was still living a harsh, spartan, if not impoverished life. He rented his tiny house, but the boat was nobody's but his. Comforts were sparse, but any improvement in his lot had at no time been coveted. As a matter of fact, Salty Sid was the happiest man in the land.

He crammed a palmful of tobacco into his pipe and set fire to it with a match. He had owned a lighter once, a rather splendid one, but had lost it, probably overboard, and had stubbornly refused to replace it. Under the tarpaulin, James and Sophie were hugging each other as usual.

Chapter 44

Hanne And Lisle

SUICIDE WAS CONFIRMED one more time in the coroner's court on the following Wednesday by Klaus Butsch, who then announced that he was holding a Swiss food delicacy party in his court the next day, Thursday, which was four days before James and Sophie's funeral. Frank, Stephen and Epic, who were present, stared at Herr Butsch in astonishment.

'There will be examples, for instance, of food from our country,' he said, holding up a small Swiss flag in the shape of a card attached to a fragile stick and pointing at this with his other hand, whilst the two milkmaids on either side of him did likewise. 'We begin at noon of the clock. Stay until five hours. Many foods we shall line across this bench for pickinks. Crepes with meats or creams in order to help yourself: much cheeses, fondue, sausages and naturally, as one knows, chocolates of superior qualities. For one time in this courthouse we forget *bumpity-bumps* and other dyinks and killinks. You are all for one day only a Swiss. Hanne and Lisle will serve you, if not you help yourself. But remember this, all the mans… squeeze only the cakes, bitte. Maids not part of feast. Squeezy is not allowed. Okay? No creamies!'

Klaus stood up as the cowbells rang out and then the blonde milkmaids, Hanne and Lisle, both of whom possessing impossibly large squeezable jugs, wiggled off after him as the coroner started to leave. He then stopped midway and turned around: 'Come to Switzerland's day of food when the clock is with Twelve!' he reminded the court. 'We will have power drinks made with fruits. Soon after one single drink, one is happy and warm also. Bring please not your auto. After two times of this drink, one blows into bag of police und *Boom!* Ja, that is so.'

Klaus looked as if he was making good his exit, but just before he disappeared, he stopped again suddenly and turned around to face the court once more. Some people resumed their seats. Many more were walking out. Klaus himself was rewarded for this sudden change of direction with a very pleasant facial collision with Lisle's tits. He bounced off and then found himself looking directly at a perplexed but clearly envious Epic. The coroner pointed straight at the Canadian and then poked Lisle's bountiful baps left and right: 'No creamies!' he roared and then, forgetting just why he had stopped and turned around, disappeared through the door probably for some creamies.

'Crazy mother!' muttered Epic to Stephen. 'What a crazy mixed-up, Swiss fruitcake mother!'

'No creamies!' Stephen smilingly reminded Epic, wagging a warning finger mockingly. 'No creamies!'

'Smart punk!' snarled Epic.

The three of them walked off towards the Inn, discussing the open invitation to the next day's little soiree at the coroner's.

'I think it would be nice if we were represented,' Frank suggested. 'Herr Butsch has been a good friend to us. His deliberations have always been most favourable.'

'You're crazy!' Epic whined. 'You're talking like we bought this guy off! Shit, Frankie, you know that this fruitcake brought in all these verdicts on account of all these guys genuinely flying off the rocks! The guy may be a space cadet, but he's only doing his job. We're not talking Watergate here!'

Frank was horrified, or at least seemingly so: 'Good God! I never suggested such a thing! That's terrible! I'm appalled you can even think about it!'

'Yeah, well when you start talking about the guy from the coroner's office being a good friend of mine, I can't *help* thinking about it, man! Jesus! You'll be sending Christmas cards to the cops next, know what I mean?'

Frank puffed his cheeks in exasperation and turned away: 'What's your opinion, Stephen?'

'I think Herr Butsch is an honest man,' nodded Stephen, not meaning to sound righteous but failing badly.

'We're not talking about that!' snapped Frank, not very happy at all. 'God! What's wrong with you two? I want to know whether we want to be represented at this function or not, nothing else! Herr Butsch's honesty has never been in question. *Really!*'

'Take it easy, Frankie!'

'Well, for heaven's sake!'

'Why don't we get Noddoes to do it?' Stephen asked. 'He'll bloody love it and will probably consider it a personal honour instead of a total wind-up, which it will be.'

Frank's mood changed immediately and he allowed himself the luxury of a chuckle. 'He'll certainly not be out of place at such an event,' he conceded. 'I have to say that.'

'Shit, Frankie, you've got *that* right, man! He's a bigger goddamn fruitcake than that crazy coroner back there! Say, that's the answer! We'll send Hamlet! Hey, how 'bout Sheba going with him?'

Frank's jaw dropped: 'No, no! Er…no…'

'Klaus said "no creamies",' Stephen reminded them, turning to Epic and grinning. Both of them were delighted at Frank's discomfort, but actually if the qualification required for going to Klaus' little shindig was to be off the wall, then Tessa (when she was Sheba) was admirably more suitable than the old luvvie. Together they would have wrecked the place.

'Yes, yes, that's it precisely!' stuttered Frank. 'No cr… No creamies! No… No…'

'I think it would be really cool if we don't tell Noddoes about the "no creamies" directive,' Stephen added. 'That way he'll probably sidle up to those two Swiss babes and try to switch on the charm. You know what the prat's like!'

'Say, that's right!' Epic said. 'And the judge will go ape!'

'And it won't do Noddoes the slightest bit of good anyway,' came back Stephen, 'because Hanne and Lisle only speak German, I think. I once saw some scrote from the Inn trying to chat up Hanne in Sainsbury's. She was just smiling at him and saying "not allowed!" over and over again, "not allowed!". So the scrote tries something else. He looks into her basket and says "see you like cheese, love. You get a cosmic selection in here, don't you?" and Hanne laughs and her baps started bouncing together and she just laughed and shook her head and said "not allowed!" again to the guy and he finally takes the hint and fucks off. It will probably be the horniest refusal he'll ever get in his life. I bet he went straight to the lav and jizzed himself into a liquid!'

'Hey, well we just gotta hope that Hamlet don't speak no German,' pointed out Epic. ''Cause if he gets off with either of them creamy babes, and he's just the kind of slime ball who can pull it off, I think I might just have to fucking shoot him!'

'No. I can allay your fears there. The odd corny French phrase will be Noddoes' limit,' Stephen assured him. 'I don't doubt that he'll most certainly try to impress himself on these girls, but they'll just tell him that it's "not allowed!" and then when he doesn't get the message, which he won't because he never does because he's a prick, Klaus will come running up, shouting "No Creamies!" and then twat him with a fuck-off family-size bar of Toblerone.'

Frank, who had recovered now from his stuttering fit, brought on by the suggestion that Tessa might accompany Noddoes to Klaus' fondue party, led his fellow musketeers into the Inn, where Tom and Kate, the tall brunette, all-smiling, moon-faced barmaid with only a mild habit, greeted them and where they encountered Thoad and Amanda already in there, Amanda well on the way to getting hammered like a good girl. They ordered themselves beers and top-ups for the others and then resumed their deliberations. Stephen was still touched with the idea that Noddoes ought to go to the Swiss function. Frank, who now feared that a rat's odour might be blowing his way, had now decided that being 'represented' at the coroner's bash was no longer so necessary as long as the representative was Noddoes. Ever since Tessa (as Sheba) had given him the key to her magic kingdom, not that he had remembered a second of it, Frank had done his utmost to fiercely regulate the appearances of the imperial cat. He considered it vital that whenever Tessa became Sheba, he must be there, or at least available to reap any dividends brought on thereby. The thought of this beautiful creature lavishing her wares unchaperoned on Klaus Butsch, whom Frank figured was the obvious potential beneficiary, not only filled him with a dread of his company being closed down due to an insane, drug-induced feline sexual attack on the town's coroner in his own courtroom by a principal member of Frank's own staff, but perhaps even more alarmingly, a dread of Klaus partaking of 'creamies', the kind of which he would never have encountered in the Alps. For some reason, unknown and nothing short of irrational, Frank was now unable to establish in his mind a differential between the idea of Noddoes going to the party (the suggestion had initially appeared to Frank as being excellent) and Tessa joining him, inevitably as Sheba. The only answer was to try to bluff the others, something at which he was never terribly adept. He suggested that perhaps sending Noddoes was not such a good idea, what with Noddoes putting the final touches to preparations for James and Sophie's funeral just three days later.

'Clearly the objective was to wind the old luvvie up,' he belched. 'I think, on reflection, that the short period between now and the next performance, and taking into account just how sensitive Noddoes is, should encourage a rethink. He has, after all, worked jolly hard on James and Sophie and he's been quite magnificent on previous occasions, notably with Peter Nash. I think it might be rather disingenuous if we dropped this one on him now. He's bound to make an ass of himself and it might impair his performance on Monday...'

Frank had started off not meaning a word of what he was going to say (he would gladly have taken any opportunity of making Noddoes look ridiculous, even though his attitude towards him had mellowed beyond recognition from what it had been previously: indeed, he now respected and admired him as a highly amusing and talented showman), but he had ended up finishing his spiel now believing that there were specific times to make Noddoes look like the ludicrous pompous bore he was and that this wasn't one of them.

Stephen disagreed.

Epic apparently didn't: 'Okay, so we'll give the guy a break. So let me go, Frankie!'

'You?'

'Sure.'

'*Just* you?'

'Sure, just me. What's the problem?'

'No, no, no. It's brilliant. *Brilliant*! You go, Epic!'

'Cool!'

'What about sending Tessa to keep an eye on him?' suddenly wacked in Stephen, reading Frank like a book as usual. But Epic, who would normally have leapt at the chance to join Stephen in tormenting Frank about Tessa, had strangely decided to adopt a decidedly different stance this time, and before Frank, who was already whimpering and shaking like a jelly, could disintegrate completely, Epic came like a St Bernard carrying brandy to his master's rescue: 'Shit, man. I don't need nobody keeping their eye on me! What am I? Some kind of little kid or something?'

Frank gasped with relief. 'By yourself!' he burbled.

It was Stephen now who was receiving a pungent whiff of rodent, as he knew exactly what Epic was up to. He now set about ruining things for both Epic and Frank, who of course was all of a sudden four square behind Epic's suggestion that he went by himself (or at least not with Tessa).

'Well *you've* changed your tune all of a sudden, I must say,' Stephen accused Epic. 'You were the bugger who wanted Sheba to go with Noddoes!'

'No more bullshitter than you, man!' countered Epic, annoyed to find himself on the unfamiliar territory of being required to defend himself. 'You didn't really want Hamlet to go with Sheba because he might have gotten some creamies. I could sense it, man. But now you want Sheba to come and hold my hand. I don't get it. Well let me tell you something for nothing, pal. I might just take you up on that, but there ain't no fucking way that one of us ain't gonna get no creamies from someplace!'

Frank very nearly screamed with terror at this prospect. Stephen had most certainly tried his best to make trouble for Epic, and so successfully had he done so that Epic, in his exasperation, had inadvertently catapulted poor Frank right back into the firing line again. Stephen recognised this immediately and could not conceal his delight at this spectacular win-double. Frank, for example, who was already half-cut, looked alarmingly sweaty and out of breath and Stephen couldn't help having the unforgiveable thought that if he didn't calm himself down, Frank might quite feasibly be involved with Klaus Butsch pretty soon in an official capacity, never mind the fondue party. As for Epic, he was furious that Stephen had jammed the works with a large spanner, just as it seemed that the way was clear for Epic to go by himself to the Swiss bash, something which he had of course been angling for all along.

Stephen, who was in a truly wicked mood, was blissfully content with things as they stood – Epic in a rage and Frank seemingly close to a stroke. But he was not to win. Frank, with an admirable late effort, staged a splendid recovery to turn everything around with one sentence, which he delivered word, gap, word, as if he were talking to a foreigner or an idiot. Epic was only one of these: 'You… are… going… *ALONE!*' he decreed in a husky sort of pant, pointing at Epic with a definite prodding motion on the delivery of each of the four words, increasing the volume as he went along. He then picked up his beer glass and practically threw the remainder of its contents at his mouth. A good deal of it went down his front.

Epic jumped off his stool and punched the air: '*Yes!*'

Stephen shrugged to himself. At least he had tried his best and had actually given both Epic and Frank a good run for their money. The only maddening thing was that Epic, as usual, had come out ahead.

But he didn't stay there. The Canadian had rushed out of the Inn and across to W H Smiths within seconds of being told by a now convalescing Frank that he and only he would be at the do tomorrow. He arrived back with plenty of change from five minutes with a small German phrase book, which he had acquired with plenty of change from five pounds. This he took with his beer into a far corner of the Inn and was soon heard to be muttering to himself as he urgently practiced phonetic pronunciations of what he considered the most important phrases for his big day.

He arrived at the coroner's court at five minutes past one the following afternoon. He was wily enough not to make his intentions too obvious by being first out of the starting gate and as it happened, one of the guests already there was none other than Arthur Snape, not that Epic would have known him, nor most certainly Snape, Epic. The absence of Noddoes and/or Tessa was fortunate indeed. The décor was magnificently Swiss. Everywhere you looked, the flag of that country was visible, even little plastic ones protruding from every bowl of eats, savoury and sweet, set out neatly along three long tables, each also draped in the flag of the host nation. Epic picked up a plastic plate and walked along the first of these, picking up odd items without really looking at them. He was already looking at something else. Hanne and Lisle had entered in traditional dress and were mingling. There was no sign of Klaus.

A slimy-looking rakish man of middle years was trying to talk to Lisle using hand signals. Epic watched his efforts whilst munching a small bar of chocolate and keeping his distance. Lisle was the one Epic himself was particularly interested in. She was smiling almost manically at the fellow who was troubling her and shaking her head continuously and wagging her finger. Every few seconds saw her breasts popping up to say hello. She was muttering something to him, which obviously Epic was unable to hear. He didn't need to hear. He knew what it was: 'She's telling you creamies ain't allowed, scumbag!' he growled to himself. 'Now take a hike. You can't even speak the babe's goddamn language!'

Reluctantly the man withdrew and Epic walked swiftly up to replace him. Hanne, the other busty milkmaid, was busily saying 'not allowed' to two young men in smart suits, who were obviously interested in more than the tray of cheese and biscuits that she was carrying. The host himself, Herr Butsch, was still not in evidence.

The lovely Lisle was standing behind a small table, which was of course draped in a Swiss flag and had plastic dishes on top of it. She saw Epic approach her and flashed a particularly wide smile at him. Epic thought this most encouraging. When he was right up to her with only the table of yoghurt separating them, he clicked his heals and bowed swiftly, European style. He then cleared his throat in order to begin his carefully rehearsed repertoire in phonetic German, which he was certain would not only impress the Swiss miss, but also charm her silly. All those other guys? They just hadn't done any research. Epic *had* and this, along with his natural good looks and charisma, was why he was going to get the girl, just like he always did. He was not only better looking than the other guys, but he was also plenty smarter. Way to go, Epic!

He leered dreamily at Lisle's luscious bazookas and gradually leaned involuntarily towards the magnificent spectacle.

'You! You!' suddenly yelled Klaus, running up. 'So you come! After all, you come! I tell you time after time, no creamies! Forget creamies! But still you come for creamies! You ist bad boy and make fun! It is duty for me in this hall to make you for a punish. Okay?'

Epic had swung around, which was an unwise thing to do. Klaus had arrived, just as Epic faced him and the incensed coroner promptly swung a long, hard triangular object, which could have been some kind of pole, at the young Canadian's head and managed a direct hit across his jaw.

'Oh, Jesus!' howled Epic and he fell backwards onto the fragile table of yoghurt which gave way on impact and allowed Epic a direct path through it straight to the floor.

'Oh fucking shit, man!' he groaned, his face covered in milky Swiss dessert of varying tantalising fruit flavours.

Lisle looked down at Epic and the yoghurt display that he had just so unceremoniously demolished and wagged a finger at the prostrate culprit:

'Not allowed! *Not* allowed!' she reprimanded him firmly, leaning over almost on top of him and wagging her finger in his face.

Epic was in genuine need of assistance. He was dazed and hurt. The last thing on his mind now was to try to get off with Lisle, even though her gorgeous tits were within sniffing distance; and so when he offered his hand, it was a request for not necessarily her but for anybody else to help him get to his feet.

But Klaus didn't see it that way, unfortunately. All he could see was this obsessed young man lifting his head from the carnage of the yoghurt display and holding up his arm to point at Lisle's chest, whilst moaning and licking his lips. This could clearly mean only one thing...

'Mein Gott, boy! Still you not learn! Even after hit, you try for creamies! You not learn! Again I must give you punish! *Again*! This new hit will bring to you sleep, bad boy! After sleep, maybe you learn!'

At this, Klaus swung back his long, hard triangular object, which could have been some kind of pole, and eyed Epic's jaw again.

'No, Man, *NO!*' begged Epic, weakly but desperately trying to wave his assailant away.

'*NO CREAMIES!*' roared Klaus defiantly and knocked Epic out. 'Ja! Das ist Bingo!'

The next thing Epic knew, he was being revived by Tessa and Amanda back at Freddo's. He was lying on a foam mattress in the candlelit viewing room, next to a larger mattress occupied by James and Sophie.

'Welcome back!' Amanda said to him after he had opened his eyes. 'Are you okay?'

Epic blinked at her. 'What the fuck happened?' he groaned.

'You were - '

'What did the crazy bastard hit me with?'

'He gave it to Stephen,' Amanda said coyly, not answering the question.

'Get Stevie in here right now!,' demanded Epic, trying to roll himself up and failing.

'I'm here,' said Stephen, suddenly appearing from behind his girlfriend.

'What the fuck did he hit me with, the crazy bastard?' demanded Epic again. 'Why did he let you have it? Where is it?'

'He gave it to me when we came to pick your doughnut up,' explained

Stephen whimsically. 'He gave it to me to give to you. He wants you to have it.'

'What the fuck *for*? He's *ker-azy!*'

'He said, and you're not going to like this, but he said that he wanted you to understand what happened to bad boys who did not accept "no creamies".'

'Shit, man. I don't ever want to hear anybody say that again. *Ever!* I just wanna lie here a while. Then I wanna take a bath. I wanna soak long!'

'I've got the thing he twatted you with,' Stephen added helpfully.

'Get rid of it, man!' groaned Epic, closing his eyes again. 'It was an iron bar or some shit. What does he expect me to do? Keep it as a fucking souvenir? Frame it on my wall next to Hendrix? Well, I don't even wanna see it. I don't need no lessons from nobody.'

Stephen nodded sympathetically: 'You might not want it, but if you really don't object, the rest of us would rather like to eat it, if that's cool with you.'

This reply brought on a prolonged fit of coughing from Epic, who after recovering from it then shook his head in disbelief: 'You wanna explain that?'

Stephen needed both hands to hold the weapon out. It was frayed at one end where Klaus had gripped it double-handed in order to twat Epic. It was a long, hard triangular object, which could have been some kind of pole. Only it wasn't a pole. It was actually more substantial than your average pole. It was a fuck-off family-size bar of Toblerone. Referigerated.

Chapter 45

Klaus

ODDLY ENOUGH, EPIC'S pride had not been hurt at all by what had happened to him. It had certainly not been as damaged as his jaw had been. The basic fact was that Epic had been clubbed into unconsciousness by a terrifyingly large fridge-hardened bar of triangular, almond-flavoured Swiss milk chocolate, wielded by a terrifyingly unstable Swiss coroner. It could easily have been true that Klaus had singled Epic out for a special warning to leave the milkmaids alone because he recognised that Epic had had a real chance of getting somewhere with them. Seeing him then turn up at the party and immediately move in on Lisle (which indeed was what Epic was attempting to do) had been more than Klaus could stand. He had considered his little social function of having nothing short of diplomatic significance, and it was certainly most inappropriate, if not provocative, for a foreign guest to hold the event in such low esteem as to behave as if he were in a sleazy Berlin nightclub. His blow on Epic's jaw (the one that had knocked him out) had been a blow for his country. For years, Switzerland had been regarded as a nation of smiling backward fence sitters, who took great pains not to offend anybody by opening their borders and banks to anybody. Switzerland meant the Red Cross. Switzerland meant cuckoo clocks. Switzerland meant blanket neutrality, a country which never disagreed with any other country, a country which made terrifyingly large bars of triangular, almond-flavoured chocolate, suitable for refrigeration; and it was with this indubitably exclusive Swiss *objet d'art* that Herr Butsch had repelled the foreign marauder to demonstrate emphatically that despite an entire history of democracy and no war, Switzerland would not be pushed around by anyone.

As for Epic, he had derived a surprisingly large amount of comfort from the fact that Lisle had not actually rejected his advances. He conveniently dismissed from his mind the fact that she had not been given any time to actually decide and concentrated his mind instead on pathetically convincing himself that he had in fact been at an advanced stage of winning the enthralled girl's favours before he was attacked so cowardly. In a particularly audacious fit of arrogance, Epic honestly believed that Klaus had come up with the only way open to him to prevent Epic scoring on Lisle. Maybe the old guy had been jealous. If there was going to be anybody who could score a bull's-eye with that creamy chic, it was going to be Epic, and the old pappy coroner guy knew that but couldn't take it. The only way that he could stop it was to take Epic out with that candy bar.

Epic may have been deluding himself, but then again there certainly wasn't any proof to the contrary and that was plenty enough for Epic. Lisle had only said 'not allowed' to him on account of him destroying her cute little display of yoghurt and this hadn't been Epic's fault anyhow.

Whatever the truth was, it was all history now, of course, although naturally enough, Epic faced a good deal of stick from everyone in the Inn (Stephen pulling the cruel stunt of waiting for Epic to go to the toilet and then replacing his pint of ale with a bar – albeit a regular sized one – of Toblerone), but largely because Epic had actually been assaulted by Klaus in a frenzy that no amount of 'no creamies' could have excused, sympathy for the Canadian was also thick on the ground. What was also established from this particularly strange event was that Epic never again had any designs on Hanne or Lisle. This, if nothing else, would have justified Klaus' actions in his own eyes.

Whatever else, everyone's emphasis had been obliged to switch now to Monday's funeral. James and Sophie, freshly dead, had been tended to lovingly by Tessa and presented to everyone the morning after the coroner's verdict, just before Epic left for his twatting, the result being that they actually looked little different from the excited young couple who had come bounding into Freddo's offices less than a month ago to submit their application. Noddoes had asked Tessa to take special care with Sophie, with whom he had been particularly struck from the moment he had first seen her on the tape. He had persisted in referring to her 'fragile beauty' and wanted Tessa to capture this quality in her work, or at least ensure that it was not significantly impaired. Tessa, who as usual wanted to be more adventurous, had therefore decided to do a traditional job on them both. Since it was important to Noddoes (and thus, Tessa assumed, to the success of the funeral) that Sophie emerged looking as natural as possible, she considered it unwise to produce anything creative with James either. When she first revealed her display, it drew spontaneous applause and other favourable noises from all of her colleagues. The lovers were sitting up stiffly (perhaps understandably) on a chaise longue, hand in hand and smiling straight ahead. They were both dressed in jeans and a top, Sophie's light blue and James' grey, and wrapped around them was a red sash with white lettering: "TO YOU I'M BORN AGAIN".

'Oh *bless*! Don't they look sweet!' Amanda said. 'You can see they're really mad about each other, can't you! I think they look really sweet!' Amanda clearly was sober. She would never have used a word like 'sweet' otherwise.

Noddoes also walked up for a closer look. 'What a lovely girl!' he sighed. 'You know, I've been thinking for some time now about who she reminds me of. It was driving me mad for ages but I have it now. It's darling Jane Birkin, of course. A soft gentle English beauty of such sophistication as to be revered throughout France as the ultimate symbol of femininity and sexuality and adopted by them as one of their own because of it. There she was an icon. Here she was practically a nobody. What a pity! Such a great pity!'

'Come to think of it, she *does* look a bit like Jane Birkin, you're right,' agreed Stephen, stepping up and pointing. 'She's like a gazelle, as frail as a flower but just as beautiful. If she was a little more toothy, it would be Jane B!'

'I could soon fix that!' Tessa said.

'Say, are you guys talking about the chick who made that record in

French back in the sixties where she was getting it off with her old man, that swarthy little Moroccan type with the king-sized snozzle?' fired in Epic.

'Ah!' purred Noddoes. 'There we see eye to eye!'

'What are you all talking about?' demanded Amanda, punching Stephen sharply on the arm just for a change.

'Hey!' Epic suddenly shouted, leaping half out of his skin and nearly causing everyone else to do the same. 'Hey, I have a most *excellent* idea! What if we-'

'No, no. Definitely not!' interrupted Frank, finding his voice at last. I'm *not* going to have them do *Je T'aime*. No. That's definitely out!'

'Aw, come on, Frankie. It would be cool!'

'It would be a disgrace. I absolutely forbid it!'

Stephen agreed with Epic: 'I think it would be going against everything we've striven for if we *didn't* let them do *Je T'aime*,' he said. 'We may well have long shifted emphasis from the doughnut critique to a more sympa-thetic system, where corpses are treated as if they were still alive with voices and everything, but surely this is precisely why we *should* press ahead with *Je T'aime*. And bearing in mind Sophie's incontrovertible likeness to Jane Birkin, which I think we all now recognise, it would clearly be a neglect of duty to say nothing of current Freddo protocol if we *didn't* go ahead with it!'

'But, Stephen!' wailed Frank, desperation setting in now. 'You know this record as well as I do. It's not just kissy-kissy. The two of them actually... well, you know!'

'They'll be wearing clothes, of course,' Stephen assured him.

'Shoot!' muttered Epic.

'Oh, it would be done *most* tastefully,' added Noddoes, showing his sup-port for the idea for the first time. 'It is, after all, a love song.'

'Oh, rubbish!' snapped Frank. 'It's a much maligned *sex* song. I won't have anything to do with it! And anyway, James looks nothing like Serge Gainsbourg. He looks more like Boris Becker, poor little sod!'

'I could soon fix that!' Tessa assured him, most helpfully. '*Purrrr!*'

'No! Oh, God! No! No!' howled Frank. 'Oh, good heavens. No!'

'You really mustn't overreact, dear fellow,' Noddoes told him. 'The song in question was really all about Jane. Not many people even remember that ghastly little Frenchman.'

'Man, that's shit!' barked Epic, distraught that even though the others were pressing Frank to change his mind, they did not want to go the whole hog (which Epic most certainly did) and have the couple perform *au naturel*. 'That record was about the French guy also. Why do you think that Jane chick was making with all them moans and gasps? Huh? That Jane chick was making with all them moans and gasps on account of the little frog boning her! Ain't no doubt 'bout that!'

'Not exactly a nice way of putting it, my boy,' reprimanded Noddoes.

'That's the way it was though, man!'

'I'm not having anyone do anything to that boy!' piously ordered Frank, careful not to single out Tessa in particular even though she, of course, was the only one who could have 'done' anything.

'Oh, but I *do* urge you to reconsider vis-à-vis the love song!' begged Noddoes. 'We need not touch a hair on the head of James. We don't need that ghastly little Gainsbourg. We already have dear little Jane. She is everything. She *is* the song! And *oh*, it would be done *most* tastefully.'

'Fully clothed!' Frank stipulated sternly, seemingly conceding defeat finally.

'Why, my dear Eddowes, *of course* fully clothed! Anything else would be terribly vulgar.'

'Shoot!' muttered Epic.

Frank breathed heavily and shook his head: 'I'll never forgive you if this ends in disgrace,' he warned. 'I'll hold you personally responsible, Noddoes.'

'I...,' Noddoes replied loftily, '... am in charge! Good heavens! One would think that you were half-hoping for a failure so that you could cheerfully censure me. Have I let you down thus far?'

Frank, taken by surprise, had no alternative but to give way: 'No. You've been excellent,' he admitted. 'It's just that a performance of this particular song, and I still maintain that it has precious little to do with singing, is so easily open to a vulgar interpretation. Indeed, to interpret it faithfully would mean doing exactly what I forbid you doing. The condensing of it actually produces a parody.'

'Oh, really, Frank! Isn't everything we've been doing here since we started a parody?' Stephen asked. 'I mean, for fuck's sake, disembark from your lofty steed!'

'Oh bugger it!' unexpectedly snapped Frank. 'Alright. Do it! Get on with it! Do it how you fucking well like!'

'In the raw!' beamed Epic triumphantly. '*Yesss!*'

'Tastefully!' overruled Noddoes.

'Shoot!' muttered Epic.

Chapter 46

The Officer Who Looked Like The Guy Out Of Blue Mink

THE CHAPS HAD to get weaving now to prepare for the double-headed funeral featuring James and Sophie, the lovers; and preparation was particularly important on this occasion, since Frank and Thoad had to be coached in the art of puppeteering by Stephen and Epic, the resident masters. Friday and Saturday were put by for rehearsals. It had been decided that Frank would be trained by Stephen and together they would deal with Sophie, whilst the unlikely team of Epic and Thoad would operate James. Frank had particularly made the point of keeping Epic away from Sophie (or 'Jane' as everyone was now calling her), knowing of the Canadian's disappointment at the intended watering down of *Je T'aime... Moi Non Plus* and the golden opportunity which would be presented to him to make mischief had he been allowed to get his paws on the girl. Epic himself had now quite recovered from Thursday's goings on and was now throwing himself full square behind the job in hand, although as usual, naughtiness was on his mind.

The training session went well. The task of bringing Frank and Thoad up to speed was indeed nowhere near as problematic as first had been feared, principally because whilst Sophie and then James performed their solos on the opening two numbers, their partner was not required to move very much, spellbound as they were in love with each other. Only when *Je T'aime* closed the show would all hell break loose and all hands be required to the deck.

The foursome worked out a cute little routine for the final number, which saw the lovers cooing at each other to the background of the instrumental track of Gainsbourg's *Je T'aime;* a piece actually entitled *Love At First Sight* for the purpose of its release as a single by a group called Sounds Nice, whilst sitting huddled together on a porch swing. As the music intensified, so Sophie and James would grip each other and hug lovingly fully clothed and thereby lead each other to the dais.

It had been possible to work out how to manipulate the corpses by the cords into a reclining position so that the love act was innocently replicated in the most synthetic of manners, just as they were tipped down the chute. This finale was accepted by Frank as being as necessary as it was tasteful, although he still retained his initial strong misgivings of having *Je T'Aime* in the repertoire at all.

The last view of the lovers would be that of the couple expressing their love for each other; not in the actual physical sense (they, after all, were both fully clothed), but in the decent, clean, Trevor Howard/Celia Johnson sort of way with all sniggering confined to the sidelines. The choice of backing music, after all, would provide more than enough clues as the real relationship of the dead couple and to the fact that it had not been a platonic *Brief Encounter*, but rather a full sexual exchange between two inseparables. Sophie and James might well have been fencing with each other in vows of love sung in French, but *Je T'aime* had been an international blockbuster and the music, even without the accompanying panting and gasping, only ever meant one thing; giving your lady a portion. This was why nudity was irrelevant, and this indeed was what Epic either could not understand, or more probably had no wish to understand, for he wanted to snigger on the sidelines as well.

The *Je T'aime* routine was worked out to Frank's strict choreography – the Trevor and Celia way. Noddoes was, once again, magnificent. His range of voice this time was demonstrated as being nothing short of sensational. For Sophie he sang like a bird – darling, fragile, gentile little Jane, overwhelmed by her experienced Latin lover. And then James, who contributed to the lyric as if he were addressing a seminar of industrialists, shielding any pleasure he was deriving from the lovemaking, perhaps because an admittance to such enjoyment would comprise and even demean him as a Frenchman. His voice remained deep and unruffled. He might as well have been brushing his hair. Frank, on reflecting on the rehearsal, could not but pronounce the act as being without fault. Everything was done and dusted by the following afternoon, and after two further 'takes' just to make sure, Frank announced to everyone that they had the performance to a T and that a trip to the Inn was in order as a reward: 'I'm a firm advocate of the work hard, play hard ethic,' he announced rather whimsically, as everyone else headed for the door, delighted at this decision.

For, after all, Saturday evening was upon them now and the Inn Crowd descended upon their temple in the most benign of spirits to find Tom and Kate, the tall, brunette, all-smiling, moon-faced barmaid with only a mild habit, *in situ*, ready for a heavy night, and Baz, the principal scrote regular, sitting down at one of the tables in some heavily soiled overalls, chatting animatedly to another unwashed young man, whom none of the others had seen before, and smoking a reefer the size of a miniature rug.

'Oh, hello! Here they all come!' Tom chided them by way of a greeting. 'Fucking Burke and Hare and Company!'

'Hey, bartender!' acknowledged Epic. 'Just rustle us up some beer and then go screw yourself, okay?'

'Ha Ha!' roared Tom. 'Get out of it!'

Everyone dropped themselves on top of their stools and Amanda and Epic immediately emulated Baz by rolling their own. Tessa walked off to find her supplier and the first round of drinks lasted less than it took Tom and Kate to produce it. All except Noddoes. Noddoes sipped his dry white wine conservatively. He had become entirely accustomed to the Inn now. It wouldn't have been a place he would have gone within a mile of in his pre-Freddo days, but he no longer belonged to those frugal inconsequential times. His star now shone brightly, his vocation discovered. The reception he had received in there, well before self-participating funerals had won him a foothold and had so dramatically catapulted him to eminence, had been most favourable. He had become spectacularly popular from the start, something which had initially infuriated Frank, who had pinned his hopes on the kids laughing him out of the place as soon as they had his number. Alas, Frank had been just as disappointed with the reaction of the clientele as he had certainly been with the reaction of his own immediate circle when they had encountered Noddoes for the first time. The old luvvie had been an instant hit. Nobody had ever come across anybody like him before and they thought he was wild. Noddoes' cult of personality had spiralled since self-participating funerals had imposed its iron grip. The crucial difference, of course, was that chief amongst his admirers now was Frank himself. Thus Noddoes was allowed to pose magnificently, basking in all his personal and professional glory, and sip his wine and smoke his cigarettes through a holder like Princess Margaret and offer air kisses to anybody who wanted them, and this in turn meant that Noddoes rarely got drunk. But this didn't matter, since he was permanently in a state of intoxication in any case, brought on by virtue of the fact that he had for many years, certainly since drama school, inhabited a faraway egotistical dream world, the territory of which had had its boundaries enlarged spectacularly since his elevation for the first time in his life to a genuine man of consequence.

The remainder of the Inn Crowd started to wire themselves into the session. Frank, who was almost always the first to get pissed, was practically gone already, delighted with his career and with his life and determined to drink himself to the point where he would need someone to take him home.

His mother had disappeared into a shell ever since her 'babies' had been incinerated, but her attitude towards Frank had changed too because of her new found first-hand knowledge of his work, which had left such an impression on her, both as a mourner at the specific occasion and also on reflection afterwards. She tended to nag him less now and tolerate his drinking more and this had sweetened Frank's life further. His domestic and professional situations being in such good shape, it only remained for him to claim a second, and this time memorable helping of kitty fondling, and he would be the happiest bunny in any warren anywhere. But Tessa was not on his immediate mind for a change. Frank was going on a bender with all of his like-minded colleagues and friends and everyone had all of Sunday to recover before the most romantic funeral in history took place the day after. Sure enough there was a time and place for everything. The time now was for a bloody good drink. And he maintained this view even when he heard Sheba purring luxuriously to the side of him.

Time passed and the Inn started to swell. Unclean children passed in and out, immersed in rings of smoke, whilst equally unappealing-looking couples chewed at each other's mouths, as studs embedded in all parts of their heads scraped together to a segue of punk classics thundering out of the speakers above them. Amanda caught sight of one of these androgonous pairs of Siamese twins and turned to Stephen, who was also looking at them by chance.

'Sweet!' she said and punched him on the arm. 'Bless!' she added and gripped Stephen's bollocks ferociously.

Epic was being amusing, charming, rude, clever, disingenuous, biting, ironic, foul, satirical, sympathetic and a wanker all at the same time. For him, this was easy. For him, not to be was virtually impossible. For him, silence was never golden. It was alien enough a concept for him never to have attempted to sample its benefits.

Thoad was politely enough pretending to be interested in Tom's photographs of his recent week in the Dominican Republic, which he assured Thoad was the happening place at the minute 'and cheaper than fucking Malaga.' Thoad smiled weakly (the only type of smiling he was capable of anyway) as he shuffled his way through images of Tom sharing nobblers and spliffs with local opposite numbers and also with suspiciously non-adult looking girls, most with crucifixes around their necks, their only way of saying sorry.

'The gear out there is blinding!' Tom enthused. 'Some stuff I never even heard of before. Funny little jungle roots and that sort of caper. Knocks your bleeding head off. Christ!'

'Who's this chap?' Thoad asked, indicating a distinctly unwell-looking fat bastard with a face as red as a beetroot, pictured with his arm around Tom and a girl no older than thirteen sitting on his lap, dressed in a savagely ripped blue T-shirt and nothing visible underneath, and the man resting a shot glass on her leg with his spare hand.

'Oh, he was a good bloke, Brendan,' confirmed Tom. 'He showed me around coz he goes every year. Scouser. Spoke a bit of Spanish. Got his number somewhere. Probably fucking lost it.'

'I suppose that's his daughter, the dirty bastard!' suddenly added Stephen, taking the photo from Thoad.

'Get out of it!' snapped Tom, snatching it back off him, genuinely cross. 'He was a top geezer. Those kids are all over the place. You can't get rid of them.'

'Some guys don't want to,' Epic added, having arrived at the bar and picking up the plot in his typically lightning manner.

'Fucking get out of it!' barked Tom again. 'Cheeky little sod! Are you saying that I went over there for *that*? You have me down as some kind of nonce? Fucking get out of it!' He spun an elastic band around the wad of photos and threw them angrily onto the shelf behind him.

'Hey, take it easy, Tommy!' Epic said. 'The kid's sitting on the other guy's balls, man. I never said anything about you. Jeez! You wanna take it easy! We all know you're cool. Okay? *Okay?*'

Tom snarled and then pushed past Kate, the tall, brunette, all-smiling, moon-faced barmaid with only a mild habit, to get at Frank, who had signalled to him.

The session continued through the evening and up towards half an hour of the first bell. The Inn was packed to suffocation and everyone within Frank's circle had had more than a surfeit of one thing or another. Stephen and Amanda had joined the snogging set and Frank noticed Epic deep in a cosy, rather canoodling, conversation with Sheba. A whiff of implication, perhaps? But he not only didn't mind, Frank actually smiled approval at them, not that either of them saw it. Frank was pissed and therefore happy.

Thoad was staring gloomily at his glass. Tom and Kate, the tall, brunette, all-smiling, moon-faced barmaid with only a mild habit, were busy behind the bar. Frank eventually caught Kate's eye and beckoned her over. She nodded, reached for a fresh glass, filled it and walked towards him. Frank glanced away to the side just before she arrived. This was a perfect night. Familiar faces at every turn. Wall to wall Inn regulars. All for him.

At this moment, the door on the station concourse side was thrown open and in marched five people who were most certainly not Inn regulars. The first two invaders looked like twins. They were large, early forties, gorilla-type blokes with intimidatingly short haircuts and wearing equally bad suits with kipper ties, which hadn't been in fashion outside fancy dress for practically a generation. They were followed in by a similarly aged, but much slimmer man in a blue jacket, grey T-shirt and tight blue jeans and brandishing a radio. He had a generous mop of shaggy jet-black hair and as an accoutrement, a rather excellent glistening moustache, which ran square down into a well-trimmed beard. Frank thought that he looked like the guy out of the seventies band, Blue Mink. The remaining two police officers were in uniform, one a female.

Within seconds, everybody was desperately trying to hide their gear and the under-aged kids were keeping their heads firmly down instead of down each other. Amanda was immediately terrified and in a flash, had removed a bag of weed and a lump of resin from somewhere and had dropped them into Stephen's jacket pocket: 'Hide them!' she gasped urgently. 'They'll be searching *everyone!*'

Epic too started to panic. He had, of course, been arrested during his days in London for possession and had been let off with a caution. At that moment, he was carrying a little more herbal than was usual to be regarded by police as being for personal consumption. He was thus immediately fearful of being loaded up on a charge of possession with intent to supply. He too jettisoned his gear. In his case, the floor was the beneficiary, the fat pouch of drugs being tossed to the foot of the stool occupied by the unsuspecting Stephen, who now looked in pretty deep shit actually. The irony was, he had never even touched a cigarette in his life, let alone a joint. Now there was suddenly evidence against him (or at least against his stool) for the drug squad (for it was of course they) to nick him big style. The only other drug taker in Freddo's party, Tessa, was free from worry. She had always been very careful not to carry any gear even for a second. Anything she bought she always consumed immediately.

Everywhere around the Inn kids were shitting themselves. Whether they had gear or were underage, innocents were fairly thin on the ground. They needn't have worried. The Old Bill were indeed raiding the place, but their brief was not to seize controlled drugs - they had more than enough evidence in that direction already - and the invasion was, in fact, the culmination of an investigation which had been ongoing for several weeks. They had arrived now for one purpose only: simply to make arrests. The first of the two gorillas marched up to Tom Beck and loomed over him: 'Alright, Peter Pan. You know who we are. You're coming with us!' he growled. Tom, who did indeed know who the gorillas were and what they were there for, folded the small towel he had been using to wipe glasses, hung it tidily over the drying rail and walked off with his escort without saying a word.

The second primate had come for Baz, whom everyone knew (especially Plod) as being a friend and close 'business associate' of Tom's. Gorilla II duly tapped him on the shoulder and led him away. Baz similarly said nothing, simply stabbed out his joint and departed also as Tom had done, through the door on the taxi rank side under benign police escort, indicating neither dissent nor surprise with regard to him being taken into custody.

The slimmer officer with the cheesy beard, who looked like the guy out of Blue Mink, had the honour of dealing with Kate, the tall, brunette, all-smiling, moon-faced barmaid with only a mild habit. Kate had just served Frank before the balloon had gone up, and because she was entirely trapped behind the bar in front of Frank just as the police burst in, the slimmer officer with the cheesy beard, who looked like the guy out of Blue Mink, was obliged to walk first behind the bar and then around it in order to get at her. When he arrived, he nodded at her with a cold stare:

'Alright, love, you're nicked as well!' he advised her without histrionics. Kate glanced upwards with a beam of a smile aimed at no-one other than the Almighty and then stepped backwards to accept her fate. The female uniformed officer, who had been brought to the scene specifically for Kate's benefit, led her away.

With both Tom and Kate now under arrest, the remaining member of bar staff was a 'casual' – a twenty-year-old Australian student called Millie, who had been employed for less than a week. Millie, a wholesome-looking girl, who swam and played tennis and didn't do drugs at all, had viewed the carnage open-mouthed with a total lack of an idea as to how to react to it, apart from being abjectly grateful that she had not been bundled off in the crossfire. For a few precious seconds, Millie, who wanted to train to be a vet once her obligatory Aussie wunderlust had been disposed of, found herself the proprietor of the Station Inn. She also, for the record, was destined to be the last one, as the slimmer officer with the cheesy beard, who looked like the guy out of Blue Mink, was only too happy to explain once he was able to knock out the taped music and then address the noble assembly in a raised voice:

'Okay. We won't waste your time. You know who we are. I imagine just about all of you know *why* we're here. Basically, this place is closed as of now. The licence will be revoked and the premises will be impounded. Now, I want everybody to leave as quickly as you can. I'm going to give you five minutes to drink up and go. We know that many of you are carrying. Some of you are still smoking it now. But we've got the people we want and so we're giving the rest of you a break. So five minutes, alright? Let's go. And don't hang around outside. Clear the area. Anyone who is still in here, or even on the concourse after five minutes, we shall assume wants to help us with our enquiries. Thanks for your attention. Cheers.'

Some of the scrotes immediately started filing out through both doors without worrying about their drinks. The slimmer officer with the cheesy beard, who looked like the guy out of Blue Mink, walked over to Millie and indicated the male uniformed policeman who had remained there throughout:

'I want you to give your details to the officer and then you can go. I'm sorry, love, but you're out of a job, I'm sorry to say.'

The Inn Crowd, meanwhile, were just finishing up and preparing to depart through the concourse exit. Stephen placed his empty bottle down on the counter and stepped off his stool. The slimmer officer with the cheesy beard, who looked like the guy out of Blue Mink, called across to him:

'Hey you! Pick up that now! That's not staying on the floor! Get it up!'

Stephen looked down and saw Epic's pouch: 'That's not mine!' he stammered, genuinely shocked and indignant. He pointed at it: 'That's got nothing to do with me!'

'Pick it up!' demanded the officer again.

'Goddamn it! Pick it up, asshole! Pick it up!' Epic hissed at him.

Stephen, feeling more than a little slighted, scooped up the offending material and dropped it into his jacket pocket, where it found appropriate company in the contribution made by Amanda earlier. He then followed Thoad and Amanda towards the door; Epic was next and then came Sheba, accompanied by Noddoes. Within a microsecond of the door closing, Epic and Amanda jumped on Stephen and retrieved their gear:

'Gimmee that thing!'

'Hand my stuff over, you thieving bastard!'

Frank remained on his stool, utterly stunned. Millie the barmaid walked past him and around the bar to pick up a few odds and ends. She too then left. Frank had approximately a third remaining in his beer glass. He stared at the liquid and blinked heavily.

'Come on, mate. Drink up!' the slimmer officer with the cheesy beard, who looked like the guy out of Blue Mink told him.

Frank looked up: 'Is it really true that this place is finished?' he slurred.

'You heard what I said. The licence is being revoked. You'll have to go somewhere else.'

'But this place is my life!' wailed Frank tearfully and pathetically.

The officer sneered at him: 'It's a shithole!' he said. 'Now I want you out, alright? Come on, you're the last one in here. If you're still here in sixty seconds, you're going to find yourself nicked. You're pissed. And that's just for starters. Now come on, mate, you're far too old to fuck me about!'

Frank glanced about him. He was indeed alone, apart from the two officers. 'This place is my life!' he repeated and finally drained his glass. He dismounted from his stool and half staggered to the door. He reached out for the handle and then turned around to confront the slimmer officer with the cheesy beard, who looked like the guy out of Blue Mink one more time: 'Please! *Please*! Don't close us down!' Frank was practically sobbing.

'You're on your last warning, my friend,' the policeman told him. 'One more word and you're coming with us. Now do yourself a favour and just go!'

Frank left, closing the door behind him and practically walked straight into Stephen, who was on his way back in to try to find out what had happened to Frank. He was fearful that he had been nicked, but was not worried about the police himself since he was no longer carrying anything naughty. He found Frank still at liberty but in tears and not in good shape at all.

'They've closed the Inn!' howled Frank. 'They've closed it, damn them!'

'I know, mate,' nodded Stephen, immediately feeling a lump in his throat. 'It's the end of the fucking world!'

Thoad suddenly appeared alongside them, tears running powerfully down both cheeks: 'What did they have to go and do that for?' he blubbered. 'How *could* they close the old Inn? What are we supposed to do now?'

Stephen then surrendered to his own emotions and the three men stood in a circle, hugging each other and heaving with grief. Amanda then walked up and suddenly burst into tears too. She punched Stephen sharply on the arm: 'You stupid, silly, useless, weak, spineless bastard! How could you stand around and let them do that to us?' She pummelled both shoulders with her fists and then flung her arms around his neck. 'Weak bastard!' she blubbered.

'What are we going to do?' choked Frank. 'Our world has been shattered. We're finished! It's all over!'

There was a heavy thud as Thoad dropped on to his knees, gasping and sniffing. 'I don't want to live!' he snivelled. 'I'm going to jump!'

Everybody looked at him. It was a most pathetic apparition, but Frank reacted as if he had been poked with a pin. 'Yes… yes. Of course. There's no other answer. *I'm* going to jump!'

Stephen kissed Amanda, who responded by kicking him on the shin and then punching him on the same part of the same arm, thereby ensuring that Stephen's physical pain complemented admirably the hurt engendered emotionally by the Inn's demise and his comrades' reaction to it: 'Shall *we* jump, sweetheart?'

Amanda glared at him. 'Of fucking *course* we jump, you weak bastard!' she spat and kneed him in the groin.

Noddoes sidled up to the hysterical quartet: 'Perhaps, dear friends, at this most hopeless of times you would not thank me for interjecting, but I feel I must remind you that before any mass action is considered and put into operation, we must fulfill our obligation to that lovely girl and her handsome young boy.'

'By God, Noddoes. You're right!' whimpered Frank. 'James and Sophie. None of this is *their* fault!'

'I'm going off the old Point!' Thoad reiterated from his knees.

'Not yet, old fellow.'

Epic, who had been just as stunned as the others by events, but had not taken it nearly as badly, came strolling up with Sheba. 'Say, have you guys been talking about totalling yourselves? Hey, don't go doing that without me, now. I've *always* been into suicide and such. Talk to me!'

'It's the only way out,' Frank assured him, calm enough now to finally dry his eyes.

'I'm going to bring back the boys from ROPSAS!' sobbed Thoad, still from the floor. 'I think *somebody* should benefit from this tragedy.'

'Christ! You guys are really serious, aren't you?' enthused Epic. 'You're really gonna do this!'

'It will be the greatest festival of self-destruction this town has ever seen,' envisaged Frank. 'We shall turn it into a carnival. Up at Rocky Point. The happiest day of our lives, as well as the last. We'll all make arrangements for our own musical choices for our farewells. I'll talk to Danny as soon as I can, for surely our suicides must have music; music as personal to ourselves as were our lives. And then to our funerals where we shall dance again. Dance and sing. Sing to other selected pieces important to us. It will be a festival which will set you, Noddoes on the path to glory... and ourselves into the annals of immortality. For Noddoes must remain, as must Tessa, as essential staff. I shall employ and train sundry staff for puppeteering duties to cover the vacancies resulting in the departure of ourselves. Are you with us, Epic?'

'Oh, man! Am I ever!'

'It's decided, then.'

'You coming over the side, Sheba, honey?' Epic asked, turning to her excitedly.

'*Purrrr!*'

'No, no,' Frank said. 'I'm sorry but, as I point out, we need Tessa most certainly to remain. She'll be embalming our corpses remember, once Sid has recovered our shattered remains. As must Noddoes remain for our mass funeral, over which he must preside. That leaves five of us to close the book on ourselves.'

It seemed perhaps the ultimate of ironies that Frank was happy to allow Noddoes the opportunity to set himself 'on the path of glory', whilst he, Frank, forfeited his life in order to set up this chance to a man he had for the best part loathed. But for once, Frank, who knew most certainly that he no longer wanted to live, was thinking far more clearly. Clouded no longer by either personal desires (Tessa) or personal prejudices (Noddoes), his reasoning was governed entirely by practicalities and pragmatism. It was certainly easy enough to recruit bearers (even though they would have to be trained as 'puppeteers' – and there would need to be several of them), but both Tessa, and especially Noddoes, were truly indispensable and Frank understood this in spades.

'Nobody's going to stop me from doing it,' grieved Thoad forever from the floor, eyes as red as tomatoes. He clearly hadn't been listening at all.

'No, old friend,' Frank assured him. 'We're *all* going to do it!'

'We'll convene after we've done our duty by James and Sophie,' Frank reminded them. 'Our lives are over.'

'We're all gonna die!' panted Epic. 'Man! That's horny!'

'Groovy! Groovy!' agreed Sheba.

'Not you!' Frank reprimanded her sharply. Sheba responded with a long catty hiss.

'We'll take this up later,' Stephen stated huskily. 'All I can say is that there are two young corpses waiting for their big day. Deal with them first for decency's sake.'

Amanda nodded and whacked Stephen on the arm again to confirm acquiescence.

'I'm going to jump!' Thoad wailed, still not paying any attention to anyone.

'Yes, yes,' Frank assured him, placing a comforting hand on Thoad's shoulder, which began immediately heaving again, as the desperate imbiber gave way to sobbing once more. 'Yes, old friend. We're *all* going to jump!'

In that instant, the door to the Inn flew open and out marched the uniformed officer, followed by the slimmer officer with the cheesy beard, who looked like the guy out of Blue Mink, who locked the door behind him. He then noticed Thoad, still on his knees sobbing, and then one by one glared at the remainder of the Inn Crowd before fixing a blank look directly at Frank.

The officer shook his head: 'You and these sad little bastards are not even worth a ride in the van!' he said before walking off to solve more crime.

Chapter 47

Serge Gainsbourg
And Jane Birkin

Aʟʟ ᴏꜰ ᴀ sudden, the charming funeral of James and Sophie meant something else. It had become inadvertently a statement, more than anything which had gone before it, including even the emotion-charged adieu to dear Harry Evans, an event which had sapped everyone emotionally to an almost sanity-losing degree. This time, they faced a goodbye to, and for, everyone. The staff, who were to preside over these proceedings, had all decided that they had no option but to end their days following the closure of the Station Inn courtesy of the Special Branch. Consequently, Sunday was a day of reflection for all of them, with poor Thoad having to be supervised closely, lest he should potter up to Rocky Point by himself and fling himself off unauthorised, so utterly uncontrollably distraught was he at the Inn's sudden cruel demise.

Frank, meanwhile, conferred with Danny the vicar and emphasised that he would soon be required to preside over a five-way suicide spectacular ere long and that the event would be something which the town would never forget.

'The ceremony will be in two parts, essentially,' Frank told him. 'The first part will see the suicide party jumping off Rocky Point. Five of us: Stephen, Amanda, Epic, Thoad and myself. Naturally we shall all be jumping to our chosen music track piped over by Keith. Your mission, Danny, if you choose to accept it, will be to officiate at this festival. *The Pendlesham Gazette* will be informed, and dear old Thoad has promised to secure the services of some associates of his to record the leaps by way of camcorder. It will be full-steam ahead as soon as we finish here tomorrow.'

'So The Exotics won't be returning then?' Danny said, sounding disappointed. 'Amanda's going over.'

'Ah! Not necessarily,' Frank told him. 'Certainly it's true that Amanda's jumping, but since Tessa isn't and she'll be embalming us all, there's no reason at all why Amanda shouldn't be in your line-up for the big event until such time that it's her turn to go over. I'd love to think that The Exotics could make a special return for this final spectacular. And indeed the suicide of one of those beauties will add, in my judgement, an unparalleled touch of class. This is going to be a suicide extravaganza and the funeral... well, the *funeral*, Danny, which is the second part of the ceremony over at the Bar and Grill, will be the greatest moment of your ecclesiastical career. I see it as the defining moment in funeral history. Oh yes. It's going to be a never to be forgotten, never to be repeated festival of magnificence, rock and roll and doom. I can't give you any precise details just now, but the second we get rid of this couple we have booked for tomorrow, I'm going to put everything into action. Full speed ahead!'

'This sounds excellent!' beamed Danny, rubbing his hands together. 'I'm so excited. Especially since the girls are coming back. It will be one of pop's greatest returns.'

'We're all very excited,' admitted Frank. 'It's quite amazing really. This has been such an astonishing and instant turnaround. When we were all banished from the Inn by a horrid policeman, who looked like the guy out of Blue Mink, by the way, we were all of us feeling as low as rats. The outlook for everyone was desperate. And then dear old Thoad announced that he was going to jump, and by doing so switched on a glorious light for the rest of us to be guided by. From desperation to delirium in two shakes of a lamb's tail. An epithany. Quite remarkable!'

'I'm happy for all of you,' Danny beamed. 'It's so nice to have some good news for a change. But your old boatman shall have his work cut out, won't he? Bless him.'

'Goodness, yes,' suddenly remembered Frank. 'Sid! I shall have to sound him out, of course. Thank you, Danny.'

The two men shook hands. Frank walked away and Sunday was completed.

On the morning of the following day, the Bar and Grill was ready to greet the arrival of James and Sophie. Everyone was in place with the puppet masters; Stephen and Epic checking the ropes and also the strength of a porch swing on which the lovers would sit canoodling during the set, up to the opening of *Je T'aime* before walking across to the catafalque for their romantic finale during the committal. The display was hidden behind a screen.

Noddoes was conferring with Keith Tate, the soundman, and Amanda was chatting excitedly to Barefoot Sally and Tessa about The Exotics' comeback for the forthcoming extravaganza at which she would also appear as a corpse:

'I'm going to be a busy, busy bee that day,' she enthused. 'Busy, busy bee! Buzz, buzz, buzz!'

'Have you got any idea about what you want me to do with you, beautifying-wise?' Tessa asked her.

'Busy, busy… I want to look like Siouxsie Sioux,' Amanda said, referring to the dark princess of punk, lead singer of Siouxsie And The Banshees, one of Amanda's principal icons. 'But I'm not sure about the track yet. I might go for *Christine*, but then again, I might choose *I Want To Be Me*. I know that was Toyah and not Siouxsie, but the song's fucking ace… sorry, Sal, really good!'

'What's Stephen going to do?' asked Barefoot Sally. 'His music, I mean. What's he going to pick?'

'Busy, busy, buzz, buzz… I'm going to pick it for him,' Amanda insisted. 'It's called *I'm A Stupid, Useless, Weak, Spineless Bastard* by one of Johnny Rotten's old bands, The Spineless Cunts!… Oh, I'm sorry, Sal!'

The families of the lovers, meanwhile, were sitting around in the crematorium, waiting for things to get going. Most were formally dressed, whilst the young friends of the couple were decked out in more Freddoesque apparel. Things were almost ready to begin, and as Stephen and Epic followed Thoad discreetly to the door, *Three Times A Lady* by The Commodores wafted softly across the room, replacing a very light organ piece composed and recorded by Keith Tate himself, which had been playing continuously up to that point. People began coughing and shuffling around in their seats like school kids at the start of morning assembly, and whilst they were doing this, Stephen and Epic delivered James through the back door, plonked him on one of the seats on the porch swing and connected him up with the ropes; this of course unseen by the congregation because of the screen.

'Okay, okay. Jimmy's cool,' whispered Epic, not wishing to drown out Lionel Ritchie. 'Let's go get Jane and get this thing on.'

'I still think we should have told Frank,' Stephen said. 'He's likely to blow his fucking stack when he sees what we're going to do.'

'No, Stevie,' Epic said. 'Frankie don't give a damn no more. Trust me. He might feel a bit sore to start with, but, hey, the guy just won't give a damn. We're gonna get this thing on. Now c'mon!'

The two men slunk off.

Three Times A Lady came to an end, followed first by silence and then the prelude to morning assembly again. During this shuffling and coughing, Sophie was delivered through the back of the Bar and Grill. But instead of joining James on the swing, she was connected up by the ropes in such a way that she was standing directly in front, leaning against the catafalque on which they would 'cuddle' to say goodbye before being tipped into the furnace. The puppeteers still needed a minute or so to prepare, and Thoad, mindful of the increasing restlessness of the audience, peeked around the screen and gave a pre-arranged signal to Keith Tate that another record was required before kick-off. Sonny and Cher's *I've Got You, Babe* came on, a significantly louder track than the one which had come before it and the guests settled down again. Within no time, everything was ready and Thoad leaned around the screen again to attract the attention of Danny and Frank, the vicar thereby notified that the funeral was ready to begin, and Frank thereby reminded that his efforts would presently be required in order to help operate Sophie on the final and pivotal track. Notice had been requested and had now been served.

Sonny and Cher were allowed to finish their pop classic...

'READY TO RUMBLE!' then roared Danny into his microphone. Up went the obligatory cheer, as set out in the 'hymn' sheet as a reply:

The Rev Hare: Does everybody in the chapel feel the force?

Everyone: We feel the force indeed, Daddy Cool!

The Rev Hare: Reggae, Country, Punk and Soul!

Everyone: Blues and Jazz and Rock and Roll!

The Rev Hare: We're gonna reveal brother James and sister Sophie in the name of the biggest, baddest DJ on the network!

Everyone: Reveal our brother and sister, right on!

The Rev Hare: Shall we do it?

Everyone: Do it!

The Rev Hare (Louder): Are we gonna do it?

Everyone (Louder): We're gonna do it!

The Rev Hare: Are we gonna Rock and Roll?

Everyone: Rock and Roll!

The Rev Hare (Louder): I said, are we gonna Rock and Roll?

Everyone (Louder): Rock and Roll!

The Rev Hare (Still Louder): Hit me, one more time! Are we gonna Rock and Roll?

Everyone (Still Louder): Rock and Roll!

The Rev Hare (In Delirium): ROCK AND ROLL, JAMES! ROCK AND ROLL, SOPHIE!

Everyone (In Delirium): GOD GAVE ROCK AND ROLL TO US!

And with that, the lights were dipped out completely, total darkness, so that Frank and Thoad could remove the screen and then go and hide with Stephen and Epic behind the catafalque. Stephen and Epic then fastened onto the wires connected to Sophie and a torch with a green light was flashed at Keith Tate by Thoad. In the same instant, the bright arc light sprung out of nowhere to reveal a leggy, gap-toothed Sophie walking demurely from in front of the invisible dais, as the intro of Jane Birkin's signature tune, *Jane B*, a classical piece actually composed by Chopin but given a distinctive arrangement and a French lyric by Serge Gainsbourg dedicated to his English wife, whom all his male compatriots idolised as a French sex symbol, began its short but sensual path up to the point where Sophie launched herself into the song just as she appeared in front of the porch swing on which already sat her betrothed.

Frank glared at the working puppeteers from behind the dais: 'What the blue blazes is this?' he rasped in as low a tone as his anger would allow.

'Take it easy, Frankie!' Epic hissed back, eyes firmly on the job. 'They're gonna love it. Trust me on this!'

'But you should have *told* me!' Frank spluttered. 'You had no right to change the programme without my consent. You know how sensitive this is!'

'It hasn't been changed, Frank,' Stephen insisted, as he pulled on a wire which allowed James to look up at Sophie, who was singing away, and wave, whilst still helping Epic to operate the chanteuse.

'It's just as well we rehearsed,' Epic whispered to Stephen. 'We've just added a bit at the start, that's all. No problem.'

'It's the number she starts all her gigs with, man,' returned Epic. 'Birkin still tours. Tommy's seen her. She's some chick! A bit goofy and old, but hey!'

Frank had started to calm down by now: 'Yes, yes. I recognise it now,' he nodded in relief. 'This is a nice touch, I suppose. But I don't want any more little surprises. One of those is quite enough!'

The congregation looked on in wonder at this unscheduled prologue: 'I didn't realise Sophie had such a lovely singing voice,' opined her proud mother. 'And singing in French too! Always a clever girl!'

Sophie duly finished Birkin's number, and as the music faded out, she turned around and sat down next to James, who then glanced sideways and smiled back at her.

The applause was rapturous.

'What did I tell you, Frankie? Huh?' positively shouted Epic backstage. 'I *told* you they'd love it. And I was *damned* right, baby!'

Indeed, *Jane B* had gone down so well, there were even one or two calls of '*Encore*', which Sophie felt obliged to acknowledge by rising slightly up, raising her hand and flashing her toothy grin before settling back down in her porch seat next to James.

Her mother turned to her husband and nudged him: 'I think she could have gone to the dentist before she killed herself, dear,' she said, being very ironic, but not knowing it.

Morning assembly again. Thoad, once more, flashed the green torch light at Keith and the pleasant intro to Stevie Wonder's *You Are The Sunshine Of My Life* was suddenly surrounding the hall, the fifteen seconds or so it lasted providing ample time for James to rise from his seat, stand over Sophie and look lovingly and longingly at her before beginning the song. This too was a deviation from the previously arranged programme. It was originally supposed to have been Sophie who had been down to begin with Jennifer Rush's *The Power Of Love*, with James responding to it with the Stevie Wonder number now in progress. This had now been reversed - (*The Power Of Love* was up next), and although Frank immediately recognised that this was only because Sophie had already been first up and deserved a break, he still couldn't prevent himself being irritated by what he saw as another little dig at his authority, even though this second change was a perfectly reasonable consequence of the first.

Whereas Noddoes had been particularly intent on Sophie singing *Jane B* as Birkin and had thus allowed Keith Tate to merely play the record, he reverted to normal procedure with James; and thus the young man delivered *You Are The Sunshine Of My Life* as himself and not as Stevie Wonder, 'Little' or otherwise. James' family and friends immediately demonstrated their support and appreciation by cooing, sighing and even with some light applause, which was pretty well sustained throughout the whole number, which itself was gradually faded out by Keith Tate with James charmingly positioned on bended knee, arm stretched out to his enchanted lady love.

The congregation rose again in acclaim and out went the lights. Within seconds, the quivering voice of Sophie (as distinct from Jane) was delivering the beautiful opening to *The Power Of Love*, a classic pop/rock ballad, which had taken the world's charts by storm in the mid-eighties. Everything remained pitch black during this intro, leading as it did to the distinctive and immensely powerfully delivered first chorus, at which point the arc lights came on again, immediately and dramatically spotlighting Sophie belting out the lyric, whilst a separate dimmer light revealed James, head and shoulders only, smiling widely and nodding his heartfelt thanks periodically. There was a clear moistening around his eyes. It was as clear as day that the lad was moved. For the middle bit of the song, Sophie sat down next to James, grasped his hand and held it firmly and lovingly to her breast. Oohs and aahs came thick and fast around the crematorium before being summarily drowned out as Sophie scrambled up rather awkwardly, due to some rarely clumsy puppeteering from the otherwise superb Stephen, in order to blast out the final chorus and then fade out.

Frank, behind the catafalque with Stephen, Epic and Thoad, was just unable to hide his emotion: 'That sounded beautiful!' he shuddered, as the roof of the Bar and Grill was lifted once again off its foundations by the cheering on-heat audience. 'Just beautiful!'

'Hey, take it easy, Frankie!' Epic said, as he and Stephen made firm the wires so that both cadavers were now sat next to each other on the swing and locked in place without the prospect of any movement. 'Remember, once the preacher's through, you and Stevie are on with the chick. It's time for the sex song. Let's get it on!'

Frank stared at Epic and emitted an involuntary gasp. But before he could say anything, the lights on James and Sophie had been dimmed, so that they were visible, but only just, and the main beam illuminated suddenly on Danny, whilst Keith's very light organ music floated around them.

'I'd just like to tell everybody here that this funeral has been as unique as it has been spellbindingly beautiful,' Danny announced.

'How so very true!' shuddered Frank, in hiding.

'Cool it!' barked Epic. 'Do you want to get into position, or what?'

'Yes, come on, Frank, it's the real thing now,' agreed Stephen, as he manoeuvred himself across to the half of the dais where Sophie's wires hung, whilst Thoad crouched down next to Epic on the other side. Frank sniffed, gave a deep breath and then nodded: 'Yes, I'm ready,' he said firmly.

'Cool!'

'Sweet!'

Danny's short sermon underlined to the crowd the obvious love shared by the corpses: 'It will last for eternity,' he assured them before leading everyone through the 23rd Psalm and The Lord's Prayer. 'James, Sophie… all I can say is… Go and be with Christ! You hear? Huh?'

He looked over at where the dais was, nodded, and out went the spotlight. Stephen, who had peered over the top of the catafalque for just such a signal, was quick to react.

'That's it!' he whispered. 'Whenever you like, Thoad!'

Thoad flashed his green torchlight at Keith Tate and immediately the arc light came on again. Sophie then announced: 'We've got something ever so romantic to finish,' to which James replied: 'It underpins our love for each other.' One split second later the unmistakable opening bars of *Je T'aime… Moi Non Plus* began invading everybody's flappers.

'Everything's going to be fine,' Stephen quickly assured Frank. 'Just pretend it's a rehearsal. Just like before.'

Sophie delivered her first line as Jane, and was immediately replied to by James, who despite not looking anything like Serge Gainsbourg (he looked more like Boris Becker, the poor little sod), could not but help singing as Gainsbourg. The song, after all, was in French and Noddoes' skills, astonishing and wide-ranging though they were undoubtedly, were always going to be considerably stretched if he attempted to get away with passing off a French accent delivering a French song as an impersonation by James and have it recognised as such by those close to him. He had thus surrendered to the only sensible alternative of aping both Birkin's and

Gainsbourg's voices, which simply meant allowing Keith to play the record.

The loving couple started embracing and canoodling as the passion of the song intensified until it was time for them to leave the porch swing and make towards the catafalque for their committal. Behind that very stage, things were going swimmingly. Thoad had taken to puppeteering superbly well under Epic's tutorage and although James, their charge, had had a far less intense workout than his lovely girlfriend, Thoad's performance had been faultless and Epic had not been slow in showing his approval and appreciation with a constant string of Barry White-style low tone exhortations peppering his performance: 'You're doing good, man!' 'Keep on doing it!' 'Right on!' 'Keep on!'

Frank had enjoyed similar success under the stewardship of Stephen, whose slight but noticeable error in the operation of Sophie, occurring just before the final chorus of *The Power Of Love*, had been the only blemish committed by either team. The four of them were now applying all of their concentration and both of their hands on the closing moments of what had been a marvellous show. James and Sophie were now lying next to each other in an embrace on the stage. Their pantings were getting rather steamy, and not at all in sync with the comparatively conservative way in which the lovers were hugging each other. Everything was most tasteful.

'I need you to help me out in a minute, Frank,' Stephen suddenly declared.

'What is it?' Frank asked nervously. 'It's nearly over. What's the problem?'

'No problem,' Stephen assured him. 'I have to admit that I need a little help, though. Do you see that little wire above you?'

Frank looked up and noticed it for the first time: 'I see it.'

'I want you to pull it twice when I give the signal. Twice, alright?'

'But what does it do?'

'It connects with one of the wires on my side,' Stephen explained. 'It's like a dual-control pedal on a car, so to speak.'

'I don't like the sound of this,' Frank admitted.

Stephen appeared untroubled by this: 'Well, as you wish, Frank. I must admit that it won't mean a total disaster if you don't help me, but things might look a little lopsided when we tip them down the chute. But no matter. Nothing can ever be perfect, can it, Frank? Forget it.'

'It won't spoil things, though, will it?' Frank muttered furtively. 'Everything was perfect in rehearsal. It was brilliant. You didn't need any help then.'

'You're right,' Stephen nodded. 'Forget about it, Frank. It's our last show, so who cares? If we fuck it up, we fuck it up... But don't worry!'

'I jolly well don't *want* to fuck it up!'

'Just forget about it, Frank,' Stephen insisted again.

'I'll do it! I'll do it!' Frank immediately rasped, reaching up to grab the wire.

'NOT NOW!!!' Stephen screamed, giving Frank a near heart attack and almost causing Epic and Thoad to drop James.

'God, not now, Frank! Not now! Fuck me! Not now! When... I... give... When I give the signal. Okay, Frank?'

Frank blinked at Stephen heavily.

'I'll count up to three, Frank, and then you pull twice on the cord. Twice. Stand by. Christ!'

'Standing by,' Frank said meekly, feeling a bit of a fool.

Stephen peered across at Epic, who winked at him and then nodded. James and Sophie were still cuddling each other on the dais and *Je T'aime* was almost at its climax in every sense of the word.

'Here we go, Frank. Pull *twice* on the count of three, okay? It's coming up. So here we go! One!... Two!...'

Stephen looked over at Epic again and saw the Canadian staring straight back at him. 'THREE!'

As quick as a flash, Frank tugged the wire above him twice, as instructed, and over on Epic's side Thoad did the same with his. Immediately, James and Sophie's kit slipped off them, leaving the cadavers naked, apart from Sophie's boots and James' trainers, and as Epic and Stephen activated the appropriate wires, so James leapt on top of Sophie and began to apparently service her in the same second that the music was turned up and the catafalque began to rise. Sophie's gasping and moaning was deafening for five or six seconds until the trajectory took the horny couple down the now tipped-up stage and sent them sailing straight down the shoot into the waiting furnace. As the doors to this slid shut, so the spotlight, under which everything had been clearly seen, was extinguished and total darkness now accompanied the total silence ensuing, since the record had also been cut in the same instant.

There was a further few seconds of nothing at all, before Keith's very light organ music returned to float dreamily around and several dim lights came on so that the crematorium was illuminated throughout.

By this time, Epic, Stephen and Thoad had scurried off. Stephen had tapped Frank on the shoulder and proffered the sage advice, 'C'mon, mate. Leg it before we're fucking carved up!' and this had been supplemented by Epic's equally sound recommendation, 'Fucking run, Frankie, goddamn it!'

Old Thoad, who had of course been in on it, had required no such prompting and had vanished already. But Frank, who had never been the most precipitate at taking good hints, remained behind the screen blubbing about how beautiful it had all been, and his eventual rising to depart coincided precisely with the delayed moment which preceded the second that all hell broke loose amongst sections of the congregation, which immediately spread to just about everyone else, resulting in an explosion of anger and outrage, which shook the Bar and Grill.

Mrs Lutz, for her part, directed her anger solely at her daughter: 'How *could* you?' she rasped, running up to the door of the furnace and hammering at it with her umbrella. 'You've gone *much* too far this time, young lady! *Much* too far! Come out! You should have kept all that sort of thing solely for the bedroom! For the bedroom! I know your dad and I taught you to be liberated, but my *God*, I never *dreamed* that you'd do something like that!'

But Sophie's mum appeared to be firmly in the minority of opinion. Everyone else seemed to be directing their wrath at the person they considered most certainly to blame and thereby began an immediate search for Danny Hare in order to enquire politely into the significance of the nude scene at the end there. But crafty Dazza, who had been tipped off from the start by Epic, had long since departed with Barefoot Sally, Tessa and Amanda, all of whom had nothing to do during the ceremony but watch and marvel at it. They were already en route by road to their respective homes.

Keith Tate had wisely fucked off as well; a move which proved even more judicious subsequently when the mob broke into his control station and smashed up all his equipment for him. Before this had happened, Frank himself had finally taken flight, but only after Noddoes of all people, seeing that his clueless boss had not taken the earlier broad hints that had been rammed down his throat, had still not departed and was quite literally in mortal danger, as of course was also Noddoes at this time, had screamed for him to get out:

'In the name of all that's holy, Eddowes, flee! Flee before you are slain!'

'What are you talking about?' Frank stammered, alone of course in not knowing what had happened.

'Run for your life, you imbecile!' Noddoes shouted back, beginning to run himself. 'Follow me!'

Frank, angered by Noddoes' tone more than anything else, and still oblivious as to why a riot was commencing around him, followed the old luvvie with no undue urgency to the back exit, there joining the others already packed into the Anglia, more than ready to go.

'Frank! Thank fuck!' gasped Stephen, revving up the engine. 'Get in!'

'Would one of you *please* have the good grace to tell me what's going on?' Frank demanded.

'Get in, you asshole!' rasped Epic.

Still Frank was not happy: 'But what's the meaning of this surreptitious departure. I demand an explanation!'

Frank showed no sign at all of joining the others in the vehicle, and it was thus left for Epic to save the day by leaping out of the passenger seat and knocking him out with a smartly delivered right cross.

'Asswipe!' he hissed, as he and Noddoes placed him in the back of the car with Thoad. Noddoes clambered in to join them and Epic jumped back into the front.

'Move it!' he growled at Stephen, and off they finally sped to safety. Nobody was harmed. They all got home.

Danny's Bar and Grill was wrecked. The congregation did everything but set fire to it. Understandably not content with this, part of the mob went around to Freddo's and put out the windows in there too. One or two of the more adventurous ones succeeded in climbing in and were still roaming around trashing the place when the constabulary arrived and nicked them for breaking and entering, criminal damage and anything else which took the rozzers' fancy at that time.

Chapter 48

Toboggan Hunt

T HERE WAS NOT a chance now that Danny would be able to host the Inn Crowd's funerals, at least not at the Bar and Grill. The premises had been practically destroyed, whilst Keith Tate's control room had fared worst of all by being utterly and irrevocably devastated. The sound system itself would need to be largely replaced. This had been the handiwork of some rather less than satisfied connections of James and Sophie, whom, whether Danny knew or not, were still looking out for him. He had been prepared for a backlash of sorts, but had certainly underestimated the feelings of outrage which had been generated over the last few seconds of what had up to that point been a rapturously well-received event. People had become incensed at this, and in an attempt to become just a little bit more outrageous, the critique of self-participating funerals had been irreversibly damaged. Word of what had happened flew around Pendlesham and the local newspaper, *The Pendlesham Gazette*, normally a staunch friend of Freddo's (indeed, Frank had penned several articles for the journal), not only lambasted Frank and his staff (it made no mention at all of Danny) but even instigated a fund for the three people who now awaited a court's decision on their punishment, having decided to plead guilty, with a further guarantee that it would buy their 'stories' once any punishment had been meted out, and in the seemingly unlikely case of any custodial sentences being handed down, these being served.

Frank himself had only finally found out the truth about James and Sophie at an astonishing post-mortem at Tessa's flat the morning after the funeral. He had been picked up by Stephen, who had driven him straight home immediately after Epic had knocked him out, and together with Epic had bundled him indoors as soon as Frank's mum had opened the door:

'How you doing, ma'am?' Epic had said (he had of course met her before in very similar circumstances). 'Can we just take Frankie to his room at this time? He's had a big day.'

'Of course you can, dear. Take him straight up.'

By the time Stephen came for him the following day, Frank had, not only recovered from his whupping, but had also spoken to the police and had, in addition, been in touch with his insurance company. These communications were not instigated by Frank. The police had turned up on his doorstep and told him that his premises had been burgled and damaged, whereupon Frank contacted his insurance guys and told them to get round there immediately. He personally would get there when he could.

Only he wouldn't, of course. Because the only mission on his mind now was reporting back to his troops. The other was he still had no idea at that time about what had really occurred at the Bar and Grill to cause such a disturbance; and further to this, had not linked the riot in the crematorium with the break-in and attempted destruction of his offices. The only thing that his hopelessly confused, plot-losing mind had managed to piece together was the fact that for some fantastic reason, which he certainly could not piece together, Epic had demanded very aggressively that Frank should leave with them immediately, as if the mob was angry with him and his staff for some reason, but remembered nothing at all after that. It had all been most curious. He had woken up in his usual way, feeling fine, as he had done countless times before following an afternoon session over at the Inn. Only he had not been to the Inn this time. He had been working. He had been to a funeral.

Stephen and Frank arrived at Tessa's *pied-a-terre* to find everybody else chatting excitedly about their imminent dooms and plans for a grand service up at Rocky Point. They may have lost the prospect of the intended second part of the spectacular scheduled for the Bar and Grill, but the Sermon on the Mount was still very much on and would now take on a much greater significance, indeed consume everything.

The general mood of the gathering was most certainly jovial. Only Thoad remained glum. This was never a surprise, but Thoad was in a particularly bad way this time because he had not stayed at home after his successful flight from the funeral, but had gone out again almost immediately to spend the rest of the afternoon and some of the early evening too sitting in the station concourse staring miserably at the bordered up Inn. He had walked gloomily around to the taxi rank side as well in the desperately forlorn hope for a miracle, but of course the same grim sight had faced him, and Thoad returned to the concourse and just sat around amongst the smelly Scottish vagrants and grizzled.

The boards covering the windows and doors on both sides had already been got at by the kids, the flakes and the opportunist billstickers. Mr Plod was the principal target, but there were also contributions from lovesick teens (or those acting unsolicited on their behalf); people offering sexual services for all sorts by people of all sorts; the regular graffiti wallahs, who in the name of art to say nothing of vanity, left their squiggly calling cards on any surface they happened across and had done so on this one; the odd obscure message perhaps from a drunk or a loon, who probably felt that they were being profound; and a rock band called Toboggan Hunt, which had placed (or whose connections had placed) a number of cheaply made fliers advertising gigs in a number of local drinkers, which themselves had been either ripped down, in whole or in part, by any of the other contributors. Not only was the Station Inn buried, its tombstone had been defaced too. And Thoad cried.

He eventually went home and cried again and then went to bed crying, remembering that everyone had agreed to meet at Tessa's place the next day. This had been earlier suggested by Stephen Mauve, who had, with what turned out to be the most fortuitous aforethought, felt that HQ would not be the widest choice of venue. The staff would need to get weaving on their suicide plans if nothing else.

But of course there was indeed something else. Quite a lot else. There was the riot for one thing, and the fact that Frank would now have to be told (he would demand to be told anyway) why there was a riot in the first place, and there was also the slight matter of the damage and break-in at Freddo's, which nobody but Frank knew about, and the turning over of the Bar and Grill, which everybody but Frank now knew about, since Amanda had picked up the news in the middle of the night directly from a devastated Barefoot Sally, who had then been instructed by Stephen, who had been woken up as well, of course, to get herself and Danny around to Tessa's flat in the morning so that everything could be thrashed out. By the time Stephen and Frank arrived, everybody, having digested the bleak news about the Bar and Grill, was deep into a discussion about a multi suicide spectacular and a service held at the same time up at the Point.

During these early exchanges, Thoad began muttering to himself more than to anyone else that he was going to jump and that he was not minded to sit around talking about it for much longer. The theme of this was immediately picked out by Danny, who in a masterstroke made the suggestion of having the funeral actually *before* their deaths:

'Since this was always going to be a spectacular, why not take this *magnificent* opportunity which the man upstairs has given us, in his own mysterious way, to do something unique? Since you guys always intended to hold a multiple self-participating funeral over at my place, hows about participating at your own funerals *before* you jump? You can all perform to your own special tracks, as arranged, but you can also deliver your own tribute… to *yourselves*! Hows about that, then?'

Everybody looked at each other and then suddenly erupted into whooping and cheering.

'Hey, that's *great*, Father' Epic shouted over the din. 'We're gonna have a party up there. And Sheba and Hamlet can now jump too! Okay, Sheba?'

'Groovy! Groovy!' squealed Tessa. 'Groovy!'

Noddoes looked less sure.

'We're gonna rock 'til we drop!' suddenly roared an inspired Stephen and everybody except Noddoes, who was in deep thought, and Thoad, who was still crying from last night, pissed themselves royally.

But this was when the merriment halted a while. Frank, whose arrival at this point went by pretty much unnoticed, announced that Headquarters had been hit, was told in turn by Danny that the Bar and Grill had been razed to the ground practically and was then told the reason for these acts of criminal damage by Stephen: 'James and Sophie went a little too far, I'm afraid...'

'What are you trying to tell me?' Frank demanded, suddenly feeling very cold.

Stephen looked to the floor, but Frank's incredulous glare remained upon him.

'What the blazes happened!' he ordered. 'Tell me!'

Stephen shook his head, opened his mouth and closed it again.

'It was Jimmy and Jane, Frankie,' Epic finally explained. 'They kinda... well... got it on. Just like on the record...'

'THEY DID *WHAT*?' Oh, God, *NO*! That extra wire! It was that extra wire you got me to pull!... Good *God*! What did you buggers make me do?'

Tessa started to giggle and this set Amanda off, which in turn caused Stephen (who was still looking to the floor like a disgraced infant) to smirk stupidly.

'And it *isn't* funny!' snapped Amanda suddenly and punched him on the arm.

'You bastards!' rasped Frank. 'Bastards!'

'Take it easy, Frankie.'

'Take it easy, is it? Take it fucking easy? By God, no *wonder* those leftovers went fucking berserk! Now I know why they were caught trying to smash up HQ! Now I understand why they fucking smashed up the Bar and Grill! They had every fucking reason to, didn't they, you stupid bastards! Now I understand why you were all running around like fucking headless chickens, desperate to fucking leave. That mob was going to smash *us* up too, weren't they? And no fucking wonder, you stupid fucking bastards!'

Noddoes and Stephen, who had been the architects of the *Je T'aime* finale, firmly against Frank's instructions (not surprisingly Epic), had every intention of putting up a defence for what they had done. It had after all been a blow for the creative arts, and indeed for the entire Freddo critique. *Je T'aime... Moi Non Plus* had been perhaps the most notorious record of the sixties. It's banning by the BBC had not stopped it topping the charts in Britain (many commentators argued that it helped it) and a condemnation of the recording by none other than the Pope had not been enough to prevent it from also penetrating Catholic Europe, so to speak. The reason for the hoo-ha was patently obvious. *Je T'aime* was a blatant (and rather well done) depiction of sexual intercourse covering the full programme of foreplay, screwing and climaxing. The objectives of Noddoes and Stephen, for arranging a faithful interpretation of the track at James and Sophie's funeral, were therefore ephemeral and done on entirely artistic grounds, whereas Epic, who wanted fidelity too, only wanted it on grounds of tasteless smut, which wasn't quite the same thing. This argument was worthy and solid and Noddoes and Stephen had long been prepared to defend it to the hilt. But they had not reckoned on Frank's cathartic explosion of anger at finding out that he had been hoodwinked into bringing James and Sophie's funeral into what Frank perceived as such disgraceful and disgusting disrepute. They had therefore concluded that it was probably less than wise to attempt a defence of their corner as intended. They had similarly not bargained on the riot and the consequent property damage, and Stephen in particular who, after all, did not have such a bee in his bonnet artistically, felt that the best interests of all parties would be served by telling Frank that what was done was done.

Frank completed his John McEnroe-style rant and Stephen prepared to deliver his shot at a diplomatic response. But he was beaten to the punch by an interjection, which not only couldn't be ignored, but which had the desired effect of switching in an instant everyone's mind back on to Danny's sermon. The interjection was not for once from Epic. It was five words sobbed out by a non-stop blubbering Thoad: 'I just want to jump!'

Frank looked mournfully across at his desperately miserable and deteriorating friend, colleague and drinking partner and immediately understood.

The business with James and Sophie now meant nothing. In fact, nothing much beyond one thing meant anything.

Frank and Stephen had only just become party to what Danny had suggested about the 'live' suicide spectacular on top of Rocky Point – a party, gig, sermon and multiple suicide all rolled into one festival. They were therefore not in the same ecstatic mood as the others; and the sight and sound of poor, dear, pathetic, beaten old Thoad sobbing continuously brought Frank himself trembling to the very verge of tears.

'Yes, mate,' Frank assured the grizzling wreck. 'Now we're *all* going to jump!'

And when Thoad wailed in acknowledgement: 'They've closed the Inn!', Stephen could do nothing other than smile softly and quizzically and say nothing, as he too was moved by the sight and sound of poor, dear, pathetic, beaten old Thoad, who had clearly gone crackers. Everyone else burst into applause, apart from the Reverend Danny Hare, who made the sign of the cross and said 'Beautiful!' in a voice he hoped sounded like Jimi Hendrix.

Chapter 49

Adrian

NATURALLY THOAD'S RAPID and continuingly worrying decline meant that he was in no fit state to contact the former members of ROPSAS with a view to commissioning their services for a one-off return from retirement for the festival on top of Rocky Point, which would go ahead as soon as could possibly be arranged. Other things had to be taken into consideration too, not least checking when the tides would be favourable for Salty Sid to sail in and scoop up all the numerous corpses. Sid had now been prepared for the multiple leap from the cliff and had serviced his tug and strengthened his nets in preparation for this gargantuan labour. His suggested leap at roughly 17.30 on the following Thursday promised the best option. The tidal prognosis for that time was ideal, the long-term weather forecast was excellent for the south coast and, in any case, it was high summer – mid August – and it would be light until eight o'clock at least. Sid, after all was done with, would then set sail with his cargo of cadavers bound for the offices of Proudfoot and Gadd for pending cremation (pending the formality of Klaus Butsch's inquiry). This, naturally, was Frank's last pie in the face for the Old Firm – the delivery of his and his comrades' mortal remains to his former employer's historic rivals. This change in plan also solved at a stroke the conundrum of training a fresh posse of puppeteers for the funerals originally planned for the service at the Bar and Grill.

The choice of a late afternoon jumping time went down spectacularly well with the participants (all except Thoad, who really just wanted his life over and done with). The timing provided everyone with the fondest of memories of the magical kingdom, which had been the Station Inn. On a weekend, or on an allocated spare day when there wasn't much work around, everyone would arrive at the Inn at noon and by half-past five (the allocated leaping time), they were all shot to absolute fuck. The Inn Crowd didn't have the Inn any longer, but there was nothing whatsoever to stop them from exporting the spirit of the place to the top of Rocky Point. They would have to make do without Tom, Baz and Kate, the tall, brunette, all-smiling, moon-faced barmaid with only a mild habit, all of whom were tucked away somewhere awaiting trial, and nobody, not even Amanda or Epic, whom distinct from all the others, retained a quota of friends and acquaintances amongst the masses of youth Inn pond life, were really very keen for any of these young folk to cuckoo in their nest by showing up and turning the whole festival into a nonsense. The 'Sermon' was certainly set to be a celebration of suicide and of the Station Inn, of which the young scrotes and slappers had indeed been an integral part, but there would also be a large dose of solemnity amongst the ingredients, and it was further assumed (correctly) that the kids, most of whom had no sense of *heimat*, had already found other places to go to pick up drink and drugs in lieu of the fabled Inn. Nobody had felt anything like the same way about the pub that the Freddo team had. If they had done, they would have been just as gutted as they were, in which case if they chose to turn up for the Sermon, they could bloody well take communion as well. When all was said and done, it was quintessentially a private party. It might well attract an audience, but as Noddoes pointed out: 'the day an audience encroaches on a stage during a performance, civilisation is dead'. The decision was taken to keep the Sermon in-house.

Stephen was nominated to make the approach to ROPSAS and he duly made contact with a man in a seaside café during lunch hour, who had been one of the most enthusiastic Camcorders; indeed the same guy who had so graphically described the heartwarming demise of the nemesis Reg Doorman, this victory spelling the end of the activities of ROPSAS on the most glorious of terms. The man, Adrian Templeman, a forty-five year old unmarried clerical officer for the South Coast Water Board, had not been the least bit idle since ROPSAS had folded. He had initially become involved in co-editing a publication dealing with the tragic hobby of collecting baggage labels from airlines and had then moved from there to a position of influence in a society called 'GO', dedicated to the promotion of the persona and works of seventies pop singer Gilbert O'Sullivan.

'I certainly don't want to prise you away from the important work you do for Gilbert,' Stephen assured him, knowing exactly how to handle this pitiful tosser. 'I thought that *Nothing Rhymed* was a great track. It was Gilbert's first hit, wasn't it?'

'Number eight in January 1971!' confirmed Adrian, smiling warmly.

'It will basically be a one-off commissioning for ROPSAS, if you agree,' Stephen explained, turning smartly to the subject of the Sermon. 'We expect six of us to jump, possibly seven. And this includes your old friend, Thoad.'

'I'm sorry. Who?'

'Ah, yes. Of course. You'll know him as Tom. Tom Hoad.'

Adrian nodded and smiled again. 'Good old Tom! Top man! So he's going over as well, is he? Top lad!'

'I think he's pretty well bagseed the first jump,' Stephen told him, thinking immediately of poor, dear, pathetic, beaten old Thoad.

'Good old Tom!' said Adrian again and then he suddenly brightened up. 'I say! Will there be any music to any of this?'

'Oh, too true there will!'

'Would you like me to take care of that for you?' beamed Adrian.

'We've got that sorted out, thanks,' answered Stephen quickly, feeling suddenly cold.

Adrian immediately looked bitterly disappointed. 'Well, I'll bring along his Greatest Hits CD just in case,' he mumbled helpfully.

Stephen, with horrendous thoughts of *Clair* and *Alone Again (Naturally)* polluting the air up at Rocky Point, swiftly changed the subject: 'Have you contact or any means of contact with the rest of the ROPSAS guys?'

'We're not 'guys' any more, actually, my friend,' answered Adrian stroppily.

'I understand that. But do you know where they are?'

'I might do.'

'Look, mate, I'm here because of Tom, right? Now it seems to me that you owe that poor old bugger after all the help he gave you with your suicide observation hobby.'

'His company didn't do too badly out of it either, did it?' sneered Adrian, still sulking.

This was actually very true.

'Alright, look,' embarked Stephen, knowing now that a deal had to be struck with this idiot if ROPSAS participation was to be secured. 'Everyone is choosing their own personal music to jump to and I'm sure that you wouldn't expect me to ask anyone to change it. I mean, that's non-negotiable, okay? You can understand that?'

'Did anyone choose Gilbert?' enquired Adrian hopefully.

Stephen shook his head. 'I'm sorry,' he said.

'*Disgraceful!*' hissed Adrian. '*Tasteless!*'

'But what I think I *can* offer you is the inclusion of a Gilbert classic during the crucial intermission between the vicar's sermon and the first leap. Come to think of it, *Get Down* would be perfect for this, it seems to me.'

Adrian's face suddenly lit up like a Christmas tree: 'Number one in April 1973!' he gushed. 'That would be a wonderful arrangement! I'll bring some of the lads from GO along!'

Stephen turned instantly pale. 'Oh shit! No, *please!*' he begged. 'Look, mate, here's the deal. *We* agree to slip in *Get Down* into the pre-jump musical programme as long as *you* round up the rest of your camcorder friends, your *former* friends, and get them all primed to film the festival up at the Point. Now come on, now. You boys used to be brilliant! I would have thought that you would all jump at a chance of a spectacular like this, if you pardon the expression!'

Adrian grunted and shook his head. 'Ah, but that was all in the past, my friend. Only Gilbert matters now. Just Gilbert. I'm a changed, milder person since I finished with ROPSAS. Strange heartless bunch! I used to swear like a fucking trooper until the magic of Gilbert's music touched me. It was as if I had been caressed by an angel. Gilbert's on a par with Mozart, you know. He has altered my perspective on life and its priorities. He has taught me what is important. I am undeniably a better, cleaner man as a consequence – thanks to Gilbert!'

'Very good. And happier?' asked Stephen.

'Pardon?'

'And happier? Are you happier?'

'Oh yes, my friend. Certainly happier!'

'Good. That's good. I'm happy that you're happier.'

'I think I'm going to be with Gilbert for a very long time. We all think that way at GO, you know. That's why Gilbert *must* be involved!'

'But Gilbert *will* be involved in his own special way,' insisted Stephen, now wishing to goodness that he hadn't been saddled with the responsibility of negotiating with this pathetic wanker. 'With *Get Down* being played just before the first leap, *Tom's* leap, no less, Gilbert will in effect be opening the whole show. He will be the raiser of the curtain, the founder of the feast. Everything which follows will all be down to Gilbert, okay? Gilbert!'

Adrian's emotions were multiple for a few seconds, as were his facial expressions, as he tried to fathom out whether this was a good deal for Gilbert or not. He then slowly nodded his head.

'I tell you what I'll do,' he said. 'Since Gilbert will be at the forefront of all this, it only seems right that GO are represented –'

'But they *will* be represented!' jumped in an increasingly desperate Stephen. 'By *you*!'

'That doesn't really help Gilbert, though, does it? You see, I'll be representing ROPSAS, won't I? I can't represent ROPSAS *and* Gilbert, can I?'

'Well, can't you represent both, for fuck's sake?' stammered Stephen, more than a little exasperated now.

'Could you support two football teams at once?' smiled Adrian smugly.

Stephen was incredulous: 'What kind of fucking analogy is that, you fucking nut job? What are you talking about?'

'There's no need for that, my friend,' answered Adrian, trying his best to sound and look hurt.

'Look, look, look, look... I'm sorry, okay? I'm just trying to cut a deal with you and the rest of ROPSAS and -'

'ROPSAS doesn't exist anymore, my friend. This is what I'm endeavouring to convey to you. It's very hard when you don't listen.'

'Look, mate. Question, okay? What will it take for you to simply pop round to the rest of the blokes who *used* to belong to ROPSAS, okay? and gathering them all up so that they and you can go back to Rocky Point and tape all of *us* having a sermon, a party and then killing our fucking selves? You tell me, okay? Although I fancy I have a pretty good idea I know already.'

Adrian smiled smugly again: 'Two conditions will have to be met.'

'*Two*? I certainly hope that you're not going to take the piss. I've had enough of all this, quite frankly.'

'I really wish you wouldn't be so rude, my friend,' snivelled Adrian, in 'hurt' mode again.

Stephen nodded a half-hearted apology. 'Alright, I'm listening.'

'Firstly, as I've already said, since Gilbert is playing a pivotal role in your celebrations, GO will have to be represented. And since I'll be working with the old ROPSAS gang, I'm going to have to insist on a couple of guys representing Gilbert.'

'A couple? Just two?'

'Just two.'

Stephen looked skeptical: 'Now, you're not going to renege on this, are you, and bus a whole load of your boys up there?'

'There are only three of us in the society,' Adrian cheerfully informed him. 'Wally, Max and myself.'

Stephen flashed a double take: 'Oh, for fuck's sake!'

Adrian seemed oblivious to Stephen being on the brink of embedding a tea set in him: 'Wally and Max are the first condition,' he reiterated.

Stephen nodded acceptance, probably involuntarily: 'What's the second problem?'

'Well, it *is* a problem, actually,' Adrian confirmed airily. 'A *material* problem…'

'Oh, bollocks, no! We're not paying you for this, mate!' jumped in Stephen. 'You can fuck off!'

Stephen, in fact, could not remember when he had been so wound up and he irritatingly was forced to acknowledge to himself that Epic would have knocked this lunatic out at least five minutes ago if he had been there instead of him.

'No, no.. my friend. You misunderstand,' corrected Adrian, sounding more unbearable than ever. 'I can find the other ROPSAS boys for you, you needn't worry about that. The problem is *literally* material, as in the sense that none of us have any.'

'What do you mean? Any *what?*'

'We don't have any camcorders anymore. We all sold them after we disbanded.'

'Oh, for fuck's sake!'

'Ken Prendergast actually gave the money to Children In Need. I thought that was a grand gesture!'

'Look, you arsehole, we're not going to buy you all new camcorders! You can fucking hire some!'

'That was precisely what the second condition was. And I'm not an arsehole,' scowled Adrian, more genuinely annoyed this time than pretending to be hurt.

'I mean, if I'd known about all this fucking about, I would have just hired Channel 4 and been done with it!' muttered Stephen to himself, still contemplating smashing Adrian up.

'These are the conditions,' Adrian advised him. 'Wally and Max and half a dozen camcorders hired for the occasion. Is that too much to ask?'

'It isn't,' Stephen admitted, nevertheless rolling his right hand into a fist.

'Then is it agreed?' asked Adrian hopefully, offering his hand.

Stephen unravelled his fingers and plonked his hand in Adrian's: 'Yeah. Go on, then.'

The two men shook hands.

'Just one thing,' said Stephen, as he got up to leave.

'I think we've just shaken hands,' Adrian instantly reminded him.

'Yes. This has nothing to do with the deal,' Stephen assured him. 'I've just had an idea.'

Adrian remained quiet and Stephen smiled at his apparent discomfort: 'You've always been banging on about not being anything to do with ROPSAS anymore, you having devoted yourself to the genius of Gilbert...'

Adrian was delighted with this description of his icon: 'Gilbert was the Mozart of his age!' he repeated with a shudder. 'As for ROPSAS... we are finished!'

'As you say.'

'... finished.'

'Yes. My suggestion is that there is no renaissance of ROPSAS, but in fact a founding of something new. A founding of a new organisation entirely. The Old Ropsasians. How does that grab you?'

Adrian's face went into the heavens and exploded like a firework: 'That's brilliant! The Old Ropsasians! *Brilliant*! We can have some blazers made up... with a badge. I'll design it myself!'

'Can I just point out that the blazers are not subject to the camcorder hiring budget we've just agreed?' quickly pointed out Stephen.

'I can see it now,' imagined Adrian, in a world of his own now. 'Ken, Malcolm, Nobby, Dick, Ted! All in pristine green blazers! All bearing the ancient noble insignia of The Old Ropsasians! And of course *you*, my friend, as our founder will be entitled to -'

'Whoa, horsey! Now, wait a minute!' jumped in Stephen, feeling rather like a drowning man who, having been rescued, had now found himself back in the water again. 'I just made the suggestion. *You're* the founder. Okay?'

'But I can't take the credit for this, my friend!' Adrian beamed. 'I would never have thought of founding a brand new club!'

'As far as the world will know, it was your idea,' returned Stephen. 'All down to you.'

'But –'

'It will be our secret.'

'That really is very good of you!' gushed Adrian, grasping Stephen warmly by the hand and shaking it for the second time.

'Don't mention it,' said Stephen, meaning every word.

'Right, well, I've got to go!' Adrian said, suddenly dropping Stephen's hand as if it were a hot coal. 'I've got lots to do. Lots to do.'

He stood up.

'Here's my card,' Stephen said. 'Keep in touch. We'll be ready to move in a few days.'

'Oh, undoubtedly!'

'And it *will* be only Wally and Max, won't it?' asked Stephen, intent on reassurance.

'Hum?' asked Adrian dreamily.

'Wally and Max.'

'Oh, I'm not worried about Wally and Max!' scoffed Adrian, taking the card. 'Fancy worrying about Wally and Max! There are far more pressing matters than Wally and Max!'

He turned to leave.

Stephen looked more flabbergasted than ever now: 'What is this? More important than Wally and Max? More important than Gilbert?'

Unfortunately, Stephen had set himself up again…

'Fuck Gilbert!' declared Adrian. And he scuttled off.

Chapter 50

The Station Inn

STEPHEN REPORTED BACK to Frank that everything had been arranged. Gilbert O'Sullivan failed to get a mention. The need to pay for the hire of six camcorders did, and Frank was as gob smacked as Stephen had been but authorised it nevertheless: 'We did, after all, commission them.'

Adrian in fact replied swiftly, which was just as well because Thoad had already made one bold attempt to reach the top of the Point but had been intercepted by Frank. A successful assault could only have been a day or so away.

'Thoad is a suicide risk,' Frank warned Stephen and Epic sternly. 'He must be watched for his own wellbeing.'

Thoad indeed would have fallen even deeper into depression (if such a thing were possible) had he been fed the rumour picked up by Amanda and conveyed to the others, although specifically hidden from Thoad, concerning proposals for the site occupied by the derelict Station Inn. The worrying word on the street was that an opportunist investor from the town had secured the lease for the property and now intended to convert it disgracefully into a spanking new 'sports bar', where overpriced 'designer' drinks and 'designer' lunchtime salads would be on offer to a target clientele - the town's supposed smartset, a category into which the pre-Freddo Stephen Mauve had fitted so snugly, much to the irritation of the core Inn regulars - and where screens would display the rapidly emerging (soon to be all-consuming) satellite and cable stations offering sporting events which were now forbidden fruit to the simple poor bastard licence payer. More astonishingly, there was talk of a dress code (no team colours or shirts would be permitted, which rather destroyed the bar's 'theme', one could reasonably surmise), and worse still, patronisation by off-duty police officers. There was to be no jukebox, a strict age limit of twenty-one (something which in normal circumstances would guarantee a place to be jammed packed full of teenagers, but certainly not this time!) and thus no 'student drinks' would be served. No snogging, no writing on the bog walls, no drunks. And anyone who fancied a bit of dealing, or even consuming would be marched straight up the road. And no poofs or slappers. Boring drinker!

The rumour of a sports bar was a live one according to Amanda's sources. Perhaps the officer who looked like the guy out of Blue Mink had an interest in it. The prospect of this stretched farther than the mere ironic, and in fact fuelled a further rumour that Tom, Baz and Kate, the tall, brunette, all-smiling, moon-faced barmaid with only a mild habit, had been loaded up, and this caused abject fury amongst a small section of youngsters who were only too happy to latch onto it. The framing of Tom was not something which had ever been seriously considered by any of the Inn Crowd, but an effective police takeover of the site on which the Inn had proudly stood would not really have surprised anyone, least of all Frank, who would have put nothing past the officer who looked like the guy out of Blue Mink short of a King Herod like slaughter of innocent babes. But when all was said and done, everything was only speculation and of no consequence really to the Inn Crowd, who would all be dead by the time anything happened anyway. Probably.

Adrian's efforts, meanwhile, had been admirable. He had managed to round up four of his five former colleagues. The fifth, Nobby Barnes, who worked in a town arcade shopping centre on the deli counter, had declined the invitation due to a pressing engagement with the East Sussex branch of *The Men From U*N*C*L*E Society* of which Nobby was the proud treasurer: 'Oh no! Mr Waverley would censure me if I didn't go to our briefing,' Nobby had warned over the phone, referring to Agent Solo and Kuriakin's benign patriarchal boss. 'He would demand to see my credentials. We can't give T*H*R*U*S*H an inch, you know! Those madmen won't stop until world domination is theirs!'

'I quite understand, Nob,' returned Adrian cheerily, quite a fan of *The*

Men From U*N*C*L*E himself. 'But how about joining The Old Ropsasians anyway? We're going to be enjoying a full programme of functions after this. I think it's going to be marvellous. And how dapper we're all going to look in our new blazers! Wonderful!'

Nobby seemed to be affronted by this: '*Adrian*! How could you ask me that? Could you support two football teams at once?'

'It's okay, Nobby…'

'U*N*C*L*E cannot and *must* not rest until our evil nemesis, T*H*R*U*S*H is immobilised. They are all mad! *Maniacs*! They will not be denied!'

'That's fine, Nob!'

Adrian thus settled for one man short, but he ordered a blazer for Nobby anyway. Two guys he certainly didn't seek to enlist were Wally and Max, the other two-thirds of GO, although he did call Max to let him know that he and Wally were now halves.

'You fucking wicked sod!' foamed Max. 'You've walked out on Gilbert then, have you? You've thrown him away like a bad carton of milk, have you? Except this carton *hasn't* gone bad. This carton will *never* go bad, you fucking evil swine!'

Adrian did not thus explain about the part of the deal he had initially made with Stephen, which had made provisions for Gilbert's *Get Down* to be played directly after the service had finished and immediately before Thoad jumped. He did however mention The Old Ropsasians as being the mistress for whom he had dropped Gilbert and this was to be a mistake.

In any event, when Adrian contacted Stephen to confirm that he had netted all but one of his Camcorder chums, and subsequently, when Stephen handed over a wad of notes to pay for the hiring of the equipment, nothing was said about Gilbert, Wally or Max at all; and so when Stephen casually brought up the subject of *Get Down*, Adrian told him that since Wally and Max would not now be present, it really was a matter for Stephen, whether he wanted to play the record or not. To this Stephen gave an honest answer and said that whilst *Get Down* had been a good suggestion with obvious comic overtones, the general consensus was in favour instead of Van Halen's *Jump*. He asked Adrian if this was okay and Adrian replied that he really couldn't give a stuff. He would, he said, be far too busy filming 'with the lads' and looking forward to the viewing party afterwards.

'I think I'm going to be with The Old Ropsasians for a very long time...'

With the Camcorders and the vicar ordered, it only remained to set a date for the Sermon. Diaries were consulted and dates were cross-referred with Sid, who confirmed that the following Thursday at 1730 was still most promising. This was now only three days away, which at least meant that the problem with Thoad, who had lost weight at a worrying rate, could now perhaps be managed safely. Danny and Keith Tate, who had built up a new mobile music station, had assured everyone that they could be ready at a drop of a hat; and now that Adrian had been given the camcorder money, and The Old Ropsasians' blazers, actually cheap off-the-peg jobs with a sad sewn-on badge depicting the letters OR, which Adrian had made himself, had been produced, The Old Ropsasians were ready too.

Proudfoot and Gadd meanwhile had been warned to 'expect some major business' and were strongly advised to 'maintain a watch of impending events up on Rocky Point'. The message couldn't have been clearer.

Headquarters had been tidied up since its understandable violation by the connections of James and Sophie, and although there was always a fear, in Frank's mind in particular, that they might return, as he was convinced that the mob was still out to get them, he suggested that meeting back at their home base was fitting, if not practical, judicious, or even safe. Even Stephen and Epic, who had been acutely aware of the need to get the hell out of the Bar and Grill as soon as things took off after *Je T'aime*, accepted that in the absence of the Inn (a silly example, perhaps, since had the Inn still been open, nobody would have been hell bent on suicide anyway!), Headquarters was really the only apt place they could meet for such a discussion in any case; and it was thus on the Tuesday afternoon that the Freddo staff, minus Salty Sid, who had already been briefed, came together to make their final arrangements. Quite literally.

Chapter 51

Frank

NODDOES STILL BRAVELY volunteered to live. This came as no surprise at all to Frank, who even after all this time, could still never feel clear into giving the old luvvie the benefit of any doubt about anything, despite his admiration for his talents. Before the idea of the Sermon had come along, it had been imperative that Noddoes didn't indeed jump, because that would have scuttled any prospect of the grand finale of the multiple self-participating funeral, which had previously been mooted and at which Noddoes would have been expected to star. This also had precluded Tessa from the suicide party. Now, of course, the funeral would be taking place *before* their deaths and thus everyone would be free to do themselves in; Noddoes included, Tessa included.

Tessa, who had always been very aroused by the prospect of being dead, had always considered double-crossing Frank and jumping anyway. She would have found it unbearable watching the others closing the book on themselves, whilst she, no less a figure than the Imperial Cat of Doom, was obliged to remain alive, and to boot, to be expected to patch them all up later. Tessa was far too charming to lodge a complaint, but she was also far too strong a character to let people take advantage of her. The chances are, she would have just jumped anyway, and this would have meant that any prospect at all of the grand self-participating funeral, fresh puppeteers having been found and trained, would have been as dead in the water as Tessa. Now, of course, she was free to jump officially and she had greeted this wonderful news with a surfeit of sensual purring from her feline alter ego.

Noddoes, by the same token, seemingly had no excuse now. Since his services would no longer be required, nor would he. But it was soon apparent (to Frank at least) that the old luvvie had no intention of joining them in any event. He was far too fond of life, and more to the point, of himself, to throw it away just as his star was beginning to rise. Noddoes still saw great things for himself, particularly so, in fact, now that he had rediscovered himself as a mimic of unrivalled brilliance. He would most certainly not be ending his days, and this was due to entirely selfish reasons. Frank for one was not fooled, but matters were certainly not helped by Noddoes coming out with a quite tremendous and feasible reason for not just why he shouldn't die, but actually why it was imperative for the benefit of everyone else that he must live. He insisted that he was required to ensure that all their corpses wound up at Proudfoot and Gadd; something which Frank had absolutely insisted upon in order to deny the Old Firm.

Noddoes outlined his reasoning during the briefing at HQ: 'Although our boatman, to whom funeral arrangements for everyone has been charged, is a truly excellent fellow and a brilliant seafarer, there remains the possibility, if not probability, that officers of Mr Snape may be alerted to events on the peak and an unsolicited delegation dispatched to intercept the cargo of corpses bound for Messrs Proudfoot and Gadd,' he warned. 'In order for any such raid to be resisted, it is vital that an officer of our company remains living, in order to supervise the safe delivery of said corpses to the prescribed firm of undertakers. Our boatman, mighty on the waves though he undoubtedly is, will need nevertheless to be aided when the cargo reaches land, where his talents are less celebrated. It would be indefensibly unfair should this burdensome task be placed on the shoulders of one single bold man. An extra is required beyond dispute to assume charge of the precious cargo once it has been off-loaded; someone who would be able to put down a challenge from any unwanted raiders; someone who has had experience in dealing with the more traditional side of our unique business and who would thus be the perfect intermediary to present this considerably valuable piece of business to the desired company, thwarting as need be hostile bids from any others, principally that of Mr Snape. And I have come to the conclusion that this man must be me.'

Frank's immediate reaction to this was to consider playfully asking Thoad whether he wouldn't like this job instead, but he just as quickly dispensed with this idea because not only would it have caused a delay to their proceedings, and that since Noddoes was clearly not going to jump come what may, it was just as well to agree to his suggestion, but just as conclusively was the position of Thoad, who was actually present in the room, still crying to himself, a good number of days now into an involuntary hunger strike and, in fact, not to beat about the bush, utterly oblivious to what was being discussed, half blind, caked in shit and half dead already. With only a matter of hours to go before their deaths, there was now a real fear that Thoad could turn out to be something of a party pooper by passing away pathetically before he had a chance to kill himself gloriously.

Epic took charge. He produced a carton of chilled full-cream milk, into which he crumbled a multivitamin tablet, rich in iron and added folic acid, plus a slow-releasing Vitamin C capsule, poured the nutritious mixture into a glass and handed it out to Thoad.

'Hey, bud! Try this!' he said. '*Dead!*'

At the sound of this magic word, Thoad came to life as if jolted by an electric current; and eyes bulging, he grabbed the glass and took the entire contents down in roughly half a second. He waited to die but nothing happened. And then his tastebuds sent in their belated report. And it wasn't good.

'Milk! *Milk!*' wailed Thoad. 'MILK!'

'See you on the cliff top, darlin'!' Epic nodded and knocked Thoad out as clinically as he had done Frank.

'Oh, bravo!' Frank applauded, as he and Stephen advanced towards the stricken Thoad to pick him up with Epic. 'That drink will give dear old Thoad all the nutrients, minerals and calcium he needs to sustain him through to his jump,' he noted, as the three men carried the comatose lump through to the viewing room. There they secured stunned Thoad to a couch by a rope, gagged him and then locked the door behind them as an extra precaution. At Epic's request, they also switched on a tape of light organ music, so that should Thoad awake, 'he would figure that he was in heaven'. It was an effective solution to what had been an encroaching disaster. Now solved.

The business with Noddoes was approved. Frank had long already guaranteed that no surviving member of staff would benefit from the Freddo estate by arranging for his mother to be named as the sole executor with proportionate sums eventually being granted to everybody else in the form of a fund to a named benefactor once the value of the estate had been realised. Everyone else's personal estates (such as they were) would naturally remain a matter for them. This "all to Mother" arrangement had been a device to preclude the unlikely threat of Noddoes, Tessa and/or Salty Sid attempting to claim the whole cake for themselves. Frank now felt that the clause had more significance. Tessa would now be jumping, and with Salty Sid never perceived as a realistic obstacle to the honouring of the agreement, which they had all signed, this only left Noddoes as a potential fly in the ointment. Frank had actually felt that Noddoes' duplicity only stretched as far as a desire to live, rather than a grand plan to enrich himself with the assets of the company. Now something was telling him that Noddoes may have been pulling a fast one. How the old luvvie was expected to have successfully challenged the legally bound document and emerge as the sole benefactor was anybody's guess, but Frank didn't care. Noddoes was capable of anything, the scheming wretch.

There was, however, not much Frank could do now. In fact, there was *nothing* he could do now. Noddoes was *not* going to forfeit his existence, and if he had indeed devised a Machiavellian plan to seize Freddo's assets, then he was on his way to a sizeable fortune without a doubt. The more Frank pondered this, the more he became satisfied that Noddoes, in the interests of fair play, really ought to die. But he thought no further on this, because this meant murder. And murder went against suicide. He simply made the following announcement: 'So you've decided not to jump, have you? Well, it gives me the greatest pleasure to finally say to you after all these years that you are fucking sacked!'

The meeting broke up and everybody left HQ (not Thoad), some for the last time. Stephen had been asked to return with Frank and Epic to scoop up the newly nourished and rested Thoad. It had initially been decided for just Frank and Epic to go, but this was eventually thought unwise, lest Thoad had remembrances of who had hoodwinked him with the bogus death drink and then punched the poor fucker on the bugle. He might have caused a scene, and it was therefore suggested that the presence of the extra man would stabilise maters given that eventuality.

In the meantime, everybody passed on their CDs of their musical choices to Frank so that he could pass them on to Keith Tate via Danny. Only Thoad had omitted to do this and it was here that the trueness of a friend was brought to the fore for everyone to see (except Thoad himself, who was unconscious). It was Frank who took it upon himself to add to the consignment a compilation of reggae masterpieces from the sixties/seventies border and underlined one track in particular as being the pick to represent the memory of his desperate colleague and drinking partner. Frank then went home and spent his final two nights quietly with his mother. On Thursday, he departed at noon for the Sermon and his death: 'Goodbye, Mother.'

'Will you be back for your tea?'

'If everything goes well, I doubt it.'

Nellie looked at him crossly. 'Don't be getting yourself pickled again, Frank!' she nagged.

Frank smiled and kissed her. 'Goodbye, Mother,' he said again. 'Watch the post!'

Chapter 52

Thoad

POOR THOAD WAS in no better shape when Frank, Epic and Stephen went back to HQ and untied him to fetch him off to his suicide than he had been before Epic had fed him the nutritious milk drink and then rocked him peacefully off to sleep with a dry slap. As a matter of fact, poor Thoad appeared to be in considerably worse shape, because in addition to crying again because the Inn had been closed, the stress and associated fear of having been trussed up and locked up in the viewing room for nearly two days also meant that he had shit himself; no small achievement for a guy who had not eaten anything for close to a week and was now at his lightest weight for sixteen years with his stomach as tight as a drum.

Notwithstanding, Thoad didn't appear to bear any grudges, although any suggestion that this was due to his renowned altruistic nature still being intact was soon dismissed as unlikely the second the gag was ripped off his mouth. Thoad was surprisingly alert despite everything.

'I just want to jump!' he immediately barbled through his tears.

Frank smiled back benignly and gripped him by the shoulder: 'Yes, mate,' he assured him. 'We're *all* going to jump! Today! Today's the day!'

'Keep on!' mumbled Epic.

By teatime it will all be over, son!' Frank added. 'Now come on, mate. One last effort! One last effort! Do you want to get something to eat?'

This question seemed to Stephen like an electric prong being poked up his arse: 'What are you saying that to him for?' he squeaked. 'He can't eat anything now! He's fucking shat himself! We've got to get the old bugger cleaned up! He'll stink out the whole fucking south coast! He must be caked in it!'

Epic agreed. 'He's right, Frankie!' he concurred. 'We've just gotta move him on out.'

'I just want to jump!' moaned Thoad as a reminder.

'He just wants to jump!' repeated Frank, almost sarcastically, who then turned to Thoad, who had not yet been untied: 'Yes, mate. We're *all* going to jump! Today! Today's the day!'

'*Jump!*' shrieked Thoad, who then farted twice.

'Say, there's a hose in Sheba's lab some place,' Epic pointed out, not quite using the right word.

'Of course!' said Stephen. 'We'll simply trash his Y-fronts, blast him up the botty with the hose, spray it, pin a towel around him and pull up his strides. That should be okay for today!'

'That's disgraceful!' tutted Frank.

'It's gotta be done, Frankie,' confirmed Epic. 'He's like a baby. He needs a new diaper, man!'

The three men cut the cords and then dragged Thoad sobbing to the embalmer's room. Unfortunately, this involved taking him down the corridor and thus away from the front door and Thoad, fearful that his suicide was going to be further delayed, which alas it was, started to struggle:

'Jump! Jump! Jump! Jump!' petulantly stammered Thoad, smelling quite unexpectedly horrid.

He started lashing out wildly. Stephen and Epic looked at each other urgently and then dropped their captive onto the floor.

'Wait in the car, Frankie,' Epic advised him. 'I don't think you're gonna want to watch this.'

Frank looked at Stephen, who smiled weakly back and then nodded to signify that for Thoad's own good they were left with no real alternative. Thus, while Frank turned his back and walked slowly and sadly back to the door, Epic and Stephen viciously laid into Thoad with their fists and feet, desisting only when their problem child's procrastinations had dissolved into a barely audible whimper. They then took an armpit each and dragged the wretch off to clean him up by blasting him with Tessa's hose.

As suggested, they wrapped a towel around his arse, sprayed it and pulled his trousers up. They then slid him out to where Frank had parked the Anglia, the back of which he was now opening.

'Say, Frankie. How would it be if we rope the old guy up to the fender just for old times?'

Stephen roared with laughter. Frank was indignant. He was not prepared to accept this suggestion even as a joke, which it might not have been at all. Epic didn't care, much less than Thoad, who once again had been cruelly and decisively smashed up.

'You two bastards have no heart. How could you suggest such a thing to poor, dear, pathetic, beaten old Thoad?'

Epic beamed at him: 'It ain't him, Frankie! It's a doughnut. How the fuck can you respect that? Just burn the shell and let it be.'

'What are you talking about, you imbecile! I can hear Thoad moaning. He's not dead, you idiot boy!'

Thoad very helpfully groaned and farted at this point for verification.

'Say, you're right, Frankie!' Epic conceded. 'But that's cool; me and Stevie are gonna beat up on him some more! C'mon, Stevie!'

At this, he and Stephen dropped Thoad onto the road and prepared to rip into him for the final decisive installment.

Frank screamed at them to stop: 'Leave that man alone! We have a duty to allow Thoad to die like the rest of us, in the way of his choice, to the music of his choice. He, after all, was the first of us to suggest such a scheme, was he not? He doesn't deserve murder. He deserves hospital. And we haven't got time for either. So just throw him in the fucking car, *gently*, and try to freshen him up. Tell him that we're taking him off to jump, which we are. *You* do that, Stephen. *Epic*, whatever you're going to say, please don't. We've wasted enough time already on this little episode. We could have run into connections of James and Sophie and then not one of us would have been alive to kill ourselves. So let's just go!'

So Epic and Stephen scooped up Thoad once more, this time quite literally from the gutter, and tossed him into the back of the Anglia. Stephen climbed in after him. He immediately began slapping Thoad across the face: 'Come on, son. Time to jump. Time to jump. Don't go to sleep now, mate. Wake you, you bugger!'

Grumbling Epic got in next to Frank and away they sped on the ten-minute drive up to Rocky Point. Nobody uttered a squeak until Frank turned the vehicle up onto the final approach road to the cliff top. Then, whether it was by sourcery, by chance, or down entirely to Stephen's sterling recuperative efforts, an unmistakable utterance gently dropped out of the mouth of only one man: 'I just want to jump!'

The other three exploded into cheers, and through what appeared to be instant tears of joy, Frank shouted back his obligatory response: 'Yes, mate. Now we're *all* going to jump!'

Seconds later, the little yellow vehicle had been deposited in the spaces up at the Point reserved specifically for patrons of either the Rocky Point museum and gift shop or the Rocky Point public house and restaurant, and whilst Frank and Epic strolled into the latter to find the others, Stephen stayed with Thoad, who had attained something of a state of karma, realising that he was now at the top of the cliff and would ere long be lying mangled and dead at the bottom of it.

It was twenty past one.

Chapter 53

Rocky Point

THE HEADCOUNT IN the pub and restaurant was impressive. Amanda, and most definitely Sheba, were both present, both of whom were jumping, and Noddoes (who wasn't) was talking to, of all people, Salty Sid, who was addressing a ploughman's lunch, his pipe and a large rum with nothing girly in it. The Rocky Point pub and restaurant was a mature, friendly establishment, which fed copiously people who did not ostensively come from Pendlesham. Coachloads of tourists and suicide jockeys seeking a last drink were the staple, and although they fitted quite obviously into this latter category, ordinarily the old Inn Crowd would have had nothing but disdain for such a conventional eatery. But today, not only was the use of it palatable, not only was it indeed ideal, but in fact for this occasion, nowhere else would have been acceptable.

Barefoot Sally, who enjoyed a drink and was proving this by sharing a bottle of dry white wine with no-one, was also in the bar, and although her husband, Danny, who unique amongst the Freddo party had not a smidgen of a tendency towards alcohol, was absent, Keith Tate had set himself steady into a session of cider, having already wired up the newly-acquired equipment in the morning and had then gone to lunch, leaving Danny to mind the house.

Keith Tate had effected the most remarkable and ironic of coups. In his search for the ideal spot to set up his sound station, his eyes had fallen upon the redundant Hut vacated by the late Reg Doorman, the man who had been practically hounded to his doom by a mixture of the non-stop supply of Freddo clients by way of suicide leaps from Rocky Point and the Camcorders' constant chiding of him as they recorded each one. The Lifejoys, that altruistic bunch of do-gooders, had practically dissolved into the sea as a consequence; the Hut had become available for sale or rent, so Keith stepped in, knowing nothing at all of the tiny premises' morbid antecedents.

Salty Sid had finished his poor man's meal and walked off, cursing away any offers of a taxi to take him down the hill to pick up his boat. Sid was a walker immediately behind a sailor and would have countenanced no such thing – and didn't. Off he went, although he didn't depart until he had recharged his flask: 'I don't wants none of you to be buggering about. Half past five!' Sid said to Frank. 'I've never pretended to be the cleverest of men, but I knows how to count from one to six, I does, and that's all I'll be needing whens you all flies o'er towards the rocks yonder. That's alls I have to say.'

'Six it is,' confirmed Frank.

'I shall rendezvous with you when you reach shore with your bountiful cargo, boatman,' Noddoes said to him.

'I don't knows what that means, but you can suit yourself!' replied Sid and he ambled off again, adding loudly for general consumption a reminder: 'I don't wants none of you to be buggering about. Half past five!' And he was gone.

Taking lunch also amongst the happy, civilised gathering were Adrian, Ken, Malcolm, Dick and Ted – The Old Ropsasians, dapper in their 'smart green blazers' and all nursing half pints of real ale.

'It's a shame that Nobby was on an assignment with U*N*C*L*E,' Adrian said. 'He would have loved this. I'm certain of it.'

'I think old Nob deserves a pat on the back for his sterling work against the evil of T*H*R*U*S*H,' offered Malcolm, thumbing through a large hardback scrapbook containing newspaper cuttings and photographs of non-league football matches. 'Those chaps are a menace. I only hope that Nobby is careful.'

Adrian picked up his glass: 'To Nobby!' he announced, glancing around for support.

'Nobby!' they all concurred and completed the toast.

'It's rather strange,' Adrian then mused. 'I can see Eddowes, but I haven't seen dear old Tom yet. I wonder why?'

'That *is* odd,' agreed Dick, looking up from his magazine on women's tennis. 'It's not like good old Tom to be absent when there's a drink to be had. Where is he, I wonder?'

'Adrian peered around the pub further: 'What's also odd is that I can't see that chap Stephen either. Something's not quite right...'

This vexation immediately gave way to a hearty cheer from all of them, as through the door swept Thoad, being 'escorted' by Stephen and Epic, who had gone out to help fetch him.

'Here he is!'

'Good old Tom!'

'Over here, son!'

Stephen, noticing this, looked at Epic. 'Now there's a blessing in disguise if ever there was one,' he said, motioning towards the waving and cheering party. 'Those are the camera blokes. They're the saddest band of no-life fuckers you'll ever see. They'll look after him.'

Epic nodded: 'Okay, man. Let's do it. I just need a drink!'

They dragged the burbling, dribbling Thoad over towards where the Camcorders were sitting and as they approached, all five men rose and applauded:

'Good old Tom!'

'How's tricks, Tommy?'

'Half pint for Tom!'

Epic grabbed Thoad's arm and waved it back in the direction of the table just as they arrived.

'Can we get this guy into a seat?' Epic enquired, as he and Stephen handed custody over to Adrian and Ken.

'Certainly!' Ken beamed, as he embraced his old comrade.

'Hello, Tom! Ooh! What a funny smell!'

Ted tapped Thoad on the shoulder with the stalk of his pipe: 'I say, old boy, you don't look quite the ticket. What *have* you been up to, hum?'

Thoad responded with some strange, unintelligible throat noises...

'Hum?' asked Ted.

'I…just…want…,' croaked Thoad inaudibly.

'Hum?' asked Ted.

'…just…want…to…,'

'Hum?'

'Here you are, Tom,' said Malcolm, as Adrian and Ken eased Thoad into a seat next to Dick. 'Here's a half.' He plonked a small glass of ale on an adjacent table.

Thoad started to shudder when he saw the liquid. 'Milk! *Milk!*' he wailed. 'MILK!'

'Hum?' asked Ted.

'*Milk?*' scowled Malcolm disapprovingly. 'That's not like you, Tom. Are you sure?'

Thoad glared at the half pint of ale with more than a little suspicion. Slowly his arms raised and a finger indicated the offending glass.

'Milk!' he managed breathlessly, and his arm dropped wearily to his side.

'Very well,' nodded Malcolm, sounding rather offended. 'Milk it shall be. Half a mo.'

Adrian, who had recognised that Thoad was looking a little different, but had been unable to put his finger on how this was, suddenly realised: 'Of *course*! You've lost weight, you old dog! Of course you have, Tom! Been dieting, have we?'

'*Milk!*' groaned Thoad again, as liquid shit began to seep into the towel pinned to his crutch.

'A milk diet, is it?' beamed Adrian. 'How extraordinary! That's a new one. All that fat! But it's certainly worked for you, hasn't it? Congratulations, Tom!'

Ken stood up and tapped the table: 'I think it would be a fine idea if we *all* have milk this time so that we can pay proper tribute to Tom and his wonderful diet!' he announced, as Malcolm arrived with Thoad's milk.

'An excellent suggestion!' agreed Dick.

'Splendid, splendid!' concurred Ted, emptying his pipe into an ashtray.

So Malcolm, who couldn't agree more, returned smilingly to the bar and emerged moments later with a tray containing five more glasses of Daisy's Special Reserve. Everyone took one, as Thoad looked on in abject horror:

'*MILK!*' he roared in utter desperation, nearly in tears again.

The Camcorders raised their glasses to acknowledge the proposed toast: '*MILK!*' they all returned and downed their milk to its glory.

Meanwhile, across the bar, the Inn Crowd (minus Thoad) had deep rooted themselves into their final session together. Sheba was in particularly fine form, displaying her beautiful curves and purring continuously. The girl was coked out of her lovely head. Amanda too had decided to mark her death with a celebratory last sniff and was in serious bollock-grabbing mood, with Stephen naturally her target. At one point, she inadvertently seized the plums of Epic…

'Hey, hey, hey, girly!' cautioned Epic. 'Not me, baby!'

Amanda acknowledged her error with a trademark punch on Stephen's permanently bruised arm: 'Bastard!' she rasped. 'Why wasn't that you?'

Frank was pissed by this time and in a soppy, nostalgic mood. Even the presence of Sheba in her most shebarist of Shebas did not seem to have any impact on him. He had never been able to work out to his own satisfaction whether the ultimate woman of his desire had actually slept with him that time following the tragedy of Birmingham and had long since given up trying to discover the truth. The incident had seemed so memorable, so vivid, which it most certainly would have been had it actually happened; and the fact that every wonderful detail remained tingling inside him to the point where even the thought of it pleasured him almost to the point of satisfaction rather than having been banished from his brain along with most other drunken escapade and thought suggested that the wonderful episode had been real.

Tessa (or Sheba) has shown no interest since then, which may or may not have been a pointer to the exchange being a dream, were it not for the fact that Tessa, as Sheba, was nothing other than a drug-induced cartoon character and therefore a mad, irrational apparition, no matter how beautiful, and capable of anything including duplicity. Added to this was the prospect that she had had her memory wiped clean and could remember nothing at all, which was why she had never mentioned it.

Frank had therefore decided to live with the even possibility (in his eyes) that the one-night-stand may have been true, instead of attempting to find out whether it had been or not, something which in itself may have been fruitless, since the only possible corroborator was Tessa who, as Tessa, had nothing whatsoever to do with it, and as Sheba, was mad and irrational and therefore an entirely discredited witness.

He had given up.

Frank instead had his eyes set on one prize only – that of the mass suicide, which was a protest to authority and most certainly in particular to the officer who looked like the guy out of Blue Mink, his superiors and cronies, those who had closed the Inn, almost certainly because they wanted to open their own cheesy watering hole in its stead on the prime station concourse. Suicide was the only option now, and so here they all were just moments away from the time that had been put aside as being the commencement of Danny's Sermon. It was half past four and all was merry.

About ten minutes later, Barefoot Sally and Keith Tate left the Rocky Point pub and restaurant and went out onto the cliff top itself. Neither were wrecked. Sally had long since retained a circumspect watch on her drinking habits and kept these days strictly to wine, whereas her early days had seen her downing anything from vodka neat to pints of snakebite - a terrible mixture of cider and lager – with her pills and weed. She was still far enough away from being even a slightly unconventional vicar's wife, but she was more conservative than she had ever been and she certainly didn't do drugs anymore.

Keith Tate was one of those short, bearded gorillas, who never seemed to be able to get pissed, no matter how much he supped. He could sit in a pub and talk about music, football, politics, or… earthenware pots and walk away as if nothing had happened after six hours and twenty pints of scrumpy. His capacity and appetite for drink was beyond the boundaries of most mortal men. Had he ever been a Station Inn regular, which he never had been (he drank in more mature quarters), Keith would not only have been an important member of the Inn Crowd, he would have been elected president unopposed. He was the one who got away. He was a man of great intelligence and honest opinions, and as an imbiber he had no parallel.

Keith had become friends with Danny Hare through a mutual friend called Gary, another gargantuan drinker, over whose father's funeral Danny had presided. After the service, Danny had casually declared that he was looking for a reliable 'sound man', as his own skills in this discipline had proved at times to be sadly inadequate. Gary immediately thought of Keith, who had done lots of work with some minor London bands, and introduced him to the Reverend. Keith Tate, like Danny, was a man of liberal views, but made it clear that unlike Danny he was not and never could be a Christian. ('God's cool with that!' Danny had assured him). Once that was understood, the two men quickly found their common ground – rock music. A deal was promptly struck and so was an impenetrable friendship. Their combined knowledge and love of the broad sweep of music of the sixties and seventies was truly monumental. Had Danny ever been a pub man, and had they been able to concoct a quiz competition, which featured rock and roll questions exclusively, the duo would have been unbeatable. Keith had played keyboards for one or two bands and eventually Danny persuaded him that he could quite legitimately play the church organ too without compromising himself ('even Satan was a musical guy'); and so Keith sat at the organ in humble dress, playing songs which meant nothing at all to him and sometimes even annoyed him, not so much for their religious connotation as for their banal and totally uncomplicated music composite; and he began to jazz them up with different tempos and chord changes, which Danny and Barefoot Sally loved and so did the majority of the parishioners. Rock and roll took over the agenda, and in that context at least, Keith Tate became truly a holy man.

Chapter 54

Freddo's

WITH SALLY AND Keith departed, this only left the staff of Freddo's to finish up and get over to the cliff top so that the entertainment could commence. At five o'clock precisely, the seven of them came tumbling out. Thoad, once again, was under escort. He had not touched a drop of liquid in all the three and a half hours he had been in there. All he had done was to fret about milk and had inexplicably ended up with half a dozen glasses of it in front of him, none of which he had touched by either hand nor lip before he was led to the door by Stephen and Epic again.

Amanda and Sheba scuttled on ahead. Their appointment was with Danny and Barefoot Sally. There was not intended to be a performance of The Exotics now. The idea, which would certainly have been appropriate had the two girls (or at least one) been already dead and the service had been held at the Bar and Grill with puppets as originally supposed, had been, to coin a phrase, put on ice, since Danny had decided that the performance would be too fragmented as a result of Amanda and Tessa both leaving the performance at the appointed time to go and jump off the cliff. Indeed it was in order to preclude mayhem that an order of play had been drawn up – a strict roster determining who would jump when. On this, Amanda had been placed third, behind Thoad and Stephen with Sheba next after her. Fifth was to be Epic with Frank to complete the show, much to his reluctance, for he still harboured a dim hope that Tessa would reconsider her position and remain so that she could embalm them all, particularly himself.

There was some surprise when it was announced that Stephen and Amanda would not be jumping together à la James and Sophie. Stephen had suggested this as being a 'sweet' idea, which it was really. But he was far too much of a romantic, and the idea was scuppered for two reasons, the principal one of which was Amanda's own veto of the idea because 'I'm going to outlive that useless bastard if it's the last thing I fucking do!'. In addition to this was the problem concerning the chosen music for them both. Amanda, for instance, had decided, as she had said she might, to leap to Toyah Wilcox squawking out *I Want To Be Me*, whereas Stephen had managed, after fierce resistance from Amanda, to select his own track without her direction or even influence. His choice puzzled the others, particularly Danny and Keith, who had tried to work out the significance of the selection for days and had come up with nothing. This itself was not surprising because the choice had nothing to do with profundity and everything to do with a personal fondness for a nice old track. It was Hurricane Smith singing (or rather growling) *Oh Babe, What Would You Say?*, a chirpy, oldy-worldy ballad from 1972. When Stephen had initially played it to Amanda, who had sworn she had never heard it before, she had smashed him so hard on his now permanently deadened arm that Stephen's mouth had shot open in pain and surprise; and although this only hardened his resolve that his musical wishes be honoured, it was a very curious choice indeed ('hardly cool', as Epic had put it). With two such diametrically opposed tracks being played (indeed *any* two tracks being played) at the same time, the event might have been seen to lose tone due to the resulting cacophony and the pivotal idea of everyone jumping to their own personal choice would have been rendered meaningless, something which Danny was not going to countenance. Of course had Amanda agreed to jump with Stephen, Stephen would almost certainly have accepted the Toyah record for them both and that would have been that. But since Amanda was having nothing of this, the prospect of a collision of two distinct sounds was avoided in any case. The one thing Danny and Keith had perhaps not considered with regards Stephen's choice of Hurricane Smith was that he simply wished to wind up Amanda by subjecting her to a track he knew she would despise following Amanda's long-held assumption that she would pick his record for him. As it happened, this was not true.

The reason that Amanda and Sheba had joined Barefoot Sally by Danny's side was nothing more really than a nod towards all the wonderful work that this very special and sexy band had done together over the astonishing times made possible by Freddo's prior to the advent of self-participating funerals when their performance was pivotal to proceedings, before the corpses began running things and stealing the limelight and all the glory for themselves. The three women hugged and giggled girlishly with each other. Whilst Frank, Epic and Stephen eased Thoad into position, Danny muttered 'Testing! Testing!' into his microphone and Keith emerged from the Hut to give them the thumbs-up indicating that everything was all set there too.

Adrian, Ken, Malcolm, Dick and Ted were all primed and had set themselves up at the precise spot which had been their most favoured one in their salad days. Not one of them had so much as been near Rocky Point since ROPSAS had disbanded so triumphantly, and indeed the first thing they had done when they had all met up outside the gift shop prior to entering the pub was to go for a stroll along the cliffs to reminisce about the times when ROPSAS was mighty, and especially of their finest hour – the smiting of Reg Doorman. It was this memory in particular which understandably caused the most poignant emotion, and in order for the full nostalgia value to be appreciated, the boys had decided to worship at the very shrine of Doorman himself – the Hut.

'I'll never forget all the times the wanker came haring out of that door like Ben Johnson on gear to try to save some bastard who had already jumped!' chuckled Adrian, clearly no longer the 'milder, cleaner, better' man he had been whilst a disciple of Gilbert's.

'Clearly a buffoon,' nodded Malcolm. '*Always* a buffoon.'

'I actually think his foolishness ceased to be entirely his own fault in the end,' Ken put in. 'I think it became a state of mind.'

'Rubbish!' countered Ted, pointing his pipe at Ken. 'Doorman was an idiot. We had a duty to dispose of him.'

Dick nodded at Ken to signify that he broadly agreed with Ted.

The Old Ropsasians trained their camcorders on the Hut and started rolling, and it was at this point that seemingly right on cue the door of the Hut flew open just like old times. This, though, was as far as old times stretched, for instead of the running, panicking, altruistic figure of Reg Doorman, there stood instead the short, stocky, hunched-up, hairy, cave-man-like figure of Keith Tate, with a reefer hanging from the corner of his mouth and an open can of cider clutched in his right hand. There was nothing but silence for thirty seconds whilst the Old Ropsasians stood in amazement and trained their activated instruments first at Keith and then through the door of the Hut at the broadcasting equipment within. Thirty seconds became forty and this was more than enough for Keith, who had been busying himself with his final arrangements when he had become aware of the intruders.

'Do you muppets want something?' he asked.

The camcorders rolled on for an extra five seconds before a hesitant voice ventured out from the one which was held by Adrian: 'Er'm... Who are you?'

'I'm Keith, the soundman,' admitted Keith, the soundman. 'You're here to make the film for the coroner, right? Why are you wasting time and film on me?'

But there still seemed to be some confusion...

'Do you work in the Hut, then?' Malcolm asked suspiciously. 'You haven't taken over from Reg, have you?'

'I thought I'd just explained to you what I'm doing here,' Keith said, flicking some ash off his cigarette end.

'He's Keith, the soundman,' Adrian reminded everyone before lowering his de-activated camera and smiling weakly at Keith, who missed this nicety because he was squeezing cider down his throat. 'You're the chap who's playing the records!'

'Hum?' asked Ted.

'Was there anything else?' Keith enquired, closing the door.

'Well, I...' began Malcolm.

Closed door.

The Old Ropsasians trooped off, grateful at least that The Lifejoys had not returned, although it had taken some of them long enough to grasp this fact, and even now Malcolm remained in a state of perplexity: 'I don't know who that guy was or what he was doing there, but he was bloody rude!' he sniffed. 'Bloody suspicious too, what's more. I vote that we instigate a campaign against him at the earliest available opportunity.'

'Malcolm, he's only the soundman,' Adrian assured him. 'And he'll only be here today. He's here to play records for dear old Tom and his friends and then he'll leave the Hut and take whatever he has in there with him. Alright?'

'How can you be sure?'

'Look, Malcolm. You seem to have missed the plot, methinks. The Old Ropsasians is not an organisation whose functions and agenda mirror the aims and aspirations of our old club...'

'Oh?'

'... We are founded purely for the benefit and derivation of nostalgia...'

'Ah!'

'... and even if that chap Keith *had* been a replacement for Reg, or indeed anything to do with The Lifejoys at all, our brief is *not* to do anything to oppose him. Our organisation is merely concerned with celebrating past triumphs...'

'Ah!'

'...Of course, if any group decided to form in order to oppose and destroy any resurrection of The Lifejoys, that would be a matter for them, and naturally we would send fraternal greetings to them...'

For Malcolm, the penny had at last dropped but still his lust had not been appeased and he looked back behind him distrustfully: 'I'm going to keep my eye on the Hut just to be on the safe side,' he vowed. 'If I find out that The Lifejoys are even *contemplating* even as much as giving it a lick of paint, thus destroying all our victory messages to Reg, I'm going to take it as a council of war and act immediately. I shall, as you've suggested, Adrian, form a new band, an entirely new group, with which we will deliver a mortal blow to our mortal enemy void of mercy. I shall break this conspiracy!'

'That's okay, Malcolm,' Adrian said. 'That's fine. But I have to tell you again that this particular guy who's in the Hut just now is only the soundman. I bet that he doesn't even know what the Hut used to be used for before he got in there…'

'He had better not!'

'… He still may not. But even if he did, it's of no concern of ours. Form your own new band by all means, Malcolm, but it may mean that you are asked to resign from the Old Ropsasians.'

Malcolm's eyes bulged: 'How do you work that one out, then?' he rasped. 'You don't know what you're talking about. No matter what happens, I'll still be a former member of ROPSAS, no matter what, won't I? Thus, I'll always qualify for membership of the Old Ropsasians, no matter what. You can't change history.'

'Actually, Adrian, Malcolm's quite right,' pointed out Ken. 'You can't just throw him out like that. He already has his blazer, and as he says, you can't change history.'

'You can't change it,' concurred Dick.

'Hum?' asked Ted.

'Yes, but Malcolm,' Adrian protested. 'Could you support two football teams at once?'

'It's the same team, you tosser!' Malcolm growled.

'It isn't!'

'It fucking *is*!'

'But it *can't* be!'

'It's the same team but a different squad,' suggested Malcolm, who was a non-league football follower and knew of these things.

'It fucking *ISN'T*!' roared Adrian. 'What a stupid fucking analogy!'

'No it isn't!' immediately countered Malcolm. 'And how would it be if we all decided to chuck *you* out of the Old Ropsasians?'

Adrian went cold: 'What would you want to do that for?' he whimpered, firmly on the back foot already.

'Well, you're always banging on about throwing other people out of clubs, so why don't we just throw *you* out? You're getting far too big for your boots, Adrian. You just can't go round barring people willy-nilly. We'll fucking bar *you*, you bastard!'

'No man's bigger than the club,' added Dick smilingly and in no way maliciously.

Adrian was on the ropes now: 'Oh, please don't!' he begged. 'Please don't make me turn in my blazer! The Old Ropsasians are my life. I had such plans. Please, *no*!'

'No-one wants to bar you, mate!' Malcolm assured him soothingly, coming to Adrian's rescue now that he had beaten him. 'I just don't want *you* trying to bar *me*. You see, I'm only really trying to protect myself from *you*, you fucking bastard. Neither of us need to hand in our blazers to anybody. Just stop trying to turn *me* over, or I'll fucking turn *you* over, son!'

'You'll be barred!' Dick reminded him cheerfully.

'Drummed out!' nodded Ken.

'Hum?' asked Ted, emptying his pipe.

'Please… Please, *no*!' Adrian trembled. 'There's no need for *anybody* to be barred. Please don't drum me out! Let's just go back to how it was. *Please!*'

Malcolm now turned to Adrian with the bitter smile of victory: 'And so if I form a new group, an entirely new group, to counter any renaissance threatened by The Lifejoys, I will not be thrown out of the Old Ropsasians?'

'No, Malcolm,' submitted Adrian meekly.

'The working name for my new organisation is "The Reggies,"' Malcolm announced proudly. 'This of course is an ironic name, giving reference to the bastard we drove to suicide so gloriously, but whom we would still blame for any return to the scene of anybody from The Lifejoys, including that guy in the Hut, who certainly looks like a Lifejoy to me, I must say.'

'He's the soundman,' Adrian said, without thinking.

'If he isn't,' Malcolm warned, raising his voice, 'I'm going to put the bearded pothead through the fucking blender!'

At this, Adrian capitulated entirely: 'I'm with you!' he suddenly insisted stridently.

'You are?'

'So you're calling yourselves The Reggies?'

'That's it,' confirmed Malcolm.

Adrian looked at him sheepishly. 'Can I join?' he asked.

'Of course you can, mate!' warmly accepted Malcolm.

'Will we have blazers?'

'Totally new colour, son!' beamed Malcolm.

'Crimson would be nice,' suggested Dick.

'We'll form a bowling team,' suggested Ken.

'Hum?' asked Ted, puffing away.

'I have an important announcement to make,' gushed Adrian suddenly. 'When we finish here today, I'm going to resign from the Old Ropsasians and throw everything behind The Reggies. The Reggies are clearly the way forward. The way ahead. An exciting and enduring concept. That fake soundman won't know what's fucking hit him! This is brilliant! I think I'm going to be with The Reggies for a very long time...'

Chapter 55

Wally And Max

A T JUST BEFORE a quarter past the hour, Danny's Sermon for Suicide began before a curious audience of about thirty people including the participants and the Old Ropsasians.

Noddoes stood to one side of the others, as if to reiterate that he would still be alive at the end of the afternoon, and Thoad was still being propped up between Stephen and Epic.

'Not long now, son,' Frank said to him, placing a reassuring hand on his shoulder.

Thoad, though, had crapped himself again and smelt grim. His eyes were glazed, lips as red as a post box and he was dribbling and still grizzling. Jumping looked almost unnecessary now.

'Okay. Testing one more time!' Danny suddenly said into his microphone, and his words came out loud and clear. Keith Tate gave the final thumbs up to verify it. 'Good. That's cool!'

Thoad croaked out for 'milk'; nobody paid the blindest bit of notice, and Danny launched finally into his Sermon for real:

'Friends! We gather here upon this peak to say goodbye to some groovy rock and rollers. God gave rock and roll to us all and it was one of His most special gifts. And our six dear friends here have all elected fittingly to enter His house through the glory of this, one of the Lord's most wondrous creations...'

For once, there was no shaking. Despite Danny's tone, jovial as ever, and despite the fact that the occasion was undoubtedly a joyous one, this sermon was like no other he had ever delivered; it was entirely special and completely unique. It was delivered paradoxically to a rather subdued, if not somber, assembly.

'The Father shall soon be entertaining six of His great pioneers, who have elected today to arrive at His right hand via the congregation. Suicide is a noble institution. It remains the ultimate symbol of self-expression. The decision taken by our six heroes and heroines to arrange and choreograph this festival of self-destruction and to link it intrinsically with a personal selection from the annals of post-war popular music, rubber stamps their right to be listed as pioneers. And it rubber stamps too their right to be called heroes and heroines. Their noble deed today will reverberate around and across this sceptred isle and subsequently the world. And it is my submission that such festivals, not necessarily on such a grand scale, will eventually become commonplace.

'As much as it wounds me to admit it, the pioneering nature of this momentous occasion does not stop with the rock and roll extravaganza which awaits us. It is not *all* about rock. Just as pioneering is (and I say this as humbly as I can), the part played by the Church itself. For surely a funeral attended by someone not yet dead, but whose funeral it incontrovertibly is represents the final spin of the ball for the industry of the funeral director? Although it is perhaps only the corollary of the now well-established self-participating funerals, when participants contribute post-death; a phenomenon in which our six pioneers specialised so remarkably.

'The conventional church funeral with floral tributes, the meaningless utterings of the minister, the false solemnity and yes, the false tears, has been revealed as being the ludicrous, hypocrisy-rich, laughable cap and bells affair it has always been, surviving so long only because nobody had neither the courage nor the imagination to challenge and then break the taboo. This remained the case until Frank Eddowes protruded onto the scene, a true rock and roll brother with a mission, a mission which he and his comrades have gloriously accomplished against incalculable odds. Their deaths here today will not just open the final door, but sledgehammer it down. Funerals will soon be for the living, every bit as much as for those who have died with no prior intention of doing so. Our Father awaits them, and so also do the late icons of rock and roll with Presley as the undisputed king. Let us pray.'

Danny Hare thus, launched into The Lord's Prayer, 'the prayer which Jesus himself taught us'. This was the only overtly religious offering which Danny had always considered sacrosanct for each and every ceremony. 'Nothing ain't *ever* gonna eradicate *that* one, baby!' he had once barked at a questioning young girl just after he had taken over the Bar and Grill. 'The Lord's Prayer is just what it says it is, little lady. It's the Man's signature tune!'

This having been accomplished (and impeccably observed it was too), the Reverend gave the pre-arranged signal to Keith Tate, which told him that the sermon had concluded and that the jumping could begin. Everyone shuffled into position. It was now half-past five.

At the bottom of the cliff, Salty Sid was waiting in his boat, puffing away at his pipe, of course; his keen vulpine eyes peering up at the very point where he was expecting Thoad to come hurtling over at any second. Back at the top, Van Halen's *Jump* was already thundering out of the surrounding speakers plugged into the equipment in the Hut. This was the track that had been finally chosen to open the show, and it was here that the Inn Crowd hugged each other to say farewell. The camcorders were now rolling.

The next thing that happened certainly shouldn't have. The curtain-raising track, stadium rock at its finest, was not more than half way through when it was abruptly terminated. At first, silence and confusion. Then Frank turned to Noddoes and delivered an immediate order: 'Find out what's happened!' he hissed. 'And be quick about it!'

Noddoes acknowledged and quickly strode off to see what the problem was with Keith. On the way, Gilbert O'Sullivan came on singing *No Matter How I Try*, and this explained everything to two people – Stephen Mauve and Adrian, the Camcorder.

'Oh God, no!' groaned Adrian. 'It's Wally and Max!' And so it was. For it was Adrian's former colleagues from GO who had taken over the Hut in order to hijack the musical festival in the name of their hero. They had crept up to the top of the Point, unnoticed by the only man who could have possibly recognised them, and had remained in the background as quiet as mice whilst Danny had delivered his historic sermon. The moment *Jump* had started to sweep across the cliff, the activists sprang into action. They had marched up to the door of the Hut and rapped on it solidly. Only they then had to do this again because Keith had a head full of earphones. The door finally flung open and Wally and Max piled in, immediately over-powering an astonished Keith by threatening him with a twatting from the Spanish truncheons they had both brought with them. The soundman wisely hit the floor, and thus immobolised (and terrified), Wally ejected the Van Halen CD and replaced it with *The Gilbert O'Sullivan Collection*, whilst Max (the 'heavy') made certain that Danny's 'verger' didn't attempt any-thing foolish. He gently tapped Keith upside the nostrils with the special issue cosh: 'Make a noise and I'll give you this!' he lisped menacingly.

Not long after this, Noddoes arrived. Wally and Max had not closed the door to the Hut behind them and the old luvvie was able to push it open and peek inside. His eyes immediately met those of Keith's who had been pinned well and truly to the floor.

'What's the meaning of this tomfoolery, Tate!' Noddoes demanded of him. 'Return to your duties immediately, or I shall see to it that you are censured most severely. This is no time for levity!'

'Have him, Wal!' ordered Max, and Wally immediately advanced towards Noddoes and belted him across the chops with his stick, send-ing the old luvvie spinning out of the Hut: 'Piss off. We're working!' Wally barked and slammed the door. Gilbert was singing *We Will* now.

Noddoes yelped like a whipped puppy, crumpled and rolled over dra-matically on his back. The blow had been hard but nowhere near decisive and Noddoes had easily retained consciousness, even though blood had been drawn from a wound to his mouth. Noddoes, though, viewed his inju-ries far more gravely:

'Good God! Am I slain?' he questioned to himself out loud. He put his hand to his lips and retrieved a light smear of blood. And then he knew...

'Oh most merciless fate!' he howled. 'I *am* slain! I am cut down! I…' And then he suddenly stopped, for he had realised that there was no-one present to witness this, the greatest tragedy and the finest interpretation of tragedy the world had ever known. Since his audience had not come to him, he would have to go to them. He picked himself up and started galloping across the grass with Gilbert O'Sullivan accompanying him all the way, although Noddoes of course was oblivious to this. As he ran, he repeated to himself the part of the soliloquy he had already delivered but which had been heard by no-one. '"Good God! Am I slain?"' he muttered.

He then remembered that the next part demanded that he put his hand up to his lip, although in this impromptu rehearsal, he didn't do it. 'Er, yes. Then I say: "Oh, most merciless fate! I *am* slain! I am cut down! I am a man destroyed! I am…" Yes, yes. This is brilliant! "Oh, most merciless fate…" No, you fool! You've missed the first bit! "Good God! Am I slain?" Yes, that was it… And *then* it's "Oh, most merciless fate! I *am* slain!" Oh, my. This is going to be a *masterpiece!*'

Meanwhile, farther along by the edge, the failure of Noddoes to secure the return of Van Halen and the advent of the second Gilbert O'Sullivan track had been more than enough for Frank. He could do nothing, though, but watch as Noddoes came skipping towards them, muttering nonsense to himself, having accomplished precisely nothing. But at last Stephen had cottoned on by then: 'Quick!' he had hollered to Epic. 'The Hut's being attacked!'

'Say *what?*' Epic retorted.

'It's being attacked by lunatics. I know them. They're nutters. They'll ruin everything. Come on!'

'But what about *this* guy?' Epic asked, meaning Thoad.

'Knock him out!' demanded Stephen. 'Come on!'

Stephen started running, and so Epic's mighty right hand thundered into Thoad's jaw once again, bringing him instant oblivion as he sank to the floor.

'Well, that was easy!' quipped Epic, as he scuttled off as well.

Noddoes arrived, being passed en-route by the other two, only to run straight into a voluble reprimand from Frank. It was nothing short of hateful and was in fact the culmination of all the contempt Frank had felt for the old luvvie over the years, up to and including his cowardly withdrawal from the mass suicide, which now lay in ruins, it seemed, something which Frank was also more than ready to blame on him. The old luvvie, still bleeding from the mouth but not badly, had not even been given the opportunity to utter one breath of his 'merciless fate' soliloquy before running headlong into Frank's explosion of vermin against him. It was because of this that everything threw at him bounced off without registering, as Noddoes remained locked into his own trance, continually composing his speech in his mind and preparing himself mentally to deliver it to maximum dramatic effect the moment his restless audience had finally come to order.

Whilst this was happening, the Hut was being gloriously reclaimed by Freddo's. Stephen had assured Epic that the two guys whom they almost certainly faced were 'what you lot call geeks or dweebs' and this revelation, if nothing else, had satisfied Epic immediately that the liberation would not last long. It didn't. They burst through the door, which was closed but not locked and Stephen, who was leading, ripped straight into Max just as Gilbert was commencing the third track on the album, the self-pitying dismal ballad, *Alone Again (Naturally)*. Epic, realising immediately that Max was the guy who needed to be taken out and that together he and Stephen could quickly overwhelm him, piled in as well, thereby freeing Keith Tate and meaning that there were now three of them available to deal with the smaller bespectacled Wally, who suddenly now appeared to have shrunk even smaller so that he now reminded Stephen of Arthur Askey, and that now that he was alone (just as much as Gilbert, apparently), he looked just about as fearful as the late 'kind hearted Arthur', even though he still brandished his weapon.

'We only wanted to make a point...' he began timidly before Stephen kicked him in the bollocks, grabbed his truncheon off him and swung it into his face, cracking the frame of his glasses and bloodying his hooter.

Keith wasted no time in laying into the prostrate Max with his boots and would have carried on doing it had not Epic intervened:

'It's okay, man! I think we've retaken the hill,' he said, and Keith stopped and then walked over and started kicking Wally.

'Hey! Stop that right now!' shouted Epic.

'Let's get this bollocks off!' added Stephen, meaning Gilbert. 'Come on, Keith. Leave him alone. We've done the pair of 'em!'

'You're a couple of bastards!' Keith barked as a final tribute to Wally and Max, both of whom had been nicely bashed up but each taking their defeat in distinctly different ways. Max was sitting up now with his back to the wall, eyeing his conquerors with almost a look of approval, whilst Wally was lying on his back grizzling softly with his damaged glasses in his hands, resembling the school weed whose function it was always sadly fated to be was to be duffed up at playtime, either by an established bully or by a lower status thug intent on promotion in the ranks. His and Max's assault on the Hut in the name of their iconoclast had been decisively put down, and with a contemptuous flick of a switch from a truly avenged Keith Tate, Gilbert O'Sullivan's mighty voice was stilled.

Not so that of Noddoes, whom Epic and Stephen had passed galloping in the contrary direction as they themselves were on their way to the Hut to put Wally and Max to the sword. After Frank was through barking at him, Noddoes, who now had his back to the cliff edge, placed his right hand on his breast, thrust his head into the air, took an exaggeratedly deep breath and away he went. It was now twenty-five minutes to six. Just gone.

'Good God! Am I slain?...' Hand to lips. No blood at all. 'Oh, most merciless fate! I *am* slain! I am cut down! I am a man destroyed! I am a person perished! I, in the prime of my existence, have been discharged from the duty of suffering further the agonies and ecstasies of life by means of a foul act of homicide from a fellow man who is a fiend! By this nefarious deed, I am murdered!...'

At this stage, Noddoes paused and took two steps backwards. He had ignored the Gilbert O'Sullivan record, which had now been forgotten by everybody else as well, as they stared open-mouthed at the greatest live piece of open theatre anywhere in the history of the world. Danny Hare thought it was wonderful and considered that what he was hearing and the exquisiteness of its delivery relegated his own superficial Sermon to the point of irreverence, irrelevance, if not plain ridicule.

'The light of life is before me becoming dim!' continued Noddoes finally. 'I cannot help myself! I am dying! I am edging back into darkness! Gradually, yet inexorably, I am edging back!... Edging back!... Edging back!... Edging back!'

Noddoes flopped into a dramatic series of bows and eased slowly backwards. He had finished and was now inviting applause. Indeed, he was demanding it and did not expect to be denied it.

Nor was he. Everybody began cheering and applauding most thunderously and cries of 'Bravo!' and 'Encore!' resounded all about the Point and far out over the waves. Noddoes' exultation of 'Edging back!' grew ever softer until it became a murmur, but he did not extinguish it completely because he was being constantly fortified by the applause, which to him, like to so many people in his narcissistic profession, was as vital and necessary to him as solid and liquid and as exhilarating as the most ecstatic sexual climax. He was now exclaiming 'Edging back!' in his mind only, but the physical accompaniment of a bow and a step back with each one of these silent prayers was still being maintained, and as the applause continued (seemingly intensifying), Noddoes' proclaimed 'edging back into darkness', snuffing out the light of life became a reality as the old luvvie made the most dramatic and definitely most final exit of his astonishing career by disappearing over the edge of the peak and plummeting to his doom, thus opening the scoring after all. Salty Sid floated in to net the inaugural catch. He had long since relinquished the patience of Job:

' 'bout bleedin' time!' he moaned.

One would have thought that this development would have caused nothing but horror and confusion amongst the assembly (with the clear exception of the Camcorders, who had captured every second of the hilarious episode as joyously as they had any of the others during the golden days of ROPSAS, including the incomparable Reg Doorman), but Frank, despite his abject astonishment, had recognised immediately that Noddoes' death had been nothing other than an accident. Others may have taken it upon themselves to believe that the old luvvie had merely had a change of heart and had mustled in on the party despite everything he had said and done to avoid jumping, but Frank knew otherwise. The fact was that Noddoes had finally fallen prey to his own gargantuan ego. His 'soliloquy' had had nothing at all to do with the reason everybody else was on top of Rocky Point that day and had everything to do with himself putting on a performance which he was convinced was a work of genius and was equally convinced that everybody would recognise as such. What irony, then that the applause for it had actually been quite genuine, for a wonderfully hammy performance it had been too, but it had never intended, of course, to be an adieu and had only become one because Noddoes, drunk with applause and oblivious to how close to the edge he had actually become as he neared ever closer to it, had quite simply 'edged back' too far. He was still bowing and muttering to himself when he was in the air and was perhaps not conscious of what had happened until he was half way down. It was a singularly ludicrous way to die, but a most suitable way in Noddoes' case, since he was singularly ludicrous. The first time he had actually brought the house down with a performance outside the confines of the much lamented Bar and Grill had instantaneously been his last. The final thing he had heard was applause, all for him. No great Thespian could have asked for more, except perhaps for not to have been killed in the first place, or indeed at all. But there you go.

Chapter 56

Keith

HE COMEDY DEATH of Noddoes shared more or less the same air-
time as the liberation of the Hut. The last act carried out by Epic and
Stephen, having taken the surrender of Wally and Max, was to invite their
defeated adversaries to leave. Wally was still in a bad way, but Max, who
harboured a quiet admiration for Freddo's boys for the way they had set
clinically about their campaign, offered his hand to Stephen as he walked
past. But Stephen was not interested:

'No, I'm sorry, but this wasn't a game. It's a wonder we didn't have you
both arrested instead of just kicking you in!'

This, needless to say, was a rather silly thing to say, even though it was
merely designed to underline to the failed invader that he and his grizzling
chum had overstepped the boundary somewhat. In any event, Keith Tate
was certainly back at the helm and he was preparing to resume with his
original playlist just as Noddoes fell to his unscheduled demise. He had come
out of the Hut again to signal to Danny that all was well now, only to see
signs of the great commotion, which had been the consequence of Noddoes'
involuntary curtain-raiser. A hint that something irregular had occurred also
presented itself to the conquering heroes returning to the cliff edge to resume
their own suicide celebrations. Everyone seemed to be very excited about
something, goodness knows what. Frank in particular looked especially jolly.

'Frankie. A couple of dudes tried to jump your sound guy, but me and
Stevie took care of it. No problemo! Say, are you okay? You look kinda
weird.'

'Daddy, daddy, daddy!' said Amanda softly.

Epic frowned and looked around amongst the assembly.

'Say, where's Hamlet?' he said suddenly. 'I don't see Hamlet.'

Frank's smile broadened: 'He's shuffled off this mortal coil,' he quipped. 'So he has.'

Epic reluctantly conceded a smile: 'Yeah okay, Frankie, go ahead and out-Shakespeare me and then tell me that Hamlet's down there with Hemmingway already!'

This time, Frank positively roared with laughter: 'That's *exactly* where he is, boy!'

'Daddy jump! Daddy jump!' sang Amanda, pointing wildly to the edge of the cliff.

'Are you two being serious?' interjected Stephen.

'Oh, perfectly,' Frank confirmed. 'Noddoes...' he said, composing himself, '... is a doughnut!'

'But I thought ...' began Stephen.

'You thought wrong. Now let's carry on, shall we?'

'The crafty old bastard!'

'I'm gonna miss that old faggot!' offered Epic as a tribute, without really considering if this news was true or not and a ridiculous statement in any case, since he too would imminently be following the same path and would therefore not be missing Noddoes at all.

Danny, with Sally just behind him came over. He was clearly puzzled, and no wonder: 'You're going to have to clear a few things up for me, guys. I want to know why you didn't tell me about that prologue there whilst you went ahead and told Keith.'

'What makes you say that?' asked Epic.

'Well, Keith pulled the Van Halen track out and put on all that awful cheese by Gilbert O'Sullivan and then Noddoes came running out over the cliff, comes out with that blinding address and then takes himself out of the game. Brilliant!'

'It was groovesville!' added Sally.

'It was,' agreed Danny. 'But it certainly wasn't on the order of service. So, what happened?'

'Noddoes wanted it to be a surprise,' quickly lied Frank.

'Well it certainly was!' Danny smiled.

'Oh, it *certainly* was!' Frank agreed. 'Anyway, we need to get on now. Thoad, I think.'

'I'll go wake him up,' Epic nodded.

'Right there,' indicated Stephen, and both men walked off to retrieve, indeed revive Thoad, who was resting none too peacefully on the grass some way from the cliff edge where he had been left by Epic's latest right hook.

'Perhaps I can give you the signal when Thoad's ready and then you can give Keith the nod and he can put Thoad's record on and off we go,' Frank hinted.

'Super!' beamed Danny, and Sally walked up and very unexpectedly embraced Frank and kissed him on the cheek.

'You actually *are* super,' she confirmed, 'for arranging this lovely day!'

Frank, somewhat taken aback by this, meekly thanked her back.

There then followed the long-awaited (by Thoad at least) suicide of Thoad; and even after all the trouble there had been with the wretched man, his final seconds brought forth yet more delays and complications. First, the bastard just wouldn't wake up and then, when he finally did, the bastard just wouldn't *get* up. The most worrying aspect was that he was no longer gurgling about either wanting to jump, or about milk, the two subjects which had dominated totally his verbal contributions (and presumably therefore his thoughts) to the exclusion of all else for the last week or so. Instead, he said nothing at all. He just groaned and moaned inaudibly but still wouldn't move.

This was ironic. For days, Epic and Stephen had practically needed to chain Thoad down in order to stop him jumping ahead of time. Now when it was finally time for him to jump, the bastard wasn't interested at all. He would need to be coerced, it appeared.

'Come on, man. The cliff's that way!' hinted Epic helpfully, jabbing the toe of his shoe into Thoad's ribs. Thoad looked up, shook his head and stayed down. His following announcement was, however, at least encouraging:

'They've closed the Inn!'

'They certainly have!' confirmed Stephen. 'And you just want to? ... Come on! You just want to?...'

'I just want to...' stammered Thoad.

'You just want to?...' Stephen prompted again.

'I just want to?...' repeated Thoad, desperate to remember what he just wanted to do but not quite being able to manage this.

Epic, any patience having evaporated by now, punched Thoad in the ribs again: '*JUMP!* You wanna fucking *jump*, okay? Now get up, asshole! *Jump!*'

He leaned down, and with a mighty effort pulled Thoad to his feet and then gripped him around his stomach to steady him, just as Stephen moved in to assist.

'Okay. We're gonna get this guy's music on and then we're gonna slide him on towards the edge until he starts running. Is that cool?'

'Yes, good!' agreed Stephen, who although was far more tolerant towards Thoad's plight, was nevertheless still rather fed up with him.

'Then let's do it!' Epic concluded.

So the signal was finally given via Frank to Danny to Keith for Thoad's record to begin, and in keeping with the lifelong love affair Thoad had had with classic reggae (which was now about to end), over the airwaves came on one of the best-loved tracks of all from that era, Desmond Dekker's *Israelites*.

Sure enough, this appeared to be something of a tonic to Thoad momentarily. He looked about to see if he could find where the music was coming from. It was coming from all around him. A crack of a smile appeared and Thoad started nodding to the beat. Stephen and Epic then pushed Thoad gently forwards but Thoad did not pick up step, which was when Stephen, by now just as exasperated as Epic, took charge:

'Thoad!' he barked, gripping him by the shoulders and shaking him. 'Thoad! Listen to me!'

Thoad's eyes were watering.

'This record,' continued Stephen, his voice sounding so dramatic, it almost appeared to be taking on an echo. 'I can see that it means much to you, Thoad...'

Thoad, understanding and agreeing smiled weakly again and his nodding intensified. But still he didn't move. Stephen pointed to the edge as *Israelites* entered its instrumental middle bit: '*RUN!*' he roared.

'RUN!' screeched Epic, less convincingly.

'RUN, Thoad!' bellowed Frank, adding a personal touch at least and worried now that Thoad may have had a change of heart.

But Thoad hadn't. He just needed something else. And so typically it was Stephen who provided it: 'Oh, *Thoady!*' he chided in a childish singsong voice directly into Thoad's left ear. 'Guess what?... They've... closed... the... *INN!*'

That did it. Thoad whelped like a little whipped pup and at last galloped gamely towards the edge. But even after all of this carry on, he was still thwarted, because in his haste to action his doom, he clipped the top of one of The Lifejoys' old plaques and fell heavily. He hadn't been the first, of course.

"THE LORD HASN'T CALLED YOU YET" said the sign.

'Fucking RUN!' immediately bellowed Stephen, infuriated at yet another delay.

Thoad obediently scrambelled grizzling to his feet and flinched as his gashed right ankle failed to take his weight without paining him. The leg was already bleeding through the ripped trousers and Thoad had to hop the rest of the way practically. With just yards to go and with Desmond Dekker just about exiting, Thoad, with near split-second timing, did so too. His jump was manful. He bravely brought his bad leg down to earth, ran the half-a-dozen remaining strides, then jumped, and with one last sorrowful howl, he was gone. The Lord had called him after all, right enough.

Salty Sid recognised Thoad in mid-air: 'That'll be that miserable ugly old bugger!' he mumbled to himself, as he drifted in to land the catch. He presently netted up the carcass and secured it before sailing clear to await the next one.

After the unexpected drama of Noddoes' exit and the painfully lengthy end of Thoad, the Inn Crowd were now hoping that proceedings would be afforded an element of smoothness hereafter. Danny hoped so too, if not the Old Ropsasians, soon to become The Reggies, who already had on tape a festival which had exceeded all expectations comfortably and were keen for these festivities to continue in the same vain. As it happened, the next two suicides ran briskly back-to-back and, if nothing else, got the whole show back on schedule again. The two to go were the incongruous lovers, Stephen and Amanda.

Stephen Mauve's life came to an end just after he had attempted to kiss his girlfriend goodbye and had been rewarded with the staple diet of a punch on the arm, a kick on the shin and a stoned girlish scream of 'Fuck off and die, you spineless bastard!', coupled with a less than tender grab of his testicles. Hurricane Smith was well away into *Oh Babe, What Would You Say?*, still an inexplicable choice in the eyes of many, just as Stephen recovered sufficiently to turn himself over in a surfeit of cool. First he turned to his comrades and shouted 'See you all later!', something which was especially appreciated by Danny, and then he ran off towards the edge in deliberate slow-mo, immediately reminding those who remembered the TV series *The Six Million Dollar Man* of the ludicrous Steve Austin. Then, just as he passed the CLIFF EDGE sign, Stephen produced a sprint into a cartwheel and launched himself high enough up into the air off his hands as to be able to wave to the already rapturously applauding audience on the way back down before he lost sight of them and they of him and he of life.

Hurricane Smith hadn't quite finished, as Stephen lay dead on the rocks. Epic turned to Frank: 'I really don't think we figured just what a guy Stevie was!' he said. Frank nodded: 'I quite agree. And to think we ignored him for so long!'

'He's mine!' spat Amanda, astonishingly using the present tense and then she started to get impatient: 'Where the fuck's Toyah?'

She had a point. Danny, who should have signalled to Keith after Stephen had gone over, had not. He and his wife had been busy applauding

Stephen's performance and had not realised that Amanda, either eager to join him or more eager to usurp him, was ready immediately to take the plunge herself. She was ready, but the music wasn't. Where the fuck was Toyah indeed?

Hurricane Smith faded out finally and it was Barefoot Sally who noticed that Amanda was less than happy at the fact that the stage apparently still belonged to the spineless bastard who was no longer with them, whilst she was impatient to entertain the masses. Sally quickly waved at Keith and on came Toyah finally.

Amanda screeched a welcome and started jumping up and down; as her pogoing intensified, spit flew out of her mouth, and in between she belched out the lyrics word perfect before the track concluded all too quickly and Amanda made a bolt for it and she too cartwheeled over the cliff edge, but did not give herself enough leverage to produce an opportunity for a wave in imitation of Stephen. She instead was drawn straight back in and was killed by her first contact with the cliff about a fifth of the way down. Salty Sid promptly secured the dead girl in his net.

Everyone now turned to face Sheba, the Imperial Cat of Doom, as she now prepared to achieve the suicidal fate which had been her avowed goal since she was a little girl, considerably longer than anyone else at Freddo's. The closure of the Inn had really meant nothing to her at all, but as soon as the rest of the Inn Crowd had decided that they couldn't live, she had instantly become the most enthusiastic supporter of the plan, if one excluded Thoad, who was just a poor, sad basket case really. Frank in particular couldn't wait to see what Tessa had in store as an accompaniment to the Stray Cats' *Stray Cat Strut*, a kitty connection clearly a prerequisite in her choice. In the end, the spectacle was disappointing, although Frank's fantasy that Tessa would slither over to him disrobed for a particularly steamy goodbye was always going to make what actually happened when his fantasy didn't (and it didn't) look a devastatingly poor substitute. Sheba did actually writhe around on the grass and purr and Frank, and indeed Epic, couldn't keep their eyes off her as she scratched and clawed the air.

But this display, as it needed to be, was all too brief, and to their further dismay, no attention was paid to either of them. Instead, she sprang up on all fours and bounded over to the very edge, screamed stridently her last words - a phrase she had used many times before, but which now had more meaning than any time previous – 'My home is with the dead, you foolish enemies!' and leapt gracefully over the side to at last prove the point. There was a ripple of applause rather than a thunderous ovation, this due in part to the rapidly diminishing congregation, but Tessa was gone.

'You were a wild woman, Sheba!' Epic said softly.

It was what she had always wanted, the Stray Cats were silenced and now only Frank and Epic remained.

The two friends fell into a hug. Their relationship had been most curious. Two such different personalities, backgrounds and age groups, but two rather special associates. Even Epic's behaviour in Birmingham, which had indeed been a disgraceful display of selfishness, had not made a dent in Frank's warm regard for the Canadian, whom despite his continuous tendency to create mischief, always had the wonderful gift to make Frank (and most other people) feel good. He was one of a rare breed - a person whom it was impossible not to like, indeed to be fond of enormously - no matter how vicious the more than occasional sting in his tail was.

The warmth of this final embrace was genuinely affectionate and Epic then nodded at Danny and simply said: 'Let's do it!' This was immediately followed by the opening strains of The Doors' classic suicide anthem *The End*, the final track (fittingly) of their brilliant eponymous first album. And Epic held court. He did not mime when Jim Morrison began singing. He actually belted out a rendition of his own wonderful performance and sustained it throughout the famous monologued middle bit. 'The killer wakes before dawn…', which includes the intentions of 'The Lizard King' to emulate Oedipus, having 'walked on down the hall', and through to the last chorus and the final, utterly final, deep thundering proclamation that this indeed *was* the end.

And so it was. And Epic held court. He bowed and then walked on, not down the hall this time, but across to the edge of the cliff and straight off to his doom. It was certainly one of the greatest self-destructions of all time. And Epic held court.

Frank stood and blinked ahead of him out over the cliff, below which had lain the broken corpses of his comrades and colleagues, safely bound up in Sid's net now. He thought of his mother awhile. He knew what he was about to do was going to devastate her initially, but he hoped that she would later recognise it as the triumph he himself knew that it was, especially after she had received the assets of the company which had made everything possible and had become finally aware of just what a phenomenal success Freddo's had been. Frank was going out a winner, and to him this was everything. The tragic closure of the Inn, its eclipse courtesy of officers of the law, the imprisonment of Tom Beck, the consequent advent of the cheesy sports bar, had been signs, not merely thinly painted, but large flashing neon lights, that the watershed had been reached. The only answer had clearly been suicide in order to freeze in time forever the salad days of their success and thereby prevent the decline. Freddo's, after all, had been a novelty, an outstanding successful novelty, but a novelty nonetheless, and novelties were always perishable goods. The use-by date for this particular item had now been reached, perhaps already passed.

Frank glanced at Danny and Barefoot Sally and smiled, he hoped, serenely. Danny blinked and beamed back, then held up his hand as a signal to Keith and on came *Something In The Air* by Thunderclap Newman, one of pop's undoubted classics, studio-created though it was and the very track deemed as unsuitable for Reg Doorman. This Pete Townsend-produced track from 1969 spoke somewhat whimsically about something special brewing, a revolution no less and of the consequent need for unity. The record, containing one of the most distinctive instrumental middle bits of the rock/pop era, was also one of the most original and was a monumental hit for a cobbled together group of misfits who were never heard of again. Admittedly Frank had plumped for it largely because of the double meaning (as far as his imminent situation was concerned) within the song's title. But how much this ultimately influenced the choice didn't alter the broad fact that the record was one of Frank's premiere tracks and always had been.

As *Something In The Air* ran its course, Frank, never one to dance or jig about, remained practically motionless, staring out to sea. He was calm, relaxed and extremely happy now. During the final stages of the piece with its clever, but not entirely original snatches of *La Marseillaise* (The Beatles had mugged the French National Anthem even more mercenarily in order to preface *All You Need Is Love* two years earlier), Frank began to march, attempting and largely succeeding in keeping in time, and marched on boldly to disappear silently over the edge of the world.

Salty Sid, meanwhile, had already set sail for land with what he considered was (and why shouldn't he have after what he had been told?) a full cargo. He had been advised to expect six. Six he had got. When Epic had come over, Salty had slipped his rum flask back into his pocket and muttered to himself: 'That'll be the last of the buggers!' before sailing over to collect the remains. He thus retrieved and secured Epic's corpse and then spent the next few minutes binding the bundle of six together so that the bounty would hold steady. He then refreshed himself once again from his flask, filled his pipe copiously and lit it and then set sail for the landing station puffing away. As Sid's boat approached the headland, plummeting Frank suddenly arrived, landing squarely on the top of the old boatman's head to starboard, squashing him and his flask and pipe into something resembling a bathmat. It was only the indomitable sturdiness of the hull of the craft that saved the vessel from any significant damage and danger of running aground.

And so Salty Sid died too.

And so did Kipper, a stuffed Danish cat Sid had only recently acquired as a bequest from a late salty friend called Ned Natkinson, who had retained Kipper as a ship's cat and general talisman even after the animal's demise. Sid, on inheriting Kipper, had nailed the moggy to a footstool and then plonked him down just inside the cabin to keep him company.

Chapter 57

The Old Firm

IT WAS THUS left to the long redundant coastguard to retrieve the eight corpses of the Freddo staff plus Kipper. The Old Ropsasians, now in the death throes themselves, filmed this too and thus had an exhaustive record of the entire sermon and its sensational aftermath. These tapes were cheerfully made available to the coroner's office as evidential exhibits, which were of course as conclusive as any evidence anyone could get for a verdict of suicide on all but Salty Sid and Kipper, whose demises were nothing but tragic accidents.

Klaus Butsch saw it this way too. In his summing up, he said in part: 'These films says everythinks as if God himself speaks. One by one, one after one, these crazy undertakers jump! Many smile as if they are on the way to fun and not rocky dooms. Some make speech. But all go off cliff with no help. *Bumpity-Bump!* Only old man in boat dies not by the own hands. He is hit by fallen corpse of Eddowes, which he not see. He is squashed. Kitty-cat squashed also. This case has many dyinks. More than any since I come in England. But even after this, it is much easy to decide, even though one counts many deads. It is a strange case and bad day for lovers of kitties.'

Herr Butsch had not forgotten to cross-examine Danny Hare during the inquest. At one stage he had asked: 'Did you and pretty wife know that all this undertakers would *bumpity-bump*?'

'Yes, we did.'

'You say yes?'

'Yes.'

'Yet you do nothinks?'

'No, we did not.'

Hanne and Lisle gasped.

'You are holy man…' Klaus continued after the court had settled down.

'You can bet your sweet booty!' winked Danny.

'… yet you take part in a game of self-killinks. On the film it looks like party. I can see it. Check the film! Your speech before *bumpity-bump* gives to me clue that you say self-killinks is okay. Then, as strange musics play, one after one, undertaker after undertaker goes for jump to self-destruct. If you holy man, why you not stop? Is it possible that you are holy man nein but man of devil?'

Danny certainly did not care for this suggestion: 'That's out of line, mein herr!' he snapped. 'These people were friends of mine. All I did was to do what they asked me to. I did *not* help them to die. And unlike the majority of the righteous bastards in my line of work, I don't regard suicide as sinful. It seems simple logic to me that if a guy or gal doesn't want to live any longer they should go ahead and close the book on themselves, just as long as they don't take anybody else out in the process. This is why I'm genuinely sorry about the old guy in the boat. But, hey, that was just an accident! And as for me being a man of the devil, where the hell do you get off saying that? Who the hell are you anyhow? What are your credentials? Along with my lady and rock and roll, God is the main thing in my life. Who are *you* to speak for *Him*? You're a coroner. You're not a theologian. You may be a judge in here, mein herr, but you're not going to start judging *my* morals or those of anyone else, I shouldn't think. Legally, neither my wife nor myself have done anything wrong. And if we *have* committed any moral offences, these will be answered on Judgment Day by our God. Okay?'

Hanne and Lisle gasped again. Certainly Herr Butsch had never been spoken to like this before in his own courtroom. He was a figure who commanded great respect. He was certainly not readily cheeked.

But Klaus also was a godly man. As a catholic, he was immeasurably more conservative than Danny Hare. Indeed, he did consider suicide to be a mortal sin and could never have accepted the reverend's liberal outlook on 'closing the book' on oneself. Klaus was certainly a godly man and he had seen clearly (and been told clearly) that he had offended another one, a fellow Christian. And after all was said and done, Klaus was a coroner. Not a theologian.

'I'm sorry, Father. Step down, please,' he said.

Klaus Butsch summed up shortly afterwards and the cowbell rang out in confirmation of his verdicts, his apology to the Reverend Hare and, inadvertently, as a tribute to Freddo's.

The Old Ropsasians, meanwhile, had already been disbanded and replaced by The Reggies, an organisation which its members all swore they would be committed to for a very long time. During the evening of the sermon, the group had quickly escaped with their tapes and gone round to Adrian's place where a buffet was waiting with eight party cans of beer. The occasion marked the drowning of birth of the Old Ropsasians, and once again 'good old Tom' was saluted and this time remembered for the remarkable man he had truly been.

'I'd like to offer you all milk,' Adrian said, 'but I've only got enough for my porridge tomorrow morning. I hope you'll forgive me.'

'Old Tom would have liked the beer,' suggested Dick.

'He would have *preferred* milk,' corrected Malcolm. 'But it doesn't matter, Adrian, the beer's fine.'

The five tragic men viewed their tapes and then sealed them up in their cases so that they could be submitted to Klaus Butsch in a professional manner. The Old Ropsasians were then dissolved by an unanimous vote and a mighty cheer went up as The Reggies instantaneously succeeded them.

'Once the blazers have arrived, we can all troop up to the Point and put the frighteners on any bastard we find in the Hut!' opened Malcolm with a snarl. 'Especially that hairy pothead. If *he's* up there, we'll fucking batter him!'

Adrian, remembering how close he had come from being barred from The Old Ropsasians even before The Reggies' very inception, nodded quickly at the man who had clearly emerged as the new group's senior officer: 'Yes, Malcolm,' he said meekly...

Despite the unquestioned pathos surrounding this woefully inadequate band of middle-aged men, at least they always seemed to have a purpose, however tragic and ludicrous, to counter their clear failures in the wider game of life.

Meanwhile, poor Nellie Eddowes emerged as the principal casualty of the suicide fest, and since her only purpose had been for nearly fifty years her most unusual but devoted son, she now no longer had any purpose left. She had been inconsolable when the news had been broken to her, and matters did not improve when she sobbingly attempted to call The Life-joys in an attempt to find some meaning to the madness, and a mechanical female voice said 'This number is no longer extant. Please redial,' and then a short bleep abruptly cut her off. In short, Nellie now had no-one, barring the mercurial company of a solicitor, whose services Frank himself had engaged in order to settle the matter of the Freddo Estate. Even here, the anticipated remuneration (contrary to what Frank had hoped) did nothing whatsoever to console his mother. She gave not one hoot to the material proof she was set to receive that Freddo's had been a monumental, perhaps historical, success. She would certainly never countenance Frank's suicide as a concluding triumph. She saw first, last and only the unnecessary, indeed insane loss of a son, and more tragically than this, blamed herself for it for not being forceful enough in weaning Frank off drink. Surviving relatives suffering extreme guilt over the self-destruction of loved ones is not at all unusual and underlines that suicide is far from being the personal matter many people who go down that route care to think it is. The acuteness of the pain naturally corresponds to the closeness of the relationship, and more often than not so does the guilt. A person who loses someone close may well convince themselves that part of the blame (if not all of it) rests with themselves and that they might even have been the cause of the trag-edy. This self-believed contribution invariably brings long-lasting despair, and thus although only one life has been lost, another has been ruined and the surviving relative or friend could well find themselves on the precipice of suicide as well, or even over it. The basic concluding fact was that Frank had tragically miscalculated his mother's reaction to 'the triumph he knew it was.' In short, his suicide had destroyed her. Nellie had indeed been obliterated, and the four and a half years she was to live before a stroke finally killed her were not rich in happiness. She died a broken woman. The whole thing was terribly sad and a wretched and lonely footnote to the suicide festival up at the Point.

Certainly the relatives of the others who had jumped were stunned and mystified when they learned of the deaths. It was however quite easy for many of them to redirect their blame onto either Frank, because he was the boss, but especially onto Danny for being the presiding minister who had done nothing to stop it. The exceptions to this were the Sharmas, who, if anything, had been surprised that Tessa had lasted as long as she had.

As for Danny, it wasn't at all long before he realised that it was necessary that he had to get himself and Barefoot Sally out of Pendlesham with exceptional haste. This was not so much to do with the need to run the gauntlet of the parents of Stephen and Amanda. It had almost everything to do with the little bit of unfinished business concerning James and Sophie, or more precisely with their still dangerously hostile leftovers. Some of the pack had waited outside the court during the inquest and were determined to confront the minister and demonstrate their well-held disapproval of what had happened to the corpses of the young couple. With the entirety of the Freddo staff now liquidated, only Danny remained. The unforgiving mob was determined to deal with him and Danny's antennae had picked this up. He therefore grabbed Sally and headed for the hills, or more precisely Market Harborough in Leicestershire, where he was finally to find distinction as well as safety. Having done a stint as a hospital chaplain, he doubled this up by running a hospital radio station, which was a significant success all across the board and attracted as a result the attentions of what turned out to be a very special patient. He was an executive of Radio Leicester, a station which reached much of the East Midlands.

The executive liked what he heard, became even more interested when he learned that the DJ was a vicar, and promptly offered Danny a trial as the presenter on the small hours' slot. This went so well that the reverend soon found himself piloting the earlier show running from 9pm to midnight, as well as a weekly Sunday morning broadcast of 'rock and roll praise', which Barefoot Sally occasionally co-presented. Later, as a person of some influence, Danny was able to recommend 'an excellent soundman' to help 'advise' the young producers and technicians. This recommendation was given the green light, so the call went down to Pendlesham, and up to Leicester came Keith Tate, who had actually only recently recovered from a brutal and very nearly decisive shoeing he had received from The Reggies, who had followed the bearded stoner out of the Rocky Point pub, after Keith had enjoyed a quiet and perfectly civilised lunch alone, and set upon him savagely, even though Keith had been stomping off towards the bus stop to get back into town and thus walking in the contrary direction to the Hut. Tate was kicked to a pulp in fine style.

It would be wrong to say that Danny became a cult, but he certainly emerged as a popular broadcaster, willing to offer his services ad hoc around other radio stations throughout the Midlands, Wales and parts of the North of England; in fact, anywhere outside London and the South East. Neither he nor Barefoot Sally were troubled again and Keith Tate could once again enjoy a cheese ploughman's and a pint or three of cider without the prospect of having his fucking head kicked in for dessert.

The fate of the cadavers of the wonderful Freddo troupe became now a matter of bitter dispute. Proudfoot and Gadd had of course been promised the business verbally by Frank, who had banked on Sid and Noddoes carting all their carcasses off to the town's second undertakers, who would then tend to them once Klaus Butsch had given the go-ahead. The sudden and ludicrous disqualification of Noddoes from this duty had not troubled Frank one iota. He knew fully well that Noddoes would have had no real part to play off-loading the cargo as he had claimed he would. Frank, therefore, as a precaution had arranged for Sid's boat to be met by two young bearers from Proudfoot and Gadd, who would have provided all the beef required to remove the corpses tidily off to the Old Firm's bitter competitors. Noddoes would have no doubt attempted to direct matters, but his role would have been entirely superfluous. However, since he had insisted on joining the party after all, his part in the proceedings had certainly subtlety altered.

Frank had never worried because he knew that Salty Sid was the pivotal, indeed only player. Old Sid wouldn't let them down! Since this vital task involved his boat and his net, the task, this most important of missions was as good as accomplished. Frank thus allowed himself as much glee as he could take over the fate of his old enemy. Noddoes' arrogance and narcissism had fittingly been his final undoing. It was a just climax and thus Frank was generally euphoric as he faced up to his own demise, which meant that when he had jumped there had been no terror for him. He had marched stridently towards the cliff, and by chance rather than by design, had exited off the point which proffered the sheerest drop of all, which meant that Frank went straight down. He shat himself, naturally, but remained conscious, and the last thing he ever saw was Salty Sid's boat looming larger and larger as he plummeted towards it. He was in direct collision with Sid's bonce and knew it. He thus realised in the final blink of an eye that he was defeated. When he landed on Sid, Sid would be dead and so would any chance of the consignment of corpses (Frank's included, of course) reaching the offices of Proudfoot and Gadd. And this tragically meant only one thing.

And so it proved. For the first time in a long while, the coastguard picked up a rare piece of business. And what carnage they found too! Eight dead plus a cat. Six of the corpses had been conveniently netted up and could thus be hoisted back up the cliff. The bodies of Frank, Sid and poor Kipper, a cat who had done no harm, were subsequently secured and Sid's faithful boat was pulled around the headland along to the landing station where the two men from Proudfoot and Gadd had long since departed, initially puzzled but ultimately greatly annoyed that their time had been wasted. They had assumed (and were quite reasonable so to do) that the promise of a large consignment had probably been a hoax, but of course it had been no such thing; and the fact that the coastguard had secured the load rather than Sid and Noddoes meant that another interested party was alerted to the likelihood of a substantial piece of business and immediately dispatched representatives to meet the boat to pick up Frank, Sid and Kipper, as well as intercepting the netted bounty up at the Point.

It was just like the good old days - the pre-Freddo days – a time when the question of who had first refusal was never a serious issue. And like a phoenix from the ashes of the brotherhood of funeral directors rose the Old Firm.

Proudfoot and Gadd issued writs.

Chapter 58

September 1996

PETER FOSTER AND his newly-recruited assistant Neil Turner eyed the eight corpses lying in their caskets in the Old Firm's viewing room. Five of them were those of strangers, but Frank, Noddoes and Tessa had at length returned.

Kipper was placed in a small basket at the foot of Sid's coffin. Since the cat had belonged to the old boatman, Peter felt that whomever identified and claimed Sid's corpse could also remove the carcass of his faithful moggy at the same time, or perhaps even leave instructions as to how the Old Firm may help, for a modest consideration naturally. But it didn't work out like that because as soon as Nellie Eddowes had entered the viewing room in order to identify Frank, she noticed Kipper resting peacefully in his basket, which had not been covered, unlike Sid's casket, which at that time was sharing space with Frank's, which was open for viewing. The sight of the deceased moggy brought back instant memories of Hansel, and Nellie immediately emitted a bitter roar of anguish before starting to sob 'My baby!' uncontrollably over and over. Peter Foster, realising that Nellie was referring to Kipper and not Frank, had no other option than to hand the creature over.

'He's already been cremated once!' grizzled Nellie, some moments later. 'It was such a lovely funeral too. Well, this time he's going in the garden. Where's his sister? Do you have his sister here too?'

'Er... no,' admitted Foster.

Whilst there was going to be no resistance from the Old Firm with regards the release of Kipper to Nellie Eddowes, there was certainly not a chance that they would even listen to a claim by Proudfoot and Gadd over the rights to the remaining eight cadavers, which as the Old Firm pointed out they had come by without trickery, despite the outrage and claims of foul from their rivals. Proudfoot and Gadd wanted the Freddo group to be made wards of court, and not surprisingly did not get to first base with this request. Silly legal documents began flying about to zero effect. The next thing Proudfoot and Gadd tried was reason. Perceval Proudfoot went personally to Arthur Snape and explained that the consignment really was theirs and that it had only been because of a freak tragedy that the collection hadn't been made. The Old Firm should relinquish their bounty. It was a question of ethics.

'The trouble with that, my dear Proudfoot,' smiled Snape, 'is that there appears to be nothing in writing to substantiate your alleged arrangement with Eddowes. And since our interception was entirely honest and legitimate, I fear that you must write this off as a loss, the result of your own, albeit unfortunate administrative error.'

Mr Proudfoot, though, held firm: 'The fact remains, and I'm going to suggest that you are aware of this, Snape, that there was no error of any sort. We had indeed made a verbal agreement with Mr Eddowes, which only failed to be honoured due to the sudden deaths of the two intermediaries with whom we were expecting to liaise, namely a Mr Noddoes and his boatman, Mr Bonniface. Both of these men unexpectedly perished in the interim and our agreement was thus thwarted.'

'*Noddoes*!' sneered Mr Snape. 'I might have known! *Noddoes*! Well, it serves him damned right. That one always was a duplicitous knave!'

The next thing Proudfoot and Gadd tried was bargaining…

'I'm going to put to you a proposition, Snape. One which will enable honour to triumph over our personal difficulties and terminate this rather ugly impasse immediately. Bearing in mind my company did not in any sense anticipate Mr Noddoes and Mr Bonniface being included in the list of clients, principally because they were the two gentlemen who were supposed to deliver the agreed load to two of my chaps at the landing station, I happily relinquish any claim on them in return for your consideration in returning my anticipated consignment once, shall we say, a further two clients have been held back by yourself with my blessing as a sign of my own goodwill. I do so hope that you accept this, as it would mean that we are each left with exactly one half of a consignment, a quarter of which I concede is legitimately yours, and the remaining three quarters, I repeat again, is ours by right and was only acquired by you as the result of a tragic accident. I am asking you as a man of honour, Snape, to accept this equitable proposition.'

This was a good play by Proudfoot. Appealing to Snape's 'honour' and sponsoring compromise rather than continuing to argue his case for the whole thing was clearly the only option that would stand any chance of bringing about any part of the feast to Proudfoot's table. Arthur Snape had certainly pulled some strokes in his time and his late partner, Herbert Woodcastle, had been in his time even worse; but nobody had ever before appealed to him in the name of 'honour,' that strange somewhat meaningless quality peculiar to peculiar old Englishmen. This put an entirely different spin on the ball. Appealing to one's spirit of fair play could only really induce one response – that of reciprocation. It was then that old Snape suddenly became aware that an even greater gesture could elicit an even greater ironic victory, for not only himself, but for dear Herbert too. Frank Eddowes, Maurice Noddoes and Tessa Sharma had not only committed an outrage at dear Herbert's memorial drinks party (something which had never been forgotten or forgiven), they had also attempted to destroy the Old Firm thereafter and had gone as far as poaching the lucrative Rocky Point intake from them, something which also had remained a constant source of fury to Arthur. They had brought abject shame to the industry and doused docile Pendlesham in a poisonous concoction of infamy. Now they had returned as corpses, the Old Firm would exact its revenge.

'I propose, my dear Proudfoot,' to relinquish all of the departed in question barring the three principals, to wit Eddowes, Noddoes and Sharma. The others are unknown to me and I must therefore conclude that they were underlings, factotums, whom I am content for you to remove as a matter of urgency. This is most certainly my final word, and allow me to assure you that beyond argument the matter of honour has been accommodated incontrovertibly.'

Mr Proudfoot brightened up immediately. He indeed could not believe his luck. He now had a promise on no less than five cadavers to the Old Firm's three.

'Mr Snape, your offer is most generous and is accepted with much gratitude,' he beamed. 'Indeed you are an honourable man, sir!'

'Indeed I am, sir, yes.'

So Epic, Stephen, Amanda, Thoad and Sid were retrieved by Proudfoot and Gadd in the coffins provided by the Old Firm. What managed to escape Proudfoot completely was old Snape charging a quite monstrous sum for these caskets, so that a good deal of expenditure was recovered quite extortionately and without Proudfoot, still overjoyed that he had won the lion's share of the Freddo bounty, knowing what had hit him. When the arithmetic had been done, the Old Firm as usual had come out on top. Arthur Snape may have been a man steeped in honour, but he had never held a claim to philanthropy. He was an old rogue.

The Old Firm's viewing room now contained the open caskets comprising the three people who had once been part of the Old Firm family. Old Snape himself and the two embalmers, Foster and Turner, were at the scene - Neil Turner flicking his eyes between them all consecutively, as if he were daring any of them to suddenly open their eyes and declare a ruse. Peter Foster stared only at Tessa, the beautiful girl who had once been his assistant. He had been genuinely fond of her, without ever having letched after her like the rest of male humanity, and Tessa, having recognised this, had liked Peter back. He immediately resolved to make his former protégé look as lovely as possible, despite the pale look on her dead face and the strange henna-like markings on it that looked somehow like a cat's whiskers. Bleak and beautiful.

Arthur Snape, meanwhile, could not suppress a look of smug satisfaction covering his similarly pale but alive face. This satisfaction warmed his system until it exceeded satisfaction and passed on through pleasure and into triumph. He stared down at all of them but lingered particularly on Noddoes. He remembered the occasion when Noddoes had appealed to him directly against his dismissal from the Old Firm, insisting that the sacking was in no way just, and indeed expressing outrage that he had ever been expected of any wrongdoing at all, whilst slimily endorsing whole-heartedly the dismissals of Frank and Tessa as sensible and deserving courses of action. Arthur, though, had not been fooled. He had realised perhaps just in time that it had indeed been Noddoes who had put the offending words into Frank's mouth (Frank's own mouth being full to the brim with vomit at the time) and was, when all was said and done, not only an unbearable sycophant, who in reality held he, Snape, in contempt, but also a duplicitous rogue, who had mercenarily attempted to cash in on the condition and consequent behaviour of Frank, already doomed because he was steaming drunk. Noddoes was a nasty, lying, cheating, dishonourable rotter, who had worst of all demonstrated just how ready he had been to even use dear dead Herbert to further his crooked aims.

The Sharma girl had perhaps been unfortunate, but she had certainly displayed, no matter how little she had been at fault with the incident in question, behaviour which bordered quite simply on madness. Old Snape had always satisfied himself that had Tessa not succumbed when she did, she would surely have snapped on another occasion in the near future. As Snape himself pithily put it to Peter Foster, whose silent reaction certainly did not indicate acquiescence: 'She's best canned up, I think, in case the worms escape.'

And then there was Frank Eddowes, Snape's former clerk; a man of seemingly no consequence who had risen to become, in Arthur's view, a nemesis of Moriarty-type proportions. An implacable enemy. A dark force who had done all he could (indeed had gone some way towards) effecting the ruination of the Old Firm, to say nothing of the integrity of the industry. But now he was dead and so was his regime.

Peter Foster wheeled the three revolutionaries off to his quarters and began to work, with Neil Turner in attendance. He had decided to do Tessa last and his first patient was Noddoes, who was lifted out of his casket and dropped carefully onto the slab.

'This chap was most odd,' Foster explained, as he started to chop the corpse about. 'He belonged to another age.'

'He certainly does now!' smiled Neil Turner, who believed in God, heaven and hell and so knew about such things.

Both Noddoes and Frank were given a conventional embalming, but both being 'Fosters', they were exceptionally good jobs. They were placed back in their coffins and wheeled back out to the viewing room.

Peter then commenced work on Tessa, who even in cold pale death (and even before embalming) looked stunningly lovely.

'A truly mesmerising young woman!' Peter confirmed, as he slid his hands down through her long black hair and then down her right shoulder and arm.

'Very pretty,' Turner said, not really having noticed.

'Do you know?' Peter continued, 'I hate to admit it, but as a professional I often wondered how Tessa would look after embalming. We talked about it many times and she even climbed into a coffin for me at one time, the lovely girl! You see, I had to try and picture her as a much older woman, and I imagined myself recreating her through my art back to the stunning beauty of her prime, creating thereby my greatest feat of art, something entirely without parallel in the field of corpse preservation. I never however believed that I would not only find myself in the position of fulfilling this daydream, being able to embalm this luscious girl, but that she would have met her death so soon, very little different from the warm, beautiful and charming young woman I was so fond of. The girl who modelled for me in the coffin.'

'Does this mean that she will not need much doing to her, then?' enquired Neil, trying to appear normal after what he had just heard.

'Ordinarily, someone like this, of this age, would require just a drop of colour,' Peter said, using this as an excuse to tenderly stroke Tessa's cheek, 'but apart from the manner of her death, which has inevitably left a certain amount of damage, Tessa's obsession with cats has caused her to apply some rather coarse make-up. Observe these strange horizontal lines crossing both cheeks from the nose. They are obviously meant to be cat's whiskers, so that's the explanation, but I'm afraid it will all have to go. Then I can make her look beautiful again. Colourful and gorgeous. I refuse to remember her like this.'

So Tessa, who had spent so much of her crazy mixed up young life as Sheba, the Imperial Cat of Doom, became converted back to Tessa Sharma for her funeral. She may have died as a Cat, but she finished up as a perfectly normal dead girl, courtesy of a friend and admirer, whose utter decency and goodness had prevented him falling foolishly in love with her. Her embalmed corpse was placed tenderly back in her coffin, sporting a beautiful smile on a full, fresh and lovely face. The Cat had been put out, not just for the night, but for eternity.

Back at Proudfoot and Gadd, work was being completed on Epic, Stephen, Amanda, Thoad and Sid. The house embalmer, a middle-aged South African called Douglas Marman, had not been long with the company, but his experience gathered from his previous position in a mortuary in Johannesburg meant that he was no stranger to dealing with those who had met their end suddenly and violently. The workload naturally meant that there was more than an element of pressure for Douglas, but as it turned out, they were all extremely professional jobs, the supreme irony of all being Thoad smiling broadly, as if he had got a coat hanger stuck in his gob. If only Marman had known.

There thus followed the funerals, and it was here that the Inn Crowd were finally separated from each other. Since the families of Stephen and Amanda had not only never met, but had not even been aware of a relationship between the couple at all, the lovers had their own ceremonies on different days in different crematoriums. In both cases, the Church of England had its way. Silly meaningless hymns were sung and well intentioned, but equally silly prayers were prayed. It was not what either of them would have wanted, particularly the girl.

Epic's folk were contacted in Vancouver, and after much tearful discussion, Mr and Mrs Seebal sent over instructions that their son might as well be cremated in England. Epic had always hinted in rare letters home his intentions never to return home most subtly: 'I never want to set foot in that icy wasteland shithole (Canada) again!' His devastated parents thus made the long, long journey across from the west coast of the North American continent for less than the three days it took to view their boy and see him cremated, with a rest in a Pendlesham bed and breakfast on either side. It was the first time they had been back in England since they emigrated. A few of the kids from the Old Station Inn made representations to attend the service and were politely but firmly advised to stay away. It was thus a particularly sad little funeral, and as with the cases of Stephen and Amanda, the complete reverse of how Epic would have desired it to be. Mom and Dad only. Hardly rock and roll.

Salty Sid's congregation, on the other hand, was a well-attended affair, surprising perhaps for such a solitary and private man. The Boat, his local hostelry at the foot of Rocky Point, was practically emptied for the morning session as Sid's grizzled, weathered, rum-drinking, pipe-smoking, Crib-playing brethren from the sea gathered to say goodbye to the old bugger. The ancient old lad with the accordion played a shanty as a tribute. The Boat's governor, a retired City broker, attended and in a nice touch, HM Coastguard were represented to pay tribute to one of their nearly own. Sid was the only one of the Freddo group to be buried, not at sea as he undoubtedly would have wanted, but in the grounds of a tiny church yards from The Boat. This at least allowed his flask and pipe, both as mortally wounded as Sid himself, to be buried with him. Sid was alone in having had received the funeral he almost certainly would have specified, attended by his own kind, and the resting place within sight of his beloved Boat, an acceptable substitute for the deep, which was never really going to be a viable option really.

Thoad, the saddest bastard of all, was taken care of with minimum fuss and ceremony in a tragic little service reminiscent to that of Eleanor Rigby, attended by absolutely no-one. It was entirely indicative of what an abject lonely man he had been, more-so than any of the others, but perhaps not that much more. The Inn Crowd, or at least the Freddo group which had splintered off from it, ostensively consisted of indubitably lonely people, who did not have the inclination to recognise that they were lonely, or rather knew that they were lonely but kidded themselves sadly and drunkenly that they were not. Even Stephen and Amanda, who had the Inn to thank for forming a lively sexual relationship, were two remote people within a plastic alliance, whilst Epic, seemingly so popular, convivial and never alone, had in reality been marooned on a desert island for much of his life due to a mixture of personal choice and a more serious condition of failing to fit in anywhere, his brashness and self-assuredness dissolving like sherbet once he found himself alone in his flat with nobody left to fool but himself.

Tessa's loneliness had been a consequence of her many complex psychological problems, which had forced her into a lunatic world only she inhabited. Only the drunks of the Inn touched, or pretended to touch base with her, but when the others sobered up and were lonely again, Tessa remained disturbed and was in effect lonely all the time like so many beautiful girls. Distinct from the others, though, she didn't know, even less care.

Uniquely amongst the group, Frank had been a microcosm of the abject lonely man. The mummy's boy who had never left home. The man with no mates. The man who could never make it with women. The man with no career. The man who had drifted aimlessly into middle age with nothing behind him and the same in front. The man who held on for dear life to an albeit genuine love for the music and time of an era long past. As long as 'the day the music died' never came, so the intervening years failed to exist at all in his eyes and Frank was therefore locked continually inside a jukebox, because he too was a selection willing to be played time and time again. In order to sustain this fantasy, Frank had drunk, knowing that once the fantasy had dissolved, reality inexorably returned and that the reality was that Frank was an extremely sad and lonely figure indeed. The Emporium had done nothing to alter this. The advent of Freddo's may have converted Frank's hitherto pitiful career into a triumph, but he had still remained, as indeed had the others, a miserable unhappy character, which made the apparent near miss he had had with Angela Stockley in Birmingham even more of a tragedy for him.

The Inn Crowd alone and collectively had had only one interest in life and that was the Station Inn. Without it, these social misfits were finished, and thus when it was taken away from them so suddenly, nobody could take it. Thoad had cracked immediately and Frank similarly felt just as cruelly slain and for a long time, like Thoad, would not believe it. The others, Noddoes excluded, quickly realised also that it was the end of the line and could only now wish for an utterly spectacular doom to firmly place a pie in the face of the policeman who had destroyed their little world.

The truth then was that the Inn Crowd, far from being a solid entity, comprising of a sophisticated group of happy and fulfilled *bon viveurs,* friends who lived varied and interesting lives, fascinated in every aspect of the world around them, had in reality been merely a mixed-up group of pitiful bar-room drunks, with no interest in anything other than remaining in the bar and thereby sustaining the toytown bubble in which they lived in a desperate attempt to fend off the bleak loneliness which had infested each and every one of them. Freddo's had provided unity, and for a time, a degree of salvation was offered in another toytown. But, alas, when a group of flawed individuals, irredeemably so because of drink, drugs and/ or psychological problems, attempt to form themselves into a unit, failure is surely never too far away. The stupendous clash of one individual psyche with another causes combustion; and even though Frank was quickly established and accepted as the leader, which met with the common good of the company, and even though their success was quick and spectacular, this did nothing to bring the individuals together as friends other than friendly adjacent barflies, which they had always been anyway. For this reason, Freddo's might just as well not have existed.

Stephen Mauve's case had been perhaps the most tragic of all, even more-so than Thoad's. In the immediate pre-Freddo days, Stephen had craved nothing more than admittance into the original Inn Crowd, then consisting of a motley band comprising of Frank, Thoad, Epic, Tom, Kate, Baz and assorted here today/gone tomorrow scrotes and slappers. He had been a largely ignored, and in some quarters disliked regular and knew it. He craved acceptance, and when this eventually came through Freddo's, so did Amanda, a large dose of self-confidence and the smelling salts of happiness. Only then did he realise that he had actually been a member of the Inn Crowd all along and that they were all as pathetic as he was. He finished up despising himself for having so ardently desired admittance to this tragic band, and even though the associated founding of Freddo's, something in which Stephen had been instrumental, changed and enriched his life, he recognised that the trap door to the whole shebang was not going to be delayed *ad infinitum*, and despite his undoubted elevation in Inn society and his consequent relationship with Amanda, who had probably never really *liked* him, Stephen had remained, in essence, alone on his bar stool, as indeed had they all. The closure of the Inn thus took its toll on him, just as vehemently as it had wounded Frank and destroyed Thoad, and thus Stephen's suicide was never in question.

It was therefore arguable that the supposed show of support up on Rocky Point was anything but and was, in fact, as Klaus Butsch put it: "One by one, one after one, these undertakers jump", taking their own lives, not together, but entirely separately because there was nothing else they could really do and nothing better either. They had killed themselves because they were sad, lonely drunks with psychological difficulties, who had certainly not met convalescence with the advent of a crazy madcap adventure, which somehow had encountered unbelievable success. Had it happened instead, the failure of Freddo's may well have led them eventually back to safety. But the ensuing astonishing period had paradoxically muddied the waters entirely and the closure of the Inn had placed the final conclusive straw on the back of metaphorical camel.

Drink, as Nellie Eddowes had always feared, had been the definitive undoing of Frank. For was it not the case that Freddo's had been a drink-induced idea, a pipedream of excitable inebriates, its subsequent monumental success being as it may? Thus, if accepted, drink had brought down them all, and in this sad aspect alone, the band were at least united, Noddoes and Sid notwithstanding. Their neverending libations had cost them their lives and they had blamed everything on the closure of the Inn for the fact that they must die rather than their bitter individual unhappiness, their bitter individual loneliness and their complete and utter madness.

As Nellie had willed, 'Hansel' was placed into a shallow grave in her back garden by a man she hired who then paved over the spot lest the animal attempted to abscond again. As an extra precaution against an escape attempt by this remarkable creature, a heavy imitation marble fountain was plonked on top.

Frank's funeral took place at Pendlesham's main crematorium, a building with which Frank had been only too familiar during his Old Firm days. Thus Frank belonged forever to the Old Firm. And the Old Firm had exacted its final revenge. A full, traditional Christian service, the absolute antithesis of what Frank would have wanted, courtesy of the people he would have wanted least to conduct it. The poor bastard's defeat was absolute. Everyone's ashes were sprinkled quite unsolicited over consecrated ground, except Sid, whose body was buried in it.

The Freddo phenomenon was now dead too and Pendlesham was finally liberated from self-participating funerals and the suicide rate inevitably dipped considerably as a consequence. The fad had in fact been played out and wasting yourself was no longer cool.

Up on Rocky Point, things returned to normal, with the public jumping at a sensible and manageable rate, the coastguard sweeping up the mess and the Old Firm staying one step ahead of Proudfoot and Gadd and any other competitors in securing the principal share of the business. Dignity was all.

The Reggies inevitably soon retired, especially since Keith Tate was no longer around to kick in, and the pitiful little club disbanded and splintered off into separate special interest groups of varying degrees of sadness, none more-so than a nocturnal group founded by Dick, which spent entire nights hiding in bushes watching foxes ripping people's black bin liners of garbage to shreds through binoculars. Additional flash photography did not fail to hinder their study. The departure of The Reggies also allowed The Lifejoys to eventually return to the Hut, something which Malcolm (who had now been taken over by a worrying obsession with the career of dancer/ singer and former child star Bonnie Langford) once swore would never happen. The new representative was a Joyce Grenfell doppleganger called Marjorie Hammersley, the sort of interminably cheerful 'jolly hockey sticks gal', whose inability to stop, not only talking, but laughing and snorting at the end of each sentence, was more than enough to make suicide seem attractive to anyone.

And it was indeed as if Freddo's had never happened: the Old Firm dominant and feeding copiously off those whom a well-meaning but entirely ineffectual organisation had failed to save; Miss Hammersley herself (for it was she) bolting out of the Hut desperately attempting to save desperate students, who ploughed over the edge before she had covered even a quarter of the ground in her always doomed quest to save them and then to turn back in abject defeat to trudge miserably Hut-bound again; the coastguard hoisting up the broken corpses to deliver ultimately to the Old Firm once the coroner had had his say; and then there was the Old Firm itself, as perennial as Rocky Point, delivering a quality service where dignity was taken as standard: where dignity was all.

The Station Inn underwent the most dramatic volte-face as the result of its conversion into 'The Sports Track'. It was September 1996. The ridiculous restrictions on dress (with particular regard to club football shirts) were soon relaxed, and as satellite television became ever more encompassing everywhere, so the pub within the railway station enjoyed a renaissance which none of the Inn Crowd could have anticipated. An appealing all-female bar staff was at hand to serve drinks and meals to an almost all-male clientele: sports fans rather than rock fans and not a reefer in sight. As a result, The Sports Track became one of the most popular pubs in Pendlesham, ironically in the main stream.

Rocky Point itself remained one of the most beauteous landmarks in England, its spectacular views and the generally warm climate of Pendlesham making it always the perfect pitch for a picnic or a walk, with the Rocky Point pub, museum (which made no mention at all of the Freddo era) and gift shop all doing bumper business. The soaring cliffs left the town behind, and in the scorching afternoons in high summer, out they all came; locals, holiday makers, daytrippers and students to wander where the sea and land collided with a light wind which refreshed the face and gave the reminder that life might, after all, be worth the candle, whilst seemingly within touching distance, gulls and other seabirds flocked effortlessly across a cloudless blue sky.